C000150503

1,000,000 Books

are available to read at

---◆---

www.ForgottenBooks.com

---◆---

Read online
Download PDF
Purchase in print

ISBN 978-1-330-40796-7
PIBN 10054939

English
Français
Deutsche
Italiano
Español
Português

www.forgottenbooks.com

Mythology Photography **Fiction**
Fishing Christianity **Art** Cooking
Essays Buddhism Freemasonry
Medicine **Biology** Music **Ancient
Egypt** Evolution Carpentry Physics
Dance Geology **Mathematics** Fitness
Shakespeare **Folklore** Yoga Marketing
Confidence Immortality Biographies
Poetry **Psychology** Witchcraft
Electronics Chemistry History **Law**
Accounting **Philosophy** Anthropology
Alchemy Drama Quantum Mechanics
Atheism Sexual Health **Ancient History**
Entrepreneurship Languages Sport
Paleontology Needlework Islam
Metaphysics Investment Archaeology
Parenting Statistics Criminology
Motivational

530

A

GEOGRAPHICAL SURVEY

OF

AFRICA,

ITS RIVERS, LAKES, MOUNTAINS, PRODUCTIONS,
STATES, POPULATION; &c.

WITH

A MAP ON AN ENTIRELY NEW CONSTRUCTION.

TO WHICH IS PREFIXED,

A LETTER TO LORD JOHN RUSSELL,

REGARDING

THE SLAVE TRADE,

AND THE IMPROVEMENT OF AFRICA.

BY

JAMES M'QUEEN, ESQ.

LONDON:
B. FELLOWES, LUDGATE STREET.
1840.

LONDON :
RICHARD CLAY, PRINTER, BREAD STREET HILL.

GENERAL CONTENTS.

PAGE

Letter to Lord John Russell—Great errors committed in the pursuit of
African Discovery—Improvement of Africa—Suppression of the
foreign Slave Trade—the immense Expense which it has cost Great
Britain—Great increase of that Trade—Increased productions of
Foreign Countries in consequence thereof—Cultivation of the Soil—
the true and only way to Improve and to Civilize Africa, &c. &c. i—xciv

GEOGRAPHICAL SURVEY OF AFRICA.

General View of Africa, Population and States 1
Great Desert, nature, extent, miseries in crossing it 6
Arabian Divisions of Africa 15
Guinea—the Pepper and Ivory Coasts 21
Ashantee, or Western Wangara—States, Rivers, Mountains, Manners,
    Customs, Wars, Slavery..................................... 28
Human Sacrifices—Bloody Fetisch rites, &c. 42
Western division of Africa, Countries, Rivers, Rokelle, Rio Nunez,
    Rio Grande, Gambia, Senegal, &c. &c. 55
The Niger, or Joliba, and its early tributaries, the Tankisso, Sarano,
    the Bagoe, the Kowara Ba, Ba Nimma, &c. &c...................... 71
Butter Tree, Colat-Nut Tree, Jinne, Massina, &c. &c. 88
Course of the Niger below Jinne, Lake Dibbie—Jinbala—the Gozen
    Zair, the Moosiaca Ba, &c. &c.................................... 94
La Mar Zarah River, Cabra, Timbuctoo, small rivers, &c............... 103
The Niger below Timbuctoo—Ghou, Haoussa, Yaoori, States betwixt
    the Niger and the Kong Mountains, Population, Lakes, Rivers;
    Boussa, Park's death, &c. &c. 113
The Niger below Boussa, the Oli, the Moussa, Wawa; Nikky, Rakkah,
    Rabbah, &c. 128
The Country from Badagry to Katungah 131

CONTENTS.

PAGE

Delta of the Niger; Rio de Formosa, the Calabar, Old Calabar, Bonny, Cameroons, High land of Cameroons, &c. &c.......................... 133

The Lower Niger and the Shadda, &c. &c. 146

Yacoba, Adamowa, Kornorfa, Biafra, &c....................................... 155

Rivers and Countries eastward from Boussa to Bornou, Mayyarrow, Coodonia, Quarrama, &c. &c. 160

Kashna, Ghana, Oongaroo, Meczara, Lamlam, Agadez, the Yeou, Old Birnie, Gambarou, &c. 175

Bornou, Kouka, Lander and Clapperton's Itineraries 194

The River Shary and its tributaries 197

Country from Mourzook to Bornou ; the Tibboos, Bilma or Domboo, Kowar, Kanem, &c. 202

Lake Shad, or Zad, Bagherme, Bahr el Gazelle, Wajunga, the Gir, the Asoo, Caugha, Kuku, Lake Fittre, &c........................... 209

Runza, Dar Saley or Waday, Darfur, Kordofan, Zagawa, Nubia,...... 224

The Bahr el Abiad, Shilluk, Denke, or Donga, the Bahr el Azreek, Abyssinia, Angot, Gondar, &c. &c. 230

African Rivers which flow to the south, Shoa and Effat, Tadjoura, Zeilah, River Hawash, Ancober 240

Berbera—Eastern Horn of Africa, &c. &c. 245

Magdosha, the Zebbee, Narea, Gingiro, &c. 246

Jaba, the Quillimancy, Limmou, the Habahia and its tributaries 250

The Zaire or Congo, Cataracts, &c. 253

The Coanza, the Cuanene, Mattemba, Cassange, Meropooa, the Fish River 253

The Eastern Coast of Africa, the Zambeze and Senna, Tatta, Zanzibar, Quiloa, Population of South Africa, Lakes in Southern Africa... 261

Concluding remarks 264

Construction of the Map 268

APPENDIX.

Distances of Places from each other in Africa............................. 275

Park's Journeys ; Time and Distances stated 278

PREFACE.

THE very great and unexpected delay (above three months) which has taken place in engraving and bringing forward the map which accompanies this work, has enabled me to reconsider a few of the numerous authorities, and frequently not very specific or clear narratives which could alone be obtained as guides for the subsequent geographical survey of Africa, in order to make such amendments as appear to approach to a greater degree of accuracy in one or two points connected with African geography.

The first is in reference to the Travels of Wargee, pp. 111 and 112. He gives the distance from Yaoori to the Niger, at Cabra, forty-one days' journey. On the fifth day he reached Karamanee, on the sixth day Cumba, where he crossed the Kowara; thence to Gourmou (the capital, of course) ten days; Gourmon to Moush, ten days; Moush to Imbolee, ten days; and Imbolee to the Niger, at Cabra, five days. The reader will perceive how accurately this distance, at $15\frac{1}{2}$ geographical miles per day, corresponds with the positions of Yaoori and Timbuctoo on the map drawn before his journey or authority was at all adverted to. Karamanee, mentioned by Wargee, is, I am convinced, the Karmassee of Park's guide, which he places in his narrative above Gourmou, instead of below it, mistakes which are quite common in the narratives of African travellers. Sultan Bello's map places Gourmon about N. W. from Yaoori, the territory belonging to which, in Park's day, stretched northward to the

b

Niger. Bowditch also places it in a similar position in a route a little to the eastward of north from Yahndi, through Matchaquadee to the Niger; viz. 25 days from Yahudi to Gooroma or Gourmou, and thence 15 to the Niger. The route which Wargee took from Yaoori, crossing the Kowara at Cumba in order to proceed to Timbuctoo, together with the positions of Gourmon and other places as given by the authorities just alluded to, all go to show and to prove the high northern course and the great angle which the Niger makes amongst the mountains of Batako, approaching as nearly as possible to the course assigned to the stream by Ptolemy, and as it is rudely, but not very incorrectly, delineated by Bello's Schoolmaster. The Moush, mentioned by Wargee, is no doubt the country governed by Mouzee, (Moush and Mouzee being clearly the same, and the sovereign being frequently named after the country,) the chief who, shortly before Park's arrival in that quarter of Africa, had attacked Jinne, by embarking his troops in canoes on Lake Dibbie. The position of the place, as given by Wargee, shows that the route which Mouzee took was the most proper which he could take in order to attack that place. There is one point further worthy of remark in Wargee's statement, and which is, that, between Moush and Imbolee, he "crossed no water," which would go to prove, either that no such river as that stated according to the Greek text of Ptolemy, as flowing into the Niger on the south side, about $3°$ to the east of Cuphae or Timbuctoo, exists, or, that Wargee must have crossed it so near its source, that the diminutive nature of the stream rendered it unworthy of notice. This last is most probable. Dupuis gives the distance from Timbuctoo to Moozee 14 days S. E.

Secondly, since the subsequent pages were written, Mr. Isenberg, the gentleman referred to in p. 242 and in the Postscript, has arrived in England, and having seen him, he confirms the view I had taken of the deep bay stretching S. W. from Tadjoura. Near its opening it is about seven miles broad, from which, narrowing, it becomes not more than two miles; and then contracting to a very narrow strait, it again expands in a circular basin of about three or four miles in diameter. Mr. Isenberg crossed the bay mentioned on his return from Ancobar. Tadjoura has a fine harbour; Zeilah has none. The country around Tadjoura is mountainous, and to the north-west of it coals are stated to be abundant. In returning from Shoa, Mr. Isenberg took a route a little more to the north, that is, nearer the Hawash than the route by which he had advanced, and in this route he describes the country as still more decidedly and distinctly volcanic than he found it in his route more to the south; so much so, indeed, that in some places appearances plainly indicated that these volcanoes had, at no distant period, been in activity. Tadjoura is about 46 geographical miles NN. W. of Zeilah. All the Arab tribes on the African coast in this quarter have a friendly feeling towards England.

The travels of Ignaz Pallme have put us in possession of a few additional facts regarding Kordofan, and the parts adjacent, especially to the south. Kordofan is a delightful country, and, in many districts, not inferior to the Brazils. Vegetation, the most variegated, exhaling the sweetest odours, overspreads the low lands, while the general surface is rather flat than mountainous. Towards the west the soil is composed chiefly of loose sands. The trees in many places are very tall. Numerous singing-birds sport in their branches. There are but few rivers. The houses are circular, made of straw, and have no windows. Cattle are numerous. Two pounds of good beef do not cost so much as a penny. Oxen are used for riding. Snakes, and other reptiles, are numerous. The country is, upon the whole, unhealthy. The natives of Kordofan are in general peaceable and hospitable, but very indolent, much given to lying, and are great thieves. The reigning religion is the Mahommedan. Six days' journey to the south and south-west of Obeid is the country of the Nuba, extending to the borders of the Bahr-el-Adda and the White Nile. The inhabitants are a different race from the population of Kordofan. They are Pagans, but very kind-hearted people. Their parental and filial affection is very great. The country is very mountainous : they enumerate above one hundred mountains. The nation forms a republic— each inhabited mountain has its own judge. They are a distinct race from the population inhabiting around the White Nile. The republic of Darhammar is amongst the Nuba mountains ; so is Tekele, which is also a republic, but with aristocratic institutions.

It is proper to state, that Cobbe, in Darfur, seems to be situated on a table land near that portion of the country where the division of waters takes place ; some to the south of it, flowing south and south-easterly, tributary to the Bahr-el-Abiad, and some on the west, flowing to the west and north-west into the Misselad, and some probably into the lakes to the north of the province of Wara.

Thirdly, my friend Mr. Jamieson has, a few days ago, communicated to me full extracts from Capt. Beecroft's and Dr. Moffat's letters to him, (dated in December last,) previous to starting again for the coast of Africa, regarding the river Formosa, where they were in June last, taking preparatory measures for a voyage up that river in the spring of this year. Capt. Beecroft, it is proper to observe, had surveyed the Nun branch from the sea, and the parent stream of the Niger to its junction with the Shadda, and had also previously visited all the rivers in the Delta and the parts adjoining ; and as the accounts given are fuller than the abstract referred to in the letter addressed to Lord John Russell, p. xii., and going more clearly and decidedly to prove the views which I have ever taken with regard to the river

Formosa, I readily and with pleasure transcribe them at length, thus :—

Capt. Beecroft.—" A few days before we left Benin River I ordered the gig to be manned and armed ; also lead line and compass. Left at 9 A. M., arrived off Jaquetine Point 9.30; after a run of six miles, sounded in four fathoms. A fresh sea breeze springing up and flood tide, with a sail we made very rapid progress. At 11 A. M. sounded off a small creek on the north side of the river, when it commenced raining in torrents. At noon passed Gatto Creek ; the river rather became contracted here. At 1 P. M. rain continued in such torrents" that, fearing to be benighted before he could regain the vessel, he turned back at a point "where there were several villages, and about five miles above Gatto Creek: sounded in 4½ fathoms; course up E. N. E. with a noble reach in sight before us about 12 miles." At sunset he regained the vessel, "entertaining a very favourable opinion of the advantage which may result from a knowledge of the navigation of this river. It very far surpasses the Brass (Nun) River in every point of view. I am quite satisfied the result will show that it communicates with the Niger above Eboe. I went to bed with a full conviction of success when the time arrives for the great work."

Dr. Moffat.—" Capt. Beecroft and myself went up the river to reconnoitre. We proceeded above Gatto Creek, and were much pleased with the appearance of the river at that part where it is about half a mile broad. Saw a reach extending for about twelve miles upwards, without any obstacle to obstruct the eye or turn the river from its placid course. From repeated soundings which we made, we never found less than 4½ fathoms water, from one side of the river to the other, and sometimes we found as much as 5½ and 6 fathoms. I have now seen all the principal rivers in the Bights of Benin and Biafra, with the exception of Old Calabar, and my opinion (sanctioned by Capt. Beecroft's) is, that the Benin is most likely to be of the greatest commercial importance in relation to the interior, and we have also come to the conclusion that the city of Benin is nearer the river than has hitherto been pointed out."

This, from two persons on the spot alive to the importance of the question and with a knowledge of the anxiety of the public about the matter, is worth volumes of London closet theories, and is to me most satisfactory. The account given of the depth of the river, 5½ to 6 fathoms, is the same that a young man, who had traded in this river repeatedly, and who had been up it to the distance of from 60 to 70 miles, gave me of it in the year 1822, immediately after his

return from Africa. The distance run by Capt. Beecroft, from the anchorage where his vessel lay to
Gatto Creek, at the junction of that auxiliary with
the Niger, cannot be less than 25 miles, or more probably 30 miles, from the sea; which is from six
to ten miles more than has hitherto been supposed,
and which will bring the eastern termination of the
reach of the Formosa, which Capt. Beecroft saw, to be
only 33 miles below or to the west of Eboe, taking
the longitude where it is placed on the map to be
correct; but not more than 15 miles, if the longitude
given to that place by Capt. Beecroft, namely 6° E.,
is correct. The supposition also, on the part of Dr.
Moffat, namely, that the city of Oedo, the capital of
Benin, is at no great distance from the river, is in
accordance with old Portuguese maps, which lay it
down at no great distance on the north side.

The same cause which has delayed the present pub-
lication enables me to notice the charge of misstate-
ment and "exaggeration" which, through Mr. Buxton's
work on the Slave Trade, Mr. Turnbull, in his recent
work on Cuba, has thought proper to make against
me. At p. 362 of his work Mr. Turnbull proceeds
thus: "He, Mr. Buxton, takes credit for extreme
moderation in not extending it to 100,000, on the
authority of Mr. M'Queen, the grounds of whose
opinion are equally indefinite."

The specific reference and returns regarding the
slave population of Cuba, given in p. xxvi. in the subsequent letter, and in the Appendix to the work,
p. 283, render it quite unnecessary to extend remark
or contradiction here. To these the attention of the
reader is requested and directed, and from these he
will learn whether "the grounds" of my "opinion"
are "indefinite" or not. It is necessary, however, to
advert, for a moment, to Mr. Turnbull's estimates,
and the authority on which he makes them. Out of
his own lips and from his own pages he shall be
judged.

Mr. Turnbull's results are that the number of slaves
in Cuba, in the year 1837, was 356,000 (p. 151); that
the yearly import is, at the utmost, 24,000 (p. 155);
while Mr. Tolmé, the British consul at the Havannah,
cannot stretch the number beyond 23,000 (p. 363).
Mr. Turnbull, p. 150, states that the parliamentary
commissioners confess the number 122,500 (p. 150) to
have been imported in ten years ending 1837; that
the present decrease on sugar estates is ten per cent.
yearly (p. 150); and on coffee estates from $3\frac{3}{4}$ to 5
per cent. (p. 295) per annum. Mr. Turnbull further
adds (p. 230) two returns of the slave population of
Cuba, which it is necessary to state and to bear in
mind, (see also general returns in Appendix, p. 283,)
namely, that in 1775 it was,—males 28,774, females
15,562, together 44,336; in 1827, males 183,290,
females 103,652, total 286,942. Such are Mr. Turnbull's conclusions, regarding which it may be observed
that those which relate to the extent of the slave
population are made not only on "indefinite grounds,"
but contrary to the most pointed and definite data
which he either had or could easily have obtained.

Why the return of 1792 has been omitted, and why
the reference has stopped short with the slave population of 1827, will readily appear. With regard to
the number stated by the slave commissioners to be
imported, it is simply necessary to observe that every
one knows they neither know nor can ascertain one
half the number that is introduced into Cuba or any
where else. The returns of the slave population for
1792, 1817, 1827, 1828 and 1830, are here reproduced:

Slave Population of Cuba.

1792.	1817.	1827.	1828.	1830.
84,590	199,145	286,942	301,000	479,000

The actual *increase* here given in Cuba, in the two
last years, is 178,000, or 89,000 per annum, to which
must be added the number imported, to make good
the decrease by deaths over births, which Mr. Turn-

bull states is, for sugar estates, 10 per cent., and coffee, 5 per cent. per annum; and also the additional number which must have been imported to make good the number enfranchised, which, in Spanish colonies, it is well known is very considerable. In fact, as is shown, Letter, p. xxvi., the increase of the free black population of Cuba, in these two years, was 25,000, and on the whole free coloured population in three years, 88,506. The proper proportion added, on account of these two items, will make the number imported for the years mentioned more than 100,000 for Cuba alone.

This authority and these returns Mr. Turnbull might have seen in Cuba. I gave them to Mr. Buxton to publish in his work; which had he done, his estimate, instead of being impugned as it has been, would have stood upon invincible grounds. This was the authority for stating what I did state to the gentleman mentioned about two years ago; namely, that such was the extent to which the slave trade had, during previous years, been carried on, especially from 1827 to 1831, that for successive years the number introduced into Cuba and Porto Rico could not be less than 100,000, not that 100,000 had been and were continually and yearly introduced into these places since 1808, the year of British abolition.

The yearly decrease by natural deaths, owing to the very great disproportion between the sexes that has always existed in Cuba, and which has been still more increased of late years, as Mr. Turnbull's pages abundautly testify, (" 3 to 1 on most estates in the island :" he mentions one estate with 700 males without a single female,) must be very great. His object is to make it be believed that only a comparatively small number of African negroes has been introduced into Cuba during a great number of years back. Had he taken the return of the number at the close of 1830, namely, 479,000, all his statements and speculations would have been scattered to the winds, and he would have saved himself the trouble of writing statements which he must, on reflection, regret.

It would be a waste of time to extend observations on this point. From 1827 to 1837 Mr. Turnbull and the slave commissioners admit the known importation of only 122,500 additional. But the former has supplied us with invincible data to show that it has been a great deal more. I shall not stop to inquire into the accuracy of Mr. Turnbull's returns, which, as regards produce exported, I know, from more correct authority, are below the mark, but take them as he has given them, published as he says they are by official authority. First, as regards general trade—

	1829.	1837.	(pp. 153, 154.)
	Dolls.	Dolls.	
Exports, value .	13,952,405	20,346,407	

equal to 48 per cent.

Next, as regards particular produce—Export :

| | 1829. | 1837. |
| Sugar, Arrobas (pp. 115, 153) . | 6,588,428 | 9,062,053 |

or 37 per cent. increase.

Mr. Turnbull (p. 231) shows, as regards Alexandria estate and others, that owing to the decrease of slaves from death the yearly produce had been reduced, even so much as four-fifths; consequently, to procure the above very great increase of produce since 1829, there must have been a proportionate increase of African slaves, because Mr. Turnbull nowhere ventures to state that any portion of the staple articles, viz. sugar, coffee, &c. &c., in which he pointedly states the greatest increase had taken place, is raised by the labour of free people.

Next, as regards particular articles of food given to the slaves, there was imported :—

		1829.	1837.
Jerked beef, (p. 154) Arrobas	. .	536,678	800,500
Codfish,	ditto . .	323,696	408,308

being, as regards the former, an increase of 50 per cent., and of the latter, 26 per cent.

: With regard to the amount of exports previously
given, it is necessary to bear in mind that the value
is stated at the rate of the customs valuation, which
gives no correct idea of the real value, but only the
comparative difference. Thus the customs export
value for coffee is one dollar the arroba, whereas the
actual value is double the sum. The following
reference to St. Jago de Cuba will show still more
pointedly the increase of produce in Cuba, and consequently the increased introduction of African slaves.

	Imports.	Exports.
St. Jago de Cuba,. 1827 . . . 1,441,048		1,270,586 dolls.
" " 1837 . . . 2,299,396		2,182,008 ,,

being, as regards exports, 73 per cent. increase.

We have seen the increased per centage on articles
of produce exported within a given period, and also
noticed, on the authority of Mr. Turnbull himself,
the great increase which has taken place in the importation of articles of food exclusively, or very nearly so,
appropriated to the use of the slave population, namely
—50 per cent. in the former, and from 36 to 45 per
cent. in the latter. The increase of the slave population, it is clear, has been in the same ratio. Let
us assume 40 per cent. as the medium, and the slave
population, at the close of 1830, 479,000 ; these data
will give us 191,600 as the actual permanent increase
of slaves in Cuba, from 1830 till 1837, inclusive. To
this, in order to obtain the number actually introduced,
must be added the annual decrease of 10 per cent. on
sugar—(p. 150, this decrease, he emphatically says,
amounts " to the total renewal of the numbers by
importation in the course of ten years")—and 5 per
cent. on coffee plantations ; and say only 4 per cent.
for enfranchisements, and, together, we shall have at
least 30,000 yearly, or 240,000 to add to the permanent increase. The whole united, will thus bring the
yearly introduction of slaves into Cuba, for the period
mentioned, to have been about 60,000 ; the number

which Mr. Buxton has stated it to be, from specific but totally different data, and not materially different from the general average which, in latter years, I have elsewhere calculated, and stated it to be; and all this, without taking into account the number lost in the middle passage, which requires to be added, in order to give the correct number which has been carried away from Africa for the quarter mentioned.

Mr. Turnbull cannot overthrow these calculations. He admits that the slaves are not better fed than they were formerly; and he states, p. 120, that the reason of the increased production of Cuba proceeded from two causes; first, chiefly " by the constant and increasing introduction of new negroes from the coast of Africa;" and, secondly, because its inhabitants looked forward to meet the calculated " diminished production of the British West Indies." In this they have, unfortunately, calculated right.

Mr. Turnbull fills up a few pages with reference to Porto Rico, where it appears he never was. In course of his narrative, he refers to the returns for that island, given in Mr. Porter's Tables, No. 7, lately published. The returns for Porto Rico in those Tables were given to Mr. Porter by me, and were brought by me from that colony three years ago. With these Tables in his hands, it is not a little surprising that Mr. Turnbull should mistate the crops of Porto Rico as he has done. The crop for 1835 was, he states—sugar, 369,539 quintals; coffee, 121,151 quintals; and molasses, 671,009 arrobas, &c. Now, from the tables referred to, the crops of Porto Rico were :—

	1835.	1836.
Sugar, Quintals	438,574½	498,888½
Coffee, ditto	72,623½	52,772½
Molasses, gallons	1,391,593	1,724,661

There is no such return as 369,539 quintals of sugar, for any year. In 1830, the export was 340,163¾ quintals of sugar. The coffee exported in 1829, was 121,800 quintals, which is, in fact, the amount taken by Mr. Turnbull for 1835 ! The coffee crops of Porto Rico have decreased of late years, because many of the coffee plantations have been turned into sugar, as being a more profitable cultivation.

The great object which Mr. Turnbull has in view, is, to state, and to prove, that the introduction of slaves into Cuba, is not by any means so great as it has been represented to be. For this purpose he brings forward the comparative exports at different periods. At p. 153, he gives us the export of sugar, 9,060,053 arrobas, in 1837; and 6,588,428 arrobas, in 1829; adding, that the export for the latter year, was " the earliest period for which I could find a corresponding return !'—that is, a return for a period of ten years, to correspond with the slave population return, as officially stated, for 1827. Now, what will the reader think, when I state, that, in the very same table from which Mr. Turnbull takes the export for 1829, namely, Don Sagra's work, p. 111, the export of sugar for 1827, the corresponding period sought there, stands 5,878,924 arrobas, being 709,802 arrobas less than the return for 1829, which he took, but which, as it goes to prove a greater increase of produce, (55 per cent. instead of 37 per cent.) and, consequently, of slave population in these ten years, than Mr. Turnbull wishes to make out, he, consequently, does not take. Is such a mode of proceeding correct, or just?

Mr. Turnbull selects the year 1837 as the scale on which he fixes the yearly importation of slaves into Cuba. Scarcely any thing can be more disingenuous and unfair than this. During the greater part of 1836, the slave traders were every where paralyzed by the reports of the very severe and stringent nature of the new British Slave Act, which came out in the month of June of that year. The Act in question authorized the capture of all supposed slave-traders, on new, but not well-explained grounds; the consequence of which was, that the British cruizers on the coast of Africa captured every vessel which came in their way. No fewer than 29 were captured, and sent to Sierra Leone, towards the close of 1836 ; the greater part, if not the whole, of which were subsequently liberated, from the want of legal proof and authority to condemn them. All these things paralyzed the slave trade on the coast of Africa, from the summer of 1836, to the summer of 1837.; and, consequently, greatly lessened the number of slaves imported into the Havannah, and other places, during 1837, as compared with previous and with subsequent years.

The public exposure of the fact of the tremendous increase of the foreign slave trade, especially by the hand from whence that exposure has come, has, no doubt, startled the nation, and made more than one official personage, and travelling *attaché*, uneasy. The public stands appalled at the fact disclosed, namely— that, after all the enormous outlay and waste of money and life—and after the belief generally entertained that the slave trade was extinguished, or very nearly so, it is greater than ever ; and is also astonished to find that ambassadors, and their subordinates, in more than one place, instead of attending to Africa, as they stated they were doing, and were bound to do, have either been doing nothing, or attending to other and less important matters ; in short, that they have been doing that which they ought not to have done, and leaving undone that which they ought to have done. Such conduct is of itself sufficiently reprehensible; but is it to be borne by our ruined colonists, and by the misled and fleeced people of England — are they, in addition, to be told by one set of officers, who have been pocketing their money and neglecting their duty, that they have been eminently successful, when they have signally failed in every point? and by another set, who have been for many years living at the public expense, with large salaries, proclaiming the slave trade is increasing, doubled, trebled, and so forth— now to come forward, when the public have been awakened to a sense of their folly, and the mischief which has been done, and tell us, We have been openly deceiving you—the extent of the slave trade is nothing —hardly deserving notice, or a name?

Yet, is not this the true state of things? Is not Great Britain paying yearly to slave-commissioners in slave-commission courts, in different parts, 14,700*l.* per annum, (formerly as high as 19,000*l.*); and after having been in receipt of this sum yearly for more than twenty years, and loudly proclaiming, as commissioners did proclaim, we are worked off our feet by the increasing labour which the still increasing slave trade brings upon us, at once to turn round, as Mr. Turnbull and his Havannah informants do, and say, it is all deception—the extent of the slave trade is not one-fourth of what it has been represented to be? Mr. Turnbull, and others, are grievously and grossly mistaken, if they think that such conduct can be any longer tolerated, or escape exposure and reprobation.

The financial accounts of Great Britain are, unfortunately for the heavily-taxed people of England, not fables. They prove, upon evidence undeniable and irresistible, the enormous extent and the undiminished extent of the foreign slave trade. Those for 1839, lately published, give us (see p. 92,) the amount of bounties paid for slaves captured last year. The charge on the year is 47,238*l.*; the sum paid, 42,454*l.*; being almost double that which I had (p. 86,) estimated it would be, and much higher than it has been in any year since 1830.

Since the subsequent pages were written, the returns of the sugar-crop of the four ports of Cuba, and of these only, have come into my hands. This sugar-crop, reduced into muscovado by the scale which Mr. Turnbull has furnished us with, (p. 126, and Don Sagra gives us, p. 125,) is equal to about 180,000 tons, exclusive of the consumption in the colony, above one-fourth more. The crop of Porto Rico will, I learn from a commercial friend, be, for this year, nearly 60,000 tons; together, 70,000 tons more than the sugar-crop of all the British sugar colonies for 1839; and in which colonies .there are. 720,000 negro labourers. The above vast increase of produce, there-fore, clearly and forcibly argues a vast and. increasing influx of fresh labourers into the colonies first alluded to.

Mr. Turnbull, surely, cannot for one moment have considered what his labours, if just, and his state-ments, if correct, go to show and to prove. It is no less than the truth, that 390,000 slaves in Cuba and Porto Rico produce, adverting to last year, one-third more sugar,—(as regards sugar only it is that 90,000 slaves in Cuba produce more than 500,000 in the Bri-tish colonies,)—ten times more coffee, exclusive of about 1,500,000*l.* in value of other articles of commerce, than 720,000 free negroes in the British sugar colonies produce. This gives a preponderance of almost four to one in favour of slave labour over free labour. Could not Mr. Turnbull see this? If his statements regarding the slave population of Cuba and Porto Rico are cor-rect, then the preponderance as regards production and returns is so great in favour of the system there established, that all hope of extinguishing slavery, or of suppressing the slave trade, while the mass of man-kind seek gain in their pursuits, must fall to the ground, and must prove utterly hopeless. Taking Mr. Turn-bull's statements to be, as he says they are, correct, then the conclusion is undeniable, that no man has ever advanced any thing so powerful in support of personal slavery, and coercive labour, or afforded such irresistible strength to the policy and profit of conti-nuing the African slave trade as in his work on Cuba he has done.

Mr. Turnbull tells us that some Spanish writers give the population of Cuba above 1,000,000, of whom 600,000 are supposed to be free people, and slaves. Even this would bring the slave population to be 480,000, about the year 1830, the period to which these writers allude. Further, all the proportions between

the classes which Mr. Turnbull gives, apply to the census of 1827, and not to the state of the population in
1837.   As one more instance of his inconsistency and
inaccuracy, take the following :—The district of St.
Jago, or the Oriental, which (see Don Sagra, p. 6,)
contained, in 1827, only one-fifth part of the population of Cuba, Mr. Turnbull tells us contains 65,658
free white, and 24,859 free coloured children; together, 90,517, from 5 to 15 years.   In the preceding
page (128) he informs us, that the number of free
children *in the island* of the same age, is assumed to
be 99,599 ! !
   Certain travellers in their researches discover mares'
nests.   Mr. Turnbull seeks after no such unprofitable
things.   He finds out an infallible plan (how could he
miss finding that which he tells us lay in his way ?) to
extinguish the African slave-trade.   It is this : the
appointment of a new British Slave Commission Court
in Cuba, with power to seize every slave in that island
that they may choose to pitch upon, and compel the
owners to prove the legality of the purchase and their
right to the property.   The discoverer of this infallible
remedy would, as a matter of course, be at the head
of the new court with a proper salary !   The government would be bold, and the commissioners bolder,
who would attempt to plant themselves in Cuba for
such an object.   Why not go to the Brazils also ?
   There is, throughout Mr. Turnbull's work, a prodigious deal of beating about the bush, clearly intended
to withdraw the mind of the reader from the fact ; and
it requires no common patience and investigation to
detect the subterfuges to which he resorts.   Yet every
now and then the real truth oozes out.   Thus, during
1837 he states 78 vessels under the Portuguese flag,
and 3 under the Spanish, landed in the Havannah
alone 24,000 slaves (p. 154).   In the following page
he adds, " the reports of the commissioners at the
Havannah for the last slaving season, from October
1838 to March 1839, are *truly appalling.*"   Again,

to the end of April 1839, five months, "the slaving season," it is presumed, just mentioned, he states (p. 355), "twenty-five vessels landed their cargoes on the southern coast of Cuba." Nevertheless, he informs us that the Havannah and Matanzas are still the greatest and the best places for the trade. Considering the importations at the times, and the places mentioned, and the "truly appalling" accounts regarding the extent of the traffic for five months, ending March 1839, where is the room or the reason for boggling at or cavilling at Mr. Buxton's account of the yearly introduction of 60,000 slaves into the whole island of Cuba? At the Havannah only, there are two slave barracoons which contain 2,500 slaves; these were constantly full during the greater part of the time that Mr. Turnbull was there. Why does he not tell us how many of these were sold daily or weekly? With such a great demand for labourers, they could not remain in these places long. We do not require to be told how the vacancy so created is filled up.

According to the census of 1827 (see Don Sagra, p. 6,) the whole population of the St. Jago or the Oriental district was 131,453, of which 47,499 were slaves. In page 129, Mr. Turnbull informs us that the number of free children in that district, from 5 to 15 years of age, was 90,517. This must clearly relate to a different, and to a period subsequent to 1827, and we are warranted in taking the children of the ages here stated as the number in 1837. This number, according to the ratio of population in other countries of the world, (see Ireland, for example,) would give 364,000 for the number of free persons in the St. Jago or Eastern district of Cuba in 1837, showing a very great, as there really has been a very great increase in that class; and, as Mr. Turnbull admits and states that the number of slaves in that and in every other portion of Cuba had increased, between 1827 and 1837, in a still greater ratio than the free population, it follows: first, that if increased only in an equal ratio, then 160,000 slaves, a permanent population, must have been introduced into the district of Cuba alluded to ; and secondly, that according to Mr. Turnbull's general statement and admission, the number must have been a great deal more. It is also well known that the Trinidad and Matanzas divisions have increased in population and cultivation to an extent equally great as the St. Jago district.

The facts here stated, and the observations here made, are deemed amply sufficient to show the errors which Mr. Turnbull has committed. They may also be taken to relate, and are, in fact, intended equally to apply, to all other cavillers, more especially to the very learned critic, who enriches by his labours the last number of the London and Westminster Review, with several assertions and contradictions relating to the extent of the whole African slave trade. " It does not," says he, p. 128, " exceed 80,000 souls," (60,000 of which are probably landed in Brazils, Cuba, and Porto Rico, and the rest lost in the passage, at the rate of 25 per cent., p. 129.) " From Africa, we accordingly," continues he, " on sufficient grounds, demur to the conclusions drawn by Mr. Buxton, though backed by the opinions of Mr. M'Lean, and Mr. M'Queen." With Mr. M'Lean, Mr. M'Queen never had any communication, either on this or on any other subject, though the Reviewer may have had, at some remarkable moment, which will account for his combining together authorities quite unconnected with, and distinct from, each other, in order to strike down both by one blow with his invincible arm. Where the oracular writer got his authority for fixing the number of negroes carried yearly from all Africa in the external slave trade, at 80,000, I know not ; nor does any other know, nor does he state. We are, however, required to bow our heads in silent submission, and in perfect humility before this superior authority; but to this even the spirit of meekness and patience itself may reasonably " demur." The only reasons adduced, inadequate as they appear, for the unqualified submission demanded are, that the writer had, at some period, been in some portion of Africa, the particular point being shadowed out under the significant declarations; " Having had some sad experience on this very river," (the Niger,) p. 163; " Cameroons mountain, and we speak from personal observation, has a good harbour, is equally eligible as Fernando Po," &c.   Now, with all deference, it was neither by being in sight of Cameroons mountain, nor even by being on the very summit thereof, that could enable any one to see or to know what was passing, or what had been passing for many years, in all Africa, and in a very large portion of America, at the same moment, or to gain a general and definite knowledge of the slave trade, either in Africa, or from Africa.   On the contrary, there are few positions in the world where the sphere of observation directed to the subject mentioned, could be more involved in clouds and mists, and so little able to perceive the truth.   The Reviewer's knowledge on these subjects is clearly circumscribed.   Granting that he has been in Africa, he has supplied us with invincible data to show that he has not gained much accurate knowledge regarding things that are in it; because he informs us, (p. 165,) that " Berbera is in the Strait of *Babelmandel* ;" that, as if the world did not know it before, "Fernando Po is wholly surrounded with water," and "Cameroons Mountain being partly" so, therefore, " we expect that it will be found separated from the mainland ;" that the unfortunate Liverpool expedition " discovered (p. 163) the eastern branch of the Niger, called Tchad, or Shary ;" and further, that, amongst other African theories, Major Rennell " carried the Niger into the marshes of Wangara, *a country that has disappeared ! !* "   Is this correct African knowledge? Wangara has *disappeared*, has it?   When?   Why, does not the critic know that the very portion of Africa, where he says he was, is situated in Wangara, a name and a large portion of Africa perfectly well known to every tyro in African geography, and to every Moslem African, or Moslem African traveller that ever crossed the Niger, or traversed the countries from the Assinee on the west, to old Calabar, inclusive, on the east, and the countries and districts extending along and around the outlets of that mighty stream. With these specimens of geographical errors we are warranted in placing little reliance upon the Reviewer's statements regarding the extent of the African slave trade; more especially when these are flatly contradicted by various authorities more comprehensive in their field of observation, and unquestionably better informed.*

Having committed such blunders in these important matters, it cannot be considered extraordinary that equally great should have been committed in other points. Take the following.

" Let us compare [says the Reviewer, p. 127 and 128] the value of the slaves alleged to be imported into Cuba" [60,000 at 300 dollars each, 18,000,000 dollars every year paid for fresh labour] " with the value of the total exports, 20,346,407 dollars yearly." And extending this song of triumph, he proceeds :—" what would be thought of Great Britain exporting 40,000,000*l.* of manufactures annually; and in order to produce those manufactures, importing 36,000,000*l.* worth of machinery? On the face of these figures the import into Cuba is impossible."

The Reviewer, in the exuberance of his wisdom, puts the capital invested, or supposed to be invested,

---

* A respectable trader, who has frequented the southern part of the west coast of Africa for several years, gives the extent of the trade last year at the following places. At Cabenda there were, and never are fewer than, 4 or 5 vessels; in the river Congo, 14 or 15; at Ambriz, 10; and at St. Paul's de Loando, 40 to 50; each of which vessels is capable of carrying from 300 to 500 slaves. They complete their cargoes in about six weeks. The places of those which depart are always and immediately supplied by fresh arrivals, so that the number actively engaged in the traffic is never diminished throughout the year. Admitting that only four voyages in succession are made in the course of the year, and that each vessel conveys 400, the tonnage alluded to would be sufficient to carry away 110,000 yearly! (See article, Colonial Gazette, June 17th, 1840, communicated from a source which the writer of this knows to be most respectable and well informed.)

in both cases, and the produce exported from the employment of that capital, as one and the same; and consequently wholly overlooks the fact, that out of 20,346,407 dollars, the yearly exports; 14,564,304 are the value of the produce raised from the application of 160,000,000 dollars capital vested in agricultural slaves, forming part too of 450,000,000 dollars of fixed agricultural capital. In this way he is making— not the manufacturers of Great Britain and the agriculturists of Cuba, but himself, extremely wrong, and extremely ridiculous; and instead of flooring Mr. Buxton, he has floored himself. He clearly considers the whole manufacturing power, animate and inanimate, in the supposed British capital as lasting only one year; and as regards Cuba, that 60,000 slaves, value 18,000,000 dollars, are exterminated, extinguished annually; a number which, together with the permanent yearly increase admitted by Mr. Turnbull, would require an importation of 74,000 annually; also that amongst the population there is no waste, and that neither it nor the productions of the island ever increase.

The following remarkable and pointed assertions regarding the insincerity and want of all moral principle in the African chiefs (p. 141) are worthy of notice :—

" We having had [says the Reviewer] personal experience of the native chiefs, both on the coast and in the interior, are quite aware that treaties may be made with all of them :" they " will sign anything, promise anything, and as long as they *are coerced*, perform that part, but no longer." " As to making a treaty in the European sense of the term with any power in the negro country, the idea is absurd." " Liberal sentiments are common in the mouths of all." " We have often listened with wonder to the just and benevolent sayings of these gentry, and have invariably found the greater the profession the more reason to distrust the man." " A confederacy of chiefs from the Gambia on the west to Bagherme on the east, and from the desert on the north to the gulf of Guinea on the south, is purely chimerical."—(P. 142.)

In opposition to these statements it may be observed, that Mr. Macgregor Laird, only a few years

ago, wrote a considerable volume in order to prove
from "personal experience" that African chiefs and
the African people were in all respects the reverse,—
the kindest-hearted and most sincere people that he
had ever met with. Take the following in proof:—

"If I had been pleased with Obie's character before, I was much
more so now.   I had been completely in his power : the vessel's
decks were crowded with his people ; they were aware that out of
the five white men I had living, three were confined to their ham-
mocks ; and yet I was received with more kindness, and had more
respect paid to me, than when I had visited the place before, with
all my crew living, and in full health and strength."—(Vol. I. p. 273.)

" The only means we can adopt with any probability of success
lies in following the only channel which nature has given us,—that of
the river Niger ; and thus, if I may use the expression, to turn the
flank of Western Africa.   I therefore propose that a chain of British
posts should be carried up the Niger as far as Sego, and from thence
by Timbo to Sierra Leone, and to Barraconda on the Gambia ; that
the seat of government on the coast should be transferred from
Sierra Leone to Fernando Po, and that the communication with the
interior should be kept up by steam-boats from that point."   This
plan " would be easy in execution, economical in practice, and most
satisfactory in its results."

The Niger " is navigable for three thousand miles. The reception
which we met with, the freedom which we enjoyed from all molesta-
tion, sufficiently attests the peaceable and amiable character of the
natives."   This "proves the facility with which establishments might
be formed in the most favourable positions for trade."—(Vol. II.
pp. 385, 386.)

" At all these places there is abundance of unoccupied land, which
could be purchased from the natives at a mere nominal rate ; and in
the part of the country I have myself been in, I am confident that
such establishments would be hailed by them with a general feeling
of good will ; that the white men would be appealed to as umpires
in all disputes ; and as long as they conducted themselves with justice
and propriety, would be looked up to with respect and affection."—
(Vol. II. p. 386.)

" I can safely assert that, as far as my experience goes, European
traders will be received with open arms by all the inhabitants of the
interior ; that no hostility, but, on the contrary, every kindness and
respect, will be shown to them ; that their property and life will be
as safe (excepting from the effects of climate) upon the Niger as
upon the Thames."—(Vol. II. p. 407.)

" I fearlessly assert, that there are no people on the face of the
globe more desirous and capable of trading than the present race of
Africans, with all their disadvantages."—P. 363.

Which is right—the Westminster Review in 1840, or Mr. Macgregor Laird in Africa in 1833, it is left to the public to determine. It appears quite incomprehensible how people so " capable of trading" should not be able to understand the nature of a treaty between man and man, and between nation and nation. Sheik el Kanemy of Bornou and the king of Ashantee both understood and maintained the treaties entered into by them with this country.

What the soil of Africa wants is labour, to render it productive. What the population of Africa require is capital, and industry, and security; with intelligence to maintain the latter, and to direct the two former. To suppress completely the external slave trade it is not necessary to plant these on every part of the immense coast, or in all the vast continent of Africa. Only raise in any more commanding and accessible portion of Africa, say on the greatest artery, the banks of the lower Niger, 300,000 bales of cotton, 20,000 tons of coffee, and 100,000 tons of sugar, at a cheap rate, and throw these yearly into the market of the world already fully supplied by slave labour, and the result will be that this additional produce would reduce so greatly the general prices of all produce in every quarter, that the external slave trade would cease to be profitable,—cease to exist; because the cultivators in Cuba, Brazils, &c., would find themselves unable to purchase so as to extend cultivation at a rate that would repay. That Europe has not hitherto found out this important but simple truth, argues no great superiority of intellect over the people of Africa.

In conclusion I may add, that it is impossible to consider or to reflect upon the labours of Mr. Isenberg and Mr. Kraaf, elsewhere noticed, without feeling the highest pleasure and the greatest satisfaction. They have not only brought to our view a correct geographical picture of a most important portion of Africa, but also of a population bearing the name of Christians,—a population and a country which, in ancient and remote times, were much more cultivated and civilized than they are now ; brought to our view, in short, a very remote portion of the Ethiopia of both the New and of the Old Testament, — that Ethiopia which the evangelical Prophet, instructed by Wisdom which cannot err, and commanded by Power which can bring every thing to pass ; has told us that, in the latter days, that is, under the Christian dispensation, " Ethiopia shall stretch out her hands unto God."

I cannot conclude these labours without again stating my conviction, that the sources of the chief branch of the Bahr el Abiad spring in about three degrees of north latitude; and that a great branch of the Zaire, or Congo, rises on the opposite side of the dividing range. The flooding of the rivers decidedly proves this, independently of every other authority.* The springs also of the Habahia, the Zebee, and the Webbe are, it is conjectured, still further to the south than where they have been placed in the map, and those also of the Shadda are probably a little more to the eastward and south-eastward. Referring to old translations of the early Dutch and Portuguese navigators, Nyandael, Barbot, &c., (I have not seen the originals,) I find that they estimate the distance of Gatto, or Agatton, from the mouth of the Formosa, to be 20 leagues; the capital of Benin to be one day's journey from Gatto ; and Arebo (certainly Eboe) on the river to be 60 leagues (not miles) from the mouth of the Formosa.

* While correcting the press for these pages, the *Times* of the 7th July published the following confirmation of the correct delineation of the map, and of the accuracy of the opinion advanced here and in p. 235, &c.

The *Gazzetta Piemontese* of the 1st July gives the following extract from a private letter, dated Alexandria, May 27th. " We have received news from the expedition which went to discover the source of the Nile. Having arrived at 3° 30′ north latitude, they found that the river divided into two branches, and the current became so rapid that no boat could resist it. The expedition was consequently obliged to return to Cartoum."

London, 6th July, 1840.

LORD JOHN RUSSELL,

My Lord,

Permit me, respectfully, to place in your hands, for the information of the British Government and the Public, the subsequent "Geographical Survey of Africa;" more especially of the tropical portion of that vast continent, containing in a space as brief as possible, a brief description and delineation of the courses of the great rivers, the chains of mountains, the general manners, character, and pursuits of the people, and also the productions and capabilities of the soil. The facts regarding these matters, collected from the best authorities, ancient and modern, have been, after long and laborious consideration and research, arranged in their present connected shape. It may, to some extent, prove a guide to Government in following out their present extended views and plans, formed for the purpose of extirpating at its roots the African slave trade, and the causes and the passions which produce it.

b

In reference to the important subject of African discovery, and the attempts to put an end to the foreign African slave trade, some observations are necessary. These are specially called for when the extraordinary and injudicious proceedings are considered, which Europe, but more especially Great Britain, has adopted and followed with regard to both. . But first, as relates to discovery, what has been done? In every single instance the wrong course and the wrong road has been taken to explore the interior of Africa, and to determine the course and termination of the great river Niger; and this wrong course too adopted, and these wrong paths taken, in the teeth of irresistible evidence and facts. For fifty years we have laboured to comparatively little purpose; and all that is really the most important African practical discovery in modern times, has been brought about as it were by chance, and in despite of ourselves; or, to use a homely proverb, "more by good luck than good guiding." What has been the consequences of these long and these continued errors? Why, that many valuable lives have been sacrificed, many thousands of the public money (in looking through parliamentary returns 60,000*l.* may be counted for this service alone) have been thrown away; the sad consequences of which are, that this country has been kept completely ignorant of the real situation of Africa, and the only way by which we can reach her to do her any permanent good. Even where that way was disclosed to us, it has, from various causes alike humiliating and reprehensible, been forsaken, or suffered to remain useless. Even where travellers, however wrong directed, have, by their perseverance, obtained information, or created a favourable impression, it has been neglected to be followed up by Great Britain. Such has been the case, in a very glaring manner, in the issue of the mission by Mr. Salt to Abyssinia, and of the mission by Denham and Clapperton to the comparatively intelligent chief of Bornou. He was anxious for a close and a friendly connexion with Great Britain, and also to aid her views; and even after our ambassadors returned to England, pressed these points upon them. Not a single step, however, was or has been taken to accord with his wishes, for even Clapperton's second journey was undertaken and gone about in a way where failure, as regards Bornou, might have been calculated upon as certain. He could and ought to have reached Bornou by a different, a shorter, and much easier route than that which he took, namely, up the Shadda so far, and then through the Domah country to Bornou. Again, as regards his mission to Saccatoo itself, look at the road which he took! He first went from Boussa to Kano, 300 miles E.N.E.; next from Kano to Saccatoo, 200 miles N. by W., both journeys by land; while he knew that from Boussa to Yaoori by water was only seventy miles north; and from Yaoori to Saccatoo, about seven days' journey, 100 miles N.E.; in short, to make out 170 miles he travelled, and in the rainy season too, 500! No wonder African expeditions fail.

Captain Tuckey's expedition, and its melancholy result, is well known. After a great expense it terminated without giving us any information of importance regarding that quarter of Africa, beyond that which was previously well known. The formidable and impassable cataracts in the Zaire, and that in consequence of these the river could not be navigated upwards, was well known to Europe many years ago. Had Tuckey been sent to the Rio de Formosa instead of the Zaire, Africa, to its utmost recesses, had at that time been completely explored. *

Ritchie and Lyon were sent out to penetrate into the interior of Africa from Tripoli, by Mourzook. The travellers were left at Mourzook neglected, and without the promised funds to enable them to go on during six months of the most sickly part of the year. In consequence of this, the ruler of that place lost respect for them, and Ritchie died of sickness brought on by chagrin and disappointment. Deprived of its most efficient head, Lyon got no further than Tegerby, where he was obliged to turn back. Major Laing was again directed to proceed by a similar route, namely, Ghadames and Twat to Timbuctoo, under the protection and recommendation of the Bey of Tripoli. Notwithstanding this, he was first attacked, wounded, and basely robbed, not far from Timbuctoo, by one party of Moors, and afterwards cruelly murdered by another party, without a single step having been taken by this great country to avenge his fate. Such is, or ought to be, our influence with the chief of Tripoli, and such his influence with the Mahommedan tribes in the desert, that 1000 dollars offered by him, and pressed by him on some of these tribes, would have, in a short period, brought both the robbers and the murderers in chains to Tripoli, there to suffer for their crimes. Such an example, promptly made, would have rendered the life of any British traveller, who might

---

* This unfortunate expedition was directed to the point mentioned by the urgent and decided opinions of Mr. Maxwell, namely, that the Zaire was actually the Niger. No one knew the mouth of the Zaire better than the gentleman alluded to ; but his error shows that a correct knowledge of a given point or district on the sea-shore of that quarter of the world, does not constitute any individual a safe guide to direct travellers to explore the interior of Africa.

afterwards have been led to visit that quarter, comparatively safe, if not wholly so. But not a single step to this has been taken—even yet it is not too late.

The fate of Mr. Park is well known. Though prudence cannot justify the course he pursued in reaching the Gambia, and proceeding into the interior of Africa at a season of the year which was certain to find him, before he had proceeded one hundred and fifty miles on his journey, overwhelmed with the rainy season, while conducting a large body of Europeans in a climate pernicious to them, and in a country without roads, and deeply intersected by flooded and rapid streams ; still that does not justify the little judicious exertion which has been made by this country to recover his papers, or to try to convince, if we could not punish for their crimes, the Africans who occasioned his death how unjustly they had acted. The routes which he took, and was permitted, perhaps directed, to take, were the most injudicious and tedious, and most dangerous, that could have been chosen to ascertain the general course, and probable termination, of the Niger. He perished, and was scarcely thought of. So fell, unlamented and unnoticed, Major Houghton ; while a very small exertion on our part, when established at the Senegal, might, by the offer of a reward amongst the neighbouring Moorish tribes, have brought his murderers to Port Louis in fetters, to have suffered the penalty of death for their crime.

It is sickening to pursue the extensive list of the errors committed during the last fifty years in the attempts to penetrate into Africa. In every thing, and at every time, we have begun at the wrong end ;—to use a homely proverb, we have "put the

cart before the horse," and we have accordingly
signally failed. It would indeed seem that as our
knowledge regarding Africa increased, we were nevertheless determined to pursue the same course of
error. The proposed expedition, the *dernier resort*
to do good to Africa, is, as I learn, to be sent up
the river Nun ; that is, I suppose, because three
expeditions have been thwarted, it may be said have
been destroyed, by attempting this route, that still
it shall again be tried. Let us attend to this matter
for a moment. Lander by chance came down this
river in his last journey, or rather he was at the
pleasure of his conductors *brought* down it from
Eboe. The scanty information which his unfortunate
situation enabled him to glean, and to give concerning the lower part of the stream, amounted to
this : that for a distance before he reached Brass, the
canoe which bore him found, at one place for a
considerable space, scarcely depth of water to pass
with mangrove arches above their heads, excluding
the light of day ! This too, be it observed, was the
case below that point, where he describes the river
as "fast dwindling away to an insignificant stream."
With this knowledge only, a mercantile expedition
from Liverpool, under Mr. Macgregor Laird, in
two steamers, went out; and although the largest of
these drew only about six feet water, they had difficulty to get on even while the river Nun was in
flood, there being for a considerable distance but
one fathom and a half, and in one place only eight feet
water, and the breadth only from thirty to forty
yards ! ! The fate of that expedition, after extraordinary exertions and perseverance, is well known.
As a mercantile business, it proved a total failure ;

in geographical information, except fixing the position of Fundah more accurately, it added but little to our knowledge of Africa; while the diseases caught in the pestilential swamps around the Nun, left only Mr. Laird and a few others to tell the mournful tale.

The mortality amongst the few trading ships, and the slavers which have of late years begun to frequent this river, is dreadful. No human constitution can stand the effects of the malaria engendered round its deadly shores, whereon for a distance of sixty miles or more only water, mud, and mangroves can be seen! The S.W. wind blows nearly throughout the year right up this stream and its numerous branches, and this wind carries after the unfortunate traveller and navigator, the accumulated malaria of the whole delta; while around the river Nun in particular, there is no produce of any description, and but a scanty population; and these, too, according to every account, the most idle, the most ignorant, the most degraded, and the greatest scoundrels on the face of the earth. The river has been frequented of late years by slavers, chiefly because our cruisers can more readily catch them in the Bonny, or near it. To avoid this, the slavers and their African allies send the slaves across from Bonny to the Nun in canoes, by the numerous creeks found in that part of the coast. At the Nun, they ship them in a day or a night, when the slaver runs out before our cruisers are aware; or, if these cruisers proceed from Bonny to the Nun, then the slaver ships his slaves at Bonny, and puts out to sea in safety.

The following extract from Lander's last voyage will give, in a short space, an accurate and true account of the ignorance, and the depravity of the

population; their character, and also the character of
the river Nun.   They appear to be very much a-kin
to, and suited to each other :—

" To convince of his (King Boy's) veracity, he produced a pocket-
book, containing a great number of recommendatory notes, or
' characters,' as a domestic would call them, written in the English,
French, Spanish, and Portuguese languages, and which had been
given him by various European traders who had visited the Brass
River. . . . . Boy's letters mention certain dealings which their
authors have had with him, and they, likewise, bear testimony to
his own character, and the manners of his countrymen.   Among
others is one from a ' James Dow,' master of the brig *Susan* from
Liverpool, and dated ' *Brass First River*, September, 1830,' which
runs as follows : . . . . ' Captain Dow states, that he never met with
a set of greater scoundrels than the natives generally, and the
pilots in particular.'   Them he anathematized as d——— rascals, who
had endeavoured to steer his vessel among the breakers at the
mouth of the river, that they might share the plunder of its wreck.
King Jacket, who claims the sovereignty of the river, is declared to
be a more confirmed knave, if possible, than they, and to have
cheated him of a good deal of property.   The writer describes
King Forday as a man rather advanced in years, less fraudulent,
but more dilatory.   *King Boy*, his son, alone deserved his confidence,
for he had not abused it, and possessed more honesty and integrity
than either of his countrymen.   These are the rulers of the *Brass*
country, and pretty fellows they are truly.   Mr. Dow observes
further, that the river is extremely unhealthy, and that his first and
second mates, three coopers, and five seamen, had already died of
fever, and that he himself had had several narrow escapes from the
same disorder.   He concludes by cautioning traders against the
treachery of the natives generally, and gives them certain directions
concerning the ' dreadful bar,' at the mouth of the river, on which
he had nearly perished."—*Lander's Travels*, vol. iii. p. 190, &c.

But as regards the manners and customs of the
people, and what is of more immediate importance to
the European.who seeks a navigable passage into the
interior, Oldfield gives the following, in the former

case sickening, and in the latter case, decisive information, regarding the impracticability of the river for
the purpose of navigation :—

"The Americans had equally felt the excitement and interest con-
sequent on the discovery of the termination of the Niger by Lander,
and saw that the vast tract of country which offered a market for
British goods might also be available to them. A few enterprising
merchants of Rhode Island had therefore fitted out the vessels just
arrived, consisting of a brig, named the *Agenoria*, of about two
hundred and thirty tons burthen, and two schooners, with sixteen
white men and several Kroomen. . . . . The captain and supercargo had a copy of Lander's chart on a large scale, and were very
sanguine of getting up the Niger into the Eboe country, with the
brig ; *a thing utterly impossible ;* for in the whole distance of the first
twenty miles up, there is in some parts only one fathom and a half
water. However the captain felt convinced he could go up the
river, and proceeded up for the purpose of examining it in his whale
boat. He had not gone far, before he was satisfied that to take the
brig up was impossible. . . . The captain of the American brig
received the intelligence of the supercargo's death, when performing
the last ceremony over the corpse of his carpenter ; and there being
no medical assistance on board, he lost nearly all his hands. Fever
had appeared among them, and in less than six weeks, his crew of
sixteen was reduced to five ! To add to the misfortunes of these
Americans, on one dark and stormy night, eight or ten Kroomen
ran away with the brig's boat, with buckets and five boarding-pikes.
. . . A short time after the foregoing transaction, the captain of the
Agenoria (Captain Pearce) died, and the mate took charge of the
vessel and sailed for Rhode Island. Their whole expedition was
thus unfortunately terminated : goods were given for nearly one
hundred puncheons of palm oil, not one quarter of which were paid."

After noticing the custom prevalent and general in
these parts, of sacrificing on the death of a chief
several of his wives, Oldfield proceeds to give us the
following account of a female, the wife of a deceased
chief, who was exposed to be devoured by sharks, for
having, as was alleged, wished the death of the chief:—

"I approached the place from whence the cries proceeded, which was about twenty yards from the water's edge, on the sand, and I there saw a woman lying chained to a log of wood, with her arms and legs pinioned, awaiting the period of high water, to be launched into the sea, there to become the unhappy prey of voracious sharks. . . I remonstrated with the brother on the absurdity of the charge; I determined to try to save the poor woman; I hastened to Dido, the pilot, who also interceded, but the chief made the following reply: 'White man's fash, no be black man's fash;' which, being interpreted, meant, that they allowed us our customs, and we ought to allow them theirs. After a palaver which lasted nearly three hours, owing to the influence of Dido, who is a good man, the chief agreed to liberate his sister-in-law, provided he might sell her to a slaver. We proceeded to the water's edge, which was now within a few feet of the poor creature. Her arms and legs were disengaged, but, owing to the severe pressure which had been used, she could not walk until she was actually under her own roof. Indeed, so unexpected and unlooked-for had been her rescue, that she could not believe we were in earnest. She then pressed my hand with gratitude, and looked what her heart felt. In a short time after this she completely recovered her spirits, and went on board a slaver without any emotion, for she had no one to live for, or no one to care for."

Such is the Nun, one of the most deadly of the many sickly rivers of Africa, and moreover, without one redeeming quality, and clearly unfit to become the channel for any great commercial communication with the countries in the interior! Such are the chiefs and the population around it! Moreover, where an American navigator in pursuit of gain could not go, even in a whale boat, does any sane Englishman think that he can find out or make a safe navigable passage? And is this the road chosen to open up the proposed great commercial and agricultural schemes, which are to civilize, to enlighten, and to cultivate Africa? Is it possible, that after all our acquired knowledge, after all our bitter and dear-bought experience, that such should be our conduct in this most important matter, and at this critical moment? yet so it is, and being so, forms another chapter in that dark and mischievous volume which records all our erroneous acts, and all our ill-digested proceedings, in Africa and towards Africa.

The points where a navigable access to the interior can be most easily obtained by the Niger, are clearly by the Rio dos Forcados, or the Rio de Formosa, or both. The former at its separation is 600 or 700 yards broad, and six fathoms deep. Slave ships go up it by the mouth named the Rio dos Escravos, or Brody, to Warree, where the river it is believed becomes one stream, and which is only thirty-eight miles from the point of separation from the Nun. But what is, in my opinion, decidedly the best, and the most open, and easiest accessible of the whole, is the Rio de Formosa. From its mouth to the point of separation of the large branch above Eboe, is a distance of only eighty-five miles. At its mouth it is four British miles wide, and the branch above mentioned, which is clearly the Formosa, at the point of separation is 800 yards* wide, and from ten feet to six fathoms deep. I have conversed with a trader who had been up this river from sixty to seventy miles, and who described it as both broad and deep, a vast and noble body of water; and have seen other traders who have traded with natives who had come down it, from very distant countries in the interior. While writing this, my friend, Mr. Robert Jamieson, of Liverpool, a gentleman to whom Africa is much indebted, and who is

---

* Through a channel connected with Laird's expedition, it was communicated to me after its return, that this branch was 1200 yards wide.

likely, by his prudent and persevering conduct, to render her more efficient service than any one I know, has transmitted me the extract of a letter which he has received from Captain Beecroft, engaged in his service, written in the Rio de Formosa a few months ago, and up which river Captain Beecroft is, by this time, engaged in prosecuting a voyage into the interior. His letter is dated a few miles above Gatto Creek. In the course upwards, says he, "we have a noble reach in sight before us, extending about twelve miles in the bearing E.N.E., (not fifty miles from Eboe): "sounded, and found four fathoms and a half." The river, he adds, is vastly superior in every respect to the Nun or Brass, and he is satisfied, from all he had seen and heard, that it communicated with Eboe. The Rio de Formosa, it is obvious, has nearly a direct course, which necessarily will render it more free from islands and sand banks than rivers, the courses of which are very tortuous. Here then is the point which, during the space of twenty years, I have always maintained is the navigable entrance into the interior of Africa. The Bonny branch is also well worthy of attention. It is very deep at its mouth, and is clearly a very large outlet of the Niger. So also I apprehend the great outlet of the Old Calabar will be found to be. Cross river is navigated by ships of large tonnage, to about 6° 15' N. lat., and the most easterly branch of it is navigable for several days farther, but the depth is not stated.

Assuming that the Rio de Formosa is the best and safest navigable mouth of the Niger, and equal to secure, as I believe it is, a commercial communication with distant countries in the interior of Northern Africa, it follows that Cape Coast Castle, or Accra, a British settlement on the Gold Coast, may be made the exterior point of defence and communication. This place is as near the Rio de Formosa as Fernando Po is; and from the prevailing winds and currents between it and the Formosa, the intercourse would be fully quicker than between Fernando Po and the Formosa. Accra is also one of the healthiest spots on the coast, and has moreover a considerable commercial intercourse with influential people in the interior. This is a point well worthy the serious attention and consideration of the British government, more especially at this moment.

The accompanying map and subsequent narrative will show your Lordship the rivers and the points through which, it is humbly conceived, from authority which cannot be doubted, Africa can only be penetrated by means of the great river Niger; but should these turn out to be as little fitted for navigation and commerce to and with the interior, as the Nun is known to be, then we may relinquish our views of doing any permanent good in the interior of Africa, because we cannot reach it; and without we can reach it, no lasting good can ever be done to Africa, nor any effectual stop be put to the African slave trade.

Individuals may still be found who will, from various motives, peril their lives in undertakings which embrace such clear and obvious dangers; but wherefore should Great Britain and her Government peril immense interests on the part of the British empire; and, at the same time, the improvement and the salvation of Africa, by listening to hasty counsels founded upon imperfect knowledge and erroneous data, and, at the same time, be saddled with a very heavy expense into the bargain? A dreadful responsibility rests upon the Colonial Office of Great Britain, if it knowingly or carelessly risks a danger and a result like this.

Connected with the subject of African discovery, there are a class of men who might be made more eminently useful in that pursuit, and at less expense than any other. These are, the missionaries who proceed to spread the truths of the Gospel into Africa. These individuals, in their noble cause, must frequently be exposed to many hardships and inconveniences, perhaps, from the want of pecuniary means, or from the want of a known channel and a responsible name through which and by which they could obtain these. Such is the name, and influence, and knowledge of the British Government throughout the world, that their servants and agents, civil, naval, military, and political, might, in almost every instance, and in every quarter where such inconveniences may arise, be made the means of relieving, countenancing, and aiding these worthy men in every way by which their wants could be relieved, or their objects accelerated. These missionaries also might be qualified to make geographical, and to take astronomical, observations, &c. A few thousand pounds—10,000*l.* annually, my Lord, spent in this way, would prove more effectual in spreading knowledge, and industry, and civilization in Africa, than half a million annually spent in external efforts to extinguish the foreign African slave trade.

It is 300 years since these portions of Africa around the delta of the Niger were known to Europeans; more than two centuries since England began to trade constantly and closely with them; during all of which period our commercial and naval marine has been in the practice of visiting all the mighty rivers on this portion of the coast, even taking surveys and soundings of them; and yet, it would appear, that no one has ever endeavoured to find out, or even to inquire, where they came from; nor has one single rational attempt on the part of a great naval power like Great Britain hitherto been made to explore streams which are known, and which might have been supposed, to lead to one of the noblest rivers in the world : a correct knowledge of which, moreover, would have conferred such inestimable advantages upon herself, upon Africa, and upon the whole human race. Yet such is the fact, and such a fact is an indelible disgrace to this country.

The present British settlements also on the coasts of Africa, are one and all of them the worst places that possibly could have been chosen, whether considered in a political, or in a commercial, or in an agricultural point of view, for the purpose of spreading industry, knowledge, and civilization amongst the population of Africa. They come into immediate contact only with the most ignorant, degraded, demoralized, and disunited portions of the African population. They open up no great line of communication with the comparatively intelligent nations of the interior. They command nothing, they influence nothing, and they are neither feared nor respected, nor followed, in Africa. They have done, it may safely be said, nothing; at least, all that they have effected, after an incredible and ruinous expense, is comparatively but as a drop in the bucket, and a grain in the balance, to improve Africa. As they stand, they are merely nurseries for the support, the aid, and the maintenance of the foreign slave trade. The goods they import and sell, form, to a great extent, the machinery by which the slaves are bought. The disposers of these goods can neither avoid nor prevent this result, if they attempt either to do business with those countries which carry on a traffic with Africa, or business with Africa herself. Further, the capture of slave ships adds to the evil. Carried into Sierra Leóne, the goods which they have on board are condemned and sold at auction, purchased in, for, or by, the slave traders, who come from other parts of the coast for the purpose, and thus, at much less than half the original cost, and, in a still greater proportion, less than these could be imported and brought from Europe to the coast of Africa, the slave trader gains the means to carry on the traffic more easily. Each slave trader thus adds so much more profit, perhaps 4000*l* or 5000*l*. sterling, on each ship, and to each voyage. Again, the credits given by British merchants and manufacturers in certain foreign countries, enable the slave traders in these countries to take either ready money or these goods, with which they proceed to Africa to purchase slaves; and on their return, the great profits which they obtain enable them to pay for the goods previously bought. It also not unfrequently happens that the agents for these goods are, to a certain extent, directly engaged in the speculation. These things are no secrets in other places, no, not even in England, where numbers of manufacturers and mechanical establishments do nothing else but get up and bring forward articles for the African markets and African slave trade, with a perfect knowledge that these articles are brought forward and sold for the purpose last mentioned. The regular merchant is everywhere beat by those connected with the traffic alluded to, because the great profits which are obtained in that trade enable those who partake of it to under-sell the legitimate traders in every article. On the coast of Africa the sales by auction of British goods are destructive to all honest commerce. The legitimate merchants can no where compete with the slave-goods traders and purchasers at such markets; while the destruction of the slave vessels captured, considering the small number that are captured, only gives additional employment to the builders in the United States. The slave trader can always get his vessel insured at ten or twelve per cent., and these are still the most profitable risks that American and other underwriters can take. Moreover, the vessels, when broken up, are taken to pieces in such a way that they can soon be put together again, when they proceed in their original object.

The whole system pursued by this country, in order to put down the African slave trade, is, in every part thereof, and in every country, wrong—grossly and mischievously wrong. Hence our failure, hence we are beaten, hence we are unsuccessful, and will prove unsuccessful so long as enormous profits array the passions, the interests, and the avarice of all the avaricious, and money-making, and money-seeking portion of our species against us.

European nations, as has already been adverted to, have been trading with and settled in several parts of the western coasts of Africa for more than 300 years, and previous to the discovery of the greater portion of the continent of America. As regards her tropical climates, Africa is in no respect inferior to the portion of the American continent situated within the same parallels. The climate is equally fine, the land

equally fertile and productive; the productions of the
soil of Africa are not only equal to, but even more numerous and valuable than those which were found in the
continent of America when first discovered. The population of both continents was not materially different in
point of knowledge and industry; nay, so far as commerce is concerned, the African population excelled
the American. In that description of wealth, also,
which Europeans then and now so generally and
greedily sought, namely, gold, Africa is, and always
was, more abundant than ever America has been
found to be. It is astonishing the quantity of gold
which is yearly collected in and exported from Africa
to various quarters. The different European nations
at this moment carry away a great amount in value
from her western shores, and which, great as it is,
there is reason to believe is small when compared to
the quantity carried off yearly from Soudan, Abyssinia,
&c., by the numerous caravans of Moors and Arabs
which cross the Great Desert to different states on
the Mediterranean, and also the Red Sea into Arabia.
These caravans are not only many in number, but each
caravan consists of a great number of traders, scarcely
one of whom but carries more or less gold with him,
all of which is collected in Soudan. Carried first to
the Mahommedan states on the shores of the Mediterranean, it next silently finds its way into Europe
and western Asia, and forms, without the civilized
world thinking or inquiring much about the matter,
the chief source of the supply of that metal which
furnishes to these states the principal means for keeping
up and extending their gold circulation. There is
the best reason, also, to believe that the same source,
namely, Africa, supplied the treasuries of the great

monarchies of western Asia, of the mighty Roman empire, and also those of the various states which, in the east and in the west, rose upon the ruins of that empire. Europeans carry away at this moment, probably, 500,000*l*. in value yearly from the western coasts; and the quantity and value carried across the Great Desert, in various directions, certainly exceed that sum. The imports into Morocco alone, thirty years ago, from Soudan, was about 10,000,000 Spanish dollars in value, a very large portion of which was gold dust. Jackson states, that a sovereign of Morocco, in the year 1590, brought away, in plunder and in tribute, from Timbuctoo and other states, the enormous quantity of 135 quintals, (the tribute of Timbuctoo yearly was 60 quintals,) 16,065 lbs. avoirdupois, 962,100*l*. of gold.* This gold is principally found in the countries around the sources of the Senegal and the Joliba, in the different provinces of Ashantee, also to the eastward amongst the hills of Jacoba, the places around the sources of the Shadda, on both branches of the Egyptian Nile, and the great rivers which rise to the southward of these and flow into the Indian Ocean. The following curious extract from Bosman's Guinea will show us the quantity of gold carried away by Europeans from that portion of Africa one hundred and thirty-seven years ago :

* If the Chancellor of the Exchequer had such an annual tribute as this in his power, it would go to save him much trouble and uneasiness; and yet, if common sense and common honesty had been attended to in our dealings with Africa, a much greater annual revenue might have been raised to Great Britain from the produce of the African soil, and this, too, produced and procured equally to the advantage of Africa and of Great Britain.

c 2

" My last treated of the inland countries from whence the gold was brought, how it was digged, its several sorts, the false gold, &c. To pursue our subject yet further, as I have told you whence it is brought, it is but necessary I should inform you whither it is carried, and how much is yearly brought to the coast. As for the last, I dare affirm it as a real truth, that they not only can, but do yearly, in time of peace, deliver the quantity of seven thousand marks of gold. This is a large sum; but it is divided amongst so many, each being sure to get some, that the whole is soon disposed of. The most just calculation of the division that I can possibly make is as follows :—viz.

	Marks.
Our West India Company yearly exports . . .	1500
The English African Company	1200

But this is to be understood of such years in which the commerce of both Companies happens to be very brisk; and I do not believe our Company hath, for several years past, carried off above the half of this quantity.

The Zealand interlopers are sure to carry off as much yearly as our Company, namely	1500
The English interlopers about . . . · .	1000

But the last have, for two or three years past, pursued this trade so vigorously, that they have exported above twice that quantity.

The Brandenburghers and Danes, in time of peace, both together, about	1000
The Portuguese and French, together, at least, about .	800

Which makes 7000

" According to our reckoning, then, there is brought hither and carried off exactly twenty-three ton of gold,[*] reckoning three marks to 1000 guilders. But, as I told you, above all, this account supposeth a prosperous time, when the passes are all open, and the merchants can pass safe and uninterrupted; but when the negroes are at war with one another, I do not believe that half this quantity

---

[*] At the present price of gold, this would amount to the vast sum of 3,406,575*l.*

is shipped off; and of this small quantity the interlopers know very well how to come by their share. And supposing our Company hath one-fifth of the whole, yet, when trade is low, they cannot get by it, but must make up the deficiency by trading to other coasts."— *Bosman's Guinea, Pinkerton's Collection,* pp. 375, 376.

The facts previously stated regarding Africa, her wealth, and her capabilities, being clear and incontrovertible, is it not strange that European nations have passed her by, and so neglected her in every way that could either have been permanently useful or advantageous to themselves or to her? Yet such is the fact. They have done so, and run after establishing themselves in quarters less wealthy, less productive, more distant; not more healthy, nor their population higher in the scale of civilization than the natives of Africa are or were when Europeans first came in contact with them, on either the western or the eastern coasts of that continent. The cause of this neglect was the fatal error into which every European nation, after the discovery of America, fell; namely, carrying away the labour of Africa from Africa to cultivate the islands and fields of America, instead of instructing and placing that African labour to cultivate the fields of Africa. What enormous and incalculable evils has this error inflicted upon Africa and upon the human race!

However dark and gloomy the true condition of Africa may appear to the inquirer—and dark and gloomy it indeed is, and must be admitted to be—still, it is not, fairly speaking, greatly worse than the condition of all Asia, and most part of Europe was in the early periods of their history. In and over both quarters slavery, as in Africa, was always the lot of the vanquished—and the murder and extermination of prisoners of war, before the shrines of their deities, in their public games, and at the tombs of their departed friends and chiefs, were carried on in the quarters adverted to, to an extent exceeded only by what is done, seen, and witnessed in Africa at this moment. African ignorance, superstition, barbarity, and degradation, is so far worse, greater, and blacker, that there does not appear, throughout all her borders, one ray of civilization that, without a foreign civilized impulse, can ever, from any internal change, impulse, or exertion, lead to a better state of things, which was not the case in the other quarters of the world.

This brings us to consider the European African slave trade. The consideration or inquiry must here be confined to the state and extent of that trade fifty years ago, what it now is, and the immense expense which this country has voluntarily, but in vain, incurred to put it down. In considering these points, errors, vastly greater and infinitely more fatal in their results than the errors committed in following out African discovery, will clearly appear.

It is now fifty years since Great Britain commenced offensive warfare against the African slave trade. The extent to which Europeans at that time carried it on, gave the number of 66,000 carried away (CARRIED AWAY, be it observed, from Africa) yearly, in the following proportions :

Great Britain (of whom 20,000 were resold)	30,000
Portugal	20,000
France, Holland, Denmark	16,000

At this day, although Great Britain, France, &c. have long since completely abolished the traffic, the number imported into the Brazils, Cuba, and Porto

Rico, according to Mr. Buxton's recent work on the slave trade, is 150,000. This is a work of great research and enormous labour, which every one should read who wishes fully to be acquainted with this subject; although he who reads must stand appalled and astonished, as I feel assured the author, in following out his subject, must have been at the result. The work alluded to leaves little for me to state on the subject. The number alluded to is the number *imported*, be it observed, into these countries and places, not the number CARRIED AWAY from Africa, which is quite a different thing. But Mr. Buxton might, from documents which I know to be correct, and which I have in my possession, have added to this number at least 40,000 more, and still not exceeded the truth. Thus, considering the mortality which takes place on the passage at only 15 per cent.—much lower than Mr. Buxton has taken it to be—it is clear that the African slave trade has really and actually TREBLED in amount, and besides increased in horrors tenfold!!

Mr. Buxton, in his able work alluded to, sets down the extent of the African slave trade across the northern desert, and that from the eastern shores of Africa, at 50,000 yearly. Had that gentleman been fully acquainted with all the facts of his case, he might have set down that portion of the African slave trade, that is, the number carried away, at 100,000 yearly, and still been within the truth. Take, for example, the reference which he has made to Lyon's account of the number he saw brought to Mourzook—6,000; but then this was only the number brought into that place during half the year, and in the portion thereof, too, during which the smallest number is brought;

and further, it is only the number brought in by two roads, and these not the most frequented, out of four roads which run from Soudan to that place. Also, as regards the number to Morocco, by a reference to Sidi Hamed; that caravan with which he travelled was, in the first place, not a regular but a supernumerary caravan, composed of stragglers belonging to the other caravans from places on the shores of the Mediterranean —the remains of the regular caravans, who, not having got their business finished in time to leave Timbuctoo before the commencement of the rains, left it, as is customary in such cases, as soon as the violence of these was over. It was not, moreover, any of the Morocco regular caravans, nor did it go by any of the direct Morocco roads, of which there are several from Timbuctoo, but took, for the reasons mentioned, the general road for the north by Mahbrook and Twat.

Let a few facts be adduced in proof of the increased slave trade. In 1791, according to Sir George Staunton, the slave population of Brazils, before the Monte Videan provinces were separated from her, amounted to 600,000. The importation at that time was about 20,000, but it rose after that period to 30,000, and before 1808, to 40,000 yearly. Take, however, the average for 17 years at 30,000; then, according to Signor Calmon's statement, made in the legislature of Bahia a few years ago, the average annual decrease, beyond the natural increase, is five per cent.; so that, with the above importations, the slave population of the Brazils in 1808, the year in which Great Britain abolished the traffic, could not have exceeded what it was in 1791. Look what it is now! According to the Government Census of 1833, the latest authentic account which I have seen, the number of slaves *registered* in the Brazils, exclusive of the Montevidean territories, was in round numbers 2,100,000, and this number, be it observed, after all the decrease which takes place in seasoning, and the numbers which have been enfranchised, and all the numbers which have perished in the middle passage. This great increase, (1,500,000) shows clearly, that during the last thirty years, more than 75,000* must have been annually *carried away* from Africa to the Brazils, or nearly *four times* as many as were carried away for that quarter of the world in 1791 ! !

Similar are the results with regard to Cuba and Porto Rico. Their united slave population in 1808, or rather at the 1st of January, 1808, could not exceed 128,785; it is now, most probably, 700,000. According to the valuable statistical work of Don Ramon de la Sarga, printed at Havannah in 1831, there were, in 1792, in Cuba 84,590 slaves. According to the Edinburgh Gazetteer, a work of great research and accuracy, the number in 1804 was 108,000. The number in Porto Rico (see official returns for that island in Porter's

---

* According to Lord Palmerston's note to Mr. Bandieria, dated April 20th, 1839, there entered the port of the Havannah in 1837, forty-eight Portuguese vessels with slaves, and in 1838, there entered forty-four vessels, and which his lordship averages at 443 slaves each, or 40,700. In the year 1837, at Rio de Janeiro, ninety-three Portuguese vessels landed 41,600 ; and in 1838, eighty-four vessels landed at the same place 36,700 negroes. The two ports mentioned do not receive one-half the number of Africans which are landed in Cuba and in the Brazils yearly, if so many; but the yearly number landed, at the rate even of one-half, will be 119,000, and about 7,000 captured and liberated. These numbers above given, be it observed, are the numbers landed from Portuguese flags alone, exclusive of Brazilian, American, and Montevidean, &c. flags engaged in the same traffic.

Tables, No. vii. p. 324,) in 1802, was 13,333, and 17,536 in 1812, which will bring out the number in 1808, in Porto Rico, to be 15,433. The number in Cuba, in 1808, or at the beginning of January, 1808, by the preceding ratio of increase, would be 113,352— together 128,785. According to Don La Sarga's work just referred to, the increase of slaves in Cuba, according to the registrations, was in 1829 and 1830, two years, 178,000, being at the rate of 89,000 per annum! All this increase, moreover, is exclusive of the number enfranchised, which in Spanish colonies is admitted and known to be considerable, (in the two years above alluded to, the number of free blacks in Cuba increased from 49,000 to 74,000—about fifty per cent.) ; the very great number lost, especially of late years, in the seasoning, and the very great number lost in the middle passage, owing to the crowded state in which the negroes are now brought from Africa ; and which, taken together by the same ratio as has been applied to the Brazils, will give the number carried away from Africa, for Cuba and Porto Rico, to have been yearly, during the last thirty years, at least 34,000 ; but as the slave trade for the Spanish colonies has chiefly commenced since the close of the war, say 1816, the number carried away yearly since that period, but especially of late years, has undoubtedly been more than double that number. The Spanish slave trade has, in fact, been wholly created since 1808. " Before the abolition by Great Britain," says Sir Henry Willis, (Despatch, Madrid, August 14th, 1814, Par. vol. xiii. of 1814-1815,) " there was literally no Spanish slave trade. No Spanish ship had been seen on the coast of Africa for a century, except one in 1797 and 1798, fitted out by the Prince of Peace." Besides all the numbers above mentioned, there is the number, at least 300,000, which must be added for the number (150,000) carried away for the French colonies, Mexico, &c., and the number (150,000 more) carried away for the United States subsequent to 1808, and until the periods when all these countries finally abolished the African slave trade, the whole together giving, during latter years, probably five times the number that was carried away from Africa for these places yearly before 1808.

Admitting that the number in 1808, in all these places mentioned, maintained itself by natural increase, (but which is by no means probable); and admitting that the loss during the passage across the Atlantic, the number lost in seasoning, together with the number required to make good enfranchisements, are only twenty-five per cent.; it is plain, that,—including say 140,000 captured and enfranchised, and destroyed under that system, as also the number carried away for the Brazils from 1834 to 1839, both inclusive, to be say 640,000,—then since the 1st of January, 1808, there must have been carried away from Africa, for different parts, by Europeans, 3,860,000 people.

Until the appointment of the mixed Commission Courts in 1819, Sierra Leone was, except for a few years subsequent to 1808, the only place where captures made could be adjudicated. According to the annexed Parliamentary Returns, the number of slave ships captured and condemned, and the number of slaves captured, and condemned and liberated, for certain periods, were as follows :—

		Vessels.	Slaves.	Average No. in each.
From	1808 to 1819 * . .	73	11,280	
„	1808 to 1814 † . .	40		
„	1819 to 1829 ‡ . .	79	12,154	154
„	1819 to 1829 § . .	16		
„	1829 to 1839 ‖ . .	244	57,073	260
		452		

From 1828 to 1838 inclusive, the number of ships captured was 258, of which number thirty-four had no slaves; and of this latter number fourteen were restored. Of this number, 244, condemned, 197, or *four-fifths* of the whole, were condemned in Sierra Leone. This affords a scale for determining the number (sixteen,) which would be condemned in the other mixed courts between 1819 and 1829. The average number of persons on board those ships condemned, from the above returns, will be 208; and,

* Par. Pap. No. 275 of 1829.—For the Sierra Leone Courts.

† Par. Pap. No. 342 of 1813–14; gives the number condemned in all parts, 112—including, of course, Sierra Leone.

‡ Par. Pap. No. 275 of 1829.—For the Sierra Leone Courts.

§ The proportion for Courts not at Sierra Leone, as after stated.

‖ Par. Pap. No. 533 of 1838' and return to House of Lords of the same year : this last thus stated :

Years.	Slaves on Board.	Landed at Sierra Leone.	Landed at Havannah.	Landed in B. W. Indies.
1828	5,582	3,309	1,033	
1829	6,607	4,927	963	
1830	7,659	3,439	287	
1831	1,851	1,468		157
1832	3,399	2,325	888	
1833	3,427	2,569	685	
1834	5,761	4,020	807	162·
1835	7,711	4,694	2,305	
1836	8,930	5,609	1,313	1,407
1837	6,146	4,017	257	1,333
Total . .	57,073	36,377	8,538	3,059

adding for the mortality on board, say ten per cent., 230 in round numbers will be the number carried away from Africa in each vessel. Dividing the total number, 3,860,000, carried away from Africa since 1808, by 230, gives 16,784 ships' trips, or voyages, that have been made; and dividing this latter number by 452, the number of ships that have been captured, gives 37,—the number which escapes for each that has been captured! Dividing, again, the number of ships, 452, that have been condemned, by 31, gives fourteen and a half, the average yearly number which have been captured since 1808; and lastly, multiplying the total number of ships captured, 452, by the average number, 230, carried away in each captured ship from Africa, gives 103,960, the total number carried away by this portion of ships engaged in the slave trade. But the average for each vessel is here taken probably too low, and 300 is, perhaps, the correct number, which will bring the captured in the proportion to one in thirty. Of all the latter number captured, also, it deserves to be remarked, that with the exception of a few hundreds scattered over the West Indian islands, only 36,700 * (including, of course, whatever natural increase there has been amongst them,) remained in Sierra Leone in June, 1838! What a scene of destruction does even this portion disclose; and who, after the picture which has been above presented to the view, can wonder that the African slave trade, notwithstanding all the obstructions which have been thrown in its way, has so fearfully increased!

Thus, to capture, say fifteen slave ships, and no more,

* The total number that have been emancipated and registered at Sierra Leone up to 30th June, 1838, is 46,887. (See Papers, Class D. of 1839, p. 5.)

annually, this country pays 600,000*l*.! This expenditure for one year, judiciously, justly, and energetically
laid out in Africa, would plant industry, and security,
and knowledge, in the very heart of that continent,
from whence these would speedily spread to the extremities, and forthwith save any additional or future
expenditure,—expenditure, too, under the present
system, to be laid out without accomplishing any
one good object, or obtaining, either to this country
or Africa, any advantage whatever.

At the above rates of loss in transportation and
seasoning, the present slave population of the different
countries will give the total number carried away by
Europeans, from the commencement of the slave trade,
to have been as under :—

Jamaica to 1808	730,000
All the other present British Colonies . . .	1,030,000
The present French Colonies	640,000
Ditto Dutch ditto	50,000
Ditto Danish ditto	50,000
Colombia, Mexico, &c.	152,000
Hayti to the Revolution	1,150,000
United States of America (uncertain) say . .	1,500,000
Cuba, Porto Rico, Brazils, and captured and liberated since 1808	3,860,000
Grand Total . .	9,168,000

Great Britain abolished the slave trade thirty years
ago, and has just emancipated, at an immediate cost of
20,000,000*l*., 780,000 Africans and descendants of
Africans.   The contest which brought round this
result commenced in 1823.   Since that period, according to ˉMr. Buxton's work, 2,400,000 Africans
have been enslaved and landed in foreign possessions,

after a destruction in the passage of fifteen per cent., (360,000) and above 80,000 captured and liberated. The real number, however, is, as has been shown, at least 600,000 more; together, above four times the number that has been liberated by this country. Thus stands the arithmetical balance of the account between Europe and Africa!

The result of all is, that the productions and exports, of all those countries more particularly mentioned, are more than *quintupled*. The value of produce at present *exported* from Cuba, Porto Rico, and Brazils, certainly exceeds 20,000,000*l.* sterling yearly, while the exports from the United States, (the produce of increased slave labour,) greatly exceeds the above sum, exclusive of the vast amount which is consumed in their own territories, and also within the other countries above mentioned. The following table, which has been taken from authentic returns in my possession,— and wherein the exports of sugar clayed from the under-mentioned places, are reduced to what is called Muscovado, in order to make the comparison accurate,—will establish the statement made.

	1808.		1837.	
	Sugar. cwts.	Coffee. lbs.	Sugar. cwts.	Coffee. lbs.
Cuba . .	600,000	18,000,000	3,450,000	69,000,000
Porto Rico.	1,420	291,200	750,000	7,000,000
Brazils. .	400,000	24,440,000	2,400,000	134,000,000

And this, be it also observed, in only two articles of production! Don Ramon Sarga's statistical work on Cuba, already quoted, states the exports, the productions of the soil of that island, in 1830, at 50,000,000 of dollars. The result of this enormous increase, coupled with the increase of cotton in the United

States, has accordingly raised up, in several kingdoms, new and enormous commercial interests, all opposed to the commercial interests of Great Britain, and the vast ramifications of which extend into and throughout all the great commercial communities of every civilized country in the world. These interests are now become so vast, so strong, and so general, that they not only influence and regulate, but have changed the public and state policy of several of the mightiest governments in the world. They at the same time tend to give an irresistible impulse to the African slave trade—an impulse which, even if these states were more inclined than they appear to be to put it down, they dare not openly oppose or resist; and which even Great Britain, my Lord, as you must know and feel, cannot venture openly and boldly to resist or to check, without producing open hostilities, or severe commercial obstructions and disasters to this country.

There is no use to blink the question. This is the present state of things, and this, too, after the prodigious sums which, during the last thirty years, Great Britain has expended, to put down the foreign slave trade. Let us, for a moment, attend to this expenditure as it relates to Africa and the foreign slave trade alone, and as it can be drawn forth from unquestionable authority.

*African Slave Trade Returns.—Expenses to England,*1808--1838.

The expense of the navy is estimated herein by the number of men employed in the service, and the proportion to the cost of the whole naval department of the year. Furthermore, and in proof of the very great extent of this expenditure, the Quarterly Review, (No. 68, for September 1826, p. 605,) in an article, written by Sir John Barrow, says, " The expense of keeping a squadron constantly employed for the suppression of the slave trade, the bounty of ten pounds per head paid for every slave captured, and the salaries and other expenses of the mixed commission, which, altogether, we should imagine, fall not far short of *half a million* a year," &c. (This, be it observed, for the coast of Africa only.)

In this statement the reader and the public will bear in mind that only a portion of the expenditure on account of the African slave trade is adverted to. There are several other heads, under which there are branches of expenditure, containing many heavy additional sums, which, when collected together, as they are in the subsequent references, selected from official documents, will make the total sum much greater than the data which the Quarterly Review gives, even after the expenditure under the three heads which he enumerates is limited to his scale. The following tables will bring the whole plainly and clearly before the reader :—

AFRICAN SLAVE TRADE RETURNS.

	£	£
Navy, African Coasts, 32 years, at 255,000*l*.	8,160,000	
Do. part W. Indies and part S. America, 32 years, at 127,000*l*.	4,064,000	
		12,224,000

Expenditure in and for Sierra Leone.

	£
Original Capital for the Company, last . .	240,000
Paid by Government for it, 1808	100,000
Ditto ditto, Sundries to Company* . . .	55,000
Ditto do. Maxwell's ravages at Rio Pongas.	20,000
Public works, Sierra Leone and Gambia, Par. Pap. 57 of 1830, and others (Church cost 50,000*l*.)	200,000
Expense of removing Maroons and black troops (Jour. H. Com. vol. 66) . . .	21,557

Amount carried forward £636,557 £12,224,000

---

* Special Report African Institution, p. 139. Mr. Macaulay's letter to the Duke of Gloucester, p. 39, &c. and further, by the same letter, p. 58, the sum of 24,474*l*. 2*s.* 5*d.* claimed, 18,000*l.* of which had been paid.

	£	£
Amount brought forward		12,224,000
Brought up	636,557	
Expense of support of Maroons & black troops, say only five years, at 10,000*l.* per annum*	50,000	
Pensions, disbanded Africans, six years, ending 1825	61,000	
Colonial Revenue spent, Par. Pap. No. 57, of 1830	62,321	
Colonial Contingencies, ditto ditto . . .	12,743	
Civil Establishment, &c. 1791 till 1800, (estimated)	90,000	
Ditto ditto, 1800 till 1807 (Jour. H. Commons, vol. 66)	90,000	
Ditto ditto, Extra Grants, 1800 to 1805, (Jour. H. Commons, vol. 6)	64,362	
Ditto ditto, 1808 to 1811	70,535	
Ditto ditto, 1807 to 1826 inclusive, (Annual Estimates)	331,536	
Ditto ditto, 1826 to 1837, ditto, (Finance Accounts)	179,670	
Ditto ditto, and Gambia, &c. 1838 and 1839, and 1840, (Finance Accounts) . . .	30,000	
		1,678,724

Gold Coast and Fernando Po.

	£	£
Gold Coast Yearly Grants, at 30,000*l.* from 1808 to 1821	420,000	
Ditto ditto, 1822 to 1825, Finance and Commissariat Accounts, &c. 1822, 1823, 1824, 1825, and 1826	140,370	
Ditto ditto, 1826 to 1832, Returns 1826, 1827, 1828, 1829, 1830, &c.	149,581	
Fernando Po, 1828 to 1833, Papers, 1829, 1830, 1831, 1832, and 1833	53,179	
		763,130
Amount carried forward		£14,665,851

* John King, Esq. stated the yearly expense to the Committee of the House to be 10,000*l.* for the year.

		£	£
Amount brought forward			14,665,854
Paid for Foreign Powers to relinquish Trade, &c. Portugal balance loan due, cancelled .		601,774	
Ditto, paid by Treaty, 1815, with Interest*.		348,904	
Portugal, paid by Treaty, 1817, for Illegal Captures, since 1814*		300,000	
Ditto ditto, Grants for ditto, Finance Accounts 1821, 1822, 1823, and 1836† .		276,399	
Spain, by Treaty, September, 1817 . . .		400,000	
United States, Slaves carried away, 1812, &c. Finance Accounts 1825, and 1828‡.		250,000	
Commissioners at Petersburgh for settling do. Accounts, 1824 and 1825		35,000	
Paid United States for Slaves wrecked and liberated in the Bahama Islands, about .		25,000	
			2,237,077

Bounties paid for Liberated Negroes.

1808 till 1825 inclusive, Par. Pap. No. 399, of 1827 §	484,344	

Paid	1826	Finance	Accounts	£35,437	
	1827	do.	do.	54,581	
	1828	do.	do.	33,411	
	1829	do.	do.	53,333	
	1830	do.	do.	81,640	
	1831	do.	do.	25,170	
	1832	do.	do.	15,153	
	1833	do.	do.	17,655	
	1834	do.	do.	19,874	
	1835	do.	do.	45,630	
	1836	do.	do.	28,128	
					410,012

Amount carried forward £894,356 £16,902,931

* The Parliamentary Papers do not enable us to distinguish if these sums are for separate purposes, or for one.

† Considerable sums under this head must have been paid, or remain to be paid, for years subsequent to 1825, the last year (except 1836) here included.

‡ 60,000*l.* more, it is stated, remain on this account. Besides other claims of a similar nature have been made, and some of them, it is thought, are paid.

§ It is uncertain whether 1826 is included in this return or not. It is thought that it is not.

	£	£	£
Amount brought forward			16,902,931
Brought up	894,356		
Paid 1837 Finance Accounts	41,274		
1838 do. do.	18,906		
1839 and 1840 do. suppose	50,000		
		1,004,536	
Paid Head Money till 1826	56,000		
		1,060,536	

Military Expenditure.

Suppose for 1808 & 1809, it to be * 72,582
1810. Par. Pap. 113 of 1811, p. 4, &c.

	Army Extraordinaries . .	36,291
1811. Par. Pap. 234 of 1812, 4 do.	41,549
1812.	147 of 1813, 4 do.	55,330
1813.	150 of 1814, 4 do.	66,968
1814.	177 of 1815, 5 do.	51,820
1815.	318 of 1816, 5 do.	58,951
1816.	319 of 1817, 4 do.	94,219
1817.	245 of 1818, 4 do.	68,475
1818.	286 of 1819, 4 do.	66,313
1819.	105 of 1820, 3 do.	41,644
1820.	187 of 1821, 3 do.	54,799
1821.	73 of 1822, 3 do.	67,130
1822.	125 of 1823, 3,4 do.	34,291
1823.	59 of 1824, 3 do.	39,294
1824.	61 of 1825, 3 do.	60,699
1825.	87 of 1827, 55 do.	59,993

————— 970,348

Amount carried forward £970,348 £17,963,467

* Probably part of this estimated sum may be accounted for in the subsequent accounts. The Commissariat accounts some years ago, were two years behind; now they are only one; thus the account for 1837 is published and produced in 1839.

	£	£	£
Amount brought forward			17,963,467
Brought up		970,348	

*Army Estimates—Sums provided
in England.*

[These run from 19,000*l.* to 23,000*l.*—
say 20,000*l.* yearly ; 18 years is
360,000*l.* From 1825 the Commissariat Accounts are taken, which
include every thing for the places
mentioned.]

1826. Commissariat Accounts . .	71,322	
1827. Ditto ditto . . .	60,852	
1828. Ditto ditto . . .	61,431	
1829. Ditto ditto . . .	51,758	
1830. Ditto ditto . . .	38,095	
1831. Ditto ditto . . .	34,261	
1832. Ditto ditto . . .	69,193	
1833. Ditto ditto . . .	60,193	
1834. Ditto ditto . . .	41,345	
1835. Ditto ditto . . .	38,647	
1836. Ditto ditto . . .	56,392	
1837. Ditto ditto . . .	56,380	
1838, 1839, & 1840, at same rate .	169,140	
		809,009
			1,779,357

Commissariat Accounts and Pay.

1812. Par. Pap. No. 128 . . .	2,018
1816. Ditto 250 for 1815	3,654
1816. Ditto 118 . . .	4,200
1821. Ditto 47 . . .	1,528
1823. Ditto 18 . . .	1,660
1824. Ditto 10 . . .	1,665
1825. Ditto 23 . . .	2,669
1826. Ditto for 1825 . . .	2,750
8 years (average 2,518*l.*)	20,144

From 1810 to 1825, inclusive, at
2,518*l.* yearly, is   40,288

Amount carried forward . . . £19,783,102

	£	£	£
Amount brought forward			19,783,102

Ordnance Pay and Estimates.

1812. Par. Pap. No. 81, p. 10, Sierra Leone	2,348	
Par. Pap. No. 81, p. 10, Senegal	12,425	
1819. Ditto 91, p. 8, Sierra Leone	6,596	
1821. Par. Pap. No. 42, p. 8, Sierra Leone	6,337	
1822. Par. Pap. No. 28, pp. 9 and 17, Sierra Leone . . .	3,724	
1823. Par. Pap. No. 69, pp. 10 and 19, Sierra Leone . . .	2,757	
1825. Par. Pap. No. 61, for 1824 .	11,050	
1826.	31,852	
Including fractional parts . . .	77,089	
Add for 8 years wanting, at the average of 1819, 1821, 1822, and 1823—4,853*l.* 10*s.*, is	38,828	
		115,917

N.B. From 1825 the Commissariat and
Ordnance Pay merge into the preceding Commissariat Accounts.

Support of Liberated Negroes.

[Till 1817 the returns given are very
defective. For the first half-year of
1814 (see Par. Pap. 64 of 1817), the
cost at Sierra Leone was 23,630*l.* 7*s.* 8¼*d.*
The expenditure everywhere was, at
that time, unchecked, and on a most
extravagant scale. It is a moderate
estimate to take it at 25,000*l.* per ann.]

From 1809 till 1815, inclusive, 7 years	175,000

Amount carried forward . .	£19,899,019

	£	£	£
Amount brought forward			19,899,019

Brought up 175,000

From 1815 till 1825, Par. Pap. 57

        of 1830 383,431

Clothing from England, Estimates

    1825, 10,000*l.*; ditto, 1826,

    12,000*l.*—average 11,000*l.*

    from 1825 to 1838, 13 yrs. 143,000

1826. Finance Accounts	40,000
1827. Ditto ditto	35,000
1828. Ditto ditto	30,000
1829. Ditto ditto	30,000
1830. Ditto ditto	35,000
1831. Ditto ditto	25,000
1832. Ditto ditto	31,250
1833. Ditto ditto	25,000
1834. Ditto ditto	25,000
1835. Ditto ditto	20,000
1836. Ditto ditto	20,000
1837. Ditto ditto	20,000
1838. Ditto ditto	20,000
1839. Ditto ditto	20,000
1840. Ditto ditto	20,000

                          ———— 1,097,681

Liberated Africans before 1826,

     West Indies*   274,370

                          ———— 1,372,051

       Amount carried forward £21,271,070

---

* See Col. Moody's Reports, 1825, &c.; Par. Pap. 73 of 1821; Par. Pap. 325 of 1823; Votes of 1826; Par. Pap. 389 of 1826; Par. Pap. 442 of 1824, &c. &c.

Moreover the sums expended in the Mauritius and in the Cape of Good Hope are wanting. These were very considerable—say 20,000*l.*

Also those liberated in Trinidad had tracts of land given to them, some as high as 16 acres, partly in cocoa cultivation, and worth a good deal of money— say worth 20,000*l.*

	£	£	£
Amount brought forward			21,271,070

Salaries, &c. to Slave Commissioners of Mixed Courts, Sierra Leone, Havannah, &c.

	£	£	£
1819 to 1826. Finance Accounts, yearly, 8 years*		155,700	
1826. Finance Account, 1827 . .	18,000		
1827. Ditto ditto	18,000		
1828. Ditto ditto	18,000		
1829. Ditto ditto	13,700		
1830. Ditto ditto	18,700		
1831. Ditto ditto	19,450		
1832. Ditto ditto	16,500		
1833. Ditto ditto	16,500		
1834. Ditto ditto	16,200		
1835. Ditto ditto	14,000		
1836. Ditto ditto	14,700		
1837. Ditto ditto	14,700		
1838. Ditto ditto	14,700		
1839. Ditto ditto	14,700		
1840. Ditto ditto	14,700		
		242,550	
			398,250
Under head, " Civil Contingencies," 1816—1833, about . .		11,000	
Addition—Public Buildings, (See Fin. Comm. Report) . .		89,121	
Lands in Trinidad		40,000	
Expeditions to explore Africa, at least		50,000	
Illegal Capture (Dibuscadore Rep. Fin. Committee) . . .		6,770	
			196,891
Amount carried forward . . .			£21,866,211

* Expense of Mixed Commission Courts was, for 1820, 24,800*l.* (See Finance Paper, 1821). The general yearly estimate then was 18,700*l.*

	£	£	£
Amount brought forward '			21,866,211

Miscellaneous Sums.

	£		
Commissioners to inquire about Africans liberated in West Indies—Sundries . . .	18,600		
Pensions—Disbanded Africans in West Indies, at 25,096*l.* yearly, till 1826 . . .	250,960		
Pensions—Ditto, 12 years, to 1838, at 15,000*l.* (Commissariat Accounts)	180,000		
Education Captured Negroes (Finance Accounts) 1836 and 1837	23,500		
Revenue—Sierra Leone, 1826 to 1840 inclusive, at 6,000*l.* yearly	90,000		
			563,060
			£ 22,429,271

Remarks.

The Grants, which in many instances have been taken for the preceding Expenditure, were generally insufficient for the particular object, when the deficiency was made up from "*the aids*" of the year and other contingencies. To bring these farther expenses forward, would require a tedious and laborious investigation through almost every public account since 1808. To judge of the sums demanded and paid for illegal captures, Par. Pap. No. 226 of 1822 shows us the sums adjudicated by the Commissary judge in London:— Claimed, 471,938*l.* 14*s.* 5*d.* ; awarded, 211,774*l.* 17*s.* 4*d.* ; and under adjudication, two claims, 69,856*l.*[*]

[*] From Par. Pap. No. 494 of 1838, it appears that the fees amongst the Public Offices on the Bounties paid for captured Africans amounts to 5*l.* 2*s.* 6*d.* per cent., exclusive of a Treasury fee of 1*l.* 1*s.* on all sums above 20*l.* and not exceeding 50*l.*, and on all sums above 50*l.* a fee of 3*l.* 13*s.* 6*d.* ; and as 1,050,000*l.* has been paid for this purpose, these fees have consequently been 60,000*l.*, exclusive of the Treasury fee just stated, at least 2,500*l.* more !!

For all the preceding enormous sums, we have on the one hand got Sierra Leone and the Gambia, the former place with 36,000 liberated Africans congregated there, and exactly for what these places may be accounted worth; on the other hand, we have relinquished more than one settlement on the coast of Guinea, while the remainder, including Cape Coast, influence nothing and command nothing in Africa, beyond the range of the few guns and trifling garrisons which are placed in them.

The whole of our present trade to the west coast of Africa, from Mogadore to the Orange River, is, as a whole, miserable; and still more miserable, when it is considered that the greater portion thereof is made up, as regards imports into Africa, of articles exclusively appropriated to the slave trade; and as regards the exports of articles, almost wholly produced by the slave labour in the native states. The following, from Porter's Tables, is the amount for 1834 :—

Exports to Africa.

	Gambia, Sierra Leone, and to Cape Mesurado.	Cape Apollonia, Cape Coast, and to Rio Volta.	Cape Mesurado and to Cape Apollonia.
	£	£	£
British and Irish articles, 1834	97,425	33,051	736
Foreign and Colonial, ditto	86,431	107,627	3,657
Totals	£183,855	140,678	4,393

The imports into Sierra Leone, from all parts, were for the same year 126,214*l.*

Of which there were, particularly slave trade articles, thus :—

		£
Guns, 20,355, value		10,981
Gunpowder, 587,950 lbs..		11,946
India piece goods		18,266
Iron bars, bolt and cast iron, 1,102,690 lbs. .		2,974
Hardware and cutlery		6,607
Brandy and Geneva, 10,932 gallons		1,496
Rum, 63,360 ditto		5,149
Tobacco, 332,750 lbs..		6,628
		£64,047

leaving only as legitimate trade 62,167*l.*, and of which sum 32,000*l.* were directly and exclusively imported, for the support and maintenance of the liberated Africans in that place; and for the use and consumption of the balance, by the civil and military establishments in the place, the commissariat accounts in the preceding pages will sufficiently account.

The exports from Sierra Leone for that year, to all parts, were (Porter's Tables, Supplement, No. 5,) 65,558*l.*, and in 1835 there were 140,006*l.* Thus :—

	£
Great Britain	84,281
All other Foreign Countries	20,779
Other parts of the Coast of Africa	35,046
	£140,106

Included in these exports are the following ; viz.—

	£
Timber, value	35,863
Ivory	4,936
Palm Oil	14,268
	£55,067

which, besides other articles, are entirely produced by the labour of the slaves to the native chiefs beyond the bounds of the colony, viz., Timanees, Bulloms,

Mandingoes, and Sherbros. Such is the state of this, the chief British African Colony, after fifty years' fostering, and in which labour for nine hours daily can, it is stated, be had for $3\frac{1}{2}d$. and $4d$. sterling per day, and yet it is at this moment consuming the slave-raised sugar of Cuba and the Brazils, refined in England, and next exported to Sierra Leone, and our other transmarine possessions!

One-third of the exports to the coast of Africa, are in fact, arms and ammunition. In 1834 these amounted to 91,407*l*. It is true that the articles themselves are, owing to the considerate care of certain *humane* individuals in this country, procured of that description, which, before shipping, are ascertained to be such as will do harm to no one (see Mr. Buxton's Memorial to Government, p. 118.) But this is only a one-sided view of the matter, because it is obvious that the African nation which, armed with these do-no-harm weapons, meets in battle another nation which is armed with similar weapons of a serviceable nature, must either be killed, or caught and sold for slaves. This result is inevitable. The value of arms and ammunition exported from Great Britain in 1835 was 405,573*l*. to all parts of the world, of which, directly or circuitously, 130,161*l*. went to Africa.

Further, as regards this African coast trade, it is most fatal to the lives of seamen engaged in it. It has been calculated that every ten logs of African timber imported from the African continental ports into this country costs one seaman's life. In the naval and commercial marine, the annual loss of seamen probably exceeds that sustained by the British navy in some years in battle, during the war. Remaining so long in the pestilential mouths of the rivers, around which scarcely poisonous reptiles and only venemous musquitoes can live, as merchants' ships do, and which, from the nature of the African trade as it is at present conducted, they must do, renders such results inevitable.

These facts are stated, not in the spirit of finding fault with any one, or of attaching blame to any quarter. They are stated merely to show the whole truth, and to prove that the course which Great Britain has hitherto pursued in this matter has been wrong, and that another and a wiser course must, and with energy and decision, be adopted. They are stated to show that all our exertions in the cause of Africa have in reality terminated in extending the miseries of that continent; tended to retain, if not to plunge her into a state of greater barbarism; have, in short, tended to enrich foreign nations, and to impoverish and to weaken our own. This is a sad state of things; a deplorable, but a correct picture; a picture, my Lord, at the sight of which humanity must mourn, and British statesmen ought to weep.

Why is it so? Why, but because Great Britain has shut her eyes to the fact, and her ears to the truth— because she has attempted to do that which is impracticable, and because she has taken the wrong road to accomplish her object—because she puts the cause for the effect, and the effect for the cause, and proceeds upon and acts upon this erroneous principle.

The African slave trade is not the cause of African ignorance and barbarity, but the consequence thereof. The latter produces the former; and when we perceive this, when we believe this, then, but not till then, can we get into the right path to do good to Africa, and through her to ourselves. Slavery and a slave trade existed in Africa 3,000 years ago, and has continued to exist, and was in full strength when Europeans first came in contact with her western shores. The whole European foreign slave trade, great as it is, is but as " a grain in the balance, and a drop in the bucket," when compared to the slave trade which from place to place exists in Africa, and for Africa herself; and which drags the unfortunate negro in chains, according as the current of the demand sets from the sources of the Joliba to the springs of the Bahr el Azreek—from the shores of Benin to the shores of the Mediterranean, or into the oases in the Great Desert. These truths are evident and incontrovertible. It is idle to maintain that a few ships from European or American powers, frequenting only the mouths of rivers flowing in the wide extended continent of Africa, create, or influence, comparatively speaking, and to any great degree, the proceedings of the powers and the millions in the interior, as regards the slave trade; which powers, moreover, probably never heard of the name of an European, or that such quarters of the world as Europe and America exist; and into which interior parts of Africa, moreover, no white man can penetrate without the utmost danger. The European slave trade certainly tends to extend the traffic, but it does not create it; nor will its cessation stop a slave trade in Africa, nor even, if utterly abandoned, dry up more than one tear of the millions which flow daily from the eyes of unhappy Africa. Thousands on thousands are daily reduced to a state of slavery, and carried from market to market, over all the continent of Africa; and millions are still slaves, yea, slaves to slaves in Africa.

Let us look at the matter in this its true light, and then all we do will be gone about correctly, take effect in Africa, and be listened to and obeyed by Africa. The miseries and the wrongs of Africa are, strictly speaking, almost wholly her own, and the means of removing them are chiefly in her own hands. The work of regeneration must principally proceed from her own exertions, otherwise it never can be permanent. To heal up an ulcer is not to cure it. A quack can do the former, but a skilful surgeon will only perform the latter. But to effect a cure the latter must know the cause of the disorder which afflicts his patient. So it is with regard to Africa. We must know her disease, and the causes which produce it, otherwise we never can administer either proper or effectual remedies to bring about a radical cure. All our medicines and prescriptions hitherto administered have failed. It is in vain to deny, or attempt to conceal the fact. This proves them to have been wrong, and not applicable to the disease which they were administered to remove. Our efforts of thirty years' duration to put down the African slave trade have not only failed, TOTALLY and SIGNALLY FAILED, but these have tended to aggravate and to increase in every way the mighty and destructive evil.

Why, it is again observed, are these things here brought forward and stated? Why, but that the truth, and the whole truth, should be made known. Errors are pointed out, that errors may in future be avoided. Truth is made known, that the right path may in future be chosen to effect the mighty and important object. Great Britain expends 600,000*l.* yearly, in one way or another, to stop the African slave trade. So long as she does so, will you ever get, or can you ever expect to get, any one engaged in receiving any portion of this sum to say that the system which is pursued is wrong? Nay, is it not more probable that the interest of such parties will bring them to mislead, in order that the errors and the profits may be continued?

What Africa wants is European intelligence, European capital, and European industry to direct and aid her. She must do the rest herself, and would, I think, do it, if the former were honestly and judiciously bestowed and applied. If she refuses to do this, no human power can extricate her from her present state of ignorance, misery and degradation. While she bends her knees in adoration to sharks and snakes, and to the horrid fetish-trees, she will continue to bend her neck to chains and slavery, foreign and domestic; and while she refuses to labour and cultivate her soil, she disobeys the commands of Omnipotence, rebels against his high and his irreversible decree, "in the sweat of thy face shalt thou eat bread;" which decree, be it observed, by toil and labour mercifully punished man for his transgression, and was instituted to keep him from idleness, which, indulged in, would inevitably lead him to transgress. Africa may revolt against this decree, and struggle to escape from it, but she cannot. She cannot be exempted therefrom. She may, however, by her conduct exempt herself; but if she does so, then she must pay, as she does pay, the penalty; she must feel, as she does feel, the bitter consequences, idleness and a slave trade and slavery. While Africa acts such a part as she has always acted, she and her population will never be out of mischief, nor ever raise their heads amongst the civilized nations of the world.

If one-half less was said and written about African slavery and the African slave trade than is said and written, and in place thereof, if one-half more were judiciously done than is done to remove them, there would be greater hopes of ultimate success in removing the one and in ameliorating the other. But there the mighty evils are—there in Africa they are planted and grow, and stand in all their strength; and the question is, how are they either first to be lessened, and secondly, ultimately removed, and the passions of Africa, and her manners and her pursuits, directed from mischievous to useful purposes. Railing at these, or their enormous evils or disastrous consequences, will not accomplish the work. Slow, sure, and judicious proceedings alone can bring and teach the power and authority which exist in Africa to turn the exercise of that power and authority to useful, honourable, and honest pursuits. Slavery and a slave trade forms the general law of Africa. These two evils reign acknowledged, sanctioned, known, recognised, and submitted to by all her population, of every rank and degree, throughout all her extended borders. Every offence and every crime, real or imaginary, in Africa, whether committed against individuals or states, merges into slavery. All this is very mischievous and very destructive to the peace and true interests of Africa, but the question still remains, how are we to convince the whole African population, 150,000,000 of people, of this fact, for it is the fact; and without convincing them that they are wrong, that they are acting contrary to their own interests, we never can succeed in getting them to depart from those errors and that course which has been undeviatingly pursued ever since population was found in Africa. The only safe

and rational course is, to teach her industry, to set
her a good example in all things—that example which
Christianity teaches us to set—accompanied by that
forbearance which Christianity teaches and commands
us to show ; and, above all, to teach her that selling
her people will never make her rich, or better, or
wiser, but that to draw them and to teach them to cultivate the ground, and exchange the productions thereof
for whatever they want, infallibly will. Do this, but do
it seriously, strenuously, and judiciously, and the end
will, it is conceived, be accomplished. But if Africa
continues obstinate—if she turns a deaf ear to such
counsels and such an example, then Africa must and
will remain always as much lost as she now is to herself, to Europe, and to the world.

Agriculture alone is the true and stable foundation
of society and civilization. Commerce must follow
agriculture in every country. It is by her agriculture
alone, the cultivation of her soil, that Africa can be re-
generated, or produce that permanent and useful commerce which will tend to extend her knowledge, tend
to make her and her people independent members of
the general human society, and remove the present
bitter evils that afflict her. Her present commerce
and system of commerce, will not only never accomplish this desirable object, but, on the contrary, it
leads, and will lead, to extend the present evils which
afflict her. Her present trade is, in fact, carried on
by the medium of the spontaneous productions of
nature. Few, if any, of the articles which she ex-
changes with other countries for the rude and limited
supplies which she seeks, are the production of human
capital, labour, or industry. So long as this continues
to be the case, so long will African commerce tend to

perpetuate that idleness and want of industry which universally prevails in Africa; and so long as this is continued, will idleness and insecurity, with their necessary consequences—violence, slavery internally, and a slave trade externally—be continued; so long will the unfortunate Africans, her princes and her people, continue to have no idea of the value of time : yet, until they are taught this important lesson—that time, honestly and continuously occupied, is the greatest of all treasure; until they understand this, and act accordingly; all efforts to bring about any permanent advantage to Africa will be fruitless and unavailing. It is melancholy to reflect upon the picture which every traveller in Africa presents to us under this head. Take one out of millions. De Caillé met a man at Douasso, on the banks of the Kowara Ba, a native of Kong, who had been thence to Jinne, carrying a basket of colat nuts on his head, to be sold at the latter place, and who, when he saw him, was returning with the small stock of merchandise which he had obtained in exchange, viz. a little salt, and a piece of cloth—the remnants, in fact, which he had saved from the several dues which he had paid to the petty chiefs. The journey altogether would occupy him six months! What a waste of time and labour! Under such a state of things can Africa ever get better? Can she ever get rich, independent, or free? Never ! !

An intelligent trader to the east coast of Africa (Captain Cook), has brought before us, in a very short space, the cause of the foreign slave trade, and of African misery and degradation. When at Zanzebar lately, and remonstrating with the people there, in their slave market, for continuing such a disgraceful practice, and advising them to betake themselves to some traffic more honourable and more profitable, commercial, or agricultural ; " Which is that ?" said they. Several things were pointed out, and looking to some ivory then in the market, he observed, " We will buy and pay you for that in preference to buying men." The reply was laconic and characteristic : " It is easier to catch a man than an elephant !" It is easier, also, or rather more agreeable, according to the same mode of judging, to catch an elephant, than to labour continuously during six days in the week in cultivating the ground. The short reply above stated, conveys, in clear words, the whole and the real cause of African misery and degradation, and of the African slave trade. If millions in Europe were to sit down and write volumes on these subjects, they could not make the point so clear or so plain as these ten words, " It is easier to catch a man than an elephant," make it.

Why is Africa poor, miserable, and degraded? Because she is idle and disinclined to regular and steady industry, especially agricultural industry. De Caillé tells us, that at Sambatiklia the people would rather pine amidst famine than cultivate the ground ; and that, when urged to labour and to cultivate, the reply was, that it would take off their attention from studying the Koran ! Lander tells us, (vol. ii. p. 133,) as regards the people on the banks of the Coodonia, " the male population of the community seemed to have no employment or occupation whatever, spending the whole of their time in lounging and loitering about their native villages, whilst the women, more laudably employed, are engaged in extracting oil from a small black seed, and from the Guinea nut." Thus we see the true cause why Africa is wretched, why her population are mischievous, ignorant, and degraded; because, in fact, more than one-half of them are idle as regards any laudable and continuous object, and the remainder have not the slightest idea of the value of time.

Thus stands the matter as regards Africa herself. Next, how stands the matter as regards this country, and as connected with her greatest interests? We have shortly adverted to what has been done, and also to that which has been left undone; we have shown that as much money has been expended, (to say nothing of valuable lives,) as could, interest included, have purchased and enfranchised almost all the slaves in Africa. We have considered our present position as regards this great question. We have failed, most signally and completely, after spending so much treasure. What, then, is next to be done? Great Britain cannot stand still in this matter; she cannot act so, and make herself the object of derision to the whole world. She must go on; she must put down the African foreign slave trade, or it will put down England; that is, reduce her to the rank of a secondary power; it will, and speedily, too, crush and destroy all her great colonial interests on which she has lately expended 20,000,000l. of money, and which colonial interests, during her late awful struggle, afforded those supplies to her marine and those resources to her finances, which enabled her to triumph over all her enemies, over the world combined against her.

Slowly, but securely and strongly, are the consequences of the continued and immense extension of the African slave trade, by the increase of agriculture and commerce in different quarters of the world, raising up into importance numerous new and great commercial interests, and consequently proportionate political power and influence in these different quarters; thereby undermining the once predominant and most powerful interests of Great Britain; changing rapidly the political interest and power of the whole of the greatest nations of the civilized world; and, at the same time, rendering each of these daily greater and more powerful than they previously were, while those of Great Britain become less. These results are obvious to the meanest and most casual observer, and will tell, in the event of either partial or general future contests between Great Britain and any of these powers, with a severe and injurious effect upon all her interests and her power, political, commercial, agricultural, and social.

Her object, therefore, so long and so expensively sought, she must accomplish. Her government, only a few months ago, were compelled publicly to confess, that they could not put an end to the slave trade, without involving this country in war with other countries in Europe. If we go to war for such an object, who can tell over what space that war will extend, how long it will endure, or how much it will cost; but any one can tell that such a contest begun would go to perpetuate, not to stop, the African slave trade, while the extent to which that trade has been carried on has increased the strength of foreign rivals, and paralyzed or weakened our own.

This country, it is repeated, cannot stand still in African matters: it must advance. In order to extinguish slavery in one portion of the British dominions, 20,000,000l. have been paid, with what result time must show; and, in worse than useless efforts to put down the foreign slave trade, even a greater sum, to say nothing about the thousands of valuable lives which have been lost, has been expended. Are all these enormous sums to be lost? for wholly lost they will be, if nothing more is done to Africa, for Africa, and in Africa. The eyes of the world are upon Great Britain, as connected with this subject, at this moment. What will the people of England—what will the whole civilized world say, if this country, after her war against slavery and slave-produced articles, go to Africa and purchase freely, from her chiefs and her people, articles and produce of every kind, raised by the degraded slaves of ignorant, degraded, and barbarous masters! This, my Lord, cannot be done without a total dereliction of every principle of honour, justice, and truth, on the part of the multitudes which have taken an interest in the slave question, and also of every principle of municipal justice, national honour, and good faith, prudence, and policy on the part of the government. You must, therefore, proceed to introduce cultivation into Africa by free labour, and by that alone; and unless you do introduce cultivation—unless cultivation is introduced into Africa, no earthly power can ever introduce civilization, industry, and knowledge into that country.

More money, therefore, must be expended for the purpose alluded to, but it must be expended with energy, and prudence, and economy in all things, and not wasted, as it has been, in senseless theories, idle undertakings, and ruinous and barefaced jobs, in all quarters in Africa, or about Africa, as has hitherto been the case.

The application of external force to crush the slave trade has been tried and has failed. External force alone will never succeed. To blockade and watch

all Africa is a vision, and compared to which the
schemes of the crusaders were wisdom itself.   From
El Arish westward to the Straits of Gibraltar, and
thence by Cape Verde, the Capê of Good Hope, and
Cape Guardafui, &c., by the coast of the Red Sea, to
El Arish again, the coasts of Africa extend 15,000
geographical miles, including seventy or eighty miles,
the Egyptian land-boundary, between the Red Sea and
the Mediterranean.   This whole extent of coast, with
the exception of the space from the Orange River, by
the Cape of Good Hope, to Delgoa Bay, 1500 miles,
is either directly engaged in purchasing and exporting
slaves, or in importing and receiving them.   To
blockade, shut up, or in any material degree to influence or to overawe such an extensive line of sea-coast,
as that just alluded to, is quite impracticable, and
beyond the power of the united navies of the civilized
world to effect, even were these cordially to agree
and to unite in the work.   The number of people
carried away from the interior parts of Africa by the
Mahommedan nations is, including the mortality on
the middle voyage, certainly above 120,000 yearly.
The number carried away by Europeans, or the descendants of Europeans settled in America, including
the mortality in the passage, seasoning, &c., cannot be
less than 250,000; of this latter number 220,000 are
carried away from those parts of the coast which
extend from the Rio Nunez to Cape Negro, 2800
miles, and of this latter number, again, 150,000, at
least, are taken from the country or coast between the
Rio Volta and the Gaboon.   While it is quite impossible for any European nation to obstruct the traffic
in every portion of the African coast, it is not impracticable to strike a deadly blow at by far the

greater portion thereof, namely, that which is carried on between the Rio Volta and the Cameroons. According to Sir Robert Mends, the number carried away in eighteen months, in the years 1820 and 1821, " from the four northernmost rivers in the Bight of Biafra," was at least 130,000, in 424 vessels, many of them carrying from 500 to 1000 slaves. From Bonny River alone, 126, and from Cameroons 177 vessels, with full cargoes, say 90,000, sailed in the short space of four months! (Sir Robert Mend's Despatch, June 22d, 1822.) The command of the mouths of the Niger by a settlement, and authority and influence planted and exerted at no great distance into the interior, might prevent—might, in a short space, extinguish all this ; or, three-fifths of the European and American slave trade would, we may say, at once be cut off. This is the point at which to aim the hardest and most deadly blow at the African slave trade. Extinguished here, as it may be extinguished, by the means recommended, and to the extent mentioned, the results would soon destroy the remainder of the American and European slave trade, by producing, for the wants and the demands of the world, produce at a cheaper rate than could be produced by any one in any distant country, who might be inclined, or attempt to carry on the trade ; and simultaneously the same proceedings would so instruct, influence, and inspirit and strengthen the heart of Africa, as to put down, in an almost equally short space, even a greater proportion of the Mahommedan African slave trade. This is the point and object to aim at. These are the means, alike simple and profitable, required to accomplish the object. From or by our present miserable and ill-chosen settlements on the western coast of Africa, conducted and regulated as these have hitherto been, nothing ever can be accomplished, as nothing ever has been accomplished worthy of notice; nor can any human power render these settlements, in any material degree, however judiciously that power may be exerted in future, instrumental in arresting the progress of the African slave trade, or of spreading knowledge, industry, and civilization, and peace in Africa.

Admitting for the moment, and for the sake of argument, that Europe or Great Britain could extinguish by force the slave trade carried on by sea under the flags of white people, how little will this do for the relief of Africa herself. The Portuguese are already exerting themselves, by means of extending cultivation in their African colonies, to raise them to wealth and prosperity, and they will succeed, and succeed, too, by extending a slave trade for the purchase of slaves in Africa. They have unlimited soil for cultivation in Africa, and they may be said to have an unlimited supply of labour at command. Great Britain cannot interfere to prevent this. Besides, will not the Brazils and other countries, admitting they agree to put down the open and *bonâ fide* African slave trade, resort to the means of carrying away from Africa (as some of them are, I hear, now doing, or about to do) labourers, under the name of free labourers? Can England prevent this? No! Moreover, were the slave trade, which is at present carried on under the flags of civilized nations, wholly extinguished, what is to hinder any African chief to hoist his flag and carry it on? Nothing, but the want of means, and these means could, in fifty different ways, be furnished him by parties interested. By the general law of nations, also, it is not in our power to prevent this, contrary to the wish and the inclination of such African powers.

That such as are here contemplated may be the results—nay, that such, under the view in which the subject has just been considered, will be the results, under the circumstances supposed, is undeniable. It is therefore of the utmost importance, especially at this moment, to consider the probable results, and adopt such a rational and reasonable course of proceeding as may prevent such from taking place. Why are things, as regards Africa and our tropical colonies, brought to their present threatening and deplorable state? Why? but because this country, in her people and her national councils, have never thought about nor looked at results. It is now a very questionable point, whether or not the fatal errors, which have been committed in all these matters, can be retrieved; and if they cannot be retrieved, it is plain that a deadly blow has been struck at the greatest and the most vital interests of the British empire.

Africa is capable of producing, and in perfection, every article of tropical produce that any other quarter of the world, situated within the tropics, can produce, besides some of superior descriptions, which are peculiar to herself. Her dyes in particular, are found to resist both acids and light, properties which no other dyes, that we know of, possess. Throughout all her central and mountainous districts, from the Atlantic to the Red Sea and the Indian Ocean, mines of gold, silver, copper, and iron, are found in abundance, of superior quality and fineness. Sugar, coffee, cotton, cocoa, Indian corn, tropical fruits of every description, and timber of various kinds, superior in quality, whether intended for ornamental or useful purposes, are or can be produced in almost every quarter, and in any quantity. The population in all these places, though very barbarous, are yet not savages, but on the contrary, many of them are some steps advanced in the road to civilization, and to a better order of things. The distance from Europe to all her tropical western shores, is even less than to some of the tropical shores of America, and a great deal nearer than the coasts of tropical Asia ; while her noble rivers, especially that sovereign of the whole—the Niger, opens up by itself, or its greater tributary streams, a navigation through the whole of the central portion of that great continent, from the sources of the Rokelle and the Rio Grande, &c., in 10° W. long., to the sources of the western branch of the Egyptian Nile, the Bahr el Abiad in 22° E. long.,—a distance from east to west of nearly 2,000 geographical miles ! Why, then, should such a country remain almost unknown to, and wholly neglected by Europe, and more especially by England ? She can easily, and at all times with her naval power, reach the confluence of the Niger and the Shadda. There let her plant her banners and her power, the future capital of Africa, which will be commanded by no power, but which will command the two great—the greatest arteries of tropical Africa—and, with these, northern tropical Africa.

The reason why the junction of the Shadda and the Niger is chosen in preference, is obvious. This position will command both rivers, and consequently give the opportunity of obtaining assistance and supplies by means of one, should those from the other at any time be, from any unforeseen or unfortunate cause, cut off or obstructed. It would also enable the place to obtain supplies from above, should it at any time be cut off from these by occurrences below the Kong mountains. This, however, is not very likely to occur, as the naval power of Great Britain is sufficiently strong, by the aid of steam, to clear the river from the sea. It would, moreover, be healthier than to the southward of the gorge of the Kong chain, as there the alluvial country begins, and the miasma from the delta is blown by the south-west winds right upon it; while, if established at the river or in it, as at Beaufort Island, as has been stated is at present intended,* the settlement would, in the first place, be commanded by the adjoining hills and heights, which rise here like walls on either side of the river, to the height of 2,500 to 3,000 feet, and hardly more than that distance apart. Thus situated, the place would, during the rainy season, be subjected to sudden, fearful, and incessant deluges of rain, from the condensation of the clouds upon the mountains, and there, as well as in the dry season, the heat during the day would be almost unbearable and suffocating; while the chill from the river, particularly in the night, would be so keen and severe, and the transitions in both cases would be so rapid and great, that no European, nor indeed any constitution, but more especially the former, could endure the changes. The mortality would, in consequence, be fearful and fatal, and utterly ruinous to the stability of the undertaking. From all these, any settlement placed at the junction of the rivers would be comparatively free. It is scarcely possible that greater want of correct knowledge

* I have looked in vain into Laird's, Lander's, and Oldfield's Travels, and Beecroft's Survey, for an account of this island, but I can find none. Mr. Oldfield assures me that he never either saw or heard of it. Beecroft places an insular rock near the S.E. side of the river.

about a tropical climate, or the proper place to choose in Africa to establish ourselves therein, could be displayed; or an error more fatal to every object which is held in view, adopted, than in choosing Beaufort Island, or any other similar position thereabouts. A settlement further down on the banks of the river below the hills, and near or at the branching off of the rivers, would, with all the disadvantages and dangers above-mentioned, still be preferable to that alluded to, and at the same time be more commanding, and even more healthy, than the other.

Without drying up the sources of supply to the slave trade in the interior, we may as well try to dam up the Niger itself, as to cut off a foreign slave trade with Africa, and an extensive slave trade in Africa itself. To effect this, the interior, at a point which will prove the most commanding, must be gained. To work in detached, and as far as health is concerned, in destructive and ill-chosen positions on the coast, as has hitherto been done, or in any position near the coast, however well chosen, without doing more, is to continue the present erroneous system, and to effect nothing whatever for the relief of Africa. The possession of the Island of Fernando Po is valuable, but it is only valuable as it is considered, and made the means to accomplish an end. Possession of it by Great Britain would prevent any mischievous foreign power, if planted in it, from thwarting our views in the interior; or, in the event of hostilities with that power, from any force belonging to it shutting up all the mouths of the Niger on the adjoining coast. The possession of Fernando Po is, moreover, only valuable more or less, according as it commands, or can command, any of the greatest and easiest navigable branches of the Niger, but which there is too much reason to believe that it cannot do. The Nun, certainly, is not a good navigable branch, and it is as yet doubtful if either the Bonny branch, or the connecting streams of the Old Calabar‑ river with the Niger, are navigable for vessels of a size which could only be profitably employed in a produce trade with the interior. This island, or in fact any other island in that quarter, such as Prince's Island and St. Thomas's, would be of no essential service for the great ulterior object in view, except so far as has been stated regarding the former. The two latter can be of no service whatever. They are, moreover, most unhealthy places, as bad as either Sierra Leone or the Nun, (to be worse is impossible,) and, consequently, they would not only become graves to British settlers, who might be induced or be commanded to go there ; but also fathomless gulfs for British treasure,—fields for expensive and useless jobs, of which there has, unfortunately both for Africa and for Great Britain, already been too many.

The object for which the interior of Africa is at present sought, moreover, goes surely much beyond a mere voyage of discovery. The Niger is known to be navigable and to be navigated by canoes and vessels of considerable burthen from Courouassa to the Atlantic. The Shadda, too, is probably navigable for vessels of the same description for 600 miles. Voyages of discovery alone will not civilize, nor cultivate, nor plant industry in Africa. Sufficient also is already known regarding Africa, and the way to reach her most interesting interior parts, to enable Great Britain to fix upon the most eligible points for putting into operation agricultural labour, without which Africa must remain as Africa has ever been. A voyage of discovery, if successful, may and can only gratify the curious; but it can render no permanent service to Africa, or the great commercial interests of England, as connected with that continent; whereas, agricultural establishments and instructions can and will permanently improve Africa, and lay, at the same time, and nothing else can lay, the foundation for a most extensive and lasting commercial intercourse, which cannot fail to prove eminently advantageous to the world in general, and to Great Britain in particular.

The real wealth of every country consists in the productions of the soil raised by the labour of the people. In this respect, what a sad contrast does Africa afford, when compared to every other quarter of the world! With 150,000,000 of people, her whole exports to every other part of the globe do not exceed in value the exports of Cuba, with only about 1,200,000 inhabitants!

Great Britain has done much, and accomplished nothing, for Africa. She must do a great deal more, and do what is done more judiciously, or she must relinquish the object altogether, and leave Africa to her fate. The measures to be taken must be prompt, prudent, and energetic. Great Britain must do something great,—like herself and worthy of herself, if she wishes, as she surely must wish, that success should attend her operations. She must no longer go on with worse than half measures, in spending money in the manner that she has done. Such a course must fearfully add to and increase every expenditure, and yet never accomplish anything. What is expended merely in the preparations for a war threatened to suppress the slave trade, if judiciously applied, would plant knowledge, and industry, and cultivation, and civilization, in Africa, so widely and so firmly, that nothing could shake or eradicate them for the future.

The way to accomplish all this, and there is only one way to accomplish it, is simple and easy. It will cost but little; will speedily in its results repay the first outlay, and will involve the country in no hostile disputes, but, on the contrary, tend to deliver Great Britain and other nations from the disagreeable and dangerous dilemma in which they are all placed. The way is this: get Africa and. Africans to cultivate their own soil, and sell the produce thereof in order to exchange that produce for their wants, instead of selling each other. to cultivate foreign countries, in order to supply their (Africans) limited and their miserable wants.

When agriculture is stated to be the true and only means of African improvement and civilization, it is not supposed that agricultural operations are to be confined to produce merely those articles which are fit for exportation to other countries in other climates. It is not and ought not to be confined to these, but to be extended also to the production in one portion of Africa, of such articles as another portion of Africa requires and cannot produce; by which means, while the operations of agriculture are extended in Africa, civilization, knowledge, industry, and commerce, would also all be extended and consolidated.

This and this only will terminate the African slave trade, inland and foreign. Is it not plain that the cheap labour which may be procured in Africa, applied to a soil equally productive as that of any other country, will beat, in every market in the world, the produce raised in other countries at a prodigiously

f

higher rate? The slave in Africa, that is, an effective
and seasoned labourer, costs on the coast five pounds,
and in the interior twenty-five shillings.   It is fair
to presume that the price of the daily labour of the
free labourer would be in the same ratio.   The seasoned slave or labourer in Cuba or the Brazils, costs,
(that is, taking into account the value of the number
lost, until they become naturalized,) 120*l.* sterling.
What chance, let me ask, could the cultivator in the
latter places have with the cultivator in Africa, where
the proportion of capital invested for labour paid, in
order to produce exportable articles, is more in proportion than twenty to one!   The cultivator in Cuba
and Brazils, therefore, it is plain, could never meet
the judicious and industrious African cultivator in any
market in the world; and if the former found that he
could not beat the latter in the market of the world,
he would, from that moment, never bring or seek to
bring another slave from the coast of Africa to Cuba,
or to any other country out of Africa.

It has been shown, that there are on the one hand,
600,000 reasons yearly—sovereign reasons—chances
against us, why the African slave trade is not to be
discontinued; and there are, on the other hand, seventy
times the above number of reasons, namely, the productions of the soil, and exports and imports of
Brazils, Cuba, and Porto Rico alone, 50,000,000*l.*
yearly, and the great gains arising from which, and
the great interests connected therewith, which impel
and induce both individuals and nations to continue the
traffic.   This is obvious to the most superficial observer.   Try, then, the never-failing remedy, gain and
interest, to accomplish the great object.   Show and
teach the nations of Europe, and other quarters of the

world, that it is equally their interest, as it is the interest
of Africa herself, to discontinue this traffic ; that 20*l.*
capital expended in African agriculture, will produce
as much, as great a return, if not a greater, than 120*l.*
expended in American agriculture. Try this plan—
in short, pitch the interests, the heads, and the pockets
of the pounds shillings and pence gentlemen in the
world, against each other, and rest assured, when this
is done, that Africa will triumph over all her compe-
titors. Such men, and such men only, will moreover
pay Africans for civilizing, and enlightening, and
regenerating Africa and themselves, and at the same
time make great gain by the transaction; and for the
same reasons bring every African to lend his cordial
assistance in order to accomplish the work.

This is the plain common-sense view of the subject,
and common-sense pounds shillings and pence ; judgment, not feeling, must at last be called in to determine this question, and can only determine it. What,
let me ask, would have been the difference to Africa,
and to Great Britain, if all that enormous value of
imports into this country and others from Cuba,
Porto Rico, the Brazils, and the United States, produced by the labour of slaves in these places, had been
raised by British capital in Africa ? A corresponding
quantity of exports from Great Britain to Africa, that
is, above 40,000,000*l.* yearly, would have been one
result, instead of the miserable traffic which this country now carries on with the west coast of Africa,
312,000*l.* per annum, above one-fourth of which,
moreover, is made up of articles (gunpowder and fire-
arms) by which the slave trade is chiefly carried on.
Another result would have been, that Africa to her
deepest recesses would have been explored ; that cul-

tivation, and knowledge, and industry, and true religion, would have been by this time widely spread in
Africa; and a city, much greater than New Orleans,
have been placed at the junction of the Niger and
Shadda. By the measures which could have effected
this, Africa would have been enfranchised, and the
British West Indian colonies at the same time both
enfranchised and saved. Is it not mournful to think
that less than one half the number of people which,
according to Mr. Buxton, have perished in the passage across the Atlantic, or died after introduction to
countries not their own, would have produced, had
they been retained and employed in the cultivation of
cotton in Africa, more, much more of that article,
than Great Britain receives from the United States, or
1,300,000 bales' yearly?

But it will be said, all this production depends upon
obtaining voluntary labour in Africa. True, it does.
But judiciously and prudently gone about, it is believed that such labour could gradually, to a greater
extent, and from the outset, to a sufficient and to a
remunerating extent, be procured for this purpose in
Africa. But if Africa will not give that labour at a
fair and reasonable rate, then the fault lies with
Africa, and she only is to blame for her continued
miseries and misfortunes, for continued they will be,
and aggravated instead of being decreased, unless her
views and conduct are changed. If she will not labour
like enlightened nations, why then she must remain
wretched and degraded; slavery and a slave trade
will continue to be followed and pursued in her, and
by her; and under such circumstances, she will and
must be left to her fate.

Europeans, it is repeated, did not create the slave

trade of Africa—they found it there, and used it, as they conceived, for their own advantage. The trade is purely of African origin, and proceeds from the views, and interests, and corruptions of Africa-herself. Hence I conceive the hope that European knowledge, and friendship, and power, and authority, (the two latter exerted as may be necessary,) could do much good in Africa, would be welcomed in Africa, and listened to in Africa; whereas, had Europeans been, through the slave trade, the sole cause of African misery, contrary to the feelings, and interests, and power of Africa herself, the former would never have been permitted, and could not have been expected to have been permitted, to enter Africa at all.

Africa, throughout all her borders, but especially near the delta of the Niger, produces cotton in abundance, and of the finest quality. It is the lightest of all kinds of cultivation, affords the speediest return, and requires less capital to carry it on, than almost any other tropical produce. It is consequently the most proper description of produce with which to commence cultivation in Africa, and it is hardly necessary to point out the advantages which would arise to this country from such a course. The imports of cotton wool into Great Britain, from the United States, in 1838, were 444,000,000 lbs., for which this country must have paid at least 16,000,000*l.* While our manufacturers are thus almost wholly dependent on these states for a supply of the raw material for the greatest and most extensive of all the branches of our manufactures, the country and the bank of England is exposed to the danger of being, at the pleasure of these states, stripped of gold, from the immense command of the money market which such a value in cotton gives to these states; and, at the same time, while our manufacturers are deeply injured and restricted in their operations, by cotton monopolies got up in America, British pockets are every two or three years subjected to be lightened to, it may be said, the extent of millions, from the same cause. This is a state of things which ought not to be suffered to exist, and which this great country ought not to endure.

The discovery of a water communication between the GULF OF GUINEA and the most populous, fertile, and civilized (if we may use the term) portions of central Africa, is of great importance to the world, and more especially to Africa itself. Without such a communication, by which European knowledge and industry could come into immediate contact with African ignorance and superstition, and barbarity, and indolence, there can be little hope of ever rescuing the population of Africa from their present disjointed, demoralized, and degraded state. The barbarous Moors and Arabs may improve the perfect savage, and advance them one step on the road to civilized life; but retrograding as these people are themselves very rapidly in Africa, they can teach no people that are in any considerable degree emerged from the savage state, the path to improvement and prosperity. When their power was in its zenith, the result was different; and though they introduced some, and continued many evils in Africa, such as a continuation of the slave trade and slavery, still they rooted out more intolerable evils, such as human sacrifices, and the lowest and most degrading kinds of superstition, amongst the illiterate and savage Pagans. The countries which they had visited, and which they at one time controlled, and over which they still maintain a tottering sovereignty, are civilized, enlightened, and industrious, compared to other portions of Africa, such as Ashantee, Dahomey, and the countries to the south of the Cameroons river, more especially the parts the most remote in the southern interior. In the northern parts of central Africa, the elements for a better state of things are found abundant; but the people, ignorant, and naturally indolent, are without protection, and without any stimulus to industry. Hence vices of every kind flourish among them; hence arise wars and violence; and hence injustice and oppression rule Africa, sweep her fields with desolation, bind her unhappy children in fetters, and cover her miserable population with every sorrow — with "lamentation, mourning, and woe."

To remove all this, and to substitute a better order of things, is highly desirable, and a work which every man would rejoice to see proceeded in and carried into effect. But it is not the work of a day, nor of an age. It must be a work of much labour, and of much time; and a work which requires much prudence, and much caution to go about. We should remember that deep-rooted evils are not to be rooted out in a day, amongst an ignorant and extremely barbarous people; and this being the state of things, it is obvious, that one precipitate step may drive us back many years in our attempts to advance the work of African regeneration and civilization. The Moors and Arabs seek slaves only in *Soudan*, and trade almost entirely for them. The princes and sovereigns of these countries have as yet no other way to obtain the luxuries, and even conveniences of life, (we speak of African luxuries and conveniences,) but by selling their criminals, enemies, and prisoners of war, to those who will buy them, and give in exchange the articles which they want. All this, it is admitted, is wrong, and contrary to their own interest, which would be greatly advanced by pursuing a different line of conduct. But the point at issue is, to get them convinced of this fact. It is obvious, that the more ignorant and barbarous they are, the more difficult it will be to convince them in this matter. It may even be easy to persuade them of the fact, and to open their eyes for the moment; but then the impression is not lasting, nor will it be lasting, till we can bring before their eyes the luxuries they want, and show them how they may obtain these, with greater profit, in exchange for the produce of the ground, than in disposing of the hands which should cultivate it. But to accomplish this we must be permanently settled amongst them. The Arabs are not only traders for the sake of slaves almost exclusively, but they are, with regard to the commerce of interior Africa, jealous, reckless commercial rivals; and, as such, it is natural to expect, they will use all the interest they can make, and the influence which they possess, over the minds of the African princes, and which are undoubtedly great, from the combination of ignorance, religion, and prejudice on account of religion, to irritate the sovereigns against us. On this account, all that should be stated for the present, is the anxiety, and the wish entertained by Great Britain to open up a commercial communication with them, by the nearest and safest road, in order to supply their wants. This effected—once planted securely amongst them—that communication once fairly opened up, then the articles which we brought, and the articles which we required, will silence Arab jealousy, beat down Moorish rivalry, and extinguish Mahommedan influence; then we may safely begin to speak to the native princes about the errors in their government; then our councils would be listened to with respect, and be attended with effect. The prudent silence, and the delay of one or two years on some points, may accelerate the great and the desirable work of African regeneration by a century.

By proceedings of this kind we can alone hope to put an end, a complete end, to the external and internal slave trade in Africa, and ultimately to bring about the extinction of slavery itself in that vast continent. The measures we at present pursue, have failed, and will fail in accomplishing our object. A navy stationed off the coast of Africa, only lops off the spreading shoots of a branch of the tree of African slavery, but the tree itself remains far from our reach, carefully protected, cultivated, and fostered, by the power, the interests, the ignorance, and the barbarity of millions. But let us try to get near the trunk, attack the roots, dry up its juices and supplies, substitute industry for idleness, peace for war, security for insecurity, and we shall then quickly strip it naked and bare, and plant in its stead trees of a different description. By advice we can only accomplish this; by force, never. Only show and convince the African princes, that we will give them more for the productions of their soil than for the sinews which should cultivate it, and the work is done. Nothing else will accomplish the object, or vanquish this wide-spread and this deep-rooted evil. The external trade thus abolished, personal slavery, under enlightened masters and enlightened governments, may rapidly raise the ignorant and savage inhabitants of Africa, to that knowledge and industry which will fit them to enjoy the blessing of freedom and the privileges of freemen.

To extinguish the slave trade, to teach Africa to extinguish it, and to civilize Africa, we might, with equal propriety, and with equal effect, have planted ourselves at CAPE SPARTEL as at the Gambia and Sierra Leone. Will this nation not open her eyes to these facts? Will the fatal experience of FORTY YEARS of delusion and failure, and the waste of millions of public money, without accomplishing any one thing which we wished to accomplish, not teach us wisdom? Teach us to plant our energies, which we may easily do, on a spot in the heart of Africa, where we can command the outlets of the *Niger?* Great Britain would then COMMAND the trade, the improvement, and the civilization of all northern central Africa. The heart, as it were, once purified, and filled, and invigorated with proper principles and energy, and health; the blood of life would quickly circulate to the utmost extremities of the frame, and carry with it and diffuse throughout the whole, through every limb, health, strength, vigour, true knowledge, industry, security and comfort, and peace.

Colonies, my Lord, more especially tropical colonies, ever have been the great source of strength, the sheet anchor of Great Britain in the hour of the greatest danger. The command of the trade of the tropical world gave Great Britain, in fact, the command of the trade of the civilized world, and with it the supremacy of the world. This our neighbour and rival, France, knew, and yet knows, well. This, her former imperial master, Bonaparte, and his arch-adviser, Talleyrand, understood well. The advice the latter, in 1801, gave to his imperious master on these points is deserving of the most serious consideration. No British statesman ought ever to forget it, and every British statesman and legislator should have it always uppermost in his memory. Let the following extract bear witness to the propriety and necessity of this :—

" Her navy and her commerce are, at present, all her trust. France may add Italy and Germany to her dominions with less detriment to Britain than will follow the acquisition of a navy and the extension of her trade. Whatever gives colonies to France supplies her with ships, sailors, manufactures, and husbandmen. Victories by land can only give her mutinous subjects, who, instead of augmenting the national force by their riches or numbers, contribute only to disperse and enfeeble that force; but the growth of colonies supplies her with zealous citizens; and the increase of real wealth, and increase of effective numbers, is the certain consequence.

" What would Germany, Italy, Spain, and France, combining their strength, do against England? They might assemble in millions on the shores of the Channel, but *there* would be the limits of their enmity. Without ships to carry them over, without experienced mariners to navigate these ships, Britain would only deride the pompous preparation. The moment we leave the shore, her fleets are ready to pounce upon us, to disperse and destroy our ineffectual armaments. There lies her security; in her insular situation and her navy consists her impregnable defence. Her navy is, in every respect, the offspring of her trade. To rob her of that, therefore, *is to beat down her last wall, and to fill up her last moat.* To gain it to ourselves, is to enable us to take advantage of her deserted and defenceless borders, and to complete the humiliation of our only remaining competitor."

On the month of June next it will be twenty 'years since I laid before the British Government a large map of northern African, showing, from distinct and incontrovertible authority, the course of the great river Niger, and its termination in the Atlantic Ocean, through the various mouths in the Delta, in the Bights of Benin and Biafra, according as recent

travellers have found it to be.   At the same time, in
various memorials, the civilization of Africa, and the
suppression of the foreign slave trade, by the means
already pointed out, were pressed upon that Government, and mercantile men were adduced ready to under-
take the work; but official prejudices and fears were
too strong, and Sierra Leone influence too powerful, for
us then to accomplish the work.   It was accordingly
abandoned, but never wholly forgotten and relinquished. It is, therefore, with great satisfaction I find
that the attention and influence and exertions of
powerful and influential men, and even of the Government itself, are now called forth and strenuously
directed to this point, and by the same mode of pro-
cedure. This great object, approached and conducted
by judgment more than feeling, by practical knowledge, and not preconceived opinions and theories, can
hardly fail of success. The opinions and views which,
at the time mentioned, I had occasion to bring forward,
have undergone no alteration, nor any change; on
the contrary, every succeeding day and year that have
since passed away have tended but more strongly to
confirm the views and opinions then formed, taken, and
advanced, and the plans and propositions then made.
This, the volume entitled "The Geography of Northern
Central Africa," &c., written by me, and published
by Mr. Blackwood, Edinburgh, and Mr. Cadell,
London, in 1821, will amply and distinctly show,
and the following extracts, probably, be accounted
sufficient to establish.

.But first permit me to lay before you the following
extracts, from a memorial presented to Lord Viscount
Melville, then first Lord of the Admiralty, and dated
London, 19th August, 1820, in proof of my early

views on these subjects. Time has but too truly verified the facts therein stated, and the opinions therein advanced:—

"Without Great Britain can spread knowledge, civilization, and the advantages of legitimate commerce, and a desire for legitimate commerce throughout the interior regions of Africa, she will never put an end to the slave trade. All external efforts will be of no avail;—and not only of no avail, but as the naval officers employed on that coast, and in that service, know, from experience, these efforts will tend to increase and to aggravate to an inconceivable degree all the horrors of that trade; and not only so, but a continuation of our efforts in this way will rouse the hatred and indignation of all the native despots and barbarous population of Africa against the British name, to such a pitch, as will endanger the lives of every British subject wherever found in small parties in Africa, and thus shut up the interior from our view and from our research altogether, and put it out of our power to be of any service to that country, or to derive any benefits from it. Such, my Lord, from a deep consideration of the subject, your memorialist anticipates will be the results. Without we can put an end to that trade, also ruin, swift and inevitable, must overtake all our West Indian Colonies, and with their fall a deep, and perhaps incurable, wound will be inflicted on other Colonial establishments.

"It is in Africa, my Lord, that this slave trade must be destroyed; it is in her bosom that this fearful pestilence which corrodes her vitals, and diseases and paralyzes her whole frame, must be eradicated. Not by force, my Lord; no! but by the simple and easy process of showing the population and rulers of Africa, that we will give more for the produce of their labour and of their hands, than for the hand that raises, or could raise, that produce. Then Africa, and the Africans, will abolish this trade. It is they alone who can do it. All the efforts, and all the navies of Europe, without their cordial support, will fail in the attempt."

The extracts alluded to from the volume mentioned, are next brought forward as follows:—

"Attention to every article of agriculture, and the demands in the regular course of trade, occasioned by the production of these, would be found the most easy, powerful, and effective engines which could be used to turn the attention of the population of Africa to understand their true interests, and consequently prove the most peaceable and expeditious mode of extending knowledge and civilization amongst them. Without roads and regular means of conveyance of goods and produce, such as we possess, the ignorant despot of the interior will never think of making his slaves, or his people, cultivate or transport produce of great bulk, and of laborious and expensive carriage, in order to procure in exchange articles which he requires, either for ornament or for use ; produce too, which is liable to be injured by the way, while, with a trifling labour, and at a still more trifling expense, the slave can be compelled to walk to the most distant market in order to be there sold and exchanged for mercantile commodities, to gratify the passions of a barbarous master. Nor have we any reason to expect any change while cut off from all ready communication with any enlightened nation; and not only so, but, on the contrary, everywhere surrounded by fanatic powers, whose interest and whose policy it is to teach and encourage these sovereigns to follow an opposite course. It can tend to little advantage to cut off a foreign slave trade, (granting that could be made effectual) unless we teach the Africans how to employ their slaves in a more useful and profitable manner. Unless we do this, the abolition of the foreign slave trade will only tend to secure a greater number of wretched victims for those bloody " *customs*," and wholesale butcheries under the name of sacrifices, which are so frequent in many parts of Africa.

" This detestable traffic must be gradually, that it may be wholly and entirely, abolished, not only between Africa and foreign countries, but in Africa between state and state. To accomplish this end effectually, it is necessary also to destroy that grovelling superstition which disgraces human nature in Africa, and which binds the minds of prince and people in the worst and most ruinous of all bondage. In fact, it is this which leads to personal slavery, and every evil which afflicts Africa. Till the chains of superstition are broken asunder, neither the fetters of slavery, nor the yoke of the slave trade, ever will. The introduction of Christianity will dispel the terrors of the one, and its benign influence root out and remove the horrors of the other. Nothing else can accomplish the object. It is in our power to do this. The blessings and the benefits which, by the exertions of men from other countries, were first conferred upon us, we are bound to diffuse amongst other nations who remain deprived of them. It is on this sure basis, the introduction of true religion, and the education of young and old in its principles and its duties, that we must build the fabric of our dominion and our fame in Africa. Every other means will prove a foundation of 'sand,' which each flood of human passions will sweep away. But, erected on the rock of Christianity, the foundation of our power in Africa will be impregnable, and our dominions spread invulnerable against every assailing foe.

"In this voyage (if I may use the expression) for the improvement of Africa, there are two fatal rocks which we must carefully avoid, if we wish to escape shipwreck. The first is, that, although the precious metals (gold in particular) abound in Africa, still, we must take care to direct the exertions of her people to those labours of greater importance, the profits of which can, at all times, command the precious metals, and which productions ought, in this case, as well as in every other, to be only a secondary object. The next is, we ought not to go to Africa with the rooted idea, that it was Europeans who occasioned slavery, and created a slave trade in, and with Africa. If we adopt this erroneous opinion, in order to act upon it we shall never take the right path or proper means to root out the one, or to destroy the other. It is Africa herself, as has already been remarked, that is the great root of the evil, though her guilt does not constitute European innocence, wherever the latter has participated in, or yet continues the traffic.

"On the United States of America, we may say, we chiefly depend for the superior cottons for our finer manufactures. War betwixt those states and this country, is by no means an improbable event. Their interests would, no doubt, notwithstanding, lead them to get their cotton to a British market; but, during war, it is evident that it could only find its way at an enhanced rate. This additional price might be such as would raise the value of our manufactures to a price beyond what continental nations could afford, or are inclined to give, and therefore lead them more and more to encourage manufactures of their own growth, and to manufacture for themselves. It must therefore be of the first importance to our cotton manufacturers to be independent of America for a supply of fine cottons. Africa, as we shall presently see more at large, can furnish that supply. The tea trade to China is a continued drain upon this country for specie. From good authority, it seems that this valuable plant may be cultivated to advantage on the rich plains which extend between the Rio Volta and the Niger. Also the old Arabian traveller, Batouta, who had visited China, states, that in the interior parts of Africa, along the Niger, which he visited, the tea plant grew abundantly. Here is another and a mighty inducement to secure, as ours, the produce of these regions. In comparison with China, these parts are at the door; and the difference in freight and insurance alone, would give the tea there produced, a decided superiority in the European market, and in the markets of every part of the western world. It could also be obtained from Africa in exchange for our manufactures, and not as from China, in exchange for specie only.

"In an undertaking of this kind, we are not to be led away by too sanguine hopes of immediate success; because, if we are so, we shall be completely and unnecessarily discouraged at any untoward circumstance which may, in the course of events, come in our way. Neither are we to imagine that the population of Africa, or indeed any other population within the torrid zone, can be brought to exert themselves in the same manner as the hardier natives of temperate climates. But were the exertions of the former only brought to equal one-half the labours of the latter, the gain would be immense to Africa and to the world. It would give a new turn and a different tone to the feelings and pursuits of the population of that unhappy country. But nothing can be done, nothing ever will be done, to alter their present indolent and inactive mode of life, till justice and general security are spread throughout these extensive regions. It would be vain to expect industry or exertion on their parts, in order to procure the comforts and the luxuries of life, when no one can call any thing he may possess his own, or where the superior wealth which he does possess, serves only to mark him out as the prey of the unfeeling robber or sovereign despot. Formidable as these two scourges are in Africa, still they are only so to the feeble and imbecile population, whom superstition and ignorance have, from time immemorial, taught to bend under the yoke. Before the power, energy, intelligence—before the firmness, prudence, and justice of Great Britain, these would vanish. Those fearful butcheries, under the name of "*customs*," at the death of any person of note, so prevalent in southern Africa, would disappear. Industry and commerce would raise their heads. Christianity would enter, with liberty in her train; and the unprincipled despot, and the sanguinary freebooter, would shrink back into the deserts, and be heard of no more!

"The rivers are the roads in the torrid zone. Nature seems to have intended these as the great help in introducing agriculture and commerce. Wherever the continents are most extensive, there we find the most magnificent rivers flowing through them, opening up a communication from side to side. What is still more, remarkable, and becomes of great utility, is, that these mighty currents flow against the prevailing winds, thus rendering the navigation easy, which would otherwise be extremely tedious and difficult. This is the case with the great Maranon and Oronoco in South America. The prevailing trade winds blow right up their streams. This is the case with the Niger, and in a more particular manner during the time it is in flood. For ten months in the year, but more particularly from May till November, the prevailing wind in the Bights of Benin and Biafra is from south-west, thus blowing right up all the outlets of the Niger. January and February are the months during which the Harmattan wind blows,—a dry wind coming from the north-east, and from the great deserts south of the Mediterranean. In the Congo, Tuckey found the breeze generally blowing up the stream. It is needless to point out at length the advantages which may be derived from this wise regulation in the natural world. The meanest capacity may comprehend this.

"There is no efficient way to arrest the progress of this deep-rooted evil, but to teach the Negroes useful knowledge, and the arts of civilized life. Left to themselves, the Negroes will never effectually accomplish this. It must be done by a mighty power, which will take them under its protection—a power sufficiently bold, enlightened, and just, to burst asunder the chains of that grovelling superstition which enthrals and debases their minds, and which, with the voice of authority, can unite the present jarring elements which exist in Africa, and direct them to honourable and useful pursuits. A small portion of European knowledge and spirit would be sufficient to rouse the Negro to assert his independence, and drive back, with shame and disgrace, any force which either the Moors or the Arabs could send against him. Till this is done—till the native princes' are taught that they may be rich without selling men—and till Africa is shown that it is in the labour and industry of her population, and in the cultivation of her soil, that true wealth consists—and till that population can see a power which can protect them from such degrading bondage, there can be no security for liberty or property in Africa; and, consequently, no wish or hope for improvement amongst her population. Slavery and a slave trade existed in all their virulence many centuries before Europeans had any knowledge of western and of southern Africa. Were the European abolition rendered ever so effectual—were all the traffic with the other places previously enumerated completely abolished, still this would scarcely dry up one tear that flows to swell the tide of African misery. Millions are still slaves—slaves to slaves in Africa. It is in Africa, therefore, that this evil must be rooted out—by African hands and African exertions chiefly that it can be destroyed. It is a waste of time and a waste of means, an aggravation of the disorder, to keep lopping off the smaller branches of a malignant, a vigorous and re-productive plant, while the root and stem remain uninjured, carefully supplied with nourishment, and beyond our reach. Half the sums we have expended in this manner, would have planted us firmly in interior Africa, and rooted up slavery for ever. Only teach them and show them that we will give them more for their produce than for the hand that rears it, and the work is done. All other methods and means will prove ineffectual.

" Granting that the navigation of the Niger was interrupted at Boussa, by reason of rapids or rocks rising amidst the stream; still, we know that the river can be navigated in safety from Boussa upwards, and from Boussa downwards. Therefore, on this commanding spot, let the British standard be firmly planted, and no power in Africa could tear it up. A trifling land-carriage would then give this nation nearly all the advantages of an open navigation, and, by such a natural barrier, place the Niger completely under her control. Firmly planted in central Africa, the British flag would become the rallying point for all that is honourable, useful, beneficial, just, and good. Under the mighty shade thereof the nations would seek security, comfort, and repose. Allies Great Britain would find in abundance. They would flock to her settlement, if it had the power and the means to protect them. The resources of Africa, and the energies of Africa, under a wise and vigorous policy, may be made to subdue and control Africa. Let Britain only form such a settlement, and give it that countenance, support, and protection, which the wisdom and energy of British councils can give, and which the power and resources of the British empire can so well maintain, and central Africa, to future ages, will remain a grateful and obedient dependency of this empire. The latter will become the centre of all the wealth, and the focus of all the industry of the former. Then the Niger, like the Ganges, would acknowledge Great Britain as its protector—our king, as its lord.

" The extent of country and population, the improvements, labours, and wants of which, would be dependent upon, and stimulated to exertions by, a settlement on the Niger, is prodigious, and altogether unequalled. The extent compromises a country of nearly 40° of longitude from E. to W.; and through the greater part of this extent of 20° latitude, from north to south, a space almost equal to Europe. Where the confluence of the Bahr Kulla with the Niger takes place, is the spot to erect the capital of our great African establishments. A city built there, under the protecting wings of Great Britain, and extended, enriched, and embellished by the industry, skill, and spirit of her sons, would, ere long, become the capital of Africa. Fifty millions of people, yea, even a greater number, would be dependent on it.

" Unfold the map of the world: we command the Ganges; fortified at Bombay, the Indus is our own. Possessed of the islands in the mouth of the Persian Gulf, we command the outlets of Persia, and the mouths of the Euphrates, and consequently of countries the cradle of the human race. We command at the Cape of Good Hope; Gibraltar and Malta belonging to us, we control the Mediterranean. Let us plant the British standard on the island of Socotora—upon the island of Fernando Po—and inland upon the banks of the Niger, and then we may say, Asia and Africa, for all their productions and all their wants, are under our control. It is in our power. Nothing can prevent us. A tenth part of the sum which our merchants and manufacturers have lost in overstocking old markets, would have been sufficient to fix us securely in Africa, and to have developed completely all the mercantile stores which she possesses, and the improvements of which she is susceptible."

The sentiments and opinions thus expressed twenty years ago have, as has already been stated, undergone no change. In the month of June, 1838, when I had the honour of first becoming personally acquainted with Mr. Buxton, and found at our first meeting, that himself and his influential friends were about to direct their attention to other and more energetic means for checking and suppressing the foreign slave trade, and for improving Africa, the same opinions were urged, and continued to be urged, while labouring closely with him, and also for the cause of Africa through him, during the period of eighteen months previous to his departure for Italy. In support of that cause, and for the objects mentioned, the subsequent geographical survey of Africa was undertaken and written, and the map which accompanies this work constructed. About twelve months ago, when your Lordship's predecessor in office, Lord Glenelg, did me the honour to inquire if I would go out to Africa, to carry the views of government into effect, and requested me to draw up such instructions and forms of treaties as might be considered advisable to enter into with native African powers; my reply to the latter part of the request was that, before any such instructions and forms of treaties could be drawn out, it would be necessary for her Majesty's government, and the other party engaged in the matter, to determine specifically the object and the duties of the mission to be sent, and the nature of the treaties, especially the commercial treaties, which, consistent with the commercial treaties existing between Great Britain and other powers, could be entered into with any chiefs and states in Africa. To accelerate, and so far to guide, the decision alluded to, and upon the understanding that the course to be pursued in all our future proceedings connected with the suppression of the slave trade and the improvement of Africa, was in that continent decidedly and expressly neither to be by conquest nor colonization, but by precept, example, instruction, and friendship; a paper, of which the following is a copy, was drawn up by me, and placed in his Lordship's hands. Soon after his Lordship quitted office; and thus, so far as the humble individual who thus addresses you is concerned, this part of the matter terminated.

AFRICA—TREATIES—INSTRUCTIONS.

There are three modes which may be followed to benefit Africa and the world. The first is by conquest; the second is by colonization; and the third is by example and persuasion—the introduction of European capital, intelligence, and industry, into that quarter by any civilized European power, or by the subjects of such a power.

The two first modes would accomplish the work of African regeneration and civilization the most rapidly; the first more rapidly than the second; the last slower than either of the two first, but judiciously gone about, perhaps equally sure, and certainly without that expense and loss of life which would attend the two first, and especially on the mode by conquest.

The latter, for various reasons, being considered the preferable plan, and that which it has been determined to adopt; the preliminary steps necessary to be taken are—for the British government to make treaties of peace and amity and commerce with the native chiefs, who rule in the most commanding positions in Africa. Next, or along with these steps on the part of the government, for certain directors to form a Joint Stock Company* with a large capital, with limited responsibility to the shareholders, and under the known countenance and protection of that government, and under the direction of well-known capitalists, and judicious and eminent and practical mercantile men.

To make these treaties with the native chiefs, a person or persons should be forthwith sent to Africa, fully authorized and instructed by the British government; and this person or persons should, at least one of them, be also instructed and empowered by the said company, to take at the same time, the necessary measures to pave the way for the introduction of their servants amongst the Africans; and to

---

* Although one agricultural Company is here spoken of, it is not supposed to limit the privileges to one. There may be fifty similar in Africa.

take all preliminary steps which may appear to be necessary to commence their operations as speedily as possible in those parts of Africa which may be pitched upon as the future field for their operations and proceedings.

While it is stated, messengers should be sent to Africa, it is necessary to remark, that one only should have the full powers to act; the others who accompany him possessing equal talents, and judgment, and experience, attending to succeed, in the event of the death of the chief messenger, in order, that under the same instructions, the objects of the mission may be carried forward. Unity of action in everything that regards Africa, is of the first and of vital importance; and everything that could, by any possibility, lead to discordant views or opinions in any mission when working in Africa, ought to be most carefully guarded against.

The messenger or messengers so sent, should be acquainted with, and accustomed to, a tropical climate; possessed of a knowledge of the negro character; well acquainted with geographical subjects in general, and with African geography in particular; together with a practical knowledge of tropical lands and tropical agriculture; and also with a general knowledge of commercial affairs; the markets of the world best fitted for colonial productions, and the state and condition of those countries which afford the largest supplies of colonial productions for these different markets, and with which the producer in Africa must come in competition.

INSTRUCTIONS.

These messengers, both on the part of the government and the company alluded to, should be instructed to form treaties and alliances with the most potent African chiefs in those parts of Africa, which are most easily reached by an European maritime power; to observe and select the parts which are best adapted for cultivation, and which have also the easiest means of transporting the produce raised, to shipping places; and choosing at the same time those points and those states where the political power and influence of rulers are greatest, in order to extend, by that power and that influence, the great objects which the British government and the projected company have in view with regard to Africa.

The treaties so made with the native powers in these parts, which the proposed company will point out as the most eligible, will, with the customary preliminaries and formalities, be either defensive, or offensive and defensive, as the British government may deem it most advisable and prudent to enter into.

If, for peace and friendship, and defensive only, the conditions should be, that the native power, or powers, as may be, should bind themselves not only to put an end to the foreign slave trade, but also to the sale of slaves in their states destined for other African states in the interior; and further, to use all their influence with neighbouring powers to do the same within their territories; that they should allow the British company or settlers to buy or rent land within their dominions wherever that might be considered the most eligible and best fitted for the intended objects; and that they should protect, with all their power and influence, the capital and property of such company and settlers from violence and disturbance, and, at the same time, give every encouragement, not only to these settlers, but also to such of their own subjects as may be inclined to follow the example proposed to be set before them.

That these powers should bind themselves to give every reasonable facility to all agricultural and commercial operations, internal or external, which may be gone into by the said company and other settlers, and to refrain from imposing duties on articles and produce commercial or agricultural, exported or imported; or such only as are reasonable and reciprocal, such as are settled or may be settled by treaty between such powers—the British government and the company alluded to. Further, that this company, and any British settlers who may settle with or under them, whatever their colour may be, shall be permitted and empowered to try, and judge, and punish, all criminals amongst themselves, in conformity to British law and usages, and in a similar manner to that which British residents at Canton, in China, were permitted to do; and to enable them to do this, the British government must provide such company and such settlers, with proper judges, armed with the competent authority.

That these native powers should be bound to permit the said company and settlers who may join them, or any British settlers, to erect forts, as may be necessary, and in such parts of their dominions as may at present, or at any future time, be considered necessary for the protection of the persons of such company, and the property of such company, and the factories established by such company; the said company and the British government paying such reasonable sums as may be agreed upon for the right to do so.

Until civilization spreads, and political power and government becomes more stable in Africa, it will be better and more prudent to rent lands yearly than to purchase; or, if to purchase, then to do so payable at the rate of so much per annum; and likewise so of all presents and gratuities which may be given to the native chiefs, according as the latter shall be fixed by treaties. This will prevent excessive and unjust demands being made and repeated, owing to the sudden change of dynasties and authority which too frequently take place in Africa.

These yearly tributes or presents must be fixed at a reasonable rate—at a low rate will make any chief in Africa a rich man. See what may be effected in this way! The price of a slave in the interior is only 25s. sterling. Of this, or out of this, the chief receives as dues equal to probably 2s. or 4s. sterling, if so much. (Muckni, the barbarous viceroy of Fezzan, exacts only one dollar and a half duty for each slave.) Give him or them 10s., and 100,000l. so spent would prevent the exportation of 200,000 slaves annually, and save Great Britain her present annual outlay, (less the 100,000l. so paid,) one way or other, above 600,000l., expended, too, ineffectually to suppress the African foreign slave trade.

On these conditions—namely, the extinction of the slave trade, so far as above-mentioned, and the protection of British subjects, property, and commerce—all the produce from such African state or states to be admitted into every British port on the same terms as that from the ports of the most favoured nations. If the British government can lower any duties on African produce, that is, admit the productions of Africa, not purely belonging to British settlers and subjects, on British territory, at lower duties than similar produce from other countries is admitted, that concession would be well, and afford great encouragement to any such company and settlers as above alluded to, to go on with the proposed undertaking. But this is a grave subject, and one which, from existing treaties and the position of this country, as connected with other civilized countries with which treaties exist, requires not only the utmost consideration, but the utmost caution, because those nations whose immediate interests may be invaded or threatened by the increased agricultural productions of Africa, as some of these certainly will be, may adopt a similar line of policy with regard to the productions of this or other countries with which they are connected, to the great and serious, perhaps insupportable, loss of great manufacturing and commercial interests in Great Britain.

This is a point and preliminary of the first and the utmost importance. It is necessary for the British government to consider and determine not only what they will do, and what they can do, but also what they cannot do, in such matters. Without a full knowledge of these points no negotiator can direct his steps with safety or right in Africa.

With the market of the world open to Africa on equal terms, the cheapness of labour in Africa need fear no competition in any quarter; and Great Britain will have a right to require of all foreign nations to admit into their ports all produce raised in Africa under her immediate auspices and protection, on equal terms as the productions of the most favoured nations. It will, moreover, for a time, be impossible to discriminate in African productions those that are raised by free domestic labour from those that are produced by domestic slave labour.

On the above conditions, a treaty of amity, peace, and friendship, or a defensive treaty also, as may be considered advisable, to be concluded between Great Britain and African princes. It is worthy of the consideration of the British government, if they would conclude with any powerful African sovereign, who may agree to put an end, not only to the external slave trade, but also to domestic slavery, a treaty offensive and defensive, with the additional privileges and immunities which such a treaty would convey and ought to convey.

These African chiefs should be bound to protect, in the strongest manner, all the teachers of the people, or preachers of Christianity, who may come from Great Britain, or any other christian country, amongst them. To aid in the same noble cause, the British government should engage, through the proposed company, to contribute for a certain time, along with the native power or powers, to the support of such teachers and preachers and their respective establishments. That these native powers, wherever human sacrifices exist, whether to the manes of friends, or to any of their grovelling deities, or bloody fetisch rites, be urged, but without threatening or violence, to bind themselves to put an end to such sacrifices throughout their respective dominions as the price of every favour, reward, or support that they receive, or are to expect from Great Britain.

That these native powers should engage to give protection to all slaves who may come into their states from neighbouring countries, and allow the proposed company to engage them as servants and labourers. It will, however, be prudent to consider whether it may be wise or politic for the said company, at least at the outset, to become the protectors, or to appear as the protectors, of such slaves, because it might tend to prejudice other states against them, amongst which states it is desirable that the company, both as agriculturists and as merchants, should obtain a footing as early as they possibly can. A hasty step may retard this; and thus the evil arising on the one hand be much greater than the good obtained on the other, even were it obtained without danger.

The government and the company must pursue their plans for the good of Africa, and for the advantage of this country, with energy, in truth, in sincerity, and honesty : and those employed under both must do the same thing. Example is more powerful than precept; and a strict attention, both in public and private, to every moral and religious duty, is indispensable amongst all that may be employed in every department. Such conduct will work wonders in Africa. The reverence which Mahommedans, even in outward appearance, publicly show to a Supreme Being, gives them a pass-port into every corner of Africa. Peace and good-will must be sought and cultivated by the greatest prudence, judgment and for-bearance, and clemency. On the other hand, every senseless or determined infraction or violation of treaties made on the part of any of the African chiefs, to the detriment of any British subject, must be instantly resented and punished by Great Britain ; and to enable her to do so effectually, and without much trouble and loss, the settlements for that object, as well as for commercial reasons and objects, should, for a time, be placed upon or near the great rivers.

The messengers sent should be instructed to collect every infor-mation that they can possibly collect regarding the probability of terminating domestic slavery, and the human sacrifices, and the degrading superstition so prevalent in Africa; and, in the first place, communicate that information to England, in order that it may there form the subject of deep consideration and consultation, and become a sure guide for the future proceeding of the Government and the company in all the regulations and directions which may be drawn up regarding these very important matters. So deeply are all these evils rooted, so widely and so universally are they spread in Africa, that the utmost caution and prudence are necessary to know how to interfere with, in order to remove them. They must either be interfered with by a most prudent, and forbearing, and patient hand; or, at once grappled by a bold, and determined, and powerful one.

The messengers sent ought to make every inquiry into the proper way to proceed with safety into the more potent and interesting countries in the interior of Africa, and ought not only to go themselves into every part where communication is practicable, but to engage and to empower others to do so; keeping always in mind not to push too far where by doing so every thing that had been learned, may be lost; but to make sure of their footsteps and grounds so far, and then return with the knowledge previously obtained to push their researches further, and with the certainty of success. The want of this precaution has already occasioned sad delays in acquiring proper African knowledge, and consequently has tended to retard every proper undertaking that might have been entered into to benefit Africa, and by benefiting her to have put an end to the foreign slave trade, the annihilation of which, is to advance the best commercial interests of Great Britain, and the general interests and welfare of the human race.

That the African chiefs with whom treaties are made, ought to bind themselves no longer to make prisoners or slaves of any European, or other persons under them, who may be passing through the dominions of these chiefs on journeys of research, or for commercial objects and other lawful and necessary purposes; but on the contrary, that they should afford every such European or other person every assistance and facility in their power to forward their views and their objects.

That the messengers so sent to Africa, and individuals proceeding under the proposed company to settle there, should use their utmost efforts to make the Africans in general comprehend the value of time, of which they have not at present the slightest idea; that time is money and property. Without they are brought to understand this, no permanent good ever will, or can be, effected in Africa. To give one instance of the waste of time, out of multitudes which could be adduced, De Caillé mentions in his travels of meeting at Douasso, on the banks of the Kowara Ba, a native of Kong, who had travelled thence to Jinne (450 geographical miles) carrying with him, on his head, a basket of colat nuts which he bartered for salt and other trifling necessaries at Jinne, and was returning with these in his basket to his country—the whole journey occupying him about six months ! !

Coffee, sugar, indigo, cotton, every article of exportable colonial produce, but especially cotton of the finest quality, can be produced in almost every spot in tropical Africa; and the messengers of government and the servants of the company should be instructed to use every effort to encourage the production of these, and of every other exportable and exchangeable article, but especially cotton; to show the natives how to rear and to prepare all these articles, and to choose persons of competent and practical knowledge to teach, both by precept and example, the Africans in all these matters. The sale of these articles will speedily procure the latter wealth and capital, and these will necessarily lead them to seek after—first, all the necessaries of life, and next its luxuries, and at the same time enable them to pay for these.

It is quite impossible to go minutely into the instructions which should be given to the messengers who may be sent into Africa, as their proceedings and movements must, in some measure, be guided by circumstances which may arise, and occurrences which may take place around them. Possessing, however, a full knowledge of the general views and objects of the British government, and the British company, much may be left—must be left to their own judgment and discretion; but in all very weighty matters which may appear to be out of the common course of calculation, (and such will arise in African matters) and where time will permit, reference should be left to England; and where time will not permit without the most serious injury and danger to the great objects held in view, then, under such circumstances the messengers must be permitted by both the Government and the company to follow the dictates of their own judgment, in every case, except such as in the result might involve the question of war between Great Britain and any African state.

London, 12th January, 1839.

Before concluding, permit me to observe, that it has been stated in the public journals, on the authority of communications lately received from Rio de Janeiro, that the captured Africans carried into the ports of the Brazils, are afterwards let out to such as may take them upon the payment of the 5*l*., the amount of the bounty money previously advanced by the British government to the captors. Can this be true? If it is so, it is the readiest way that has yet been contrived to give the slave trade wider scope, and enable those who wish it to be continued, to obtain slaves at a very cheap rate. People in the Brazils have only to combine together; fit out a ship for Africa; fill her with slaves at 6*l*. or 7*l*. sterling each, (the price on the coast of Africa,) and suffer the whole to be captured, and then pay 5*l*. for each of the people so captured; when, even after defraying the loss of the ship, supposing she had gone to sea without being insured, they will obtain the slaves at the rate of 40*l*. sterling each, instead of 70*l*., which they pay to the regular slave merchant.

The experience of many years has shown, in the clearest manner, that while there is a demand for African slaves, there will be found the means to supply that demand in one shape or another. Rather than that things should go on as they are; and as they have been going on during the last thirty years, and supposing that nothing further is to be done for Africa to ameliorate and change her internal institutions and pursuits, it would be better, far better, for Great Britain to withdraw her ships from the African coasts, abandon all her expensive slave trade suppression machinery, and keep the 600,000*l*. she yearly expends in vain in this matter, in her pocket. No more negroes than are carried from the coast of Africa, would be carried away (the supply would be regulated as it now is by the demand); while the number that might, under such circumstances, be subsequently carried away, would be transported from Africa to America in such a manner, as would prevent the horrid sacrifice of human life which is at present witnessed in the African slave trade, almost wholly owing to the manner in which it is carried on.

I am, &c.

JAMES M'QUEEN.

LONDON,
    30th January, 1840.

GEOGRAPHICAL SURVEY

OF

AFRICA.

GENERAL
GEOGRAPHICAL SURVEY
OF
AFRICA.

AFRICA, one of the four quarters of the world, and the third on the scale in point of magnitude, extends north to south from Cape Bianco in 9° 48′ E. long. and in 37° 20′ N. lat., to the Cape of Good Hope in 34° 22′ S. lat. and 28° 24′ 24″ E. long.; and east to west from Cape Asser, 11° 48′ 50″ N. lat., and in 51° 14′ 30″ E. long., to Cape de Verd in 14° 44′ 40″ N. lat., and 17°·32′ 20″ W. long., being in its extreme length from north to south 4302, and in its extreme breadth from east to west 4127 geographical miles. This important and vast portion of the world, hitherto but little known, and less attended to for any good or beneficial purpose, stretches through the whole of the torrid zone, and includes within its borders 11° lat. of the southern, and 14° lat. of the northern temperate zones; thus enjoying the finest and most productive climates on the face of the globe.

The countries extending throughout by far the greater portion of the vast surface just mentioned are, as regards soil and capabilities, amongst the finest in the world; but the population of the whole, with the exception of Egypt in ancient times, and the population on the shores of the Mediterranean when under the Carthaginian, the Roman, and the brighter days of Arab sway, have through every age been, and yet are, sunk into the lowest depths of ignorance, superstition, disorganization, and debasement; the glimmer of civilization which for a time appeared in Nubia and Abyssinia, scarcely, as compared with the whole, forming an exception.   If it was possible also to sink Africa into a worse state of disorganization, ignorance, and distraction than that in which she has hitherto been, the present is the moment when such a state of things is eminently and particularly witnessed.   Her state cannot be worse or more unfavourable ; while the hope and probability is, that from this time forward matters will improve, and it is to be hoped rapidly improve, in her favour.

The history of Egypt, the conspicuous part which for many centuries she acted on the theatre of the world, and the history of the countries along the shores of the Mediterranean, long the granaries of Rome and support of the Roman Empire in its proudest days, are so well known that it is considered quite unnecessary to say much about these countries here.   Egypt, as early as the days of Sesostris, had extended her conquering arms far to the south of Cape Guardafui, and deep into the interior of Africa, as the figures representing the people, the animals, and the productions of the soil of Africa on the sculptures, and on the paintings found in the ancient temples of Egypt and on her mummies, clearly show.   During the pride of Roman power, and under the previous government of the Ptolemies, Egypt contained 7,500,000 inhabitants; the cities were numerous and very populous—Alexandria alone containing 700,000 inhabitants.   In Western Africa 300 cities owned the sway or superiority of Carthage, each vying with the other in wealth and population, and some of them scarcely yielding to Carthage in splendour, while that city measured itself almost with Rome in the zenith of her power and her glory (see Gibbon, &c.).   Under the reign of Seidy Mahommed, Morocco exported in one year grain which loaded 250 sail of ships from 150 to 700 tons, the duties on which, at 1 doll. per 80 lbs., amounted to 5,257,320 Mexican dollars.   Such, even yet, is the fruitfulness of that part of Africa.—(Jackson's Shabeeny.)

The population of Africa is composed of various races of men, and of an intermixture from each of the different races. The original inhabitants of the northern parts remain under the name of Berbers.   This people are scattered over Africa north

of the Great Desert from Morocco into Bornou, and along the
Red Sea and coast of the Indian Ocean as far as Mozambique.
They are supposed to be the same as the ancient Numidians.
Their language is original, and different from any other. They
themselves assert that it is the same language as was spoken
by the patriarch Noah. The Arabian writers assert that these
people are descended from Ham, and that their ancestors were
expelled from Palestine and Syria and Phœnicia. There is in
the north-west portion of Africa, and in the west from the
Senegal to the Rokelle, the remains of the old Numidians or
Berbers, the Carthaginian and Roman provincials driven across
the desert first by the Vandals, and next by the Saracen arms.
They are of a copper colour, and found under the general
name of Foulahs. They are chiefly a pastoral people, and
extend in their original and connected dwellings or country
from the sources of the Rio Pongas, &c. along by the sources
of the Gambia, the Senegal, and the eastern branches of that
stream to the confines of Benowm and Beero. They are the
same people as the Fellatahs, who have become warriors.
Their armies, consisting of cavalry, have, within the last 100
years, extended their sway over all central Africa, eastward as
far as Bagherme and Mandara, spreading ruin and desolation
wherever they came. Clapperton was told by one of them,
that they are the same people as the Wahabees in Arabia,
which, if so, is a very curious fact. The descendants of the
Arabs are found over a vast extent of the interior of northern
Africa and along the shore of the Indian Ocean. They everywhere follow the tenets of the Mahommedan religion in its most
rigid and fanatic code, and consequently Christians are everywhere held in the utmost detestation, and are always in danger
amongst them. The Arab tribes dwell in or bear the sway
over Bornou, Bagherme, Dar Saley, Darfur, Kordofan, and
over the greater portion of the course of the Bahr-el-Abiad.
South of the parallel of 10° N. lat., with the exception of the
lower course of the Bahr-el-Abiad, the population is almost
wholly black, and of the pure negro race; until, approaching
the southern tropic, the Hottentot race which spreads to the
southern extremity of the Continent in the western division of
that portion of Africa, and the Caffres in the east portion of

that quarter, a distinct race from the Negro, and who seem to be descended from some one of the numerous Asiatic tribes, are severally met with. The whole Negro race, the Hottentot, and the Caffre, are Pagans, and of the most degraded and debased class, in all their religious creeds, many of them, in fact, having scarcely any idea of religion at all. Abyssinia, a considerable empire in the east quarter of Africa, adjoining the straits of Babel-Mandeb and the western coast of the Red Sea, professes to be Christian, of the tenets of the Alexandrian Church; but isolated as that state has in a great measure been from the remainder of the civilized world for many centuries, superstition and ignorance are fast obscuring the light which once spread in it. With this exception, Africa (what exists in European colonies is not, as compared to the whole, worth taking into account), in religious belief, may be divided into Pagan and Mahommedan, the former far outnumbering the latter. A considerable number of Jews are found in the interior of northern Africa, and in some places, such as Goober and Saccatoo, and places adjoining, we find the remains of the Copts, the original inhabitants of Egypt, who, at one time, held a considerable dominion in Africa, from Lake Shad, or Zad, westward, to the borders of the Niger; and who, moreover, there is reason to believe, at one time professed the Christian faith. The belief is universal in that portion of Africa, that Gamberou, once a great capital, belonged to the Christians from Egypt.

The authority of Egypt in early times, as already alluded to, and as early probably as the days of Moses, extended deeply into the interior parts of Africa, and at later dates, there is reason to believe also, far into those countries situated to the south of Abyssinia on the shores of the Indian Ocean. The eastern coasts of Africa beyond the straits of Babel-Mandeb, and to the southward of Cape Guardafui probably as far as Sofala, were certainly well known both to Egypt, to the enterprising merchants of Tyre, and to the sovereigns of Judea, from the days of Solomon downwards. In latter periods the conquering Arabs, when they had become Mahommedans, extended their sway over all the eastern coasts of Africa, to probably 25° S. lat. The remains of their power and civilization and religion are found over all these places at the present day, and although their authority had considerably declined when the Portuguese discovered these parts 400 years ago, still it was then strong and extensive; so much so, that their commercial intercourse with India was frequent and very considerable. There can also be no doubt that, about 600 years ago, their arms and their power and their authority extended southwards from Gana to the delta of the Niger. The Portuguese pilot, in the narrative of a voyage undertaken from Lisbon to the Isle St. Thome, about 1520 to 1530, says, that the population of Benin were partly Mahommedans and partly Pagans. Arabic words and customs are yet found intermixed with the language and the customs of the different nations and states in that part of the African coast; and unless the delta of the Niger, and the salt places therein, are the mouths of the Nile of the early Arabian geographers, distant from Gana forty days' journey and navigation (the distance given between Kano and Benin at this day), their Gana must be removed to a very different portion of Africa to that wherein their authority clearly places it, and to a position, a resemblance to which can nowhere be found in any portion of Africa.

The power of Abyssinia was at one time very great, and extensively known and felt in Africa. The might of the sovereigns of this country was known even to the delta of the Niger; and it was upon the discovery of this delta, and the communication which, in consequence of that discovery, the Portuguese had with the sovereign of Benin, that they first heard of a great Christian power in eastern Africa, at a distance of a journey of *twenty moons*, or Prestyr John as their early writers styled him. That a communication existed between Benin and Abyssinia, and countries on the upper part of the Egyptian Nile is certain, and admitted, and well known in Africa. That communication no doubt took place by the Shadda or Shaderbah, and the Bahr-el-Abiad rivers. Dupuis has, in fact, given us this route and distance as still known in Africa, namely, 100 days' journey, partly by land, and partly by water. This distance, 1,600 miles, is just the distance between Benin and the frontiers of Abyssinia near Senaar.

It is here necessary and proper to remark, that the period of

"*twenty moons*" is so stated in Murray's Africa, while in
Clarke's Maritime Discovery, the distance given to the capital
of Organe from Benin is 250 Portuguese leagues, in which
case, the capital alluded to must be Kano or Gana, and not
Abyssinia.   The fact however appears to be, that the accounts
relating to the two places have been, by the carelessness of
translators and transcribers, blended in one; and that while
the sovereign of Benin was, to a certain extent, dependent
upon Gana, the former was also acquainted with Abyssinia.

These introductory and general remarks are considered sufficient for the present purpose.   The subsequent geographical
review of Africa will, in consequence, be confined to the
countries and places to the south of Egypt and the Barbary
States, and in an especial manner be pursued to open up, as far
as possible, and as far as the present state of our information
will enable us to accomplish, the following subjects, namely, the
condition of the countries in Africa within the torrid zone, the
physical features of the country, the sources, the courses and
the termination of the great rivers which flow therein, the productions of the soil, the capabilities of the country, and the
moral and social condition of her people, and other matters
illustrative of her trade and commerce and productions; what
these have been, what they are, and to what, under proper directions and impulse given to the energies of Africa herself, these
may, by judicious proceedings, be brought.

THE GREAT DESERT.

The first point for consideration is the Great Desert, the
invincible barrier of central Africa to the north, and the all
but impassable barrier between her and the more civilized
nations of the world.   Mount Atlas rises as a rampart against
the encroachments of this desert to the north.   The mountain,
or rather this great chain of mountains, which run, it may be
said, in a general bearing from N.E. by E. to S.W. by W.
from Cape Bon, on the Mediterranean, to Cape Nun, on the
Atlantic Ocean, are in the more southern and western parts
greatly elevated, so much so as to be, to the eastward of the
capital of Morocco, perpetually covered with snow.   From

this chain there descends, S.W. and S.E., several streams,
which speedily, and at the distance of 100 to 150 miles,
approach the limits of vegetation, and are absorbed in the
sands of the desert. The Draha alone has a course of about
200 miles, and is finally absorbed in the sands of the Zahara
to the E.N.E. of Tatta. From these points on the west, in
about 28° N. lat., to the limits of Soudan, south, a distance of
nearly 700 geographical miles; and from the Atlantic Ocean,
it may be said, to the shores of the Red Sea, with the exception of the bed of the river Nile, a distance of about 3,100
geographical miles, the surface of Africa is covered with this
desert, the eastern portion thereof, or Libyan Desert, being
nearly 100 miles broader than the broadest part of the western
division. The greater portion of this vast space is, generally
speaking, one mass of bare rocky hills and scorching sands,
" without," says Batouta, " water, bird, or tree," and without
even the semblance of vegetation. Here and there, there is to
be found scattered over it, but widely distant from each other,
fertile spots, or wadays, or oases, having wells of good water,
and a considerable portion of tropical African vegetation.
The portion of the desert where these are most numerous, and
nearest to each other, is that portion between the Mediterranean
and Bornou and Kashna, through Fezzan and Agadez, and
amongst the hills of Tibeste, and some parts to the north and
to the south of Bilma, &c. The wells and fertile spots are
more numerous in this division of the desert, and consequently
the road is better frequented and safer than in any other caravan
route from Soudan to the exterior or northern countries of
Africa. This portion of the desert was best known to the
Romans, whose early writers compared the appearance thereof
to a leopard's skin. Fezzan, of which Mourzook is the
capital, is a kind of oasis, about 200 miles square, where,
amidst many barren wastes and bare ridges or hills, there is
generally water and vegetation, although the former is frequently found deeply impregnated with salt. It was from this
point that the Romans penetrated into central Soudan, and
from this point that the hardy Arab, about the year of the
Hegira 160, first penetrated into the same quarter. Superior
as this route is to others, the accounts which will presently be

given will show even its appalling dangers. South of Mourzook, and eastward in the parallel of from 25° to 20° N. lat.,
the country is exceedingly rugged, and hilly, and barren; and
from the countries and places afterwards mentioned, situated
N.E. from Lake Shad, to Egypt, we know ‚very little of the
country; a proof, it is conceived, that it is worse than in other
parts, and consequently owing to this, and some other unknown causes, that it is considered or found to be impassable.
To the westward of the meridians of Mourzook and Agadez,
the desert becomes more cheerless and appalling, the watering
places and the oasis are at a greater distance from each other,
and in the latter, with the exception of Twat, the scanty vegetation is even more scanty. The wells, in this portion of the
desert, frequently become dry, which occasions, in such instances, to the caravans scenes of misery and horror which
beggar all description. This western portion also is more
sandy than the middle, and consequently is not only more subjected to the fearful simoon, but to furious tempests of wind
which roll the sands before them like the billows of the agitated
ocean, and which in a moment cover districts and bury whole
caravans to rise no more. To such a degree of heat are the
sands raised by the perpetual glow of, it may be said, a torrid
sun, and to such a degree of fineness is the sand brought by
perpetually shifting about, that the atmosphere becomes impregnated with it; and to a great distance in the Atlantic ocean,
westward of the African coast, ships find their sails, as it were,
choked with it imperceptibly and insensibly.

The destruction of human life in the journeys and in the
attempted journeys across this desert is enormous. In 1805
a whole caravan from Soudan for Morocco, consisting of 2,000
persons and all their camels, were totally lost. In 1811 and
1813, two whole caravans, between Augela and Waday, with
but few exceptions, perished amidst indescribable misery.
Sidi Hamed gives a fearful picture of the misery and the
massacre which ensued in a caravan with which he travelled,
when they came to the wells of Haherah and found them dry.
At the same time both the caravans from Tripoli and Tunis to
Timbuctoo were wholly destroyed. Denham and Oudney
give us a terrific picture of the ravages in caravans amidst

these deserts, where so many perish from want and thirst. From the well of Omah to the wells of El Hammer inclusive, a distance of 140 miles, they travelled amidst and over human skeletons, crushing at every step below the feet of the camels and horses (the camels eat the bones with avidity) many of them with the flesh so entire as to render the features, and the age, and the sex distinguishable. Around the wells of El Hammar in particular, the skeletons lay " in countless numbers." Lyon gives us a similar picture, so far as came under his review. But it is unnecessary here to dwell on these horrors at greater length. The following extracts from Park's and De Callié's travels will tend to give the reader a clearer idea of the nature and the terrors of the desert itself.

" Ludamar has for its northern boundary the Great Desert or Sahara. From the best inquiries I could make, this vast ocean of sand, which occupies so large a space in Northern Africa, may be pronounced almost destitute of inhabitants; except where the scanty vegetation, which appears in certain spots, affords pasturage for the flocks of a few miserable Arabs, who wander from one well to an other. In other places, where the supply of water and pasturage is more abundant, small parties of Moors have taken up their residence. Here they live, in independent poverty, secure from the tyrannical government of Barbary. But the greater part of the desert, being totally destitute of water, is seldom visited by any human being; unless where the trading caravans trace out their toilsome and dangerous route across it. In some parts of this extensive waste, the ground is covered with low stunted shrubs, which serve as land-marks for the caravans, and furnish the camels with a scanty forage. In other parts the disconsolate wanderer, wherever he turns, sees nothing around him but a vast interminable expanse of sand and sky, a gloomy and barren void, where the eye finds no particular object to rest upon, and the mind is filled with painful apprehensions of perishing with thirst..... Surrounded by this solitude, the traveller sees the dead bodies of birds that the violence of the wind has brought from happier regions; and as he ruminates on the fearful length of his remaining passage, listens with horror to the voice of the driving blast, the only sound that interrupts the awful repose of the desert."

" The wild animals which inhabit the melancholy regions are the antelope and the ostrich; their swiftness of foot enabling them to reach the distant watering places.   On the skirts of the desert, where water is more plentiful, are found lions, panthers, elephants, and wild boars.

" Of domestic animals, the only one that can endure the fatigue of crossing the desert is the camel.   By the particular conformation of the stomach he is enabled to carry a supply of water sufficient for ten or twelve days ; his broad and yielding foot is well adapted to a sandy country ; and, by a singular motion of his upper lip, he picks the smallest leaves from the thorny shrubs of the desert as he passes along.   The camel is, therefore, the only beast of burden employed by the trading caravans, which traverse the desert in different directions, from Barbary to Nigritia."—*Park's Travels,* Vol. I. p. 155.

" A boundless horizon was already expanded before us, and we could' distinguish nothing but an immense plain of shining sand, and over it a burning sky.   At this sight the camels uttered long moans, the slaves became sullen and silent ; with their eyes turned towards heaven, they appeared to be tortured with regret for the loss of their country, and with the recollection of the verdant plains from which avarice and cruelty had snatched them."—*Caillé's Travels,* Vol. II. p. 107.

" Our situation was still the same ; the east wind blew with violence ; and far from affording us any refreshment, it only threatened to bury us under the mountains of sand which it raised ; and what was still more alarming, our water diminished rapidly from the extreme drought which it occasioned.   Nobody suffered more intensely from the thirst than the poor little slaves, who were crying for water.   Exhausted by their sufferings and their lamentations, these unhappy creatures fell on the ground, and seemed to have no power to rise ; but the Moors did not suffer them to continue there long when travelling.   Insensible to the sufferings which childhood is so little fitted to support, these barbarians dragged them along with violence, beating them incessantly, till they had overtaken the camels, which were   already at a   distance."—*Caillé's   Travels,* Vol. II. p. 114.

" What distressed us most during this horrible day was the pillars of sand, which threatened every moment to bury us in their course. One of the largest of these pillars, crossing our camp, overset all the tents, and, whirling us about like straws, threw us one upon another in the utmost confusion ; we knew not where we were, and could distinguish nothing at the distance of a foot.   The sand wrapped us in darkness like a thick fog, and heaven and earth seemed confounded and blended into one.

" In this commotion of nature, the consternation was general ; nothing was heard on all sides but lamentations, and most of my companions recommended themselves to heaven, crying with all their might, "There is no god but God, and Mahomet is his prophet!" Through these shouts and prayers, and the roaring of the wind, I could distinguish at intervals the low plaintive moan of the camels, who were as much alarmed as their masters, and more to be pitied, as they had not tasted food for four days. Whilst this frightful tempest lasted we remained stretched on the ground, motionless, dying of thirst, burned by the heat of the sand, and buffeted by the wind. We suffered nothing however from the sun, whose disk, almost concealed by the cloud of sand, appeared dim and shorn of its beams. We durst not use our water, for fear the wells should be dry, and I know not what would have become of us if, about three o'clock, the wind had not abated."—*Caillé's Travels,* Vol. II. pp. 114, 115.

" Near the wells of Omah, numbers of human skeletons, or parts of skeletons, lay scattered on the sands. Hillman, who suffered dreadfully since leaving Tegerby, was greatly shocked at the whitened skulls and unhallowed remains ; so much so as to want all the encouragement I could administer to him."—*Denham's Travels,* p. 7.

" The depth of the well at Meshroo is from 16 to 20 feet ; the water good, and free from saline impregnations : the ground around is strewed with human skeletons—the slaves who have died exhausted with thirst and fatigue. The horrid consequences of the slave-trade were strongly brought to our mind, and although its horrors are not equal to those of the European trade, still they are sufficient to call up every sympathy, and rouse up every spark of humanity. They are dragged over deserts ; water often fails, and provisions scarcely provided for the long and dreary journey. The Moors ascribe the numbers to the cruelty of the Tibboo traders : there is, perhaps, too much truth in the accusation. Every few miles a skeleton was seen through the whole day ; some were partially covered with sand, others with only a small mound formed by the wind : one hand often lay under the head, and frequently both, as if in the act of compressing the head. The skin and membranous substance all shrivelled up, and dry from the state of the air ; the thick muscular and internal parts only decay."—*Ibid.* p. 8.

" About sunset we halted near a well within half a mile of Mesh-roo. Round this spot were lying more than 100 skeletons, some of them with the skin still remaining attached to the bones—not even a little sand thrown over them. The Arabs laughed heartily at my expression of horror, and said, ' they were only blacks,—*nam boo !*' (damn their fathers) and began knocking about the limbs with the butt end of their firelocks, saying, ' This was a woman !—This was a youngster !' and such like unfeeling expressions. The greater part of the unhappy people, of whom these were the remains, had formed the spoils of the sultan of Fezzan the year before. I was assured that they had left Bornou with not above a quarter's allowance for each ; and that more died from want than fatigue : they were marched off with chains round their necks and legs :—the most robust only arrived in Fezzan in a very debilitated state, and were there fattened for the Tripoli slave market.

" Our camels did not come up until it was quite dark, and we bivouacked in the midst of these unearthed remains of the victims of persecution and avarice, after a long day's journey of 26 miles, in the course of which one of our party counted 107 of these skeletons." —*Denham's Travels*, pp. 9, 10.

" El Wahr. The surface sandy till we approached the hills, then it changed to stony. The black hills, with cones, peaks, and a columnar-looking cap, reminded us of what we had seen before. The gloom of these places in the dusk has something grand and awful. We winded up, with the light of a moon not a quarter old, and that lessened by a cloudy sky, some sandy and pebbly beds, as of a stream, and in one place high clayey banks, with iron ore underneath. Skeletons lay about, mingled in a shocking manner ; here a leg, there an arm, fixed with their ligaments, at considerable distances from the trunk. What could have done this ? Man forced by hunger, or the camels ? The latter are very fond of chewing dried bones, but whether they ever do so to those with dried flesh on them I cannot say.—*Ibid.* p. 10.

" One of the skeletons we passed to-day had a very fresh appeai-ance ; the beard was still hanging to the skin of the face, and the features were still discernible. A merchant, travelling with the kafila, suddenly exclaimed, ' That was my slave ! I left him behind four months ago, near this spot.' ' Make haste ! take him to the fsug' (market), said an Arab wag, ' for fear anybody else should claim him.' We had no water, and a most fatiguing day."--*Den-ham's Travels*, p. 11.

" We moved before daylight, passing some rough sand hills mixed with red-stone, to the west, over a plain of fine gravel, and halted at the maten, called El-Hammar, close under a bluff-head, which had been in view since quitting our encampment in the morning. Strict orders had been given this day for the camels to close up, and for the Arabs not to straggle—the Tibboo Arabs having been seen on the look out. During the last two days, we had passed on an average from sixty to eighty or ninety skeletons each day; but the numbers that lay about the wells at El-Hammar were countless: those of two women, whose perfect and regular teeth bespoke them young, were particularly shocking; their arms still remained clasped round each other as they had expired: although the flesh had long since perished by being exposed to the burning rays of the sun, and the blackened bones only left; the nails of the fingers, and some of the sinews of the hand, also remained; and part of the tongue of one of them still appeared through the teeth. We had now passed six days of desert without the slightest appearance of vegetation, and a little branch of the sonah was brought me here as a comfort and curiosity. On the following day we had alternately plains of sand and lose gravel, and had a distant view of some hills to the west. While I was dozing on my horse about noon, overcome by the heat of the sun, which at that time of the day shone with great power, I was suddenly awakened by a crashing under his feet, which startled me excessively. I found that my steed had, without any sensation of shame or alarm, stepped upon the perfect skeleton of two human beings, cracking their brittle bones under his feet, and, by one trip of his foot, separating a skull from the trunk, which rolled on like a ball before him. This event gave me a sensation which it took some time to remove. My horse was for many days not looked upon with the same regard as formerly."—*Denham's Travels*, pp. 12, 13.

The boundary north of this extraordinary scene of desolation, unknown in any other quarter of the world, is from near Cape Nun on the Atlantic, in a line running nearly E.N.E. to the Mediterranean, to the south of Tripoli, where the coast of Africa stretches away to the eastward by the Syrtes and Desert of Barca; and on the south from the Atlantic in lat. 19° N. to the southward of Cape Blanco, the line advancing N. in the meridian of Agadez to perhaps 20° N. lat., and thence declining southerly as it approaches the meridian of Lake Shad, to about 17° N. lat., and continuing in the same parallel from

thence to the banks of the Nile, and, in fact, it may be said to
the shores of the Red Sea. This is its general bearing, but
the line to the west of Timbuctoo descends a little to the southward. (*See Map.*)

This desert is traversed in various directions, by numerous
routes, by the trading caravans, the chief of which have been
marked out on the Map, which consequently renders further
reference unnecessary. The routes are laid down straight or
direct from place to place, but the caravans in several instances
deviate from these routes, according as trading towns lay nearly
in their way; and where these deviations take place, the distance
more or less on the general line, according to the distance measured by a day's journey of the customary length, will readily
appear. The routes in the western division of the desert
require, however, particular notice. From Timbuctoo, &c. to
Morocco, there are several. One goes from Wednoon near
the shores of the Atlantic, southward as far as Cape Merik and
the river St. John's, from which point the caravans strike off
nearly due east along by the boundary of the desert to Timbuctoo, branching off as may be from Tisheet to Benowm.
Another route goes from Wednoon, for a long distance, close
to the Atlantic, and then proceeding south, it comes to Western
Tegazzá, which is six days' journey east of Hoden, which is
again six or seven days' journey east of Arguin. From Western
Tegazzá to Timbuctoo is a journey of 40, some say 44 days. There
is another place named Tegazzá (eastern), which lays, according
to Jackson, 16 days S.E. of Akkah, and, according to Batouta,
25 days' journey south of Segelmessa, and in the road from
Akkah to Timbuctoo by Taudenny. According to De Caillé,
this Tegazzá is seven days' journey N.W. of Taudenny. Not
distinguishing these two places, namely, Western Tegazzá from
Eastern Tegazzá, has led into several errors and doubts
regarding the routes alluded to, and also to the geography of
this portion of Africa.

Gualata, according to Leo, is 300 Arabic miles from Cape
Nun and 500 from Timbuctoo, in the direct line from the
former place to the latter city. This will place Gualata (centre
thereof) in 24 40' N. lat. and 8° W. long., 130 miles N.W. of
Amool Gragim of Arrowsmith's map, and also of the Map
accompanying this work. Sidi Hamed, in his second journey,

enables us to fix with tolerable accuracy the wells of Haherah. When the caravan with which he was travelling reached tnem, they were found dry, and which in consequence occasioned much bloodshed and misery. They set out from Wednoon in the direct course for Timbuctoo, travelled first six days south round the great Atlas, then entered the desert, travelling fifteen days south-easterly, the surface baked so hard and smooth that the camels could not make a track on it. At the end of this time they reached a fine deep valley with twenty wells in it, six of which had water; travelled thence three days first through hard sand, next sand as fine as dust and as hot as coals; travelled six days among this sand, when the hot wind began to blow, which occasioned a great loss of men and camels; pushed on as fast as they could through the dry, deep, hot sand, without meeting or seeing one green thing, when they reached the wells of Haherah, all of which they found dry, no rain having fallen there for one year. The distance will place Haherah, after proper allowance for the worst 24 days, in 19° N. lat. and 6 30' W. long. From this fatal spot they, in order to reach a place called Teshla, (certainly the Tashala of Batouta) journeyed 12 days S.W., here and there meeting with a hollow with a few prickly shrubs, when they were overtaken by a dreadful tempest of thunder, lightning, and rain, which supplied them with abundance of water. From this point they steered south to the borders of the desert; then to cultivated land; then south to a little river of fresh water, and soon after reached Wablet or Walet.

ARABIAN DIVISIONS OF AFRICA.

Leaving the Zahaara, or desert, we come to the other great divisions of Africa, as known to the Arabian writers and geographers, ancient and modern. Without considering and knowing these, we cannot understand or elucidate the geography of interior Africa; and to the want of which knowledge, together with the want of attention to this part of the subject, is to be attributed most of the errors prevalent, regarding the true geographical features of Africa. The early Arabian geographers and writers, such as Edrisi, distinguished Africa, or rather Central Africa, to the south of the desert, by the name of Belad-el

Sudan,* or the country of the Blacks, from the Arabic word,
" asswad," black.   To the south thereof, on the east, lay interior Ethiopia; and to the west of the portion then known,
those infidel countries, of which they had scarcely any knowledge, either of their position or extent, except from very vague
and indefinite information.   The Joliba, or true Niger, and all
the western rivers, such as the Senegal, &c., which flow into
the Atlantic, were either wholly unknown, or but imperfectly
known to Edrisi.   His knowledge, and the knowledge of his
immediate successors, seem to have been confined to the eastern
rivers of Ptolemy, or to what they more particularly denominated the Land of Kanem, and the Land of Ghana.   Subsequently, when the more western parts of Africa became known
to the eastern Arabian writers, after the conquests in that quarter by their brethren from Morocco ; Northern Africa, south of
the desert, was divided into three great divisions; viz. First,
the Land of Kanem, which extended from the boundary of
Nuba, or Nubia, near Dongola, on the east, to the Lake Shad,
including perhaps that lake on the west; and north to south,
from the confines of Barca and Zeilah, north, to the utmost
limits of the modern Bagharme, south.   Secondly, the Land of
Ghana, which extended from Lake Shad on the east to the
borders of the Niger on the west, and from the Great Desert
on the north to Lamlem and Meczara, twelve days' journey to
the south, where the Land of Ghana was bounded by infidel
countries.   Interior Ethiopia is that portion of Africa now denominated by the Arabs of Africa Soudan Dakhlata.   Thirdly,
the great division named Melli, or Maly, which extended from
the Land of Ghana, on the east, to Damloo, containing all the
countries situated on the shores of the Atlantic Ocean on the
west, and from the borders of the desert to the countries reaching to the range of hills generally known as the Kong range
on the south.   In this great portion of Africa, and the first
place of importance below Timbuctoo, was situated, according
to Batouta, the city of Kuku, or Kawkaw (the modern Ghow),

* The African Mahommedans know and admit this in conversation, but they
reject it in their geography, and confine their term Sudan from Bornou to Bambara inclusive, from E. to W., and N. to S. from the desert to the Atlantic.
South of Bornou they further have Sudan Dakhlata.—*Dupuis.*

then, according to him, one of the finest cities in Soudan. This Kuku, or Kawkaw, in the Land of Maly, is a very different place from either the Kuku, or the Kawkaw, or the Cauga of Edrisi, situated in the Land of Kanem ; which land of Kanem, Macrisi explicitly tells us, was at " a very great distance from the Land of Maly," the distance generally estimated being *three* months' journey.   Such, it appears, from Abulfeda, were the great districts into which Central Africa, to the south of the Great Desert, was divided in his days, and to which divisions opportunities may hereafter occur to require special reference.

The next and most important points to attend to are the names and the nature of the divisions into which the Mahommedan nations which now inhabit, and the descendants of those Mahommedans who have for many centuries inhabited Central Africa, divide that quarter of the world from the desert on the north to Benin and the Atlantic on the south ; and from Darfur on the east to the State of Damloo, and even including the most part of that country on the mouths of the Rio Grande, the Gambia, and the Senegal on the west.   In these we find one important term Tokrur or *Takrour*; the ignorance regarding the meaning of which has created much confusion in African geography.   The term is very fully explained, and that too by a competent hand, Sultan Bello, in his Geographical Memoir, or Survey of Africa (see Appendix, Denham's Travels, &c. p. 158).   The true word is *Takrour*, and this appellation comprehends, or is used to designate, the centre of Northern Central Africa, or the middle portion of what is technically called Soudan, from Darfur to the mouth of the Gambia inclusive.   In it is included the following great divisions :—Darfur, Waday, Bagherme, Bornou, Adamowa, Haoussa, Zegzeg, Nafra, Kornorfa, Jacoba, Gourmon, Moushee, Sanghee, Bambara, Melli, Tourooth, Foota, and Damloo, on the coasts of the Atlantic, where Christians come in ships to trade, as they also do to a port on the ocean, in Melli. Besides these, there are several other minor states, as noted in the Map, and which will be more specifically alluded to hereafter.

Another division, as regards the geography of Africa, is of still greater importance, that is Wangara.   No word or term in modern days ever occasioned so many errors in African geography as this word. It was, and is confounded with the province now known under the name Oonghor, or Oongooroo, or Ungura, the Guangara of Leo and Owencara of some Arabian writers, situated to the north-east and east of Ghana or Kano, but with which it has no connexion, and from which this modern Wangara is far distant. Wangara being, however, fixed in the point mentioned, was made the point where the Niger was stated to terminate, about the place where we now find Lake Shad. In Wangara the Niger does indeed terminate, but then modern Wangara is not the same as Owencara or Vancara, mentioned by Edrisi, nor is it situated in the same portion of Africa. The term, as regards the space which now bears the name, was in fact unknown to the Arabian geographers, and is chiefly used by the Mahommedan population, who now dwell on the Niger, and in the countries to the south of that river, particularly by those who inhabit Dagomba, Kong, and Mandingo. In its most comprehensive meaning it designates all Central Africa from the desert south, or the cultivated and inhabited country, through which rivers flow, and, in its restricted and specific meaning, all those countries from Gaman on the west, to Biafra on the east, and from Dagomba, and the neighbouring states north, to the Atlantic Ocean on the south. The following extracts from Dupuis will set this matter completely at rest, even if these were unsupported by other authority. Page xxv. he says—"It is an undoubted fact, authenticated by the testimony of every Moslem in Coomassie, that Wangara or Wankara is a mighty district, spreading over all that tract of land from Gaman inclusive, or the Madingo states of Enkasse and Ghombate in the west to Kimbee and Ajeeasie on the east, and from the north to the south from Ghofan and Tonouma down to the margin of the Atlantic Ocean." Continuing the subject, he says (pages xlii. and xliii.), that he inquired particularly of Bashaw Mahommed, a native of Gamba, a man who had travelled over almost all Northern Africa, very intelligent and far advanced in years, if there was such a place as Wangara, and where it was situated. The reply was, " Wangara is a large place, it is not a kingdom, neither is it a city; but it contains many kingdoms and many cities; the ground you now tread on is Wangara." Betraying surprise and doubt at the statement made, M. Dupuis was farther answered, " Can you doubt what I tell you ?" replied the chief; " if you do, inquire at our people whether I do not speak what is true." More than half a dozen voices confirmed the statement " in terms the most positive and convincing." " There is no doubt about it, and God knows it is true," was the expression of every Mussulman present. In course of subsequent and repeated conversations on this curious point, the replies and statements were uniform. " This is Wangara, and we believe there is no other country of that name on our side of the Great Desert; but if there is, we never heard mention of it, and therefore it must be a very small place."—" The rivers of Wangara are numerous; they are such as we have already described, running into the great salt sea of Benin, and from whence you come Cape Coast. The greatest river of Wangara runs south behind Dahomy direct to Warree, and is fifteen long journeys to the east of Abomey," &c. But this is not all: Leo Africanus tells us, that to reach this country travellers had to cross high mountains. Ritchie (see *Quarterly Review, May* 1820) was told that it was a great district in Southern Africa, and that it lay twenty-five journeys to the south of Timbuctoo. Denham was informed, that Wangara meant all the country south of Timbuctoo and Haoussa, containing mountains and rivers, stretching to the gulph of Guinea. Hutchison was told at Coomassie (*see Bowditch,* p. 206) the same thing. He is very pointed in this matter. " Wangara is the name of a region comprehending Kong, Moosee, and other neighbouring countries south of the Niger (if not some to the north of it); but Oongooroo is the name of the country laying between Kashna and Bornou." (*Bowditch,* 206.) Ritchie was farther told, that much of the gold that came to Timbuctoo came from that quarter. This we also learn from other and disconnected authorities, and we shall by-and-by see the particular places, such as Gaman, &c., which furnish it.

According to the curious and important information regarding the countries of Central and Western Africa, which Mr. Dupuis received at Coomassie, he further informs us, respecting

the great division into which the Mahommedans of Western
Africa at present divide it, that Ghunjah includes the whole of
Ashantee, exclusive of Gaman on the west and Banna on the
north, or N.E.: Salgha, or Salagha, is the capital of Ghunjah
Proper. The portion of Africa in its immediate neighbourhood,
and including Yahndi, is also sometimes denominated Inta, or
Intaa (see Bowditch). Salgha is said to be twice the size of
Coomassie, and the Rio Volta there is as broad as the Thames
at Battersea - bridge. Sarem includes Gaman, and all the
country from Cape Palmás in a semicircular direction towards
the N.E. to Kong and Enkasse, where it meets the S.W. limits
of Dagomba. This last-named division is a very great district
in southern Central Africa, separating Ghunjah from Bambara
and Fillany on the W., N.W. and N.; and Sarem from Killinga
or Borghoo and Yarribah on the E. and S.E. It is well cultivated
and highly populous, and chiefly a champaign country. Yahndi is
the capital of Dagomba Proper. It is a town much larger than
either Coomassie or Salgha. Horses and cattle are exceedingly
numerous in this great district, and very large flocks of sheep are
owned by even the lower classes of the population. Dagomba
is bounded S. and S.W. by Ghunjah and Sarem, S.E. and E.
by Killinga and Haoussa; N. by Fillany, and W. by Melli and
Bambara. Haoussa, one of the largest districts, is bounded E.
by Bornou and Yacoba, and S.E. and S. by Soudan-Dakhlata,
Benin, and Dahomy, S. by Dagomba, and W. by Fillany, and
N.W. and N. by Marroa and the Desert. Marroa is another
great division. It is bounded E. by Haoussa, N. by the
Desert, W. by Fillany, which latter includes Ghou, and thence
S. by the Niger eastward to Haoussa. Fillany is another
very great and important district. It is bounded S E. by Ha-
oussa, N. by the Niger to the environs of Ghou, thence E. by
Marroa, till it reaches the Desert to the N.; thence N. by the
Desert, W. by Beeroo, and S.W. and S. by Massina, Bambara,
and Dagomba, embracing both banks of the Joliba from below
Ghou on the E. to Lake Dibbie inclusive on the W. and S.W.
Bambara is another great division of Africa, comprehending in
its modern limits part of the country of Melli. It is bounded
on the N. by Fillany and Massina and the Great Desert, and
N.W. by Beeroo and Ludamar, and W. by Kaarta and the

Foulah country, and on the S. by Melli, and S.E. by part of
Dagomba. Melli, or, as it is called, Maly, is bounded E. by
Dagomba, S.E. by Sarem, S. and S.W. by Sarem and Ganowa; W. by Damloo and the Atlantic about the mouths of
the Rio Grande, &c.; N. by the Foulah country and Bambara, and part of Fillany. It is an immense district in Africa,
and comprehends the whole country inhabited by the Mandingoes, stretching from the Niger in its middle course about 150
miles below Timbuctoo, south-westerly to the Atlantic Ocean.
This was its extent in the early ages of Arabian conquest and
Arabian geography; and at the time (1352) that Batouta, and
subsequently at the time that Cadamosto, and other early
European navigators, first visited the western and south-western coasts of Africa.

These great divisions are again subdivided into numerous
kingdoms, states, and provinces, more or less powerful and
extensive, and which will frequently be referred to in the sequel
of this inquiry. A general knowledge of these important
divisions clears up much of the confusion which has hitherto
existed in the geography of Northern Central Africa, or Soudan,
and will enable the reader to see his way clearly, and judge of
the general accuracy of the Map which accompanies this work,
and which has been, with a vast labour and painful research,
constructed for the purpose.

GUINEA.—THE PEPPER AND IVORY COASTS.

Having thus, as briefly as possible, adverted to the great
geographical divisions of Africa, as known to and made by both
the Asiatic Arabs and the African Moors and Arabs, both in
ancient and in modern times, it is time to turn to the more minute
geographical details of Africa, and those countries in Africa
situated to the southward of the Great Desert and of the
ancient kingdom of Egypt. To make these details more clear,
and the situation of Central Soudan and the courses of the
great rivers that flow through it (the chief object of the present
inquiry) more apparent, it will be best to commence with the
countries and districts on the south and south-west, bordering
on the Atlantic Ocean, and adjoining those very mountainous

districts which give birth to the great rivers of Western Africa,
and especially the mighty Niger and all its tributary streams,
until we come to its most eastern and southern course.   The
first in order will be that portion of Africa known to Europeans
under the general name of the Coast of Guinea.

The first river of importance in this district of Africa, and
which may be said to bound it on the east and north-east, is the
Rio Volta.   This river rises in the great range of mountains
called Jibbel Sargha, situated in 9° 30′ N. lat. and 1° W.
long., flowing first past Salgha, where its breadth is about the
width of the Thames at Battersea-bridge, and afterwards by
Odonte, where there is a ferry; it runs into the Atlantic a little
to the westward of Cape St. Paul, in a wide and rapid stream.
From the rapidity of its course, the Portuguese gave it the
name which it bears.   It is a fine wide river, discharging its
waters so violently into the sea, that the current is sometimes
visible three or four miles from the shore.   The force of the
stream, meeting the swell of the Atlantic, which runs here
with great force, occasions such an agitation or burning of the
waters, that it is at all times dangerous to attempt the passage.
During the rainy season it is generally impracticable.   The
soil around the banks of the river is very fine, and on it grow
innumerable lofty trees, producing very fine timber, particularly teak-wood.   A short distance upward from its mouth
there is an island of considerable size, formed by the mud
which has been brought down by the stream; and, at times,
floating islands are borne along on its surface.

Westward from the Rio Volta, and from that river to the
Rio Nunez, inclusive, a great number of rivers enter the
Atlantic, but none of them are of any great magnitude or
importance.   The largest is the Assinee, in the east, and the
Rokelle, or Sierra Leone river, on the west.   But the course
of neither of these is much more than two hundred geographical
miles, and both are only navigable for small vessels, for a short
distance from their mouths.   The whole of the rivers in this
portion of Africa spring from that elevated range which extends
from the Jibbel Sargha, S. by W. and W., along by the sources
of the Niger and the southern boundary of the early course of
that stream to the neighbourhood of Teemboo.

All this portion of Africa is exceedingly mountainous; the hills approaching near the coast, and thence rising rapidly in elevation as the interior is approached. The country also is amost in every part known to be very populous; and from the Camaranca on the west, to Cape Lahou river on the east, to be generally well-cultivated. The soil, in almost every place, is good, and very productive of all the necessaries of life, known in, or suitable for tropical climates.

From the Kamaranca river to the Assinee river, a dozen of rivers, besides several small streams, enter the Atlantic Ocean in the coast just mentioned; but none of these are of any considerable magnitude, or equal to the Rokelle, " the river of Sierra Leone," a proof that, in comparison with the rivers in the interior and in other parts of the coasts of Africa, they are mere mountain torrents; that the courses are not, and cannot be long, and further, that betwixt the great eastern branch of the Niger, called the Ahmar, and the Atlantic Ocean from the Assinee east, to the Camaranca west, there is abundance of room left to form and to supply every one of the rivers in that portion of Africa at present under consideration. All this portion of Africa is exceedingly mountainous, the hills approaching near the coast, and from thence rising rapidly in elevation, as the interior is approached. The country also almost in every part is known to be very populous, and from the Camaranca on the west, to Cape Lahou river on the east, to be in general greatly superior to the country from Cape Lahou to the Rio Volta. From the Camaranca, the rivers in their respective courses are found first to run from east to west, thence their courses incline from south-east to south-west, from the ridge of which, Cape Palmas is the termination. Beyond that cape, their general course is from north-west to south-east, unto the river Assinee, the general course of which is from north to south, through the territories of Ashantee, although its principal springs, in their upper course, descend from the north-east, as the courses of the more eastern rivers of Ashantee do. Beyond Cape Coast Castle, where a ridge descends from the high chain of the Jibbel Sargha, the rivers, along to the Rio Volta inclusive, incline in courses from north-west to south-east.

The springs and courses of these rivers, carefully considered and attended to, disclose the great natural features of this portion of Africa, and enable us more clearly and particularly to judge of and to estimate her internal capabilities.

The rivers also in that part of the coast of Africa under our immediate consideration are proven to have short courses, by the fact of their sudden rise and fall during the tropical rains, by the comparative fulness of some of their streams in the rainy and the dry seasons, by the fact that their courses are all rapid and rocky, that there are no bars of mud in the mouths of any of them, and hardly any safe anchorage in any part of that coast. The names of the chief of these rivers, extending from the Kamaranca eastward, are the Bagoo, the Gallinas, the Cape Mount, the Half Cape Mount, which is said to be the largest of the whole, the St. Paul's, the St. John's, and Junk rivers, the line of the bed of the former bearing N. 30° E., and of the latter N.E.; they flow from one parent stream, at the distance of seventy to eighty miles from the sea. The Junk is rocky and scarcely navigable for small vessels. The country between their mouths extends twenty-seven miles, and is called Little Bassa, (see *Journ. Geo. Soc.* Paris, Nos. 67, 68, p. 99); then the Sesters, the Escragos, and, passing Cape Palmas, the Cavally, the St. Andrew's, and the Cape Lahou. The kingdom of Cape Mount is bounded by the river Gallinas on the north, and by Grand Bassam on the east or south-east; it extends inland about eighty miles, and to the north is bounded by a country called Conchy or Cotcha. The capital Couseca is two days' journey by water up the river, and is said to contain 20,000 inhabitants. The river at Half Cape Mount has fourteen feet water at the entrance, with shifting bars, composed of sand. This river is navigable to a greater distance into the interior than any of the others, and, from its local position, may be made a place of considerable commercial importance. At Cape Mesurado there is a good landing place for boats, a convenience found nowhere else between that point and Cape Palmas. The river at Cape Mesurado is shallow, and of little commercial value. St. John's river is navigable for small craft. Cape Mount is well-calculated for agricultural purposes, because the land is diversified with elevated plains, and is all well watered. The Sesters is narrow, and the entrance difficult, but it is navigable for a short distance. The people on this part of the coast, and in the kingdom of Senguin, pay tribute to Soko.

In this portion of the coast is situated the new American settlement or colony, named Liberia. It has been begun and settled by a considerable number of free blacks from the United States, who, finding themselves living in these states in a degraded and dependent state, without any chance of rising in society, have been induced by their own feelings and spirit, aided by advice and pecuniary assistance from the Colonization Society established in those states, to place themselves in Africa. These colonists are yearly becoming more numerous. Their principal settlement is Monronia, situated on the banks of the Mesurado river; but they claim as American the coast from Cape Mount River to Cape Palmas, a distance of 300 miles. Themselves and their patrons in America speak highly of their prosperity and prospects, and of the good they are accomplishing in Africa; while others, amongst which is Mr. Macgregor Laird, give a more disheartening account of their condition and prospects. Truth may be said to lay between these different accounts. Such a settlement, by people with little or no capital, and in a country where produce for exportation and commerce are to create, and where there are no roads and no navigable rivers, must have many difficulties to encounter and to overcome. Nevertheless, by energy and perseverance, they may do much good in Africa, both to themselves and to the native population, with which they have as yet lived in peace and amity. The soil is fruitful, the climate better than on most other parts of the coast, and the population inland quiet and inoffensive, and more inclined to industry than in other portions of the African coast. Still the position chosen for this new colonization scheme is a great drawback to its advance and prosperity, and must, in fact, prevent it from ever becoming a civilized settlement of the first-rate importance.

Eastward on this part of the coast is the country of the Kroomen, so well known in all the recent notices regarding the African coast. These people never enslave each other, and readily engage in any description of labour, except continuous and steady agricultural labour. The greater part of

them can speak the English language. The principal part of
all labour, more especially field labour, amongst these people,
the same as amongst all other barbarous tribes, devolves upon
the females: the males hire themselves out on every part of the
coast where they can obtain the employment which they like,
and afterwards expend the wages that they gain in purchasing
for wives females of other countries, who are obliged to labour
for them; and when they have thus obtained twenty, thirty,
forty, or more, according as their views may extend, they then
settle in their native country, and live upon the produce of the
labour of their wives, who are, in fact, their labourers, their
slaves, and their property. The neighbourhood of the river
Sesters produces vast quantities of rice, and it is here that the
Spanish and the Portuguese slave ships purchase that article
as the food for the slave cargoes which they intend to carry across
the Atlantic. Cape Palmas has the only harbour which is to
be found on the coast of Africa from Sierra Leone to Benin.
It is spacious, secure, well sheltered, and protected from the
swell of the ocean by a reef. The population is numerous,
docile, and peaceable; the soil good; the production spontaneous and numerous, amongst which is mellegette, pepper,
and other aromatics. The necessaries of life may be procured
here with very little labour. The situation of Cape Palmas, in
every point of view, and especially as a naval and commercial
place, may be rendered of great utility and importance. The
natives around would readily go along with any European
power in extending agricultural commerce. The entrance to
the harbour, either from the east or from the west, is easy and
safe, except in the case of tornados, during which, however,
the wind never blows with a force sufficient to drive a vessel
from a single anchor. These tornados also only blow for
fifteen or twenty minutes at a time, and always afford notice of
their approach. Amongst the strange customs known about
Cape Palmas, one is, that the son inherits his father's wives,
and thus his own mother becomes his property. They are all
pagans, of the very lowest caste as to religious views and
principles. The rains commence in May, and continue with
violence till October.

The town of Cavally, on the river of that name, about fifteen miles to the eastward of Cape Palmas, contains about 10,000 inhabitants, and is a place of considerable trade for ivory, grains of paradise, beads, and red pepper. The river is navigable for small craft; and in the month of May, after the commencement of the rains in the interior, immense numbers of dead fishes are brought down, which it is supposed are killed from the effect of the putrescent leaves and other vegetable matter accumulated in pools of the smaller branches of the river, into which the fish, as in other instances, had been obliged to confine themselves, owing to the decay of the water in these streams during the dry season. St. Andrew's river, to the eastward, is shallow during the dry weather part of the year, but brings down a vast body of water during the tropical rains. It was formerly a place of considerable trade. The inhabitants have little or no idea of any religion. In their manners and their pursuits they are much the same as the population about Cape Lahou and eastward to Apollonia. Cape Lahou is a place of considerable trade, and the population follow it with greater perseverance than the population of any other part of the coast. The river has nine feet water at the entrance, and the tide rises in it about six feet. The course of the river upwards is very circuitous. The character of the population about Cape Lahou is good, and they are further removed from a state of barbarism than any of their neighbours on the coast. Their lives are passed in comparative innocence. The traits of feeling and paternal affection which are witnessed amongst them would do honour to a civilized people. The inhabitants keep every sixth day sacred.

The river Assinee is by far the largest in this southern portion of the coast of Africa, and formerly bounded the kingdom of Ashantee on the west. It may now, however, from the late conquests made by that formidable power, be said to flow through its dominions in the whole length of its course. This river, at its mouth, is broad but shallow; the main course near the entrance is about 200 yards wide. Inland it has the appearance of a lake with numerous little islands in it, which have been thrown up by the eddies. The country, in the interior, on the banks of the Assinee, as well as to the westward of the river, is delightful. The inhabitants are an industrious, a clever and economical people, and some of them are wealthy. They dress better, and keep themselves cleaner than any other natives on the coast. The females are always clean and well clothed, and the men treat them with kindness and respect. The soil is a red loam. The general appearance of the country is very fine, and in the vicinity of the towns and villages it is pretty well cultivated. They do not allow their priests to interfere with matters connected with trade or polity.

ASHANTEE, OR WESTERN WANGARA.

Passing the Assinee to the eastward, we come to the great kingdom of Ashantee, decidedly the most powerful and extensive country in all this portion of Africa. It is composed of a great number of smaller states, many of them of late conquered by its arms and subjected to its power. The works of Dupuis and Bowditch, the former in general the most accurate, are our chief geographical guides regarding this portion of Africa; the one in some instances tends to elucidate and to correct the other; and where the days' journeys of travellers are given in an attentive manner, the positions of places of note become known and settled with considerable accuracy. Coomassie is from tolerable data placed in 6° 32′ N. lat., and 1° 23′ W. long. From thence to Buntokoo, the capital of Gaman, is, according to Bowditch, eleven days' journey, (Dupuis has fewer,) but ten days' journey may be taken as the correct number and distance. Eight geographic miles per day, or eight and a half made good each day on the general bearing, is, after much attentive examination and research into these matters, taken as the measure of a day's journey in mountainous, uncultivated, and wooden districts of southern Africa. At this rate, distant points have been ascertained and fixed; at this rate they are found to correspond with a surprising accuracy. At this rate Buntokoo will be eighty-eight geographical miles from Coomassie, on the bearing N.W. The river Offim is crossed on the second day, and the Tando on the fifth, in proceeding from Coomassie towards Buntokoo.

The principal rivers of Ashantee Proper, are the Tando, which rises in rocky hills called Toofeea, near the town of Ainkroo, between the Banda and Inta paths, five days' journey,

or about fifty miles NN.E. from Coomassie, and enters the
sea to the westward of Cape Three Points under the name of
Ancobar, Rio Cobra, or the Serpentine-river, so called by the
Portuguese from its extremely winding course for upwards of
twenty miles inland from its mouth.   Rice is cultivated along
its banks to a great extent, and which grows here above all
other places in incredible abundance.   Its mouth is very wide
but very shallow, scarcely admitting navigation by a boat; but
inwards it grows deeper and narrower.   Its banks are as
pleasant as any part of the Guinea Coast, not excepting Fidah
itself.

Each of its banks, says Bosman, is adorned with fine lofty
trees, which afford the most agreeable shade in the world, de-
fending the traveller from the scorching beams of the sun.   It
is not unpleasant to observe the beautiful variegated birds and
the sportive apes diverting themselves on the verdant boughs
all the way.   To render it yet more charming, having sailed
about a mile up, you are entertained with a view of a fine populous village extending about a quarter of a mile on its western
shore; of such villages hereabout are a great number.   The
Offim, above mentioned, is a branch of the Tando.   The next
river of importance, is the Chamascian river, or Rio de St. Juan,
called by the negroes Bossum Pra, which they adore as a god,
(so the word Bossum signifies,) rises about seventy miles N.E.
of Coomassie, on the eastern confines of the province of Akkeya,
and enters the Atlantic about ten miles to the westward of Cape
Coast Castle.   It is rather less than the river Ancobar, but
wide enough to admit boats laden coming into it from the sea,
if the pilot be but so careful as to avoid a rock near its mouth,
which the sailors call the Sugar.   The river upward contains
several islands adorned with fine towns and villages, but the inhabitants are described as a very barbarous race, and their chiefs
very often particularly ferocious, drinking the blood of their
enemies, and offering it to their gods in their savage sacrifices.
This portion of the coast of Africa, extending eastward from
the Camaranca river to the boundary of Ashantee, and the Rio
Volta, forms what is technically called by Europeans, the Guinea
Coast, but which name is wholly unknown, as Bosman informs
us, to the natives of that portion of Africa.   " Guinea," says

he, "is a large country extending several hundred miles, abounding with innumerable kingdoms and several commonwealths;" but he adds, "The very name of Guinea is not so much as known to the natives here, nor the imaginary Guinea monarchy yet to be found in the world."—*Bosman,* p. 340. The name, in fact, was imposed upon it by Europeans, from what cause and for what reason is doubtful or unknown. It is, in fact, that part of the coast of Africa which is now comprehended under the Mahommedan African name of Wangara. This coast has always been found extremely fatal to Europeans. Bosman gives the following very powerful and very just reasons for the insalubrity of this coast. "The unwholesomeness of the coast, in my opinion," says he, "is chiefly owing to the heat of the day and the coolness of the night, which sudden change I am induced to believe occasions several contrary effects in our bodies, especially in those who are not accustomed to bear more heat than cold, by too hastily throwing off their clothes to cool too fast. The second and greatest cause which I can find is, that the Gold Coast from one end to the other so greatly abounds with high mountains, in the vallies betwixt which every morning a thick, stinking, and sulphureous damp mist rises, especially near rivers or watering places, which mist so spreads itself, and falls so thick on the earth, that it is almost impossible to escape the infection; and while we are fasting our bodies are more susceptible than the natives. This fog happeneth most frequently in the ill season of the six months which we here call winter, but more especially in July and August, wherefore we are more seized with sickness in that time than in the good season, or summer." —*Bosman, Pink. Coll.,* vol. xvi. p. 381.

Ashantee, as has been stated, is at present the most powerful state in all Western Africa, and in fact rules over a considerable portion of it. This being the case, and also the manners and customs of its people, in a public and national point of view, being similar to the manners and customs of all the states, whether great or small, which are Pagan in their religion, and which extend south from about 9° N. lat. to the Atlantic, and from Biafra on the east to the borders of Sierra Leone on the west; a brief notice of its state and condition, as regards manners and customs, may suffice for all the rest. Ashantee is a monarchy of the most despotic description; the sovereign there rules over all his subjects by the terrors of superstition and the sword. Their religion is Paganism, in its lowest and most degraded forms; and in many of the districts and the countries adjoining, the people are so ignorant and degraded as to worship the shark and the snake. Amongst other customs which were known and practised amidst the most barbarous nations of Europe and Asia in the most ancient times—that of sacrificing their enemies taken captive in war, to gratify their deities, to appease the manes of their chiefs who fell in battle, or to attend them as slaves in the invisible world, is retained in Ashantee, and in all that portion of Africa to which we have just alluded. This custom is practised to an extent that is both fearful and incredible, and probably with a deeper and stronger ferocity than ever was known in ancient times in any other quarter of the world. Thousands on thousands of human beings are daily sacrificed in this part of Africa, amidst horrors and sufferings unutterable, under one species of religious pretence or another. The bones of relatives are dug from their graves, or these graves saturated with, and these bones washed in the blood of the butchered victims. The scenes that Dupuis and Bowditch witnessed at Coomassie are such as defy description and petrify the mind with anguish and horror. Yet the people of Ashantee are not savages, nor the sovereign thereof a perfect barbarian; on the contrary, they are considerably advanced in civilization; but such have been for ages the customs of their country, and these they continue to follow as religious duties and moral and meritorious acts. It is also a curious and remarkable fact, that in Ashantee some of their customs are the same which prevailed in Asia during the days of Moses, and which he enacted as laws for the Jews in their civil and domestic policy.

It is now about two hundred years since Ashantee began to raise her head above her neighbours in that quarter of Africa, and since that period her power has continued to increase and to spread, through wars the most bloody and destructive. State after state has fallen under her sway; rebellion after rebellion, and confederacy after confederacy against her by neighbouring states, have, after varied success and tremendous scenes of carnage and desolation, been crushed and broken to pieces; and but few powers in that quarter of Africa are now willing or anxious to measure their strength with her, though occasionally bloody conflicts do still take place between them. Besides the slaughter on the field of battle and the destruction of life in burning their towns, thousands and thousands of all ages and sexes of people are taken captives, reduced to a state of slavery, and some of them are subsequently sold to the European slave dealers, who carry them across the Atlantic. But, except the reservation of part of the youth of the male sex, spared to recruit their armies, by far the greater portion of the unhappy captives are butchered by thousands at a time, and in a day, in the sacrifices for the purposes and the objects above alluded to. Not one nation or one state, in all this quarter of Africa, is better than another in this respect. The victor to-day may be the vanquished to-morrow; and when vanquished, that nation suffers from the hand of the victors the butcheries and the cruelties which, if it had been successful, it would have inflicted upon the other. It is not only common, but almost the daily custom for the sovereign and chief men in every nation to soak their thrones and footstools with the warm blood of their butchered fellow-creatures; to carry their bones bared of their flesh before them in triumph, and to adorn their war drums, their war accoutrements, their palaces, and their apartments, and above all the temples of their grovelling deities, with human skulls and human bones! Such are the scenes which are every day presented to the eyes of the beholder in the delta of the Niger; at the courts of Benin and Dahomy, and at Ardrah, Badagry, Coomassie, and other places, independent of the horrors witnessed about their fetish temples and above all their fetish trees, of which Lander gives such an appalling but such a just picture.

The real Negro race, and who remain unconquered by the Mahommedan arms, and unconverted to the Mahommedan faith, were, from six to eight centuries ago, driven into this portion of Africa, where the very high mountains and native forests which run east and west in the parallel of 9° to 10° N. lat. have hitherto sheltered them from the incessant attacks of the fanatic Moor, and the more fanatic Negro Mahommedan convert.

The contiguity also of these Negro states with the Atlantic, from which they have been abundantly supplied for 250 years with powder and fire-arms by their trade with Europeans, has enabled them, even more than their natural barriers and defences, to oppose the restless Moors, who are only enabled to obtain such supplies of the munitions of war, to a limited degree, by the caravans across the Great Desert from the shores of the Mediterranean. To this cause chiefly is it owing that this portion of Africa has hitherto escaped from the Mahommedan faith and from the Mahommedan yoke—a circumstance in one point to be regretted, because, wherever that faith and that yoke have been introduced, an end has been put to all those grovelling superstitions, and human massacres, and human sacrifices, to which we have alluded.

Gaman and its provinces of Baman, Safoy, and Showy, contain the richest gold mines in Africa. Besides large quantities of gold dust, found on the banks of the Barra, which stream flows into the Tando below Kherabe, a large Mussulman town, gold is found in other parts of Gaman in large lumps, denominated rock gold, some of which lumps seen by Mr. Dupuis at Coomassie being equal to four pounds in weight. The king made a present to Mr. Hutchinson of three pieces, one of which weighed twenty ounces. The ore, which is of a very deep colour, is dug out of large pits from five to nine feet in depth. In Dinkira and Wassaw, the metal is found in a similar manner, but at a greater depth. On the banks of the Barra, about 10,000 slaves are busily employed for a period of two months each year collecting gold; and the dust thus procured, in very considerable quantities, is higher coloured, cleaner, and better than that which is gathered in any other country. The principal part of the metal is carried away by traders to countries in the interior, particularly Salgha, Yandy, Wabia, Kong, and Mandingo, where it is manufactured into trinkets; or carried to Jinne and Timbuctoo, and thence across the Great Desert to the shores of the Mediterranean. Boure, Gaman, and the parts of Africa adjacent, are clearly the country Belad el Tibri, mentioned by the old Arabian geographer Iben al Vardi, or the country of pure gold, where gold, as he states, came out of the earth like as plants do in other countries; and which country, he informs us, was distant three months' journey from Segelmessa, a town on the borders of the Great Desert belonging to Tafilet, a province of Morocco, and on the south-east side of Mount Atlas.

Soko, formerly a province of Gaman, is eleven days' journey from Coomassie, and Banna four days' journey beyond that place, but a little further to the eastward. The river Offim is crossed on the second day, and the Tando at the end of four days' journey beyond Tandosoo, on the route from Coomassie. From Coomassie to Boopee is sixteen journeys, about N N. E. Four hours' march south of the latter place the river Adirrai or Volta is crossed, 120 yards broad, its course in this part being towards the S.E. The source of this river, according to Bowditch, is in a very high mountain called Koondongaree, one of the Jibbel Sargha range, eight days' journey to the north-west, and in the eastern portion of which range Dupuis also places the source of this great river. This range rises to such a great elevation, that the cold upon it is very severe, while it gives birth to many rivers which flow in various, and some in opposite directions. Three days' journey from Boopee is Daboia, the capital of the great province of Ghobago ; and one day's journey to the south of it, at the town of Moronco, is the river Addifoosoo, which has its source also in the Jibbel Sargha. It is here about sixty yards broad, and flows into the Adirrai or Volta, above Salgha or Sallagha. Two days north of Daboia, upon the route thence to Yngwa, is found another considerable river, which has its source in the same . mountains, and which, under different names, bends its course E.S.E., and then S.E., passing to the S.W. of Yandi, where it assumes the name of the Komashar, so called from a kind of gum which is found on its banks. This river is the parent stream of the Lagos, and where it crosses the road from Salgha to Ghofil, about six days' journey from the former place, it is a very considerable river, and navigable for canoes. The country through which it flows in its upper course is extremely mountainous, and in general very fertile and very populous. From Buntokoo to Kong is twelve days' journey, say ninety-six geographical miles, in a bearing a little to the eastward of north. There is another and more direct road to it from

Coomassie by Enkassie, fourteen days' journey, and from Enkassie to Kong, six journeys more; together, twenty days' journey. By the first route the river Zamma, running west, is crossed on the seventh day, and described to be as large as the Volta is at Salgha, or equal to the breadth of the Thames at Battersea. At the same distance from Buntokoo to the N.W. is the Mussulman town of Kherabe already mentioned, situated on the river Barra, which rises near it, and is unquestionably a branch of the Zamma; which latter is again a principal branch of, or rather, the parent stream of the Assinee. One day north of the Zamma, and four days south of Kong, the traveller crosses the small river Woora, a branch of the Zamma; both these streams take their rise on the S.W. side of the Jibbel Sargha. In the province of Kong, as De Caillé was informed, there are no great rivers, but many small streams, which streams probably flow south to the Barra and the Zamma, because very high mountains are found to the north of Kong. The country known under this celebrated name is represented as well cultivated, well watered, fertile, and populous, and the capital situated at the foot of a very high mountain.* Nine journeys north of Kong is Kaybee, which place is also very populous; the soil is chalky, and the country is particularly famed for the number and the breed of asses which are in it. At the distance of seven of the -above-mentioned journeys from Kong, several high mountains are crossed. Three days' journey from Kaybee, over a large mountain named Saboopoo, and across a large river, is Kaywaree. The people are represented as robbers and depraved. The river mentioned as flowing here is doubtless the Kowara-Ba mentioned by De Caillé, as will be particularly adverted to in the sequel. Three journeys from Kaywaree is Garroo, a powerful kingdom, the capital of which is named Netaquolla. In his journey from Jinne by Garroo Wargee, the Twarick says he crossed the river in his route between Garroo and Kong, and that when he crossed it, it ran " from the rising to the setting sun." Twenty journeys from Garroo is Dowarro, the people of which are indifferent warriors, but superior agriculturists, and plant extensively;

* Kong is the Mandingo word for mountain. It also signifies "*forest.*" The word for hill is "*konko.*" Konkodoo is "*hilly country.*"

so De Caillé found the population of this portion of Africa. Five journeys north of Dowarro is the Niger, and the town of Jinne, situated on an island. The journey from Buntokoo is thus fifty-four days, or, at eight geographical miles made good each day, is 432 miles, corresponding well with the position of Jinne as placed on the map by other authorities, and in travels undertaken from quite different quarters. Salgha, or Salagha, the great market town of Inta, and the capital of the country properly denominated Gunjah, is seventeen journeys north-eastward from Coomassie. On the ninth day the rivers Kirradee and Oboosoom are crossed, being each about sixty yards broad, and flowing so near to each other, as to appear one during the rainy season. A high mountain, which bounds Ashantee and Booroom, rises immediately behind them. On the tenth day the river Sannee is crossed, which afterwards enlarges considerably by the addition of the two rivers just mentioned; and to the S.E. of which junction it enters the Rio Volta at Odente, where there is a public ferry. The source of the Sannee is five days' journey north of Coomassie, between the Boopee and the Salgha roads. The Booroom country is quite open, and Goya, the capital, is a considerable town. On the seventeenth day, and at a little distance from Salgha, the Adirrai, or Volta, is crossed, being, according to the accounts received by Mr. Dupuis, here about the breadth of the Thames at Battersea bridge. In this part of its course it is much interrupted by rocks, but has abundance of hippopotami in it. Salgha is a place of great commercial importance, much larger than Coomassie, and the country around is very populous. Agriculture is encouraged in all these countries, which are thus comparatively clear of forests. South-west of Salgha, and on the west side of the Rio Volta, is the large lake called Bouro, three hours' march from the river, with which it communicates during the rains. It abounds with fish of a superior quality, and which are daily carried from it to the Salgha market. A small river from the north-west runs into the lake, the source of which river is in the desert of Gofan, which, though barren and sandy, has abundance of water from wells.

Seven days from Salgha, on a bearing N.E., is Yandi, the capital of the great district of Dagomba, a city much larger

than either Coomassie or Salgha. The population is said to
be very great. The markets of Yandi are described as ani-
mated scenes of commerce, and constantly crowded with merchants from all the countries in the interior ; horses and cattle
are very numerous, and even the poorer classes possess large
flocks of sheep. About six days' journey beyond Salgha, on
the route to Yandi, is the Komashar river already mentioned,
and though the accounts are rather confused, it would appear
that on this part of its course it receives a branch from the
north-eastward.

Eight days' journey north-westward. of Yandi is the Dagomba town and district named Yngwa. Four days from
Yngwa is a river, the parent stream of the Komashar, sixty
yards broad; and two days north of the Komashar is another
Dagomba town called Konboro. Five journeys to the north-
eastward of Yandi is the small kingdom of Gamba, formerly
a much more considerable state than it now is, and without
doubt the Kombah or Kambah of former maps and of Major
Rennell. Northward of Yngwa is the kingdom of Foobee;
before reaching it, a river, which Bowditch calls Kontoroora, is
crossed, and which, in the customary strain of African amplification, he was told was half a mile broad—from certain data
we can reduce this to a more moderate magnitude. Thus
Bowditch also states, that the Rio Volta at Salgha was half a
mile wide (he states the Zamma to be of the same magnitude),
while Dupuis reduces the breadth of the Volta at Salgha to be
equal to that of the Thames at Battersea-bridge. This magnitude, with perhaps some trifling deduction therefrom, we
may take as the true breadth and magnitude both of the Zamma
and the river Kontoroora, at the points mentioned. This
latter river, he states, has an eastern and a western branch, the
united streams of which doubtless form the river Gulbe of
Magho. One day's journey from the river is a large mountain,
and one day beyond it is Foobee. Five days' journey northward from Foobee is the independent kingdom of Chouocha.
Foobee is fifteen days' journey to the westward of Gooroma,
the capital of Magho, and nine days' journey eastward from
Kayree, certainly the same as Kaywarree. Five days' journey
from Yngwa is the kingdom of Mousee, a warlike state, which

is passed by the Moors in their route from Yandi and Yngwa
to Jinne. This is the kingdom of which, according to Dupuis,
Aughgoa, twenty-five days' journey from Coomassie, eighteen
from Yandi, and fifteen from Zogho, is the capital. It is
doubtless also the great state called Mouchee, mentioned by
Sultan Bello as lying in these parts, and to the right or south
of which state lies the empire of Ashantee. A few days'
journey from Foobee, through Chambay and Kobafoo, is Kallana, rivalling Yandy as a market. Kallana is situated at the
foot of a mountain abounding in iron. Hereabouts Sultan
Bello has placed a country where muskets are made. A state,
called by Bowditch Komshalloo, is thirty days' journey from
Dagomba. The traders to it from Ashantee pass through
Mousee, and cross only one river, the Teshinga, in their route,
and that not very large. In the parallel of Salgha, and beyond
the Komashar river, is a lake of great extent. Travellers
going either from the east or from the west, journey along its
shores for the space of two days. There are several inhabited
islands in it. It lies six days' journey due south of Zogho, or
rather the capital of the country of that name, which is also
called Hio, and sometimes Eyoo. This lake is seven days'
journey from Abomey, the capital of Dahomey. It is distant
from the ford· on the Komashar, three days' journey east, and
is said to have no communication with any great river. To the
south of the lake the country is flat, and that country, together
with the towns and the villages on the islands in the lake, are
subject to the sovereign of Zogho.

Along all the coast of the Atlantic, in the Gulf of Guinea,
the country from the Assinee river eastward is in some parts
fifteen, and in others so much as eighty miles inland, exceedingly woody—in fact, a natural forest uncleared, and without
many inhabitants; inland beyond the distance mentioned, it
becomes cleared, cultivated, very populous, and covered with
large towns and villages. The country in the districts of Inta,
Tonouma, Yngwa, &c., and all about the range of Jibbel Sargha,
is exceedingly elevated, and the cold so much felt, that the
inhabitants are obliged to wear woollen garments; and Robertson states, that some of his informants told him, the mountains
in this part, as well as those further to the westward, were

covered with snow. The Quarterly Review, No. 58, tells us, that a seaman belonging to the Owen Glendower frigate travelled from Kashna to Anamaboe, in 1805, and that ten days' journey before he came in sight of the sea towards the Gold Coast, he passed over a very high chain of mountains, a peak of which was covered with a " white cap," or snow. Leo Africanus also states, that in the country of Gago, situated certainly on the northern base of these mountains, the cold in winter was so severe, that the population were obliged to wrap themselves up in sheepskins.

In studying the courses of the rivers in this portion of Africa, it appears that the rising ground commences in the neighbourhood of Cape Coast Castle, and running north-easterly, increases in height as it advances to the north; afterwards it runs northerly, about fifty miles to the eastward of Coomassie, and thence it runs about NN.W. between Banna, Soko, and Ghofan, till it joins the lofty ridge of Jibbel Sargha, which ridge divides the waters that flow eastward to the Rio Volta, and westward to the Bossempra, the Tando, &c., from those which flow N.W. and N.E. to the Niger. From Coomassie the route south-eastward to Accra is exceedingly mountainous and rugged, so much so that, according to Dupuis, p. 33, although the two places are only 140 geographical miles distant from each other in a direct line, yet the distance travelled is at least 240 miles. The same thing may, from one cause or another, be said of all African travelling.

It has been observed, that, with the exception of a small portion of the sea coast, this portion of Africa is exceedingly populous. Coomassie contains 100,000 inhabitants (Bowditch); Yandy, Salgha, Wabia, Callana, and several other towns, are still larger than Coomassie. In fact Africa here, and as we shall also see in other places, swarms with population; and this, notwithstanding the terrific and destructive wars which are almost yearly taking place amongst the different states in it. Allowing for African exaggeration, these national wars are truly bloody and destructive; according to Bosman, about a hundred years ago, in one battle which produced the subjugation of Dinkira, 100,000 men fell upon the field of battle; towns and villages were obliterated from the face of the earth, and thousands and thousands of the population of all ages and sexes were carried off as prisoners and slaves by the conqueror. About twenty years ago the subjugation of Gaman led to a similar bloody result, and 30,000 of its population were carried into slavery by the sovereign of Ashantee. Subsequent wars with the Fantees led to equal scenes of destruction and desolation ; but it would be endless, and is considered unnecessary to go further into the history of such bloody struggles which, in one place or other, are, it may be said, yearly occurrences. It is quite a mistake to suppose that these wars are undertaken for the sole purpose of procuring slaves; the king of Ashantee repelled this supposition with scorn. These great national wars proceed from causes not very dissimilar to those which produce national wars amongst the civilized nations of the world ; but the result in Africa is, that the conquered who are not slain on the field of battle, or massacred in the sacking of the towns and villages, become slaves at the disposal of the conqueror. It is true that in petty differences people are made slaves in Africa by their neighbours, from a spirit of retaliation or for the sordid love of gain, for which parents will even sell their own children. This the laws of all the African states either tolerate or directly sanction : it is equally true that wherever the Mahommedan religion prevails, predatory incursions are made into the territories of neighbouring infidel states, in order to make slaves of as many of the people as they can catch, and which these Mahommedans consider to be a religious duty. And although the number of people reduced to a state of slavery in Africa by the causes just mentioned, and although the destruction which these proceedings create, is very great, both as regards life and property, still the whole combined are but as a drop in the bucket and a grain in the balance, when compared with the slavery, the destruction, and the desolation which the great national wars betwixt state and state are daily entailing on Africa.

Lander has preserved two curious documents, namely, the hostile manifestoes of Sultan Bello and the Chief of Fundah against each other, which may serve as a correct specimen of the causes of the national wars, and the spirit in which, together with the object for which these are undertaken in Africa.

" The Sultan (Bello) accordingly, assembling all his forces, marched with a formidable army towards the devoted Fundah; and halting about half a mile from that city, sent the following singular and characteristic message to the king:—

" Bello's Message.

" 'Ruler of Fundah! deliver up your country, your riches, your people, and your slaves, to the beloved of God, Mahommed Bello, King of all the Mussulmans, without reluctance on your part; for if you do not suffer him quietly and peaceably to take possession of your kingdom, in order to propagate the religion of the only true Prophet in it, he will shed your blood, and the blood of your children, and the blood of your household; not one shall be left alive : while your people he will bind with fetters of iron, to be his slaves and bondsmen for ever—God having so spoken by the mouth of Mahommed!',

" King of Fundah's Answer.

" 'Sultan of the Fallatahs! the King of Fundah does not know you or your Prophet; he laughs your boastings to scorn, and despises your impotent threats.　Go back to your country, and live in peace with your people; for if you persist in the foolish attempt to invade his dominions, you will surely fall by his hands; and instead of him or his subjects being your vassals and bondsmen,—your slaves shall be his slaves, and your people his people.　Your chiefs and warriors, and mighty men, will be slaughtered without mercy, and their blood shall be sprinkled on the walls of his town; while even your mallams and emirs will be thrust through with spears, and their bodies cast into the woods, to be devoured by lions and birds of prey!'"

In reference to the subject of human sacrifices so prevalent in Western Africa, it is merely necessary, in order to show their prevalence, their nature, and their extent, to adduce the following extracts from the journals of Bowditch, Hutchison, Dupuis and Lander; they speak for themselves.　It is only requisite further to observe, that these practices prevail in Ashantee, Dahomey, Benin, and in every other country and state in that quarter of Africa where the Mahommedan religion and the Mahommedan power does not prevail, and greater or lesser, according to the magnitude of the state or country, and the strength of the power thereof.

HUMAN SACRIFICES.—ASHANTEE.

Let us look at the picture presented to our view in the customs and ceremonies in Ashantee, one of the most powerful and civilized nations in southern Africa, a nation with which Britain has entered into treaties, as these customs have been laid before us by an eye-witness, namely, Mr. Bowditch, the British envoy to the court of Coomassie in 1817.

" The population of Ashantee," says he, p. 250, " possess little humanity, and are very avaricious and oppressive. The lower order of the people are ungrateful, insolent, and licentious. The king repeatedly said, he believed them to be the worst people existing, except the Fantees, and not comparable with many of their inland neighbours. They listen to superstition with the most childish credulity, but they only cultivate it for the preservation of life and the indulgence of passion.....Men accused of witchcraft, or having a devil, are tortured to death.....Their fetisches or subordinate deities are supposed to inhabit particular rivers ; the king, caboceers, and the higher class are believed to dwell with the superior deity after death, enjoying an eternal renewal of the state and luxury they possessed on earth. It is with this impression that they kill a certain number of both sexes at the funeral customs, to accompany the deceased, to announce his destination, and to administer to his pleasures. The spirits of the inferior classes are believed to inhabit the houses of the fetische, in a state of torpid indolence, which re-compenses them for the drudgery of their lives, and which is truly congenial to the feelings of the negro, &c.....The states on the coast revere different animals as fetische ; the hyena at Accra, the alligator at Dix Cove and Anamboe, and the vulture universally."

Minds, manners, and society do not improve in Africa. Jobson, in 1620, and previous to the European slave trade, saw exactly what Park, Bowditch, Lander, &c. saw in 1798 to 1834. But to proceed with Bowditch—

" The Yam custom is like the Saturnalia ; neither theft, intrigue, or assault are punishable during its continuance, but the grossest liberty prevails, and each sex abandons itself to its passions. The principal caboceers sacrificed a slave at each quarter of the town, on their *entrée* on Friday the 5th of September. On Saturday, the 6th, the ceremony commenced.....The crush in the distance was awful and tremendous. All the heads of the kings and caboceers whose kingdoms had been conquered, from Sai Tatoo to the present reign, with those of the chiefs who had been executed for subsequent revolts, were displayed by two parties of executioners, each upwards of a hundred, who passed in an impassioned dance, some with the most irresistible grimace, some with the most frightful gesture ; they clashed their knives upon the skulls, in which sprigs of thyme were inserted to keep the spirits from troubling the king. I never felt as grateful for being born in a free country. . . . About 100 persons, mostly culprits reserved, are generally sacrificed in different quarters of the town at this custom. Several slaves were also sacrificed at Bantama over the large brass pan, their blood mingled with the vegetable and animal matter within (fresh and purified), to complete the charm and produce invincible fetische. All the chiefs kill several slaves, that their blood may flow into the hole from whence the new yam is taken. Those who cannot afford to kill slaves take the head of one already sacrificed and placed in the hole..... The unhappy victims on these occasions are led to execution with knives thrust through their jaws and tongue from side to side, and afterwards literally hacked to pieces ! . . . The decease of a person is announced by a discharge of musketry proportionate to his rank or the wealth of his family. In an instant you see a crowd of slaves burst from the house and run towards the bush, flattering themselves that the hindermost, or those surprised in the house, will furnish the human victims for sacrifice, if they can but secrete themselves until the custom is over. One or two slaves are then sacrificed at the door of the house. . . . On the death of Quatchie Quoffie's mother, the king Quatchie Quoffie, and Odumata, each sacrificed a young girl directly the deceased had breathed her last, that she might not want for attendants until the greater sacrifice was made. We walked to Assofoo about twelve o'clock ; the vultures were hovering around two headless trunks, scarcely cold. . . . Troops of women were advancing, dancing, &c. . . . Now and then a victim was hurried by, generally dragged or run along at full speed ; the uncouth dress and the exulting countenances of those who surrounded him likening them to as many fiends. I observed apathy more frequently than despair or emotion, in the looks of the victims. The victims, with large knives driven through their cheeks, eyed Quatchie Quoffie with indifference, he them with a savage joy bordering on frenzy. Thirteen victims, surrounded by their executioners, whose black shaggy caps and veils gave them the appearance of bears rather than men, were pressed together by the crowd to the

left of the king.   The drums announced the sacrifice of the victims.
The executioners wrangled and struggled for the office, and the indifference with which the first poor creature looked on, in the torture
he was in from the knife passing through his cheeks, was remarkable.
The nearest executioner snatched the sword from the others, the
right hand of the victim was then lopped off, he was thrown down,
and his head was *sawed* rather than cut off; it was cruelly pro-
longed, I will not say wilfully.   Twelve more were dragged forward,
but we forced our way through the crowd and retired to our quarters.
Other sacrifices, principally female, were made in the bush where
the body was buried.   It is usual to *wet the grave* with the blood
of a freeman of respectability.   All the retainers of the family being
present, and the heads of all the victims deposited in the bottom of
the grave, several are unsuspectingly called in a hurry to assist in
placing the coffin or basket; and just as it rests on the heads and
skulls, a slave from behind stuns one of the freemen by a violent
blow, followed by a deep gash in the back part of the neck, and he
is rolled in on the top of the body, and the grave is instantly
filled up," &c.

" On the death of a king, all the customs which have been for
the subjects who have died during his reign must be repeated by
the families, (the human sacrifices, as well as the carousals and
pageantry,) to amplify that for the monarch, which is also solemnized,
independently, but, at the same time, in every excess of extravagance
and barbarity.   The brothers, sons, and nephews of the king, affecting temporary insanity, burst forth with their muskets and fire pro-
miscuously amongst the crowd; even a man of rank, if they meet
him, is their victim, nor is their murder of him or any other, on
such an occasion, resisted or prevented; the scene can scarcely be
imagined.   Few persons of rank dare to stir from their houses for
the first two or three days, but religiously drive forth all their
vassals and slaves, as the most acceptable composition of their own
absence.   The king's Ocras, who will be mentioned presently, are
all murdered on his tomb, to the number of a hundred or more, and
women in abundance.   I was assured by several that the custom for
Sai Quamina was repeated weekly for three months, and that 200
slaves were sacrificed, and twenty-five barrels of powder fired each
time.   But the custom of the king's mother, the regent of the kingdom during the invasion of Fantee, is most celebrated.   The king
himself devoted 3000 victims (upwards of 2000 of whom were
Fantee prisoners) and twenty-five barrels of powder.   Dwabin,

Kokofoo, Beequa, Soota, and Mampong furnished 100 victims and twenty barrels of powder each, and most of the smaller towns ten victims and two barrels of powder each.....The king's ocras are favourite slaves, or favoured commons, who stake their lives upon the king's, to be kept free from palavers, &c.....Several of the hearts of the enemy are cut out by the fetische men, who follow the army, and the blood and small pieces being mixed (with much ceremony and incantation) with various consecrated herbs, all those who never killed an enemy before eat a portion, for it is believed, that if they did not, their vigour and courage would be secretly wasted by the haunting spirit of the deceased.....On the eve of the Adai festival, early in January, similar butcheries to those already described take place, and continue for several days and nights successively; but the scenes and deeds are too painful and disgusting to pursue them further; sufficient has been shown and adduced to show their fearful frequency, their terrible extent, and their dreadful and degrading and destructive atrocity." — *Bowditch*, pp. 275—290.

"At day-break the firing of guns, music, &c. announced a custom for the husband of the king's sister (the second woman in the kingdom,) he having died in the bush on Friday. About 7 o'clock, the king went to the market-place to make custom, and sacrifice two men; several others were killed by various caboceers. In the evening, Apokoo and the other captains who are to exhibit their gold, paraded the streets, firing musketry, &c.; the crowd was great."— *Bowditch*, p. 394.

"After drinking coffee, &c., they took a hurried leave, as one of the king's people came to tell me one of his majesty's daughters was dead, and shortly after, a constant discharge of musketry announced the custom. The king in the afternoon came to the market-place close to the house, to make custom with his chiefs. I understood that human sacrifices were to be offered, and walked out to avoid the uproar.

"On my way I paid a visit to Baba, who was performing ablution; he said he was going to prayer, but would soon have done; I told him I would sit down till he had finished.

— "There was something solemn and affecting in it, contrasted with the heavy discharges of musketry and shouts of the populace in the distance, which proclaimed the bloody sacrifice was begun, while the vultures and crows wheeled in mazy circles, expecting their usual share of the banquet, and the sun shot his last gleams through the heavy fogs that encircled the town.

"As I went home, I passed the headless trunks of two female slaves, lying neglected and exposed in the market-place, that had been sacrificed, one by the king, and one by the deceased's family. The vultures were revelling, undisturbed, amidst the blood."—*Bowditch*, pp. 405, 406.

"The greatest human sacrifice that has been made in Coomassie during my residence, took place on the eve of the Adai custom, early in January. I had a mysterious intimation of it two days before, from a quarter not to be named. My servants being ordered out of the way, I was addressed: 'Christian, take care and watch over your family: the angel of death has drawn his sword, and will strike on the neck of many Ashantees; when the drum is struck, on Adai eve, it will be the death signal of many. Shun the king if you can, but fear not.'

— "Whilst I was with the king, the officers, whose duty it is to attend at sacrifices, and are in the confidence of the king, came in with their knives, &c.

"This sacrifice was in consequence of the king imagining, that if he washed the bones of his mother and sisters, who died while he was on the throne, it would propitiate the fetish, and make the war successful. Their bones were therefore taken from their coffins, and bathed in rum and water with great ceremony; after being wiped with silks, they were rolled in gold dust, and wrapped in strings of rock gold, aggry beads, and other things of the most costly nature. Those who had done anything to displease the king, were then sent for in succession, and immolated as they entered, 'that their blood might water the graves.' The whole of the night the king's executioners traversed the streets, and dragged every one they found to the palace, where they were put in irons: but (which is often the case) some one had disclosed the secret, and almost every one had fled, and the king was disappointed of most of his distinguished victims. Next morning being Adai custom, which generally brought an immense crowd to the city, every place was silent and forlorn: nothing could be found in the market, and his majesty proceeded to the morning sacrifice of sheep, &c. attended only by his confidants, and the members of his own family. When I appeared at the usual time, he seemed pleased at my confidence, and remarked that I observed how few captains were present. He appeared agitated and fatigued, and sat a very short time.

"As soon as it was dark, the human sacrifices were renewed, and, during the night, the bones of the royal deceased were removed to the sacred tomb at Bantama, to be deposited along with the remains of those who had sat on the throne. The procession was splendid, but not numerous, the chiefs and attendants being dressed in the war costume, with a musket, and preceded by torches ; the sacred stools, and all the ornaments used on great occasions, were carried with them ; the victims, with their hands tied behind them, and in chains, preceded the bones, whilst, at intervals, the songs of death and victory proved their wish to begin the war. The procession returned about three P. M. on Monday, when the king took his seat in the market-place, with his small band, and ' death ! death ! death !' was echoed by his horns. He sat with a silver goblet of palm wine in his hand, and when they cut off any head, imitated a dancing motion in his chair ; a little before dark, he finished his terrors for that day, by retiring to the palace, and soon after, the chiefs came from their concealment, and paraded the streets, rejoicing that they had escaped death, although a few days might put them in the same fear. I had been attacked with a violent fit of the ague in the morning, from having stood so long in the sun the day before while with the king, it being unusually hot. I dared not send out my people to procure anything, lest they should be murdered, and, in fact, there was nothing in the market to be had : there was not even a drop of water in the house. The sacrifice was continued till the next Adai custom, seventeen days.'—*Bowditch*, pp. 419, 420, 421.

" The king's sister entered my quarters in the forenoon, bringing in her train a troop of about one hundred and fifty women and young girls, many of whom were described as the daughters and wives of men of high rank. This woman's relationship naturally established her in an elevated rank, but she was doubly dignified by an employment which, perhaps, may not be improperly termed governess of the Harem, or queen over the females ; all of that sex being responsible to her government, and subject to an arbitrary control under her vice-governesses.

" With this employment she had been invested only a few months, and since the king's return from Buntokoo. Her elevation proceeded from a cause somewhat remarkable.

" When the king was about to open the campaign against Gaman, he collected together his priests, to invoke the royal fetische, and perform the necessary orgies to insure success. These ministers of superstition sacrificed thirty-two males and eighteen female

victims, as an expiatory offering to the gods, but the answers from
the priests being deemed by the council as still devoid of inspiration,
the king was induced to *make a custom* at the sepulchres of his
ancestors, where many hundreds bled.   This, it is affirmed, pro-
pitiated the wrath of the adverse gods.   The priests then prepared
a certain fetische compound, which they delivered to the king,
with an injunction to burn the composition daily in a consecrated
fire-pot within the palace, and upon no account to neglect the fire,
so as to suffer it to go out; for as long as the sacred flame devoured
the powder, he would triumph over his foes.

" When the king joined his army, he commissioned his eldest sister
(then governess of the kingdom), to attend strictly to the sacred
mystery, telling her that his crown and life both depended upon
her vigilance, and the fulfilment of his order.   He selected also
three wives, to whom he was more attached than the rest, to watch
by turns over the mysterious rites, in conjunction with his last-
mentioned sister.

" During the king's absence, this arbitress of his fate formed a
connexion with a chief of Bourmay, whose ambition suggested a
plan to seat himself upon the throne.

" In this conspiracy seventeen of the king's wives and their
families are said to have joined; the fire-pot was broken to pieces,
and the chief commenced arming his party.   But the king, added
my informer, who had sustained heavy losses in the early part of
the war, *and was unable to account for the audacity of the enemy*,
performed an incantation over a certain talisman, which gave an
insight into what was transacting in the capital.   He therefore
despatched a body of men under Audo Cudjo, who, after an impotent struggle on the part of the enemy, effectually crushed the
rebellion.   When the king returned home, he called a council
to deliberate upon the punishment due to the offenders, and it was
finally decreed that his wives should suffer death by decapitation.
His sister, to prevent the profanation of spilling royal blood, was
ordered to be strangled.   The chief, her paramour, and those of his
party, were doomed to the most cruel deaths at the grave of the
king's mother.   These sentences were carried into prompt execution, and, it is affirmed, that above seven hundred people were
sacrificed, or fell in resisting the royal forces.   After this, the
younger sister, my present visitor, was made governess.

" While these butcheries were transacting, the king prepared to
enter the palace, and in the act of crossing the threshold of the

outer gate, was met by several of his wives, whose anxiety to embrace their sovereign lord, impelled them thus to overstep the boundary of female decorum in Ashantee; for it happened that the king was accompanied by a number of his captains, who accordingly were compelled to cover their faces with both hands, and fly from the spot. This is said to have angered the monarch, although his resentment proceeded no farther than words, and he returned to embrace his wives. But being afterwards told by some of the superintendents, that these women were more or less indisposed from a natural female cause, he was inflamed to the highest pitch of indignation, and in a paroxysm of anger, caused these unhappy beings to be cut in pieces before his face; giving orders at the time to cast the fragments into the forest, to be devoured by birds and beasts of prey.* Nor did the atonement rest here, for six more unhappy females were impeached of inconstancy, (a failing, I believe, very common among them,) and they also expiated their faults with their lives. Like another Ulysses, his majesty then devoted himself to the purification of his palace, when, to sum up the full horrors of these bloody deeds, two thousand wretched victims, selected from the Gaman prisoners of war, were slaughtered over the royal death-stool, in honour of the shades of departed kings and heroes."—*Dupuis' Residence in Ashantee*, pp. 114—117.

" The bashaw and Abou Becr called in the evening; they cursed the sanguinary disposition of the government, alleging that six men and nine women had been sacrificed in the morning to the king's household gods; that these butcheries were kept from my knowledge for two reasons: the one, that they concerned the Mission, as the king had been imploring the aid of his idols, to incline the heart of the great king of England towards him—the other, that I should not have to report that the sovereign of Ashantee delighted in spilling human blood, which it was well known gave as much offence to white men as it did to Moslems."—*Dupuis*, p. 128.

---

* The law of Ashantee, although preserved only by tradition, is equally influential over the morals of all ranks. That regarding the treatment of women is of some interest, from its approximation to the Levitical, or, perhaps, more intimately to the Mahommedan law, as related in the second chapter of the Koran, where it is enjoined, that the men shall separate' themselves from the women when naturally indisposed, this being deemed a pollution. In Ashantee, a woman is unclean from the same cause, and cannot approach her husband, or any male branch of her family, until the disorder has left her, and she has undergone certain purifying ablutions.

E

" On the 13th, this [the Adai] custom was ushered in by the discharge of fire-arms, and the sound of many barbarous instruments. Numbers of victims were offered up to the gods, although secretly in the palace and the houses of the chieftains. The poorer classes sacrificed cattle or poultry. The city itself exhibited the most deplorable solitude; and the few human beings who were courageous enough to shew themselves in the streets, fled at the approach of a captain, and barricadoed the doors of their huts, to escape the danger of being shot or sacrificed. The doleful cries of the women vibrated from several quarters of the city,—and the death-horns and drums within the palace seemed to stupify the obnoxious prisoners and foreign slaves with horror, as they contemplated the risk they were exposed to. I wandered about during this awful day, until fatigue and disgust led me to seek my quarters.

" The following day, one of a similar train of horrors succeeded, and still I was left in suspense, for my own linguists and messengers were not hardy enough to knock at the royal gate. They dreaded, they said, the fetische men, who guarded the avenue, and who alone were suffered to enjoy free ingress. The society of the Moslems, however, in some degree reconciled me. By these people I was given to understand that seventy men and women had been put to death the day previous in the palace only; besides those who were sacrificed in private houses, and in the forest. Most of these unhappy beings were Gaman prisoners of war, who had been purposely reserved as an offering to the gods; the others were criminals or disobedient slaves. Such was the explanation I received."—*Dupuis*, pp. 141, 142.

" Upon receiving the king's hand, which he presented with the utmost affability, I noticed a streak of dried blood upon his forehead, and this token appeared to be universal, as well among officers of distinction as their slaves and retainers. It denoted their participation in the late sacrifices. The royal death-stool, clotted with the still reeking gore of its victims, stood on one side of the king, under care of the captain executioner, who attended with his band of assistants. At the feet of the sovereign, stood a small fire-pot, and a trunk fitted up with a compound medley of relics and charms soaking in blood."—*Dupuis*, p. 142.

" ' Now,' said the king, after a pause, ' I have another palaver, and you must help me to talk it. A long time ago, the great king liked plenty of trade, more than now; then many ships came, and they bought ivory, gold, and slaves ; but now he will not let the ships come as before, and the people buy gold and ivory only. This is what I have in my head; so now tell me truly, like a friend, why does the king do so?' 'His Majesty's question,' I replied, 'was connected with a great palaver, which my instructions did not authorize me to discuss. I had nothing to say regarding the slave trade.' 'I know that, too,' retorted the king; 'because if my master liked that trade, you would have told me so before. I only want to hear what you think as a friend : this is not like the other palavers.' I was confessedly at a loss for an argument that might pass as a satisfactory reason, and the sequel proved that my doubts were not groundless. The king did not deem it plausible that this obnoxious traffic should have been abolished from motives of humanity alone ; neither would he admit that it lessened the number either of domestic or foreign wars.

"Taking up one of my observations, he remarked, 'the white men who go to council with your master, and pray to the great God for him, do not understand my country, or they would not say the slave trade was bad. But if they think it bad now, why did they think it good before? Is not your law an old law, the same as the Crammo* law? Do you not both serve the same God, only you have different fashions and customs? Crammoos are strong people in fetische, and they say the law is good, because the great God made the book; so they buy slaves, and teach them good things, which they knew not before. This makes every body love the Crammoos, and they go everywhere up and down, and the people give them food when they want it. Then these men come all the way from the great water,† and from Manding, and Dagomba, and Killinga ; they stop and trade for slaves, and then go home. If the great king would like to restore this trade, it would be good for the white men and for me too, because Ashantee is a country for war, and the people are strong ; so that if you talk that palaver for me properly in the white country, if you go there, I will give you plenty of gold, and I will make you richer than all the white men.

"I urged the impossibility of the king's request, promising, however, to record his sentiments faithfully. 'Well then,' said the king, 'you must put down in my master's book all I shall say, and then he will look at it, now he is my friend. And when he sees what is true, he will surely restore that trade. I cannot make war to catch slaves in the bush, like a thief. My ancestors never did so.

* Moslem law. † Niger.

But if I fight a king, and kill him, when he is insolent, then certainly I must have his gold, and his slaves, and the people are mine too. Do not the white kings act like this? Because I hear the old men say, that before I conquered Fantee, and killed the Braffoes and the Kings, that white men came in great ships, and fought and killed many people; and then they took the gold and the slaves to the white country : and sometimes they fought together. That is all the same as these black countries. The great God and the fetische made war for strong men everywhere, because then they can pay plenty of gold and proper sacrifice. When I fought Gaman, I did not make war for slaves ; but because Dinkera (the king) sent me an arrogant message and killed my people, and refused to pay me gold, as his father did. Then my fetische made me strong like my ancestors, and I killed Dinkera, and took his gold, and brought more than 20,000 slaves to Coomassie. Some of these people being bad men, I washed my stool in their blood for the fetische. But then some were good people; and these I sold or gave to my captains : many, moreover, died, because this country does not grow too much corn, like Sarem : and what can I do? unless I kill or sell them, they will grow strong and kill my people. Now you must tell my master that these slaves can work for him, and if he wants 10,000, he can have them. And if he wants fine handsome girls and women to give his captains, I can send him great numbers."—*Dupuis*, pp. 163, 164.

FETISCHE SACRIFICES.—BADAGRY.

After relating the atrocious butchery of two young females, wives of the chief, and slaves, merely for having expressed themselves freely on some palace proceedings, Lander goes on (Vol. II. p. 249) to say,—

" The murder of a slave is not considered even in the light of a misdemeanour amongst them ; and the frequency of this crime has not only taken away all sense of its enormity, but steeled the breast of the multitude against every compassionate feeling ; whilst the king and government encourage savage principles and pastimes by setting them the example. .... Badagry being a general mart for the sale of slaves to the European merchants (who are now almost exclusively confined to agents of the Portuguese nation), it not unfrequently happens that the market is either over-stocked with human beings, or no buyers are to be found, in which case the maintenance of the unhappy slaves devolves solely on the government. The expense incurred by this means is oftentimes murmured against by the king, who shortly afterwards causes an examination to be made, when the sickly, as well as the old and infirm, are carefully selected, and chained by themselves in one of the factories (five of which, containing upwards of one thousand slaves of both sexes, were at Badagry during my residence there), and next day the majority of these poor wretches are pinioned and conveyed to the banks of a river that runs up the country, where, having arrived, a weight of some sort is appended to their necks, and being rowed in canoes to the middle of the stream, are flung into the water and left to perish by the pitiless barbarians. Slaves, who for other reasons are rejected in the markets, undergo the same punishment, or are left to undergo more lively torture at the sacrifices; by which means hundreds of human beings are annually destroyed. . . . . In the private fetische hut of the king Adilee, at Badagry, the skull of that monarch's father is preserved in a clay vessel, placed in the earth. Human blood, as well as the blood of birds and beasts, is occasionally sprinkled on it, and when the king goes to war, the same skull is invariably carried with him, with which he frequently converses, and gently rebukes it if his success does not happen to answer his expectations. . . . . . There is another fetische hut at Badagry, the interior of which is positively ornamented with rows of human skulls, and other emblems of mortality, whitened by time, and having a most terrific appearance. At a short distance from this gloomy hut, stands a fetische tree, on the branches of which the headless bodies of human beings, slaughtered under them, are invariably suspended.

" Thieves and other offenders, together with the remnant of unpurchased slaves, who are not drowned along with their companions in misfortunes and misery, are reserved by the barbarians to be sacrificed to their gods, which horrid ceremony takes place at least once a month. Prisoners taken in war are also immolated to appease the manes of the soldiers of Adilee slain in battle ; and, as of all atrocities the manner in which these wretches are slaughtered is the most barbarous, it may not, perhaps, be improper or ill-timed to give a detailed account of it in this place. Each criminal being conducted to the fetische tree, a flask of rum is given him to drink, whilst he is in the act of swallowing which a fellow steals imperceptibly behind him, with a heavy club or bludgeon, and inflicts a violent blow on the back of the head with the murderous weapon, and, as it often happens, dashes out his brains, so that the execu-

tioner has no occasion to repeat his stroke. The senseless being is then taken to the fetische hut, and a calabash, or gourd, having been previously got ready, the head is severed from the trunk with an axe, and the smoking blood gurgles into it. Whilst this is in hand, other wretches, furnished with knives, &c., cut and mangle the body, in order to extract the heart entire from the breast, which being done, although it be yet warm and quivering with life, it is presented to the king first, and afterwards to his wives and generals, who always attend at the celebration of these sacrifices; and his majesty and suite making an incision in it with their teeth, and partaking of the foamy blood, which is likewise offered, the heart is exhibited to the surrounding multitude.....The bleeding heart, after being bitten by the king, and his principal wives and head men, is affixed to the head of a tall spear, and, with the calabash of blood and headless body, paraded through the town and followed by hundreds of spearmen and a dense crowd of people. Whoever may express an inclination to bite the heart or drink the blood has it immediately presented to him for that purpose, the multitude dancing and singing.....What remains of the heart is flung to the dogs, and the body, cut in pieces, is stuck on the fetische tree, where it is left till wholly devoured by birds of prey. Besides these butcheries, they make a grand sacrifice once a year under their sacred fetische tree, growing in a wood a few miles from the city. These are offered to their malevolent demon, or spirit of evil, at whose shrine hundreds of human beings are annually immolated, their corpses undergoing the same horrid process as that which has already been described; only, in this instance, they are not removed from the spot, but quartered and hung on the gigantic branches of the venerable tree, and the skulls of the victims suffered to bleach in the sun round the trunk of it. By accident I had an opportunity of seeing this much talked of tree a day or two only after the celebration of one of the grand yearly sacrifices, and it was the most ghastly and appalling object which I had ever beheld.....
We had travelled about seven miles from Badagry, when the so much dreaded fetische tree suddenly burst upon our sight, its enormous branches literally covered with fragments of human bodies, and its majestic trunk surrounded by irregular heaps of hideous skulls, which had been suffered to accumulate for many years previously. It was standing in the centre of a large piece of open ground in the heart of the forest, and was actually the largest tree I had ever seen. Thousands of vultures, which had been

scared away by our unwelcome intrusion, were yet hovering round
and over their disgusting food, and now and then pouncing fearlessly
upon a half-devoured arm or leg. I stood as if fascinated to the
spot by the influence of a torpedo, and stupidly gazed on the ghastly
spectacle before me, the huge branches of the fetische tree groaning
beneath their burden of human flesh and bones, and sluggishly waving
in consequence of the hasty retreat of the birds of prey; the in-
tense and almost insufferable heat of a vertical sun; the intolerable
odour of the corrupt corpses; the heaps of human heads, many of
them apparently staring at me from hollows which had once sparkled
with living eyes; the awful stillness and solitude of the place, dis-
turbed only by the sighing of the conscious wind through the
sombre foliage—or, at intervals, by the frightful screaming of vöra-
cious vultures as they flapped their sable wings almost in my face—
all tended to overpower me; my heart sickened within my bosom,
a dimness came over my eyes, my legs refused to support me, and,
turning my head, I fell senseless into the arms of Jowdie, my faithful
slave, &c."—*Lander*, pp. 250, 268.

THE WESTERN DIVISION OF AFRICA.

Quitting the positions of the places and the high lands
above noticed, let us, before entering upon the important
points regarding the countries more into the interior and towards the sources and course of the Niger, turn to the consideration of the countries to the north of the Camaranca river,
including Sierra Leone and the places adjacent. A due consideration of, and attention to these points is necessary, in
order to fix more specifically the positions of the high lands
and minor rivers in the more western parts of Africa, while the
inquiry will also tend, most eminently, to show the accuracy of
the positions fixed upon as the sources of the mighty river
Niger, and the course north-eastward and eastward of that
important stream through Central Africa.

Major Laing's journey from Sierra Leone to Fallaba, the
capital of Soolimana, is, under this division of the subject, the
first point for consideration. On the 16th of April (the height
of the dry season), Major Laing and his party left Sierra
Leone, and, proceeding by Rokon and Roketschik, on the 5th
of May arrived at Mayosso, situate by chronometer in 11° 54'
W. long., and by reckoning, 8° 28' N. lat. The nature of

African travelling will be well understood when the time is considered in which Major Laing accomplished this part of his journey. From Freetown, Sierra Leone, the Major was nineteen days till he reached Mayosso, during nine days of which only he travelled and made good nearly seventy geographical miles in direct line, in longitude rather less than eight miles per day; the difference of latitude, seven miles, not being worth taking into account. At a point a little to the east of Roketschik (8° 30′ N. lat., and 12° 11′ W. long.), twelve miles distant to the south, two eminences appeared, in which were the sources of the river Kates, which flows thence W.N.W. and enters the sea near the southern boundary of the small territory of Sierra Leone. Mayosso is situate on a rising ground on the right bank of the Camaranca, or Kabanka river, flowing from thence west by south, from fifty to seventy yards broad, and so far navigable for canoes. Mabroom, seventy geographical miles in a direct line from Freetown, is one day's journey, eight miles north of Mayosso, and two miles from the village of Mabiss on the Rokelle, there 300 feet broad, very deep in the middle, and with a current of three miles per hour. From this point the traveller first beholds the Blue Mountains of Kouranko to the eastward, and stretching as far as the eye can reach in a direction from north to south. One day's journey east of Mabroom Major Laing reached Kooloofa, three miles south of which was the Kabanka, 200 yards (it should be 200 feet) broad, and with very lofty banks. Beyond Kooloofa he came to Seemera, at which place the Kouranka Hills commence very high, extending from north to south sixty miles, and to the northward running in a north-east direction through the Kouranka country, but opening in ridges, running in the direction from east to west, through which the rivers and their various tributaries direct their course westward to the ocean. Kouranka is bounded west by Timanee and the Bullom coast; north by Teembo and Soolimana; east by Kissikissi, the Niger, and unknown countries; and south, by other countries bordering on the Atlantic. Its extent to the eastward is great—said to be more than thirty days' journey. Beyond Kanato, where the Rokelle was crossed, proceeding north-east to Fallaba, it was 100 yards broad, but much flooded. The next town was Kania, situated in 9° 22′ N. lat. by observation. Proceeding, they came to Konkodoogoree, where they found all the surrounding country in a high state of cultivation. They next reached Fallaba, the capital of Soolimana, situated in 9° 49′ N. lat. by observation.

During his progress through the mountainous districts, Major Laing everywhere found the land deeply and thickly intersected by branches of the Rokelle and the Kabanka, which rivers, from the great number of springs in the hills, become, within a short space, considerable streams. The country on all hands was exceedingly picturesque and beautiful, with a considerable population, and also cultivation. The magnitude of the Rokelle and the Kabanka has been shown at points nearly equal, or, it may be said, at equal distances from the ocean; and the former is found to be one-third broader than the latter. This fact has been noted, in order to prove that, as their sources and their upper courses are in countries, or rather in a country corresponding in every respect with each other; so it is plain that the course of the latter must be shorter than that of the former, and that the course of the Kabanka, as in Major Laing's map, and in the maps hitherto constructed, has been laid down from fifty to sixty miles too much to the eastward. The source thereof has accordingly been altered, and in doing so it will be readily perceived, that it corresponds better with the nature of the country, and with the certain sources and the course of the Niger in its upper part. The source of the Kabanka will therefore be found to be in 9° N. lat., and 10° 18′ W. long.

The magnitude also of these rivers, while running so close to each other, will enable us to estimate the probable course of all the rivers, from the Camaranca eastward to the Assinee; and further show, that even had the course of the Upper Niger been brought still nearer to the coast than it has been, there yet remains ample room for the formation of all the rivers mentioned; for it may be taken as certain, that not one of them is equal in magnitude to the Rokelle.

At its source the Rokelle springs from under a large rock, and scatters itself over a bed of red clay, after the manner of the bursting of a water-pipe in a street. About 100 yards from

this spot it collects into a channel about a foot in breadth, and
runs off rapidly to SS.E., which course it continues for a few
miles, and then making a circuitous sweep, it shapes its course
to the S.W., between Setacolia and Tigiatamba, by which
time, having received considerable tributary assistance, it
assumes a respectable appearance, and is (*Laing*, p. 320)
barely fordable. From thence it bends its course on the general
bearing about W.S.W. to the sea at Sierra Leone, not more
than 200 miles distant. From its mouth it is navigable for boats
as far as Rokon, and during the rainy season, to a considerable
distance farther upwards, and by which means Camwood and
other timber is sometimes floated down it to the sea. Beyond
the Timanee country to the eastward of Mabung, Major Laing
entered the country of the Mandingoes, who are all Mahommedans, and, comparatively, an industrious and civilized people.
The chiefs generally expressed an anxious wish to have a
regular and steady communication with Europeans, and prof-
fered every assistance to bring that about. Fallaba contains
10,000 inhabitants.

The next part which merits our consideration, is the interesting journey of De Caillé into the interior of Africa; con-
fining ourselves for the present to that portion which extends
from Kacundy on the Rio Nunez unto Cambaya on the Tankisso. The time occupied by De Caillé, in his journey along
with a caravan of merchants proceeding to the interior, was
eighteen days, and, as near as can be ascertained from perusing
his work attentively, 130 hours of active travel. He himself
estimates the number of English miles that he travelled, and
allowing the same rate per day for those few days where the
number is not exactly given, and upon reducing these to geographic miles, and protracting his daily course upon the bearings which he has given, as has in this instance been done, the
result will place the source of the Bafing and Teembo rather to
the westward of the point where Major Laing's bearings, taken
at Fallaba, places the latter, and where other authorities have
placed the source of the stream mentioned. But the difference
is so small, being only about twenty miles, that the positions in
which Major Laing has enabled us to fix them, have not been
altered. In his progress eastward, the march of the caravan

with which De Caillé was, must necessarily have been exceedingly slow, and, as he himself states, it really was; because, throughout the greater portion thereof, they had to climb over high, steep, rugged mountains. De Caillé, in his march along by the sources of the Rio Nunez, the Rio Pongos, and, in fact, of all those rivers which flow into the Atlantic, between the Rio Nunez on the north and the Rokelle on the south, and to the sources of the Bafing and the Tankisso, gives a very interesting account of the country through which he passed. He describes it everywhere as peculiarly interesting, picturesque, and beautiful; covered with high mountains, amongst which are fine fertile valleys, with numerous beautiful streams of water, which flow to form the rivers alluded to. The inhabitants are principally pastoral Foulahs, who are rigid Mahommedans, but who, with the exception of the acrimony which the tenets of that faith give to the mind of its votaries against those of a different faith, especially the Christian faith, seem to be a simple and kind people. The Tanklita he describes as the parent stream of the Rio Nunez, and the Kakiriman, near Pandayah, as the river named Rio Pongos. Where he crossed it, its bed was from seventy to eighty paces broad, with a very rapid current, and the water in it at the end of April nearly up to their waists. Eastward he passed the Coucola, a beautiful stream from forty to fifty paces broad, the water in which came up to their knees; it runs amongst high hills, the same as all the neighbouring streams do, forming beautiful cascades. The course of the Doulinco is described as particularly beautiful, and from Kacundy he had not, he states, seen so beautiful and fertile a tract of country as that around its banks. " Instead of rocks, I now beheld on every side delightful plains, which required only the labour of the husbandman to produce every thing necessary for human life." The hill of Loma, near Dougue, he says, is 600 paces high, and to the westward, and in the neighbourhood of the town of Lantague, is a range of mountains called Lantague, each of which rises perpendicularly to the height of nearly 1200 feet, and they exhibit scarcely any trace of vegetation. To the east of the village of Lantague, some of the mountains in the range rise to the height of 2400 feet above the level of the plain, but without any snow being

seen upon them. In the neighbourhood of Bafila, not far from
the Bafing and its sources, the appearance of the country, says
De Caillé, was such, " that I might almost fancy that I was in
a fairy land" (vol. i. p. 197). The land is generally fertile
and well cultivated, abounding with towns, villages, and
population, a number of whom follow the pastoral life; they
are nearly all Mahommedans. Pandeyah, and the country
about Lantague and some distance to the eastward, forms the
country called Irnanke, which country lays to the west of
Foota Jallon and to the east of Kakundy. It has on the north
side the negroes who inhabit the country of Cassemanka, and
on the south the Timanee negroes, who occupy a tract of
country not far from Sierra Leone. Irnanke is covered with
lofty mountains, and the population thereof are pastoral Foulahs, part of a nation which has, of late years, overspread, or
rather overrun, Western Africa.

The next point for consideration is the most western portion
of inhabited and cultivated Africa, through which the larger
rivers, Senegal, Gambia, &c. flow. Park's Travels, together
with those which the corrections from Mollien, De Caillé, and
other authorities, as well as the corrections which a greater
degree of attention to Park's Travels themselves enable us to
gather, will place this portion of Africa pretty correctly before
us. But it may here be simply observed, that the corrections
made, agree in a most surprising and satisfactory manner, when
checked and compared with the journeys of other travellers who
have penetrated into the interior of Africa in various and opposite directions. But to proceed to the minute details and survey
of this the most western portion of Africa, called by the Africans
dwelling upon the upper and the middle course of the Niger,
The Land of the West, or, " Land of the Setting Sun." The
Bafing, or Senegal river, becomes the first object of attention.
The Tankisso, which was formerly believed, and which Mollien set down as its parent stream, has been found to have no
connexion whatever with it, but to be a mighty tributary to the
Joliba. The Bafing, or, as the word signifies, Black River, or
real Senegal, rises at a short distance to the west of the source
of the Tankisso, and about twenty-five miles to the W.N.W.
of Teembo. Where De Caillé crossed it in his route to Cam-

baya, the stream was about 100 feet wide, and a foot or eighteen inches deep, the current rapid, and the bed very rocky. Its course, for a short distance from its source, is eastward, under the name of Gangore, but it quickly turns to the N.E., and then to the north, which is the general bearing of its course for nearly 300 miles. Its bed, to a considerable distance from its source, is almost a sheet of foam, from the rapidity with which it flows amongst the rocks which interrupt its stream.

The mountains to the east of the Bafing are lofty, and, seen from the west, extend further than the eye can reach in the direction from north-east to south-west. The country to the west of these mountains is an elevated plain, well watered, fruitful, and populous. The country of Fouta Jallon is a very remarkable country. " Walking over these districts," says Mollien, " the earth resounds under your feet;" and, what is singular, Laing found the same thing round the sources of the Rokelle. A short distance from the source of the Bafing, to the north, are found the springs of the Rio Grande and the Gambia rivers. They rise very close to each other ; the Rio Grande flowing in a winding course on the general bearing of west into the Atlantic, after a course of about 300 miles. It is a considerable stream, and near Faran is several hundred feet broad. The Gambia flows first east, then north-east, then north; afterwards it turns, and, upon a general bearing, pursues a winding course towards the west, entering the Atlantic Ocean in about 13° 30' N. lat. The length of its course on the general bearings is about 400 geographical miles, and though a considerable, it is by no means a first-rate river ; for at Teleecorra, half-way betwixt Madina and the Narico, or at the spot named by Park, " Walter's Well," it is only 100 yards broad, and so far the tide flows up it. The country towards its source is more romantic than in its lower course. In its early course it meanders through a rich country ; the soil on both sides is of an alluvial formation, and astonishingly fertile. The banks are adorned with trees of the greatest beauty, and both rice and tobacco are cultivated in the upland districts around it to a great extent.

From Fouta Jallon, the country where it springs, the Bafing, or Senegal, pursues its course northwards through Dentilia, first about NN.E., and next about NN.W., until it approaches very nearly 15° of N. lat., where it turns, first west, next north-west, and then again west by Podor, and from thence W.S.W., till it flows into the Atlantic at St. Louis, the capital of the French colony of Senegal. For nearly sixty miles the stream flows due south at a very short distance from the sea; in fact, during all that distance, a sand bank only intervenes between the sea and the river, which sand-bank, extending by degrees, has been thrown up by, as it were, the contention betwixt the sea and the river. From the S.E. it is joined near the fifteenth parallel by the Faleme, and from the eastward, and near the parallel of 14°, by the Balee (Honey River), on the west side, and by the considerable river the Kokoro, formed by the union of several powerful streams on the east. Several other streams join it more to the southward; and several more from the south and from the east run to form the Kokoro, such as the Ba Wonda, the Comeissang, and the Ba Woolima (Red River), and the Ba Woolli. The Furkama and the Boki flow to the Bafing. The Ba Woolli springs in the hills to the northward of Bammakoo, and the Kokoro rises to the south-west of Kamalia. Where Mr. Park crossed the Kokoro, on his return in his first journey, he found it a stream only sufficient to turn a mill; this was in the month of April, the very height of the dry season; but the marks on its banks indicated a rise of twenty feet during the rains. The Ba Wonda, &c., are smaller rivers in this part of their courses, which shows that these courses from the southward are very short. The Faleme, where Park crossed it in the same journey, and during the same season, was easily forded, being only two feet deep, but found running rapidly over a bed of sand and gravel. Where he crossed the Bafing at the same period, it was found very deep, but with scarcely any current; and its breadth may be judged by the fact, that it is there crossed by a bridge, constructed by bending two tall trees on the opposite banks till they meet, when they are fastened together. This temporary bridge is yearly swept away by the floods, and yearly replaced when these subside. The point where the passage is thus effected was in about 12° 48' N. lat., and the point where the Faleme was crossed lay in about 13° N. lat., and its sources were stated to be only a few days' journey to the south-east.

In his second journey, Park crossed the two latter streams, the Faleme about twenty, and the Bafing about forty miles more to the north, and this second time also at the close of the dry season. The Ba Faleme he found, June 8th, a little discoloured by the rains, to the south—its current, four knots per hour, and its sources said to be distant six days' journey to the south-east. Of the magnitude of this stream at this point, we have no further account, but that which is furnished in his first journey, when he crossed it nearly in the 15th parallel, December 20th, very early in the dry season, and which enables us to ascertain this point satisfactorily. Then, its current was rapid, the depth up to the knees on horseback, and the bed rocky. In his second journey, he found the Ba Lee not sensibly swelled, and easily stepped across it from rock to rock, which proves that its course is not so far to the southward as the source of the Ba Faleme. The latitude, where it was crossed at the time adverted to, was 13° 35' N. The Bafing, in the same journey, he found risen about two feet, a proof of its remote southern source, where the rains commence early, for as yet there had been no rain in that parallel, 13° 27' N. The river is described as large and navigable; the current, then in the middle of June, three knots per hour. Where he crossed the stream, December 28th, on his first journey, about ninety miles more to the northward, 14° 30' N. lat., he found it, as he says, a beautiful but shallow river, the banks about forty feet high, and in breadth like the river Tweed at Melross. Above Kayee, where he at this time crossed it, about five miles and a half, there is a considerable cataract called Felow; and thirty miles higher up, is the fall or cataract called Govinea, still larger than the other; but westward from Kayee, the bed of the river is composed of sand and gravel. A little below this place, the Senegal is joined by a narrow but deep stream called the Krieko, which rises in the range of hills to the eastward of Kooniakary, the capital of Casson. At Podor, the Senegal, after the junction of all its tributaries, is about one thousand English feet broad, and twenty-four feet deep, the tide proceeding some distance above this place.

Proceeding on his second journey from the Bafing, Park came to the Ba Wonda, 14° N. lat., which he found, July 4th, swelled from the rains to the southward about two feet, shallow and rocky, and, he adds, "it cannot, even in its present state, be called a large river." The rainy season had now begun in earnest, and all the streams he next came to were very much swollen. The Kokoro, called Balee by mistake, was the next which he reached, in 14° 1' N. lat.; it ran with great velocity, and broke into small cataracts. He next came to the Ba Woolima, in latitude 13° 41' N., here from fifty to sixty feet broad, but swelled to the depth of twenty feet. Lastly, he came to the Ba Woolli, in 13° 16' N. lat., a stream exactly similar to the other. In the intermediate space between the two last-named rivers, he passed smaller streams running to the westward, but all clearly of very short courses, which determines the high grounds to the eastward to be not far distant.

It has been found necessary to be thus particular about these rivers, in order to point out to the reader the facts which the evidence they afford establishes, namely, that with the exception of the Bafing, none of them have courses of any great length; while from the scale of magnitude which they give, we are better enabled to determine not only the greater distances than those that have hitherto been supposed of the more remote sources of the Niger, but the probable distance from Courouasso of its main stream, subsequently to be mentioned, as all these streams flow from countries in every respect similarly situated to those countries which give birth to the Senegal, Gambia, &c. All this portion of Africa, in the upper part of these rivers, is very mountainous and rugged, but in many places has a good soil and is fertile; large quantities of gold dust are also found in various places, in the hills and about the streams, in Bambouk and Mandingo. The mountains to the north-west of Fobea are very high, and those to the eastward are still higher, and the east wind blowing over them is felt exceedingly cold. On the summit of Tangue (10½° N. lat.), the air is so keen that exposure to the sun is sought at noon-day; and near Bourre and Bandeia, the air, from the great elevation, is so pure that Mollien found respiration to be difficult. The principal chain of hills runs north to the eastward of the Bafing, passing east of

Kamalia, and west of Kancaba to Bammakoo. Beyond this, the ridges run—one eastward to the northward of Maraboo, until approaching the neighbourhood of Yamina, where it sinks into the level country; another ridge runs northward by the sources of the Ba Woolli, separating into two chains, one running N.E. to the high mountains (12,000 feet) south of Walet (Beeroo), and the other W.N.W. not far distant from the Ba Woolima, till approaching the meridian of Benowm, they run north to the eastward of that place, finally sinking and disappearing in the Great Desert.

It is necessary here generally to state that all the west coast of Africa to the southward of the Great Desert, but especially about the mouths of the rivers, is low, very marshy, and swampy, and consequently exceedingly unhealthy for Europeans. This is particularly the case at Sierra Leone, and about the mouth of the Gambia. The English settlement at the latter place, called Bathurst-town, is founded amidst surrounding swamps, and on a sand and mud bank scarcely rising above the surface of the river. The country, also, in all the lowlands in this quarter of Africa, including almost all the country which goes by the name of Senegambia, is by no means so fine, so fertile, or so well cultivated as the countries in the interior: nor is the population thereof so intelligent and industrious as the population more inland.

This western portion of central Africa has, till very lately, been extended in all maps much too far to the eastward, even more than 5° of longitude. Mr. John Arrowsmith alone perceived and corrected this error: the consequences of which had been, that the upper course of the Niger, Lake Dibbie, and Timbuctoo, have been laid down about 5° (300 geographical miles) too much to the eastward. These errors, as has already been mentioned, were made and perpetuated by too great distances being allowed for the day's journey made by Park and other travellers.

Pisania also, the point from whence Mr. Park started, was laid down a great deal too far to the eastward. The late accurate survey of the west coast of Africa has placed Pisania 2° 1′ to the eastward of the flag-staff of Bathurst-town, at the mouth of the Gambia, and consequently in 14° 40′ W. long.

F

from Greenwich. As regards African travelling, it is here necessary to observe that a few miles each day is the very utmost that any European can make out in a protracted journey. Park, as it may be observed, sometimes travelled only four or five miles in a day. De Caillé frequently did not travel more; and the latter tells us, that even when travelling at the rate of only six miles a day in continuation, he found himself scarcely able to move.

The time taken by Park, namely sixty-eight days, really occupied in daily travelling, shows the slow progress of African travelling under such circumstances. The time calculated, or rather taken by the natives, who always travel during the dry season, in a journey from Madina, the capital of the kingdom of Woolli, on the banks of the Gambia, to Ségo, the capital of Bambarra, on the banks of the Niger, is thirty-six days. The distance in a direct line is 450 miles, or at the rate of about twelve and a half geographical miles per day. The time stated in Mr. Park's journey last alluded to, would give for the distance eight and a half geographical miles per day, made good in the general bearing; which is the utmost that can be allowed for African travelling in the mountainous countries during the rains.

Park states that Boure is six days' journey by water from Bammakoo; and this time, the old schoolmaster who came from Kammalia to meet him took to perform the journey. He also states that Jarra lay N.W. from Kammalia, distant about ten days' journey. From Benowm to Walet, the capital of Beeroo, he states that water was not wanting on the journey, a proof that the route betwixt the two places was beyond the limits of the pure desert; while from Walet to Timbuctoo, it was stated to him that water was found more abundantly, a proof that that route lay through a cultivated country. Walet, he states, lay nearly in the line of the bearing from Benowm to Timbuctoo.

With respect to the distances travelled by Park, and consequently the positions of places, in a most important but the least determined part of his route during his first journey, we have some curious information; and a good check furnished by consulting the journal of Isaaco, the person who acted as his guide from the Gambia to Sansanding during his second journey. The same individual was sent by Mr. Maxwell, the governor of Senegal, from that place, in 1810, to inquire after the fate of his former master. That part of Isaaco's journal from Kooniakary to Yamina on the banks of the Joliba, is considered sufficient to advert to for the object at present under consideration. The distance from Kooniakary, the capital of Kasson, to Yamina took him twenty-five days (184 hours) daily travel, in the month of July and part of the month of August, and consequently in the worst portion of the rainy season. His route lay more to the south than that taken by Park in his first journey, yet in the middle part thereof, he could not have been far distant from it. There is no town, the name of which he gives, that we can recognise as any of those that Park passed through, except Wassiba, which sounds like Wassiboo; but as Isaaco reached Wassiba on the sixth day after leaving Kooniakary, it could scarcely be the Wassiboo of Park, hitherto laid down as distant from the former capital 135 miles to the east, too much for six days' journey, even by an individual native traveller ; but, on the other hand, if the place should be the same, the Wassiboo of Park, it would establish the fact, that Kooniakary and Wassibo are not so far from each other as even Mr. Arrowsmith conceived them to be when he constructed his last map of Africa, and which consequently go to restrict the distance between Pisania and Sego, and to confirm the propriety and accuracy of the reduced scale given to the journeys performed by Mr. Park, and the accuracy of the positions which have been assigned to the bed of the upper Niger and the towns on that part of its banks, settled from these and from other authorities. From Wassiboo to Sego Mr. Park was ten days (about 100 hours), while from Wassiba to Yamina, Isaaco was, as nearly as can be gained from his journal, nineteen days (143 hours). The two places, therefore, can scarcely be the same, the journey of both in these parts being performed at a corresponding period of the year, and it may be said, by travellers equally unencumbered, except that Mr. Park, under the circumstances in which he was placed, was compelled to travel at a quicker rate than Isaaco had occasion to do.

To the east of Kooniakary Isaaco crossed five rivers, and afterwards on the third day, he climbed over a ridge of high mountains, unto their eastern base. The rivers or streams here mentioned, no doubt, join the Krieko. On the 6th day, and between Geocha and Wassiba, he crossed seven rivulets, after having travelled forty-one hours from Kooniakary. On the tenth day (sixty-nine hours from Kooniakary) he crossed a small river, and afterwards a large forest, situated to the east of the village of Amadi-Fatuma-Bougou. On the thirteenth day, and at five hours' journey from Giangounde, he came to lakes Chouava and Ferrinee, which are never dry, and afterwards, nearer Giangounde, he came to another lake. Beyond Giongay five hours' journey, he, on the fifteenth day, crossed Lake Sorme. At Magnacora, on the seventeenth day, he saw some fine round palm-trees, and a fine doualle-tree. Here at a distance of 129 hours' journey from Kooniakary, there is a river, and at a little distance from Magnacoro there is a cataract in it; but this cataract is not so great as the cataract of Feloups (the Felou supposed) on the Senegal. On the eighteenth day, and before coming to Sirecamie, situated between two mountains, he crossed two small rivulets; and near Serboosa he passed a fountain, and next a large lake. Gangare, to which he came on the 22d day, is also situated on a large and beautiful lake. At this place he met a caravan coming from Kankary, and proceeding northwards for Benowm and Morocco. On the twenty-fifth day (184 hours) from Kooniakary, he reached Yamina, on the banks of the Joliba, where he had formerly rested with Mr. Park. From Yamina he went in a canoe by water to Sego, which latter place he reached in from thirteen to fourteen hours.

It has been considered necessary to be thus particular with Isaaco's narrative, both as proving a check upon the distances travelled, and the positions as fixed from the travels of Mr. Park, and also as it tends to show the physical features of this portion of Africa. From Kooniakary to Yamina is 250 geographical miles, which would give ten geographical miles per day as the distance which Isaaco travelled, and made good on the general bearing, after allowing stoppages, and every circumstance considered, nothing certainly can be added, while this is probably too great. From Yamina to Sego, admitting that he travelled or sailed at the rate of five knots per hour, and throwing off one quarter of the distance so travelled for the windings of the stream, the distance between the two places in a direct line cannot be more than fifty geographical miles, which will be ten miles less than even the most restricted allowance hitherto taken has given it.

The route which Isaaco travelled in his journey just alluded to probably—nay, certainly lies along the eastern base of the range of hills which approach very near the northern banks of the Ba Woolli and the Ba Woolima rivers. The small river, therefore, which Isaaco crossed near Magnacoro, and eight days' journey from Yamina, is probably the parent stream of the river which enters Lake Dibbie from the west, and the rivulets beyond Satile which Park alludes to, are in all probability some of its tributary streams. It is clear from the journal of his second voyage, that those cannot, and do not run to the westward.

That elevated land approaches near the banks of the Ba Woolli, we have invincible proofs from Park's narrative. During his second journey, at five miles east of Nummasalou (east of the Ba Woolima fifteen miles), he passed a small stream flowing S.E. During the preceding day it had been deeply flooded, but the water had then subsided, and was only eighteen inches deep. A short distance to the east of this, and at the town of Sobee, he came to another river, running SS.W., so deep, that the bundles and baggage were obliged to be carried over on men's heads. The asses were made to swim over. He reached this stream immediately after heavy rains. Shortly after crossing it, they reached Balinding. Ballandoo, next come to, was four miles E. by S. of Balinding, and from the former place to the Ba Woolli was two good days' journey. A few hours after leaving Ballendoo, Park crossed a small stream running S.E., and one and a half hour after crossed the same stream running E. by N. the banks of which were steep and slippery, and gave them much trouble. Six hours' travel beyond Ba Woolli, crossed a stream running west, the water up to the middle, and four hours' travel further came to another *small*

stream, with very steep broken clayey banks, and beyond
which was the town of Koomi-Koomi. It was during the
heaviest of the rainy season that Park crossed all these streams,
and their then magnitude and the direction of their currents,
showed that they were mere mountain torrents and tributaries
of the Ba Woolli, and consequently, also, that they could have
no connexion nor communication with the rivers which Isaaco
crossed at least sixty miles further to the eastward, and on the
east side of the range of mountains from whence the Ba
Woolli flows.

Isaaco in his journal gives a very favourable picture of this
portion of Africa, extending from Kooniakary to Yamina.
It is populous, fertile, and well watered, instead of being, as it
has hitherto been considered to be, composed of barren deserts
or impenetrable forests.   Mr. Park gives us a similar account
of this portion of the country in his first journey. At Wassiboo,
he says, (p. 183,) cultivation was carried on to such an extent
that, as the natives themselves expressed it, "hunger is never
known." Beyond Satile, the country he states "was very
beautiful, abounding with rivulets which were increased by
the rains into rapid streams."   At Moorja, corn was very
abundant; and some days before he reached Sego, he found
the roads covered with people, either going to or returning
from the Sego market, amongst which he one day met a
caravan of merchants, with seventy slaves, going by Benowm
to be sold in Morocco.   The following additional observations
by Mr. Park regarding the countries to the south of Benowm
are worthy of attention.   "East of Kooniakary," says Park,
" January 26th, in the afternoon, I went to the top of a high
hill, southward of Soolo, where I had a most enchanting prospect of the country.   The number of towns and villages and
the extensive cultivation around them surpassed every thing
I had yet seen in Africa."   The country was very populous.
(First Journey, p. 86.) Again he proceeds, "February 4th,
departed from Soomo, and continued our route along the
banks of the Krieko, which are everywhere well cultivated, and
swarm with inhabitants," (p. 87.) Again he says, at Kanjee,
" the Krieko is here but a small rivulet: this beautiful stream
takes its rise a little to the eastward of this town, and descends

with a rapid and noisy current until it reaches the bottom of the high hill called Tappa, where it becomes more placid, and thence it winds gently through the lovely plains of Kooniakary; after which, having received an additional branch from the north, it is lost in the Senegal, somewhere near the falls of Felow."

THE NIGER OR JOLIBA, AND ITS TRIBUTARY STREAMS.

The most important and the most interesting portions of the geography of Africa remain to be considered, namely, the course of the mighty river Niger and his numerous tributary streams, and the termination of that great river in the Atlantic. The position of Fallaba, of the sources of the Rokelle, and also of Teembo, having been fixed with considerable accuracy by Major Laing, the sources of the Niger are the next objects requiring attention. By a series of bearings taken by him near Fallaba, and also from the hill where the Rokelle has its source, the hill of Loma, where the western branch springs, (it is said *western* branch, because it will speedily be shown that there is an eastern and much more important branch,) lays in 9° 18′ N. lat. and 9° 42′ W. long.; the elevation about 1600 feet above the level of the Atlantic. The spring on this hill is said to be about one foot and a half in circumference. The stream which issues therefrom bends its course N. for a considerable distance, and afterwards to the N.E. The name of this stream, which issues from the hill of Loma, is called Teembie, which, in the language of that country, signifies *water*. The accounts which Major Laing received at Fallaba regarding the source of the Niger were various. Some said it was three days' journey, some six days' journey, and some twelve days' journey distant from Fallaba, according, it is presumed, as the time relates to the sources of the different branches to which the different informants alluded. From Kowia, a town on a branch of the Niger or the Joliba, called Falico, is three days' journey to Fallaba west; and from Kowia to the source of the stream in the hill of Loma is three days' (thirty-two hours') journey. Northward of Fallaba the mountains rise very high. Major Laing calls those in which the river Munga springs, "lofty hills;" and to the northward of

Teembo, the mountains round the early course of the Bafing, as has already been shown, rise to a still greater elevation. From Fallaba the fine country of Kissi-kissi bore, by compass, from SS.E. to E.S.E.; the country of Sangara from E.S.E, to E.N.E.; and the country of Kouranka from SS.E. to S.W..

According to Dupuis, (pp. xci. and xcii.) the real springs of the Joliba rise in a high mountainous chain, about eighteen days' journey to the west of Kong, and thirty-eight days' journey from Coomassie. From Kong, the country westward, during the space of six days' journey, rises, but not very abruptly: afterwards the traveller commences ascending a chain of lofty mountains, extending throughout a period of six days' journey. These mountains are said to be bleak and barren, inhabited only half-way up, and so high and steep that no one can ascend to their summits, which are moreover covered with snow. When Mollien was in Foota Jallon (see p. 242) he received similar information, viz. that there were mountains to the S.E. or in those parts under our consideration, always covered with snow. Amidst this mighty range springs the great river Joliba, and is here known under the name of the Ahmar, or the *River of Savages*, as the African Mahommedans designate it. Dupuis was farther informed by the Mahommedans of Kong and Mandingo, that the sources of the Joliba were "behind their country," that is, to the southward of it. Numerous branches flow from the ridge mentioned, first westward, next north-westward, then northerly, and next to the N.E., through the valleys of Ganowa, Maly, and the country of Bambarra. Until clearing the mountains on the south, the bed of the Ahmar or Joliba has, like the beds of its tributary streams, many cataracts. The source of its principal stream is laid down in 5° 40′ W. long. and 7° 54′ N. lat., which is still further west than the distances given by Dupuis would indicate; but this position agrees exactly, or very nearly indeed, with the apparent direction of the ridge or chain running south-westward to Cape Palmas. It is remarkable that from this position, Ptolemy, d'Anville, d'Lisle, the maps by Robert d'Vaugondy, and old Dutch charts, bring a river running, first westward, then northwards, and thence N.E. called Guinola by the three latter authorities, while

Ptolemy mistook it for the parent stream of one of his rivers in western Africa, the Rio Grande, or Gambia. The features of the country; the fact that on the sea-coast, westward from the Assinee to the Rokelle, or, it may be said, to the Rio Grande, no river of any importance enters the Atlantic; and the fact of the great magnitude of the Joliba and his early tributaries, at points just to be alluded to ; render the position assigned to its most distant stream quite certain.

In lat. 10° 18′ N. and in long. 9° 18′ W. from Greenwich, the Joliba passes Courouassa, coming from the S.W., or, allowing for the variation, about SS.W. At this point, on the 11th June, De Caillé, when he crossed it, found the stream 900 French (nearly 1000 British) feet broad, the depth 9 feet, and the current from 2½ to 3 knots per hour. This, be it borne in mind, was the magnitude of the river at the period mentioned; immediately after the commencement of the rains in the mountainous districts, and before, as regards either breadth or depth, it was at all affected by them. In fact, in those districts, from Cambaya to the Joliba, there had been no rain of any consequence : while it is necessary to observe, that such is the state of aridity to which every part of Africa, even the mountainous districts, are brought by the dry season; so greatly are the springs and streams everywhere dried up from the same cause ; that although the rains begin from the end of May, (for two or three weeks after their commencement they are not, however, very violent,) yet such is the dryness of the earth, and such the rapid advance of all vegetation as soon as they do commence, that for several weeks they are absorbed almost as quickly as they fall, and without in the slightest degree affecting the streams that are of any magnitude. It is necessary to bear this in mind, in order to show that the Joliba, at the point mentioned, was not increased, or certainly but very little increased, from the effect of rains, and therefore that De Caillé saw the stream almost at its very lowest point of depression. The place where he crossed the stream has been carefully ascertained by protracting his daily course from Kakundy, and from Cambaya to Courouassa (connected with the positions, as determined by Major Laing), viz. Fallaba and Teembo, &c. The magnitude of the Joliba at this point, therefore, may

fairly be taken as a proper scale to estimate the distance of its
more remote sources, and also, as we shall by-and-by see, to
estimate the early courses and distant sources of other African
rivers.   From the hill of Loma to Courouassa the distance is
only sixty geographical miles, with the certainty that no river
of any magnitude does join or can join the Joliba from the
westward in that space, which distance it is scarcely necessary
to observe is by far too little to afford room for the formation
of a river of the magnitude which we find the Joliba to be at
Courouassa; while, as has been shown, it is limited as to
space from receiving supplies from the south, and, as we shall
presently see, it is so also on the north.   From the point in
which the main source has been placed to Courouassa, is about
300 geographical miles.   On turning to the Bafing, which
rises and runs through a country in every respect similarly.
situated, and after its having received numerous tributaries,
deriving their sources from the same country as the parent
stream, we yet find this river, after having traversed a space
still greater, or at least equally great as the Joliba, scarcely
more than half the magnitude of the latter river at the points
so often mentioned.   It requires, therefore, no further observation or comment to show, that the principal sources of the Joliba
must, at least, be as far to the eastward as the point where they
have been placed, and that the accounts which Dupuis received
at Coomassie regarding its real sources are substantially correct.

From Courouassa the Joliba pursues its course for a few miles
nearly E., when it turns in a direction generally N.E.   At the
distance of five days' journey by canoe, the Joliba receives from
the S.W. near Boure, the Tankisso, which rises to the N.W.
of Timboo and passes Cambaya, as has previously been stated.
According to Mr. Park, Boure is four days' journey S.W. of
Kammalia, and is a place very famous in Africa for the abundance
and purity of its gold.   Above the junction of the Tankisso, the
Joliba receives a considerable river from the S.E. named the
Milo, and another named the Linn.   Pursuing its course northwards, the Joliba receives, near Kancaba on the east side, a large
navigable branch called the Sarano or Kankary, and very probably at this point a small stream from the S.W.   Proceeding N.E.
the Joliba reaches Bammakoo, lat. 12° 48′ N., and 7° W. long.

Here Park in his second journey came to the stream, and found it, in the month of August, at which period it was in high flood, *one British mile* broad, and at the rapids, a short distance to the northward of that place, the stream was two miles broad; still the river had in no part overflowed its banks. Bammakoo is six to eight days' journey by water from Boure; De Caillé says seven or eight days'; Park's African schoolmaster says, that he made out the distance in six days, this being early in August. The rapids here alluded to, are occasioned by a chain of hills through which the river bursts to the west of Marraboo, and which run N. on the one side, and S.E. on the south side of the river. From Bammakoo the Joliba pursues a course about E.N.E., passing first Marraboo, then Yamina, then Sego, situated in 13° 10' N. lat., and 5° 35' W. long., and from thence in a N.E. direction, past Sansanding and Silla to Jinne. About half way betwixt Marraboo and Yamina, the Joliba receives from the N. a small river called the Frina, which has its source in the chain of hills to the N. of Maraboo, which gave birth to the Ba Woolli. In passing down the stream from Marraboo to Yamina, Mr. Park was greatly struck with its magnitude, and designates it, in this part of its course, as a much greater river than either the Senegal or the Gambia near their junction with the sea. Isaaco, in his journal, also remarks that the river below Yamina "was very broad."

From Courouassa Mr. De Caillé pursued his journey about E.S.E. to Time, situated in 9° 17′ N. lat. and 6° 45′ W. long. About twenty-eight miles on this bearing from Courouassa the traveller crossed the Yendan, a stream, though then scarcely moved by the rains, about half the breadth of the Joliba, with a current at the rate of three miles an hour. It flowed to the north, and joined the Joliba three days' journey distant. From the Yendan, thirty-six miles east, is Kankan, a town, the capital of the province of that name, near which, on the east side, is the river Milo, still larger than the Yendan, and coming from the southward. This river is broad, deep, and navigable for vessels drawing six or seven feet water. It must be observed, however, that when De Caillé crossed this river, it was a good deal flooded. It comes from the south, runs N.E. from Kankan, and then turning north-westward, it flows into the Joliba, five days' journey by water distant from the town just mentioned. The canoes on this river are fifty feet long, which is double the size of those used for crossing the Joliba. Six days' journey south of Kankan is the beautiful country of Kissi-kissi, which is very mountainous, but very fertile, and abounding with streams, the population of which are all Pagans. Forty-two miles beyond Kankan is Deicouro, a considerable town. Between the Milo and this town De Caillé crossed no fewer than eight large streams, all running to the Joliba, and which in their progress probably join the river Linn, which flows past Deicouro, one mile to the east. Two miles from the river Linn is the large river Sarano, which comes from the south, and pursues a circuitous course past the town of Kankary to the Joliba, near Kankaba. The Sarano, where De Caillé crossed it, was from eight to nine feet deep, with a current of two miles and a half per hour. It is navigable from thence the whole way by Kankary to the Joliba. From the Sarano to Time De Caillé crossed several small streams, but none of any magnitude, except the Oulada, near Sambatiklia, which, though not very wide, was so deep as not to be fordable. All these streams bend their course N.E. Immediately to the eastward of Time a chain of hills, 2000 feet high, run in a direction from north to south. The country round Time is intersected by numerous small streams. From Time Mr. De Caillé pursued his journey in a direction about NN.E. to Jinne. Immediately beyond the chain of mountains just mentioned, the traveller fell in with another of equal height. The land in all this part of Africa is greatly elevated, for De Caillé found in the month of December, at Time, the cold so keen as to render both constant fires and warm clothing requisite. Proceeding onwards De Caillé crossed several small streams, some of them knee deep, in the month of January, all bending their course for the Joliba. In his route he passed Tangrera, no doubt the Teng-gera of Mr. Park, a village of considerable commercial importance, and in the neighbourhood of which are several villages called Jeuille villages, also mentioned by Mr. Park, and which tend to settle clearly the positions of both Bædoo and Maniana. At a distance of ninety miles from Time, Mr. De Caillé crossed the great river

Bagoe, or *White River*, which is about as wide as the Milo at Kankan. The stream even at that season of the year was very deep, navigable, and the current one knot and a half per hour. The banks were from thirty to forty feet high. It comes from the south and passes Teute, doubtless the Totti of Mr. Park, where Colat nuts are abundant. Its course, where crossed, was from E.S.E. to W.S.W., after which, and at a short distance, it turns to the northward and pursues its course, having first received the Oulada, to its junction with the Kowara Ba, near Kayaye. From the Bagoe to the Kowara Ba is a distance of about 100 miles. In this space De Caillé passed many small streams which pursue their course north-westward, and especially one in about the centre of the space mentioned, called the Koua, which comes from the S.E. The nature and the direction of these streams show that there is elevated land at no great distance to the eastward. Near and to the northward of the village of Cowara is the large river Kowara Ba. At the point where crossed the river flows rapidly from the N.E. to E., but it comes from the southward. The banks are high. At that time, February the 10th, near the middle of the dry season, the stream was 360 feet broad, and 10 feet deep. It is here navigable for vessels of sixty or eighty tons burden. It inundates and fertilizes the country during the rains, but the flood frequently commits great ravages. The shea, or butter tree, abounds on its banks. The country adjoining the river is in general level. On the right bank there is a chain of hills which, seen from the village of Cowara, appear to extend from the S. to the E.N.E. The Kowara Ba is clearly the river which passes near Kaywaree or Kayree, (see *Bowditch*). Wargee, the Tuareck, says this river passes between Garaloo, or Garoo, and Kong, and that when he crossed it in his journey from Jinne to Kong, he found it running "from the rising to the setting sun." Pursuing its course from the village of Cowara, the river passes Kayaye, situated five days' journey NN.W. of Douasso, and near which place (Kayaye) it is joined by the Bagoe or White River. From thence pursuing its course north-eastward, it receives in its progress a considerable river from the west-ward, called the Ba Nimma, which rises in the mountains to

the south of Marraboo, and passes the town of Deena, situated
one day's journey to the south of Sego. From its junction
with the Ba Nimma, the Kowara Ba pursues its course to
Galia or Cougalia, a village on its south bank, and not far
from Jinne. The stream at this place was, in the beginning
of April, 500 feet broad. A little to the northward of this
river is situated the celebrated town of Jinne, in a kind of a
double island, formed by arms of the Joliba, which passes about
ten miles to the westward, and is here about 3000 feet broad.

From Douasso to Cougalia De Caillé crossed no rivers, but,
as he approached Cougalia he passed through marshes and
some fresh-water lakes, apparently of no great depth, the
remains probably of rainy-season streams flowing from the
mountains already mentioned to the eastward. As regards
the river which passes Cougalia, M. De Caillé makes the important remark, that the stream, though very clear, was " of a
whitish hue." The kingdom of Bambarra stretches along both
banks of the Joliba, to the eastward of Sansanding, where it is
bounded on the north bank of the river by the kingdom of
Massina, in which the island of Jinne and the town of Jinne
itself are situated.*

With these observations, it is now time to consider the point
of the junction of the Kowara Ba with the Joliba. Mr. De
Caillé's informant stated the junction of the Bagoe to take
place a little below Sego ; but the nature of the country renders it almost certain, that the Bagoe and the Kowara Ba
unite before they join the Joliba. Had such a junction as this
taken place " a little below Sego," Mr. Park, who journied on
the north bank, it is true, opposite to Silla, and then crossed
the stream to Silla itself, would in all probability have heard of
this ; and if he had done so, it would at once put an end to the
account which he received, that the Ba Nimma and the Ba
Maniana flowed eastward beyond Silla, and joined the Joliba
below Jinne. There is indeed one passage in his travels which
would seem to indicate such a junction, where, he says, that
at Modiboo, below Sansanding, the river appeared to be larger
than what it appeared to be at Sego ; but this, probably, arose

* The authorities for this section of the work are :—Park, De Caillé, Dupuis,
Bowditch, Sultan Bello, and several native travellers.

from the fact, that at Sego it is separated into more than one channel; whereas, at the point where he subsequently alluded to it, and made the remark just referred to, it was an united stream. A closer attention to these matters will, it is believed, clear up these apparent contradictions and this seeming confusion. Maniana, we learn from Park himself, is situated to the south of Sego and to the west of Bœdoo, which latter country, he also informs us, was thirty days' journey from Sego about SS.E.* Mollien was informed, that Maniana lay east, distant one month's journey from Foota Jalon, and De Caillé informs us, that it lay one month's journey east of Cambaya, and fifteen days' journey east of Kankan: this will place it in the country through which the Upper Bagoe flows. This stream, therefore, is doubtless the river of Maniana mentioned by Mr. Park; for it is quite a customary thing for negro nations to give to a river the name of the country or district from which it comes. On these points, the information which Mr. Park received, when coupled or connected with the information which De Caillé has given us, becomes of great importance, and requires the closest attention. South of Jinbala, says Mr. Park, is the great negro kingdom of Gotto, and to the west of this kingdom is Bœdoo, which he fixes, giving all the stations and towns on the way to the capital of the country, also named Bœdoo, at thirty days' journey from Sego, and clearly to the eastward of South. One day's journey north of the capital is Totti, the first Bœdoo town, and no doubt the town called Teute by De Caillé, past which town, he was informed, the river Bagoe came. We have also another and invincible proof of the position of these countries, in the statement made by Park, that two days north of Bœdoo the capital, there lay some towns, called *Jeuilli towns*, inhabited by Mandingoes, and so called, from their acting as interpreters to those traders who went to Kong and the distant countries beyond that place. Now De Caillé (vol. i. p. 376) informs us very pointedly, that to the south of Tangrera he passed several

* Dupuis says, that Baddim, which he supposes to be the Bœdoo of Park, is a district of Mandingo, to reach which from Coomassie the travellers take a circuitous route by Enkasse in order to avoid Kong, the inhabitants of which are Mussulmans and enemies.

villages inhabited by independent people, (independent of Bambarra) called Jaulas or Diaulas, who employed themselves as interpreters and travellers, clearly the Jeuillies of Park, and not far from the capital of Bœdoo. Thirty days' journey from Sego, in the direction alluded to, will bring us to the country to the eastward of Time and to the N, W. of Kong, and consequently to the northward of Time, which is to the westward of Bœdoo, and where is situated the country of Maniana, or Miniana, in that position which different authorities concur in placing it in this portion of Africa : the result of the inquiry into these matters becomes thus very clear, and at the same time very satisfactory.

Mr. Park was also very pointedly informed, that a river, called the Ba Nimma, rose in the high mountains to the south of the Joliba, at a considerable distance south from Marraboo. Bending its course north-easterly, this river runs to the east, passing one day's journey to the southward of Sego, at a place called Deena, where it is crossed in canoes; that it afterwards receives a branch from Maniana; after which the united stream, described to him as not half so wide as the Joliba, empties itself into Lake Dibbie. Mr. Park also states, that at six days' journey from Sego, on the route to Bœdoo, the traveller comes to a town called Guandoo, on the banks of a small (small, compared to the Joliba of course it would be) river called Badingfing,* which river comes from Maniana. In this, both from position and name, we readily recognise the Bagoe of De Caillé, " Fing" being a general Mandingo adjunct of rivers. Further, twenty-one days' journey from Sego, on the route to Bœdoo, is, according to Mr. Park, the town called Teng-gera, a great Jeuilli town.. In addition to these authorities, Mr. Dupuis gives us, on the information from the travelling Moors which he met with at Coomassie, a route from Daboia, the capital of Ghobago, to Sego ; in which the traveller, at five days' journey distant from Sego, comes to a large river, called by them the Bahar Yasser, which runs to the eastward, and on an island in which is the town of Borma, where the traveller rests himself for some days. What they call an island, is more probably the

* " Badingfing" is a Mandingo word. *Ba* signifies *mother* as well as *river*; *ding* is child. The literal name here seems to be " Child of the Black River."

forks of the rivers Ba Nimma, and the Kowara Ba at the point of junction; for the Moors and the Arabs almost invariably describe the towns and countries so situated as being placed on islands. Further on this subject, the Old Somonie traveller who had navigated the Joliba from Jinne to Timbuctoo eight times, gave Mr. Park a fac-simile of the course of the stream and its tributaries, representing the Ba Nimma, &c. exactly as these have been here described.

Connected with this subject, Kankary and the river Sarano require further attention. The course and termination of this river is sufficiently fixed by the following facts and authorities: First, that there are mountains near Bammakoo, through which the Joliba bursts as it were, and which extend on both banks of the river, while those to the south rise very high, as seen by Mr. Park both from the heights above Bammakoo, and also from the town of Maraboo. Secondly, the following accounts from Park, which show that Kankary is situated upon a navigable branch of the Niger, and above Bammakoo and Kancaba. " There is," says he, " no wood proper for boat-building in this neighbourhood (Bammakoo); the best wood is near Kankary, on a large navigable branch of the Niger, and almost all the Bambarra canes come from thence; many of them are of mahogany." (*Second Journey*, p. 262.) Again, as regards prisoners of war made by the king of Sego, Park says, " From Sego, they were sent, in company with a number of other captives, up the Niger in large canoes, and offered for sale at Yamina, Bammakoo, and Kankaba; at which place the greater number of the captives were bartered for gold dust, and the remainder sent forward to Kankary. Some of these slaves were from Koarta, and others from Wasselou." (*First Journey*, p. 310.) Thirdly, De Caillé states, that Kankary was on the Sarano, and that the Sarano, a navigable stream, flowed into the Joliba. The town of Morella, he says, was four days' journey east from Deicouro, at which latter place he crossed the Sarano; and adds, that Kankary lay E.N.E. of Morella, but without giving the distance between them. We are, however, helped to it, and to a further proof of the course and termination of the Sarano, in the following statement respecting a Serracolet Moor, who pressed De Caillé to accompany him from Kankan to Sego; "but I allowed him to depart," says he, "for Kankary, where he was to embark on a river which flows into the Joliba, and on landing take the road to Sego."— *De Caillé*, vol. i. p. 259.

The mountain seen by Mr. Park to the south of Maraboo, naturally turns the course of the Sarano below Kankary to the westward. These mountains continue their range E.S.E. and S. beyond Kankary towards Sambatiklia and Time, dividing the waters which flow into the Oulada and the Bagoe, from those which flow into the Sarano and the Ba Nimma. The physical features of this portion of Africa are thus laid plainly before us; and further, and to the same effect, Dupuis was distinctly informed, that to the east of Jinne there was a large range of high mountains (these will be considered by-and-by) which sent the waters from the eastward to the Niger, and in a line nearly parallel to its eastern course. This is very curious, and also very probable.

The course and termination, therefore, of the Sarano to and from Kankary, and thence to the Joliba near Kankaba, is thus clearly established, and the course, junction, and termination of the Bagoe, the Kowara Ba, and the Ba Nimma, left clear and unembarrassed. The united stream which Park mentions, was described to him as being not quite half so large as the Joliba, which will agree well with the magnitude of the united streams of the rivers above mentioned, and with the magnitude of the river which De Caillé found and crossed at Cougalia. It must be borne in mind, that when De Caillé crossed the two first-mentioned streams, it was about the middle of the dry season, when all the rivers are very low. Of the course and junction of these rivers and the Joliba, Park gives us an additional proof, in the fact stated in his last despatch on the eve of leaving Sansanding, viz. that from information he had received, in proceeding thence to Timbuctoo, he should not, in descending the Joliba, "see Jinne." But, according to his guide, he did see Jinne, and presented its chief with a piece of baft and went on. No doubt, when he descended the Joliba to the neighbourhood of Jinne, and found that a small branch flowed from it to the Kowara Ba, and forming the island on which Jinne stood, and that by it he could continue his voyage, and regain the main stream, and at the same time see the celebrated city of Jinne, he would embrace the opportunity of doing so. In corroboration of all these points, Mr. Hutchison was informed by Moors from Jinne, that " the Niger was called Quolla at Jinne and Sansanding." Quolla is the negro pronunciation of the word Quorra, the corruption of the word *Kowara*. Quolla, therefore, at Jinne, is in reality the Kowara Ba. Sultan Bello's schoolmaster, moreover, in his rude delineation of the Kowara, has the great branch of the Niger flowing north-eastward past Jinne, as De Caillé found it, and also joining another great branch below and to the north of Jinne. In the evidence given before the Committee of the Lords on the African Slave Trade, 1789, at part vi. it pointedly states, that Jinne is situated on an island near the junction of the rivers alluded to, and nearly placed as described. The account is curious, and runs thus: " The inhabitants of Jinne send their boats laden with their commodities; they choose to barter on account of the separation of the rivers about half a league from Jinne, Jinne being almost an island. One of the rivers from Jinne runs into the country of Bambarens (Bambarra,) the other into that of Betan," &c.

Before proceeding to consider the further progress of the Niger to the northward and eastward, it is necessary to advert to the features of all that portion of Africa through which those streams, the courses of which we have just been considering, flow; the cultivation which is found in the different districts; and the condition of the population who dwell in these, so far as these have been brought before us by information on which we can rely. Mr. Park, in both his First and Second Journeys, gives several interesting references as to the state of the country, and of the population in western Africa. Sego, he states, contains about 30,000 inhabitants. The houses are built of clay, of a square form, with flat roofs: some of them have two stories, and many of them are white-washed. Besides these buildings, Moorish mosques are seen in every quarter. A great number of canoes are constantly plying on the river. " The view of this extensive city," says Mr. Park, " the numerous canoes upon the river, the crowded population, and the cultivated state of the surrounding country, formed altogether a prospect of civilization and magnificence which I little expected to find in the bosom of Africa." And of the country between Sego and Sansanding, he states thus:— " About eight o'clock, we passed a large town called Kabba, situated in the midst of a beautiful and highly-cultivated country, bearing a greater resemblance to the centre of England than to what I should have supposed had been in the middle of Africa. The people are everywhere employed in collecting the fruit of the shea-trees, from which they prepare the vegetable butter mentioned in former parts of this work. These trees grow in great abundance over all this part of Bambarra." Sego, for many centuries, has been a stronghold for the Mahommedan faith; but, notwithstanding the progression of that faith, the mind of the population is debased by many superstitious and cruel customs. Thus, for instance, as Isaaco in his Journal informs us, they immediately cut the throat of every male child that is born on a Friday. A king or chief of that or any neighbouring state, taken prisoner, is confined till the fasting moon is over, when he is carried out and laid on the ground, and his throat cut across, the blood allowed to flow and saturate the earth around, when the body is left to the beasts of prey: and for eight days after these executions every one passing the spot must pull off his shoes or cap. Each fasting moon, one or more are thus sacrificed.*

In passing betwixt the Ba Faleme and the Bafing, Mr. Park, in his Second Journey, presents us with a very interesting picture of the country betwixt them, particularly of the Konkodoo mountains. " The day was cool," says he; " but after fatiguing ourselves, and resting six times, we found we were only half-way up to the top. We were surprised to find the hills cultivated to the very summits; and though the people of Dindikoo were but preparing their fields, the corn on the hills was six inches high. The villages on these mountains are romantic beyond any thing I ever saw. They are built in the most delightful glens of the mountains, they have plenty of water and grass at all seasons, they have cattle enough for their own use, and their superfluous grain purchases all their luxuries; and while the thunder rolls in awful grandeur over

* Batouta states that they eat human flesh.

their heads, they can look from their tremendous precipices over all that wild and woody plain which extends from the Faleme to the Black River. This plain is in extent, from north to south, about forty miles." To the south, however, the country is not so well cultivated. By the side of the river, at Maniakoro, latitude 14° N., Mr. Park found " a- great number of human bones (more than thirty skulls) : on inquiring the reason, I was informed that Mansa Numma (the chief) always inflicted punishments himself, and that the bones I saw were those of criminals," (p. 213). The natives of this and the surrounding districts are most incorrigible thieves.

In his progress from the Joliba, at Courouassa, by Time to Jinne, Mr. De Caillé also gives a pleasing account of the appearance of the country, and some curious notices with regard to the condition and manners of the people. In addition to that which has been already stated with regard to the great elevation of that part of Africa, he informs us that at Kankan, fires were necessary in the houses all the year round. The country of Wassalou, situated to the east and north-east of Kankan, is described as being very fine; it is "generally open, and diversified by a few hills; the soil is very fertile, and partly composed of a rich black mould mixed with gravel; the country is watered by the Sarano and by many large streams, which fertilize the soil, and it brings forth in abundance all that is necessary for man in an unsophisticated state. The inhabitants are gentle, humane, and very hospitable, curious to excess, but much less teazing than the Mandingoes. Their food is very simple—rice, and Indian corn, and pistachio nuts, &c. The women manufacture earthen pots for their house-keeping; for this purpose they use a grey clay which they find on the banks of the streams. They knead and clear it; and having brought it into the right form, they polish it by degrees with their hands; and the vessels when finished are placed in the shade to dry slowly, or the heat of the sun would crack them. The vessels are usually round, with a little rim round the top, and no handle; they very much resemble what are made throughout all Foota Dhialon and Kankan. The amiable inhabitants of this happy country live as if they were all of one family. Each hamlet is composed of twelve or fourteen huts, or even fewer, surrounded by a clumsy and tasteless wooden palisade.   In the centre of this little group of huts is a court, into which they all open; the cattle are shut up in this court at night.   The women who are employed in cooking perform their operations in the open air.   Small hamlets are to be seen at short distances from one another all over the country.   The inhabitants grow a great quantity of cotton, of which they manufacture cloth, and sell it to the dealers, who carry it to Kankan.   The looms which they use for weaving cloth are like ours, but smaller.   The women sit in their courts and spin cotton; it is their business also to milk the cows.   They grow a great quantity of tobacco.   The inhabitants generally are very dirty and ill-clothed; they form a great contrast to the inhabitants of Kankan in the article of cleanliness, for they are altogether filthy and disgusting, and never wash their clothes, which are always of a black or yellow colour.   The women have no other covering than a pagne, which they wrap round their loins.   The young men shave their heads like the Mahommedans.   The children, who are all naked, are early addicted to bodily exercise.   The inhabitants are Foulahs, but do not speak the Foulah language.   I tried to discover whether they had any religion of their own, but I could never perceive any religious ceremony amongst them, and I suspect they are careless of the subject, and trouble themselves very little with theology.   The inhabitants of Wassalou carry on little traffic, and never travel.   Their idolatry indeed would expose them to the most dreadful slavery if they did.   Gentle and humane, they give a friendly reception to all the strangers who come among them." — (*De Caillé's Travels*, vol. i. pp. 301—305.)

The inhabitants to the eastward resemble the former very nearly in every respect, but are in general very poor.   " Yet I have not seen a single beggar," says De Caillé, " between Kankan, or indeed Beleya, and this place (Sambatiklia).   The greater part of the land is a black mould, intermingled with gravel; cultivation is almost entirely neglected."   " Sambatiklia is a large village, surrounded by a double wall; it is independent, and inhabited by Mandingo Mussulmans.   The soil, composed in some places of black mould, and in others of grey sand mixed with earth, is very fertile, but very little cultivated. The inhabitants are engaged entirely in commerce; they go a few days' journey to the south of their village to buy colatnuts, and these they carry to Jinne and barter for salt. The average price of a slave in these parts is thirty bricks of salt, (a brick is ten inches long and three wide, and two, or two and a half thick; there are larger and smaller bricks, and the value varies accordingly,) a barrel of powder, and eight parcels of beads of a bright chestnut colour; or a gun and four yards of rose-coloured taffeta are also the price of a slave. The inhabitants are poor; their crops are not sufficient to last from one year to the next. The Mandingoes would rather go without food part of the day than work in the fields; they pretend that labour would take off their attention from the Koran, which is a very specious excuse for their laziness." From this to Jinne, they calculate that it takes two and a half months to travel. Salt is scarcely to be procured about Time, and when to be got is procured at an exorbitant price. "The air is always cool and damp, which renders it very unhealthy; in the months of December and January, a variable but northern wind prevails which still further cools the atmosphere. The soil consists of good black mould and sand; in some parts it is irrigated by a number of small rivulets, the overflowing of which fertilizes the land." (*De Caillé*, vol. i. p. 315.) "The Mandingoes, who are naturally lazy, make their slaves work hard. A Mandingo who has eight or ten slaves is reckoned rich. Their harvest does not maintain them during the whole year; they therefore purchase from the Bambarra negroes, who sell their surplus grain to procure salt. The Mandingoes of this part of Africa are all traders; they travel much even in the rainy season, but being obliged to carry their merchandise on their heads, they take little with them, and journey at a slow pace. When they return from their journey, they indulge in idleness and gormandizing, leaving agricultural labour to their slaves. The Bambarras, who are all Pagans, marry as many wives as they are able to maintain, but the Mandingoes have never more than four. The women are always the victims, for the men, looking upon the other sex as an inferior order of beings, are always absolute masters in the domestic

circle.   These unfortunate women may.indeed be considered
on a level with the slaves as to the severe labour imposed upon
them.   They go to distant places for wood and water; their
husbands make them sow, weed the fields, and gather in the
harvest.   When they travel with a caravan they carry burthens
on their heads, while the husbands proceed at their ease on
horseback.   While pregnant they continue to perform the
severest labours until the very last moment of their time.
They give birth to children without uttering a complaint, and
one would almost believe that they are delivered without pain,
for on the following day they resume their usual occupations.
The fathers and mothers are extremely fond of their children,
and they in their turn have a great veneration for their parents."
In his journey from Time to Jinne, De Caillé gives an account
very nearly similar of the country and its inhabitants, but as
regards the face of the country itself, he represents it as everywhere being extremely beautiful, except when approaching
Jinne it becomes in some places bare and marshy.   The
following description of the state of the slave-trade and the
causes of slavery in these countries, and also of the colat-nut-
tree and the shea or butter-tree, are particularly interesting,
and with which may be concluded the present portion of our
inquiry and our subject.

" The butter-tree, or cé, is very abundant in the neighbourhood
of Time.   It grows spontaneously, and in height and appearance
resembles the pear-tree.   The leaves grow in tufts, supported by
a very short foot-stalk.   They are round at top, and when the
tree is young, they are six inches long.   When the tree grows old
the leaves become smaller, and resemble those of the Saint Jean
pear-tree.   It blossoms at the extremity of its branches, and the
flowers, which are small, grow in clusters, and are supported by
a very strong pedicle.   The petals are white, and the stamina are
numerous, and scarcely perceptible to the naked eye.   The fruit,
when mature, is as large as a guinea-hen's egg, of oval shape, and
equal at both ends. It is covered with a pale green pellicle, beneath
which is a green farinaceous pulp, three lines thick, of an extremely
agreeable flavour.   The negroes are very fond of it, and I liked it
myself.   Under this pulp there is a second pellicle, very thin, and
resembling the white skin which lines the inside of an egg-shell;

this covers the kernel, which is of a pale coffee-colour. The fruit being disengaged from the two pellicles and the pulp, is enclosed in a shell as thick as that of an egg, and the kernel is of the size of a pigeon's egg. The fruit is exposed several days to the sun, in order to dry it, then pounded in a mortar, and reduced to flour, which is of the colour of wheat bran. After being pounded, it is placed in a large calabash : luke-warm water is thrown over it, and it is kneaded with the hands until it attains the consistency of dough. To ascertain whether it is sufficiently manipulated, warm water is thrown over it, and if greasy particles are detached from the dough and float, the warm water is repeated several times, until the butter is completely separated, and rises to the surface. The butter is collected with a wooden spoon and placed in a calabash. It is then boiled on a strong fire, being well skimmed, to remove any pulp that remains with it. When sufficiently boiled, it is poured into a calabash with a little water at the bottom to make it turn out easily. Thus prepared, it is wrapped in the leaves of the tree, and will keep two years without spoiling. The butter is of an ash-grey colour, and as hard as tallow. It is an article of trade with the negroes, who use it both for food and for anointing their bodies. They also employ it to burn for light ; and they told me that it was an excellent ointment for pains and sores. The fruit of the cé is much larger in Baléya and Amana than in Time. The seed of this tree, which is so valuable to the people of these countries, could not be transported to Europe for sowing, unless packed in small earthen vessels, otherwise it looses its germinative power, which does not last long. I have already mentioned that there is at Time a fruit called *taman*, which also produces an unctuous substance, very good for eating, and more firm than the cé. It might be advantageously employed in Europe for burning. The grease or fat, called by the natives *taman-toulon*, is extracted by the same process as that employed with the cé. The tree which produces the *taman* grows on the banks of rivulets, and is very common in the south. These two trees are so abundant at Cani and Teuté, that the inhabitants of those places, I was told, though possessing plenty of cows, never eat any butter except that produced by the trees. Palm oil is also met with here, though not in great quantity. The kernel of the taman is of the size of a horse-chestnut, somewhat elongated, of a beautiful pink colour, deepening a little towards the outside. It is exceedingly hard; and the women, after setting it on the fire in earthen pots, crush it between two flints, previously to pounding it in a mortar. The butter of the taman is of a light yellow colour. It is firmer than that of the cé, and has no smell. I preferred this to the other.

" Indigo grows spontaneously in the environs of Time. The women use it for dyeing their cotton thread, which the men weave into clothes. The process employed to extract the dye is very simple. They do not take the trouble to cut the plant, but gather the leaves, which they bruise ; and then making them up into small cakes, they lay them in the sun to dry.

" This process has been followed for a very long period. When the dye is wanted, the cakes are bruised, and put into a large earthen pot, made for this purpose ; cold water is poured over them, and time 'is allowed for the leaves to soak. After leaving them twenty hours to ferment, lye is made with the ashes of the foigné, and cold water is added. This has the effect of dissolving the indigo. The dye being thus prepared, the articles to be dyed are put into the pot. Cotton requires to be thus soaked for a whole night, or even longer ; and when taken out, I have seen it of a beautiful blue colour. In proportion as the water diminishes, more is added, and the same leaves serve to dye for a whole week ; but the first tint is always the finest.

" The inhabitants of Time are Mandingoes ; and they all make journeys to Jinne. I inquired of them the distance from one city to the other, to ascertain whether they agree on this point with the people of Sambatiklia. They all assured me that I required two months to go, and two months to return ; but that they could only make two journeys in the course of the year, because they were obliged to travel to Teuté and Cani, a fortnight's journey to the south of Jinne, to purchase their colats. I also learned that the inhabitants of those villages themselves go very far to the south, to a place called Toman, to procure these colats. On their return, they cover them with leaves, and then bury them under ground to preserve them. This fruit may be kept fresh for nine or ten months by taking the precaution to renew the leaves. The colat-tree flourishes in the south ; it is very abundant in the Kissi, the Couranco, the Sangaran, and the Kissikissi. It is a general article of trade in the interior ; for the inhabitants, having no kind of fruits, highly esteem the colat, and indeed regard it as a sort of luxury. Old men who have lost their teeth, reduce the colats to powder by means of a small grater, consisting merely of a bit of tin, in which they make holes very close together. The Bambarras are very fond of colats ; but as they have not the facility for going to the country where they grow, they purchase them with cotton and other produce of their agricultural industry.

" The colat-tree resembles the plum-tree in size and form. The leaves are alternate, and about twice as broad as those of the plum; the flower, which is small and white, has a polypetalous corolla; the fruit is covered with a brownish yellow husk or rind, within which is a pulp, which is at first pink or white, but which, on attaining full maturity, acquires a greenish hue. The same tree bears fruit of both colours. The colat-nut is of the size of the chestnut, and of the same degree of hardness. At first it appears to have a bitter taste; but after it is swallowed, it leaves a sweet flavour, which the negroes like very much. A glass of water taken immediately after one of these colat-nuts, has the effect of having been sugared. The nut easily splits in two without changing colour; but if one of the two halves be broken and exposed for a moment to the air, the pulp which was previously pink or white, becomes of a rust colour."—*De Caillé*, vol. i. pp. 311, 312.

" On the 29th of July, we had nothing to eat the whole of the day; I bethought myself of calling upon the Almany, who seemed to have forgotten that he had strangers in his dwelling, or thought that they were accustomed to fasting. He did not hurry himself, however, for it was six o'clock in the evening when he sent us some yams, boiled and pounded, with a little bad sauce; and we were unluckily obliged to share this light repast with a Mandingo, who happened at that moment to be prowling about our hut; he came and sat down by us, and needed no pressing, for he had probably tasted nothing since the evening before. I have often been obliged, in the same way, to share the little food I could get with these hungry and idle parasites, who would rather starve than work for themselves. As our host neglected us so completely, we went out to procure some rice and yams for ourselves; but we could find nothing in the village, for the devout Almany had forbidden the customary market twice a week, under pretence that it interfered with prayers. We sent to a neighbouring village, but were equally unsuccessful; so we were forced to be content with the small portion which our host allowed us. We were informed that provisions were scarce, that there was not enough to last till next harvest, and that the scarcity extended to the neighbouring country.

" On the 30th of July, a caravan of saracolet merchants arrived at Sambatiklia, on their way to Foulou to purchase slaves, whom they sell again in Foulou or Kankan. All the goods which are sold at the European settlements on the coast are destined for this infamous traffic : the slaves are not exported, it is true, but they are no better off than if they were. Slavery may perhaps be abolished in civilized Europe ; but the wild and covetous African will long continue the barbarous custom of selling his fellow-creatures. It is so pleasant to live in idleness, and to enjoy the fruits of the labours of others, that every negro does all in his power to become a slave-owner ; their ambition is limited to the possession of twelve or fifteen slaves, whom they employ entirely in agricultural labour. These poor creatures are ill-clothed, and work very hard; but I never saw them ill-treated. They are commonly obliged to provide for their own support, and have a field to themselves, which they cultivate for this purpose ; they grow maize and cassava round their huts, and find them a great resource."—*De Caillé*, vol. i.

The whole country, from the latitude of 8°. N. to the banks of the Joliba near Sego, in the direction from north to south, and from the mountains of Foota Jallon on the west to the Kowara Ba on the east, is generally exceedingly mountainous, but in many parts, such as Wassalou, Time, and Douasso, &c., interspersed with broad districts of what may be called table lands, which are everywhere very fruitful, and must, from the circumstances just mentioned, be very healthy. The whole surface of the vast district mentioned is thickly studded with towns and villages.

Jinne is a place of considerable commercial importance and celebrity in Africa. Centuries ago it was denominated by the Moors and Arabs the country of gold; and Lyon informs us, that to this day the name which it bears in the countries in and adjoining the northern parts of the desert is Belad el Tibr, or the country of gold. The gold, however, obtained there is not produced in that country, but is brought from countries far distant to the south and to the west, in exchange for salt and other articles of merchandise. All that great portion of Africa called Maly or Melli was situated to the south and to the west of Jinne, and, in fact, the latter place is supposed to have been in early times included in it. About the time the Portuguese first appeared on the west coast of Africa, the kingdom of Melli extended to the Atlantic. To this day, as Dupuis and other travellers have been told, the Moors and Arabs of Africa, include in the kingdom of Melli, all Bambarra, Foota Jallon, in fact, the whole country inhabited by the people called Mandingoes. This fact tends to explain much of the early Arabian geography regarding the interior of Africa, for the Mandingo population extends from Timanee' and the middle Gambia, considerably to the eastward of the Kowara Ba and the Bagoe. Jinne is stated by Dupuis to be in the kingdom of Massina, and to form part of the great district of Safany, extending eastward to Konbory. The town is situated in the eastern part of the island, on an elevation of seven or eight feet, which preserves it from the periodical inundations of the river. The town is full of bustle and animation; every day numerous caravans of merchants are arriving and departing with all kinds of useful productions. All the inhabitants are Mahommedans. They do not permit infidels to enter their town. The people of Jinne know no other writing than that of the Arabs: almost all can read, though few understand it. There are schools for youth like those which I have already described. "In going round the market," says De Caillé, "I observed some shops pretty well stocked with European commodities, which sell at a very high price. There was a great variety of cotton goods, printed muslin, scarlet cloth, hardware, flints, &c. Nearly the whole of these articles appear to be of English manufacture." The Moors of Jinne do not keep shops: they employ confidential agents, or even slaves, to sell goods on their account. The town is about two miles and a half in circumference, and contains 9000 inhabitants. It is surrounded by a very ill-constructed earthen wall, about ten feet high and fourteen inches thick. There are several gates, but they are small. The houses are built of bricks dried in the sun; the greater part have only one story; they are all terraced, have no windows externally, and the apartments receive no air except from an inner court. The inhabitants of Jinne live well; they eat rice boiled with fresh meat, which is to be procured every day in the market. With fine millet they make cous-cous; this is eaten with fresh or dried fish, of which they have great abundance. The expense of maintenance for a single individual is about twenty-five or thirty cowries per day. Meat is not dear in this place: a piece which costs forty cowries is enough to furnish a dinner for four persons. One thousand cowries are equal in value to one dollar. There are also butchers in the market, who lay out their meat much in the same way as their brethren in Europe. As there are no inns in this country, the strangers are obliged to lodge in houses of private persons, whom they pay in merchandise.' Three days' journey N.W. of Jinne is situated the kingdom of Massina, inhabited by Mahommedan Foulahs. According to Sultan Bello, it has many rivers, and also mountains, two of which he particularly mentions as being exceedingly high. The people of Massina often come to Jinne for the purpose of trade, and sell oxen and sheep for the daily consumption of the town. Their sheep are the finest that I have seen in the interior; they are large, and have wool like those of Europe (this proves that the sheep are reared on high and elevated lands); their fleece is used for making wrappers, which sell at very good prices. These Foulahs also bring milk and butter to Jinne. Massina is very productive in rice, millet, pistachios, water melons, giranmous, and onions. The inhabitants rear a good deal of poultry, and have a fine breed of horses. Every Moor on the island has his own horse." (De Caillé, vol. i.) According to Mr. Park, the kingdom of Massina approaches to within a short distance of the Joliba to the northward of Silla.

COURSE OF THE JOLIBA BELOW JINNE.

But to return to the progress of the river downward. From Jinne Mr. De Caillé proceeded on his voyage to Timbuctoo in a large canoe of about eighty tons burthen, deeply laden with merchandise, in company with several other canoes of equal magnitude, accompanied by many passengers, and, during the latter part of the voyage, in a fleet of about eighty vessels. Their course was with the stream, and chiefly by day, but generally very slow. He left Jinne on the 28th of March, and reached Cabra on the 19th of April. From Cougalia, the Cowara, or White River, first bends its course, nearly N.E., for upwards of forty-five miles, and thence in a general bearing to the northward of west to Lake Dibbie. Near the village of Soufara, situated on the right bank, and about eighteen miles from Cougalia, a little stream runs in from an eastward direction; and at Taguetia, about thirty miles above Isaca, Mr. De Caillé states, a branch from twenty-five to thirty fathoms wide, and forming two little islands at its entrance, runs off to the eastward. On this it is scarcely necessary to observe, that branches flowing from a river rarely, if ever, make islands at their outlet; while, on the other hand, islands are always formed at the entrance of a smaller stream into a greater. We may, therefore, fairly set down this branch, which De Caillé says runs from the Niger, as a river running into it from the east, and which river will naturally flow from Mount Dombori, to be more particularly noticed hereafter, and will, in the Moor and Arab acceptation of the term, make out the water communication which these travellers stated to Mr. Dupuis existed uninterrupted from Jinne to the Gulbe of Magho. One or other of the streams just mentioned, no doubt, forms the so-called communication. A little above Isaca the Joliba itself joins the White River, or rather, more properly speaking, the White River at that point joins the Joliba. At this junction the Joliba is very broad, has a gentle current, comes from the westward, is navigable for very large canoes, and forms a very large island at its mouth. Considerably to the southward of this, and some distance to the northward of the village of Kerra, De Caillé states that he found the river, which he descended, broader than what it was at Cougalia, owing, undoubtedly, to the two branches of the Joliba, which form, with the White River, the island of Jinne, and which branches join the latter immediately below the Cougalia. The banks of the river also, it is proper to state, were not, until after passing Isaca, so low as to render it at all probable that the stream could throw off any branches in that direction. Below Isaca the banks, however, were almost invariably low, and, as far as the eye could reach, retained the strongest marks of being widely and deeply inundated during the rainy season. Above Wouza a branch runs off to the west. In lat. 16° N. and 4° 28' W. long. De Caillé passed through Lake Dibbie, a very large body of water. Where he crossed it from south to north it was more than fifteen miles wide, and from twelve to fifteen feet deep. When in the middle, the land, though everywhere low, is seen on every hand, except to the west-

ward.   Near the course which the canoes take through the
lake a tongue of land runs inwards on the south side, and
penetrates so far into it, that it may almost be said to separate it
into two lakes. The whole breadth from west to east, according
to Scott, who crossed it in that direction, (see *Edinburgh
Philosophical Journal*, No. 7,) is sixty miles, and its deepest
part twenty fathoms.   From Isaca to Lake Dibbie the general
bearing of the course of the river is north, and from that
point to Cabra, the course on the general bearing is N. 40′ E.,
in which latter part of its course the river has many remarkable
windings.   Below Lake Dibbie Mr. De Caillé found several
arms or branches flowing off from the river on the west side,
which, no doubt, rejoined it again ; and it a curious fact, that
Sultan Bello's schoolmaster, who was a native of Massina, lays
down in his rude delineation of the course of the river, one
branch running off to the westward from the main stream north
of Jinne, and subsequently re-entering the main stream a
considerable way down by several mouths in the country of
Massina.

Before noticing the long sought-for city of Timbuctoo, and
other matters connected with African geography, in the countries
adjacent, it is first necessary to consider the supplies which
the Joliba receives, (for considerable supplies it certainly does
receive,) on both the east and west side below Isaca, and
which must necessarily join in Lake Dibbie, and more to the
northward.   The first, and the chief, is the river called Gozen
Zair by the negroes, and by the Moors and the Arabs El
Wad Tenij.   This stream comes from the mountains to the
south and S. W. of Walet, or as Sidi Hamed designates it,
Wablit.   These mountains, he further states, seen at a great
distance from Walet, are as high as Mount Atlas near Suse,
which is about 12,000 feet above the level of the sea.   Such
mountains must, as a matter of course, give birth to rivers.
To the S. E. of Walet, where Sidi Hamed and his party fell
in with the stream, in the dry season it was 250 yards broad.
The party travelled four days to the eastward, along its
northern bank, where, being much encumbered by the numerous hills and thick woods which they found thereon, they
struck off to the north-eastward, in order to reach the more

open country towards the confines of the Desert, and afterwards proceeded east, ten days' journey more to Timbuctoo. Sidi Hamed further describes this part of the country as hilly and fertile. He had left Morocco with a large caravan for Timbuctoo, and after one month's travel a burning wind assailed them, and when they came to the wells of Haherah, they found them dry. All subordination ceased in the caravan; amidst the horrors of thirst, mutual slaughter ensued, when Sidi Hamed and a few companions, mounted on the fleetest camels, fled to the south; they, fortunately, were soon visited by a fall of rain, and shortly after reached the boundary of the cultivated country, and after crossing a small river, next the town of Walet.

After the most mature consideration given to the point of the existence of rivers in this part of Africa, the conclusion is come to, that there are really two considerable rivers which flow east, and join the Niger, or Joliba, on the west side, betwixt Lake Dibbie and Timbuctoo. We have the authority of Sultan Bello to state, that the country of Massina has many rivers and mountains. Dupuis also informs us, page cx., that there are several rivers in this quarter; and he adds, that the people of Jinne and Sego have distinct names for the other rivers which flow into and from Lake Dibbie, but that they called the great river the Joliba, while the Arabs name it the Bahar Neel, or Neel Zakhar, or the Swelling Nile. The first and greatest of these rivers is the Gozen Zair; and the following are the authorities which establish the fact that there is such a river:—First. Ptolemy brings his main branch of the Niger from N.W. to S. E. over these parts, from Mount Mandrus, clearly the high mountains to the south of Walet, to the Lake Nigrites, and another branch of the river in the same quarter; and he gives the names, the latitude, and the longitude of several cities along its banks. Secondly. The old Arabian traveller Batouta, states as follows:—He left Taffilet for Soudan; in twenty-five days he came to Thagary, or, as it has been more properly translated by Kosegarten, Tegazza, and in thirty-five more to the cultivated country at a place called Aboulaten, or Ayoulaten, Eiwalaten, certainly Walet. *

* The name Tegazza for the station mentioned, settles the point regarding

H

Departing thence, he soon after came to a river running east, which he immediately set down as a branch of the Nile, and adds that it flowed down to Rakbara, Timbuctoo, &c. Aboulaten was thus clearly a long way to the west of Timbuctoo, and, as he informs us, twenty-four days' journey N. of the country of Maly, to which, in the first instance, he was bound. This distance corresponds well with the distance which Walet is from the country of Maly, to the south of Sego. Departing from Aboulaten, he came, as has been stated, to the river which he mistook for the Nile, at a town called Karsendjour; and thence proceeding south, he came in ten days more to the river Sansera, and continuing his journey he reached Maly; where, after a residence for a considerable time, he proceeded by another river, it would appear, in his course downwards and eastward to Timbuctoo, &c.; for during this journey, he tells us that he examined " a gulf which branches out of the Nile," &c., which gulf is clearly the Lake Dibbie. Thirdly. Le Brue states, that about 100 miles above Gallam, where the Senegal ceases to be navigable, a route proceeds to Timbuctoo, a journey of thirty-four days by the following places : Jaga, Beyogne, Kingurie, Sabaa, Baramaya, Goury, and Gabania. After travelling twenty-seven days on this route, the traveller quits the river, as Sidi Hamed did, and for the same reason; and in six days' journey more, he reaches Timbuctoo. According to the maps of Delisle, French travellers make the distance from Gallam to Timbuctoo thirty-two days' journey, passing through Timbe, five days short from Timbuctoo, where they leave the bank of the river to avoid too great a *détour*. Fourthly. D'Anville laid down a river in

the direction which Batouta took in his journey, and also the point at which he reached Sudan. Tegazza (eastern), he says, was twenty-five days' journey from Segelmasa. There is another part of this narrative which still more clearly elucidates and confirms the route which he took, and the point at which he reached Sudan. This is the station named Tashala, or Tasahla, which he states was ten days' journey to the north of the beginning of the cultivated land towards Eiwalatan or Walet. This place is certainly the watering station alluded to by Sidi Hamed, under the name of Teshlah, which lays, he says, twelve days' journey S.W. from the fatal point where his caravan found all the wells dry, and where the quarrel and massacre took place. He pursued his course S.W. to reach it, and thence south, till he came to the borders of the Desert, and afterwards to Wablit or Walet.

this quarter, but which, at an early period, he, as well as others, believed to be a branch of the Senegal, or the Senegal itself. Of this latter error, however, he was afterwards fully satisfied; but still the information which he had, gave him clearly to know that there was a river in this quarter, but which ran to the Joliba, and not the Senegal. Fifthly. The evidence of a witness given before the Committee of the House of Lords on the African slave-trade, 1789, gives this river running east, under the name of Gozen Zair, and its breadth 240 yards. Sixthly. The very clear and positive account given of this river by Sidi Hamed, as has been previously noticed. Seventhly. Sultan Bello, in his map of central Africa, lays down a large branch, as coming from the west, and joining the Joliba a little to the south of Timbuctoo. Eighthly, De Caillé tells us, that travellers going from El Arroan to Sansanding, pass on the seventh day from Arroan a large river. This must be the large arm which De Caillé tells us he saw seven miles west of the separation above Kabra, running W.S.W. with an island at its mouth, which was, in all probability, the junction of the Gozen Zair with the Joliba. All the distances and facts previously referred to point out this very forcibly.

Next, with regard to a river more to the south, and a tributary to the Joliba, we have the following facts and authorities. First, we have the nature and the large extent of the country itself, which intervenes between the northern banks of the Joliba at Yamina, and the high mountains situated to the southward of Walet. Here there is abundance of space for the formation of a considerable river, and both Sultan Bello and Dupuis tell us, that there are rivers in this quarter, and in the kingdom of Massina. Secondly, we have, as has already been particularly adverted to, the authority of Isaaco, who certainly travelled to the eastward of those rising grounds which supply the Ba Woolli with springs, that eight or nine days' journey to the north of Yamina he passed a considerable river, and to show that the country where he did pass it was considerably elevated, and that the passage was effected at an early part of its course, he states that it flowed over a considerable rapid or cataract. This river may be fairly taken as the parent stream of the river at present under our consideration, and its course will be to the

north-eastward. Thirdly, we have Mr. Park's authority, that
there is in the neighbourhood of Satile, about N.E. from the
point mentioned by Isaaco, several streams, then swelled by the
heavy rains running to the E. and N.E. which must necessarily
form tributaries to the river under consideration. Fourthly,
Dupuis pointedly tells us, that he was informed by the Moor
and Arab travellers, that the Arab tribe of El Moghata, who
dwell in a pastoral country on the west bank of the Joliba,
cross, in the north, on the 10th day after leaving Jinne, a large
river there, where they cross it, running to the south-eastward.
From Jinne to a point a little to the westward of Lake Dibbie,
this time and distance will exactly correspond. Fifthly, we have
to add the previous statement made by Batouta, that ten days
after leaving the river nearest to the Desert, he came, in his
southern course to Maly, to the river Sansera, in all probability
the very river which we now have under review.   There is one
point and one authority which would appear to militate against
the two rivers mentioned being separate streams at their junction
with the Joliba: it is that of Scott, the sailor from Liverpool,
who was wrecked near Cape Nun, carried captive by an Arab
tribe across the Desert into Soudan, and who, during that
journey, crossed Lake Dibbie. In his route to the lake, he
makes no mention of having passed any large rivers; but the
question was probably never asked him, and, in the next place,
his route from Wednun would be by Hoden and Benowm, and
consequently he would pass through that country where Park
travelled after his flight from Jarra, to the southern side of the
river we have been adverting to, and at a point so high in the
course of either it or any of its tributary streams, that being in
the dry season, he would necessarily see no streams of any
consequence, and which, in fact, Park scarcely found in the
rainy season.

  The next point to consider is, the country and the tributaries
which the Joliba probably, we may add certainly, receives from
the eastward between Jinne and Timbuctoo. One or more of these
has already been mentioned.   Above Lake Dibbie, on the east
side, is the village of Coria, the first village in the country of Bannan,
which the negroes sometimes call Thonga, or the land of Bannan.
It is an independent state, and stretches far inland from the

east bank of the river. Cotton is very abundant and good in it. Considerably below Lake Dibbie, on the same side of the river, is the country of Diriman, which stretches eastward a considerable way into the interior. The capital called Alcodia, is one and a half day's journey from the river in that direction. In going down the river, Mr. De Caillé appears to have heard nothing about the kingdom of Jinbala, which it is reasonable to suppose he would have done had it been situated immediately upon the river; but when at Timbuctoo he did hear of this place, that it was an extensive state, situated at a great distance inland to the south of Timbuctoo, and to the east of the Joliba in its course from Jinne. Le Brue was distinctly informed regarding this place and kingdom, that it lay to the eastward of the river and Lake Dibbie or Maberia. Park, in his first journey, was distinctly informed that this country lay to the north of Ghotto, by him placed considerably to the eastward of the Joliba, and which we shall by-and-by see is a country situated to the northward and the westward of Magho. The early French traders on the Senegal distinctly state, that the island of Guinbala, within which was the river of Guien, lay to the east of the Lake Maberia or Dibbie; and this statement is adopted by D'Anville as correct. Dupuis states, that this country is a district or principality; that it has a town called by the same name, situated about one day's journey from the Lake Dibbie, which lake, he states, is called the sea of Jinbala; but he appears to believe that it stood on the northern shores of the river, the course of which he conceives to be about E.N.E., whereas we know it is in that part of its course to the westward of north, which brings the position of this country, as it should be, to the right bank of the river, instead of the opposite bank, as he seemed to believe. He, in fact, however, enables us to correct this error in his map, by stating in the body of his work, that Taslima is a town in the country of Konbory (so is Fadanky), and which town his informants give as one in the route from Jinne to Wakwari, the capital of Jinbala. Bowditch states, that Jinbala is a country adjoining the river below Massina; and it would appear that the province of Massina comprehends both banks of the Joliba for some distance to the northward of Jinne. The inhabitants of Jinbala are

Mahommedans, and very industrious. Cotton is abundant in this country, from which they manufacture cloth to a considerable extent. Park and other travellers were told, that the land was alluvial, but swampy and full of creeks ; and that Wakwari, the capital thereof, was a place of considerable trade, and a resting-place for the merchants which traded betwixt Timbuctoo, Jinne, and other places to the S.W. Its situation is just about half way betwixt Jinne and Timbuctoo. Wakwari, there is reason to believe, is situated upon the river called by the Somonie traveller to Mr. Park, the Moosiaca Ba, and which he repre-sents as entering the Joliba from the east side, about half way betwixt Jinne and Timbuctoo. This junction most likely takes place to the south, above Diriman, at the east point of the great bend of the river to the eastward, and to the north of Lake Dibbie. This will form, according to the general Arab accep-tation of the term, the country of Jinbala into an island, and also at once account for the alluvial, marshy nature of the coun-try. It is a fact well known that the Arabs call every country situated on the forks of rivers, or a country surrounded by rivers, we shall say on three sides, islands.

This river, the Moosiaca Ba, will be found to spring from the great range of mountains which Dupuis was informed lay to the eastward of Jinne, and which mountains send off a large river to the east. Dupuis mentions particularly the state of Konbory as situated to the east of Jinne, and on the road from that place to Deboia, the capital of Ghobago. This country and this range of mountains alluded to are certainly the same as the country of Hajri, stated by Sultan Bello to be seven days' journey to the eastward of Jinne and Massina; and which country of Hajri, he especially mentions, is very mountainous, and particularly notes one, which he calls Dombori, the like of which, he states, is nowhere else to be found, and on which, according to him, the capital of the country called Onbori is situated. From the description he gives of this mountain it seems to be some great volcanic production. It is remarkable, also, that in this country he makes no mention of any deep rivers, as he does in his description of other countries ad-joining, but he states that water was abundant; and these facts will of themselves show, and go to prove, that this mountainous district, while it contains, like other countries more level, no deep streams, is merely the source of various springs which afterwards form such streams. These mountains also, be it here observed, lying in the direction mentioned, naturally bar the Joliba in its progress eastwards from the parallel of Jinne northwards, and compel the stream to pursue a northern course to Timbuctoo; and in which place, barred as it were by the ramifications of the range mentioned, and those proceeding S.E. from the mountains in Walet, it forms in the deep valley betwixt them the lake Dibbie, with the low and swampy shores around it.

That a river joins the Niger to the west of Timbuctoo, and which has its source in the mountainous country to the N.E. of that place, is, from the facts already stated and those about to be mentioned, almost certain. Sidi Hamed says, that it passes at some distance west of Timbuctoo, and that it is dry in the dry season, which might be the reason why De Caillé did not observe its bed in his journey from Timbuctoo to Arroan, part of which, moreover, was accomplished by night. Six or eight miles south of Arroan, De Caillé mentions that they pitched their tents near some water, and near which were bulrushes, which would indicate the sides of a stream. Sidi Hamed further says, that returning from Timbuctoo in his second journey, he went by way of Twat, and that he journeyed from Timbuctoo in the direction or bearing *a little to the eastward of north* for twenty days through a hilly country, when they came to a fine fertile valley, where the caravan rested. The country he had passed through was fertile, and grain plenty; and it being in the wet season, or rather at its close, he found many streams of water running S. and W. to join the great river, and which streams are no doubt the sources of the small river which flows to the Niger to the west of Timbuctoo. D'Anville heard that a river, exactly in this quarter, and flowing in a similar direction, did join the Niger a little to the west of Timbuctoo. Boubeker, a Foulah, calls the river in question " Caillorem," a branch of the Joliba, and near which, he says, Timbuctoo stood. Bowditch also heard that there was a small river near Timbuctoo, which was crossed on the third day near Azibbie, the frontier town in the route to the country of Haoussa.

He also states that a small river goes nearly round the town during the rains; and further (p. 194), that during this period, it is let out into the city by small canals or watercourses. Leo Africanus states the same thing. In his rude representation of Timbuctoo and the Joliba given to Mr. Park, the old Somonie Moor has a small river nearly encircling Timbuctoo. Shabeeny states, most pointedly, that there is a small river which runs within two miles of the city, almost encircling it, and which is lost in the sands to the west of the city. De Caillé, from the appearance of a watercourse, expressed an opinion that the Niger had, at an early period, run close by the city; but the appearance which led him to form this opinion is more probably the bed of the river alluded to, or rather, of a rainy-season branch of it, then (April) dry. Major Rennell, in his map of Africa made for the African Association, has more than one river coming from the northward near Timbuctoo, but especially one a little to the west of that city, and entering the Joliba at the bend or elbow of the latter stream to the westward of Cabra. This (namely, the river mentioned by so many different authorities) is most probably the La Mar Zara of Adams, which has so much puzzled African geographers. Connecting his account with the authorities just referred to, it will appear clear and plain. This man, a sailor, was wrecked at Cape Blanco, and carried by the Moors as a slave, on and with a marauding party, into Soudan. He confirms the account of Sidi Hamed and others regarding a river descending from the N.E. and passing to the west of Timbuctoo. In Soudan, however, they were taken prisoners and carried to Timbuctoo, at which place he was subsequently liberated. From Cape Blanco they came, after forty-four days' travel, to a negro village named Soudeny, on the confines of Bambarra. At this place they were taken prisoners, and marched in twenty-five days more to Timbuctoo. This distance, for the route which they took, is very exact when compared with the distance by what is considered the direct route from Cape Blanco to Timbuctoo, and agrees with the time occupied by Sidi Hamed—*two moons*. When liberated, they set out from Timbuctoo, and travelled, he says, for ten days, at the rate of from fifteen to eighteen British miles per day (the party being small), along the banks of a river called La Mar Zarah, in the bearing east of north, not north of east as is stated in the notes taken from him; at the end of which time they struck off to the north, and in thirteen days reached Toudeny, in their journey thither meeting only with negroes bringing salt from that place. In twenty-nine days more they crossed the broadest part of the Desert, and in ten days more reached Woled d' liem. Inspecting the map, the distances here given will be found to be very correct. It is the bearing taken by Sidi Hamed to Mahbrook in his way to Twat; and the river alluded to must be that formed by the small rivers running amongst the hills between Timbuctoo and that place. The name Mahbrook means joy and gladness, or congratulation, the caravans on their reaching it from the north congratulating each other on having got clear of the Desert.

There is another remarkable feature of Western Africa, or rather the western part of it, on the southern boundary of the Great Desert, going eastward from the Atlantic. It is this. Sidi Hamed states, that in journeying eastward (nearly E.) from the bay of Arguin (for about this point it was he left the coast) towards Timbuctoo, mountains were seen on the right hand throughout; which shows that the country is not, as has been supposed, a bare sandy desert. His words are,—travelled "to the east on the border of the Desert, close by the low country, with mountains in sight most of the way. In two moons came to Timbuctoo," which city is surrounded with hills on all sides except towards the south. Mr. Park goes to confirm the account that the fertile country stretches further north in this quarter of Africa than it had previously been admitted to do, when he informs us, that at the period when Ali fled from Benowm and carried him (Park) along with him, they travelled to the northward two or three days, and then pitched their camp in a large wood, which certainly could not be found in a burning desert. The period also when this took place was at the very close of the dry season, when every thing, even in cultivated and fertile countries, in the torrid zone, is completely burnt up, and the land reduced almost to a complete desert.

Three hours, say seven miles, above Cabra, the Joliba divides into two branches. One hour, two miles, above this, is a large

island; and two and a quarter hours above this, say five miles,
"a large branch," says De Caillé, "runs off to the W.S.W.
for a little space." The direction given to this branch, and the
state of the river at this point, render it much more probable
that a river joins the Joliba, than that a branch runs from it;
and this river is most probably the mouth of the Bahr el
Ahmar, or Caillorem, and of the Gozen Zair, increased by the
former stream.

Immediately to the westward of Cabra the Joliba turns to
the eastward, separating into two streams; the one a deep but
narrow branch, about 120 feet broad, flowing E.N.E. a few
miles to Cabra, the port of the celebrated city of Timbuctoo;
and the other branch, about three quarters of a mile wide, flows
E.S.E. and then E. until it is joined by the small branch
already mentioned a few miles to the eastward of Cabra.
From Izaca, downwards to Cabra, the Joliba in the month of
April, during the very height of the dry season, was from half
a mile to three quarters of a mile broad, and from ten to twelve
feet deep, and in some places even deeper, and this too with
branches running off to the westward, but which afterwards
rejoined the river. De Caillé, who descended the river at the
period of the year above mentioned, was greatly struck with
the magnitude of the stream, and remarks, that the Senegal
and the Gambia, even near their junction with the sea, were
"ordinary rivers compared to this." The current of the
Joliba in the part mentioned was from one mile and a half to two
miles per hour. From Jinne to Lake Dibbie, on the general
bearing, the distance is 115 geographical miles, and from Lake
Dibbie to Cabra the distance on the general bearing is 120
geographical miles, making the distance from Jinne to Cabra,
by the river line, 225 miles. This distance, it may here be
observed, is not much greater than what it was previously
stated to be, but then the course of the river betwixt the two
places is very different indeed to that which Europe had been
taught to believe—in truth, nearly N. in place of E.N.E.*

The banks of the Joliba above Timbuctoo, on both sides,

---

* Authorities for these sections—Ptolemy, Batouta, Le Brue, D'Anville, Park,
Bowditch, Dupuis, De Caillé, Scott, Sultan Bello, Report of the Committee of the
House of Lords on the African Slave Trade, 1789, and several native travellers.

are, to a considerable distance, deeply flooded during the rains. The country along the Gozen Zair, to the eastward of Walet, is represented to be fruitful and well cultivated; and the land west of the Joliba from the last-named river southward, including the whole of the kingdom of Massina, is both fertile and populous, and has numerous rivers and mountains, some of the latter being very high. Immediately to the west of Timbuctoo, and to the N.W. from the acute bend of the river above Cabra, the country is less fruitful and populous, gradually, and at no great distance, merging into the sands of the Desert.

Timbuctoo, so long the object of European research, is at present greatly reduced from the splendour and the importance which attached to it in former times, when the Arabian and the Mahommedan power was more extensive and strong than what it now is in Africa. According to the most accurate accounts which have been received, and from which the map accompanying this has been constructed, it is situated in 17° 40' N. lat. and 2° 30' W. long. being, as regards the latitude, nearly in the spot where Ptolemy placed his town of Cuphæ. This is very curious, and also very important. However longitudes and latitudes may err in the hands of the best calculator, the great features of nature do not change, and, in this respect, the course of the principal stream of the Niger to the south of Cuphæ, or the modern Timbuctoo, and to the eastward of that place, is shown, by incontestable modern authority, to have been exactly delineated by Ptolemy. Timbuctoo is not very large, containing only about 13,000 inhabitants, but these live in superior circumstances to the population of most other African towns. It is situated about ten to twelve miles due north from Cabra, its port on the Joliba. Sidi Hamed states, that the town is " built in a plain, surrounded on all sides with hills, except to the south; the plain extends to the river." The following is De Caillé's narrative of his first view of it, and after his entrance into it. " I now saw this capital of Soudan, to reach which had so long been the object of my wishes.....I looked around and found that the sight before me did not answer my expectations. I had formed a totally different idea of the grandeur and the wealth of Timbuctoo.

The city presented at first view nothing but a mass of ill-looking houses, built of earth.   Nothing was to be seen in all directions but immense plains of quicksands of a yellowish white colour.   The sky was a pale red as far as the horizon; all nature wore a dreary aspect, and the most profound silence prevailed, not even the warbling of a bird was to be heard." On this description, however, it is necessary to remark, that when De Caillé arrived there, and during the period when he resided there till he left it on his journey to Morocco, it was the very height of, in fact the close of, the dry season, (April 19th to May 4th,) when every thing in open tropical countries is burnt up, and when every spot, in places much more favourably situated than Timbuctoo, has the appearance of a desert.   The commencement of the rains soon changes the whole face of nature, and speedily clothes the earth with resplendent verdure.   This will fully explain the different accounts which other travellers give of this portion of Africa, namely, that for fifteen journeys to the N.E. from Timbuctoo the country is generally verdant and fruitful, though not so much so as parts more in the interior.   It is the position in which Timbuctoo is placed which renders it so much talked of, looked after, and celebrated.   It is the great central point to which all the commercial travellers from Morocco to central and southern Soudan, also to which all those from Algiers, Tripoli, Tunis, Mourzook, Egypt, and eastern Soudan, bend their steps for western and southern Soudan, and from whence they all again, on their return to the places and countries already mentioned, shape their course.   Hence its position is more readily ascertained than the position of other places, and hence, when this has been ascertained, it becomes of much importance, and enables us to fix with considerable precision the position of other important places in Africa.

" Timbuctoo," says De Caillé, " though one of the largest cities I have seen in Africa, possesses no other resources but its trade in salt, the soil being totally unfit for cultivation. The inhabitants procure from Jinne every thing necessary for the supply of their wants, such as millet, rice, vegetable butter, honey, cotton, Soudan cloth, preserved provisions, candles, soap, allspice, onions, dried fish, pistachios, &c.   Fire-wood is very scarce, being all brought from the neighbourhood of Cabra. It is an article of trade, and the women sell it in the market-place. It is only burnt by the rich: the poor use camel's dung for fuel. Water is also sold in the market-place; the women give a measure containing about half a pint for a cowrie. The city forms a sort of triangle, measuring about three miles in circuit. The streets are clean and sufficiently wide to allow three horsemen to pass abreast. Timbuctoo contains seven mosques, two of which are large; each is surrounded by a brick tower. In consequence of the oppressive heat the market is not held until three o'clock in the afternoon. It is very unusual to see any other merchandise except what is brought by the vessels, and a few articles from Europe, such as glass wares, amber, coral, sulphur, paper, &c. I saw three shops kept in small rooms, well stored with stuffs of European manufacture. The city of Timbuctoo is principally inhabited by negroes of the Kissoor nation: many Moors also reside there; they are engaged in trade, and, like Europeans who repair to the colonies in the hope of making their fortune, they usually return to their own country to enjoy the fruits of their industry. They have considerable influence over the native inhabitants of Timbuctoo, whose king or governor is a negro. This prince, who is named Osman, is much respected by his subjects: he is himself a merchant, and his sons trade with Jinne. The Moors resident in Timbuctoo receive consignments of merchandise from Adrar, Taffilet, Towat or Twat, Ardamas (Ghadames), Tripoli, Tunis, and Algiers. Timbuctoo may be regarded as the principal *entrepôt* of this part of Africa. All the salt obtained from the mines of Toudeny is brought hither on camels. To the W.S.W. of the town there are large excavations, from thirty-five to forty feet deep; these are reservoirs, which are supplied by the rains. Hither the slaves resort to procure water for drinking and cooking. This water is tolerably clear, but it has a disagreeable taste, and is very hot. These reservoirs have no covering whatever, the water is consequently exposed to the influence of the sun and the hot wind. The slaves draw the water from the reservoirs in calabashes, with which they fill leathern bags, which are carried on asses. I am inclined to think that formerly the river flowed close to Timbuctoo, though at present it is eight miles to the north (south) of that city, and five miles from Cabra in the same direction. All the native inhabitants of Timbuctoo are zealous Mahommedans: their dress is similar to that of the Moors. The inhabitants are exceedingly neat in their dress and in the interior of their dwellings."—(*De Caillé*, vol. ii. p. 53, &c.) They are, however, represented to be very licentious in their manners. On the east, north, and west side of Timbuctoo the place is surrounded by the Tooariks, or Tuaricks, a warlike nation, who render the inhabitants of the towns their tributaries. This people is spread over the Great Desert, from the banks of the Niger and the banks of the Yeou, north to Mourzook and Ghadamés.

Shabeeny gives the following account of Timbuctoo and its environs: " Close to the town of Timbuctoo on the south is a small rivulet, in which the inhabitants wash their clothes, and which is about two feet deep. It runs in the great forest on the east, and does not communicate with the Nile, but is lost in the sands *west* of the town. Its waters are brackish . . . . . On the east side of Timbuctoo there is a large forest, in which are a great many elephants. The timber here is very large. . . . . The winter lasts about two months, though the weather is cool from September to April. They begin to sow rice in August and September, but they can sow it at any time, having water at hand: Shabeeny saw some sowing rice while others were reaping it. Lands are watered by canals cut from the Nile; high lands by wells, the water of which is raised by wheels worked by cattle, as in Egypt. Dews are very heavy. . . . Goats are very large; sheep are also very large. Cattle are small; many are oxen. Horses are small; they have dromedaries which travel from Timbuctoo to Taffilet in the short period of five or six days. . . . They have plenty of fish. Ostriches are very numerous; their feathers are very cheap." When he left Tim- buctoo for Haoussa, he crossed the small river close to the walls, and reached the Nile in three days, travelling through a fine country abounding in trees; he embarked on the Nile in a large boat, at a place called Mushgreelia. It was during the height of the rainy season that Shabeeny left Timbuctoo.

De Caillé tells us, that amongst the countries known at Tim-

buctoo, there was the country or town of Salah, situated ten
days' journey to the E. and the country of Zawat, the capital
of which is called Bousbiby, situated two days' journey to the
N.E. It was the barbarous and fanatic chief of this district
which captured and murdered the unfortunate and lamented
Major Laing, not far to the south of El Arroan, which town is
about eight days' journey N. by W. of Timbuctoo. Lyon
mentions a town called Douna on the banks of the Niger, one
and a half day's journey east of Timbuctoo, and another large
town called Eizawen, twenty days' journey distant in the same
direction. Haoussa, or the country of Haoussa, all accounts
agree in stating, lays S.E. by E. of Timbuctoo. Le Hadge
Mahommed, a great traveller, states that from Timbuctoo to
Butoo, the port or frontier town of Haoussa on the Niger, was
forty-eight days' journey by land, thus :—eight days to Agadez, a
negro town built with reeds and rushes; fifteen days to Hum-
bie, another town, and thence to Butoo twenty-five days; to the
eastward of which the river was obstructed by rocks, as we find
to be the case below Yaoori. This traveller also states, that
the country of Butoo was bounded east by the territories of
Goober. Both De Caillé and Bowditch were informed, that
from Cabra to Haoussa was a navigation of twenty days. Park
heard that it was twelve days, and Shabeeny says, that this
was the time he took; but he adds, it was " when the river was
full." Park's guide, one of the greatest travellers in Africa,
says that from Jinne to Kashna was a journey of two months,
partly by land and partly by water, which, after deducting the
land journey in the country to the west of Kashna, would leave
about forty-five days for navigation by the Niger. Dupuis was
also informed, that from the country of Alfine, situated to the
east of Lake Dibbie, to the point where the travellers cross the
river " at the great rocks" near Atty, and S.W. of Kanka-
wansa, was a journey of thirty days. Wargee, the Twarick,
gives the distance from Yaoori to Timbuctoo through Gourmon,
forty-two days, thus :—Yaoorie to Gaigah three days; Fogan
one day; Karamaneè one day; Cumba one day. Here crossed
the Kowara in a canoe, and took one hour to cross it by this
mode of conveyance; much larger river than the Yeou. From
the Kowara to Gourmon ten days; Gourmon to Moosh ten

days; Moosh to Imbolee ten days; Imbolee to the Niger (Bar-neel) five days; ferried over in half an hour, and in three hours more reached Cabra. Thus every account goes to establish and to show the very great extent of country between Timbuctoo and Yaoori.

There is a point of considerable importance, as it regards the travels of Batouta, which here properly merits attention, as clearing up still further the routes which he took, and thus fixing the positions of other places in this portion of Africa. From Timbuctoo, he proceeded by the Niger to Kawkaw, Kuku, or Ghou, the capital of which, he says, was large, and one of the most beautiful cities in Sudan. From Kawkaw he went to Bardama, or Burdama; the females of which were chaste and handsome, and the population of which protect the caravans. From Bardama he next went to Nakda, or Takdha, or Takadda, which is handsome, and built of red-stone. Its water runs over copper-mines, which change its colour and its taste. Here is another confirmation of the existence of the Mar Zarah of Adams. The population of Nakda traded largely with Egypt. From Nakda Batouta proceeded to Segelmasa in the month Shaaban (A. D. 1353). The distance from Nakda to Segelmasa was seventy stations or journeys. He travelled by way of Tekeddam and Twat. The first place he reached was Kahor, a stony country: thence he travelled three days through a country without water; thence, fifteen days through a desert without inhabitants, but with some water; thence, in a short time, he came to the point where the road for Twat and that for Egypt separates; thence, in ten days he reached Dehkar, and next Twat.—(See *Lee's Batouta*, p. 242.)

How far Batouta travelled eastward from Kawkaw, or Ghou, either on the Niger or through the countries situated on the northern bank of that river, it is quite impossible to determine, as he has not, or rather the abridger of his work has not given us the time occupied in travelling between Kawkaw and Bardama, and thence to Nakda; nor can we now recognise the names of these places in African maps or among African travellers, but from the time which he took upon leaving Segelmasa until he returned to it again, in about twenty-one months, and the time which he states he stopped at different places, &c.; it could not be far, and probably terminated 360 miles (if so much) eastward of Timbuctoo, and near to the mountainous district where the Niger bursts through the chain to the westward of Atty, which district probably then formed the frontier in that direction of the great kingdom of Yaoora, or Yaoori, which no white man or Arab, at that time, durst enter, the reason probably why Batouta proceeded no further down the river to the east or south eastward.

On the north bank of the Niger, and from Ghou to Kabi inclusive, is situated the great country, called by Dupuis, Foulaha, from the Foulahs, or Fallatahs, its rulers, and some time ago accounted their great stronghold or head quarters in Central Africa. This leads us to ascertain more correctly that part of Africa below " Gottoijege a long way," on the Niger, where Park's guide tells us they perceived an army of the Poul nation (Foulahs or Fallatahs) stationed on one side of the river, but which, however, did not molest them. Gottoijege is the same place which Sultan Bello calls Ghourouma in the country of Sogho, or Sheego, where Park was attacked, and where, according to both Amadi Fatouma, and Sultan Bello, he killed a great number of the natives, and lost one white man on the occasion.

From Timbuctoo the Niger continues its course first east, then E.S.E. and S.E. and next southerly to Yaoora or Yaoori. The distance between these two places is now found to be much greater than was generally or hitherto supposed. De Caillé says, that from Timbuctoo to Haoussa is twenty days' navigation. The space, however, that intervenes, has been determined with considerable accuracy. Thus, Timbuctoo is situated in 17° 40′ N. lat., and say 3° W. long. Saccatoo, seven days N.E. of Yaoori, is placed by Clapperton in 6° 21′ E. long. and in 13° N. lat. but 7° E. long. may be taken to be its correct position. Yaoori has been ascertained to be in 11° 24′ N. lat. and 5° 6′ E. long.; thus leaving a space of 8° 6′ distance from the meridian of Timbuctoo. It is a remarkable fact that from his town named Cuphæ, in E. long. 23° 20′, to Panagra in 31° 20′ of E. long., Ptolemy gives a space of 8° long., corresponding very nearly indeed with the distance and longitude between the modern Timbuctoo, which is on the very spot where Cuphæ stood and Yaoori, &c. Cuphæ he places in about 18° N. lat., and Dudum in 15° N. lat., and 31° E. long.; thus, giving a rapid declination of the river to the south; for Panagra, in 16° N. lat., is placed by him in 31° 20′ E. long., and which town is on the north bank of the Niger. Modern discoveries and researches have thus realized in a very remarkable manner, as we shall by and by see more at large, the accuracy of the accounts by this, we may say, the parent of Geography, 1700 years ago.

From Timbuctoo the Joliba runs under the more general name of the Kowara. The best account that we have of the progress of the river from Timbuctoo to Yaoori, is that given by Sidi Hamed,* who travelled over the whole of the distance. From Cabra the river flows about seventy-five miles in a direction a little to the southward of east. At this point, a mountain on the north bank turns the stream more to the south. On a line drawn from this point about E.S.E., Sidi Hamed travelled, the river at a considerable distance to the southward, describing a curve like the arch of a bow. The country in the intermediate space was very hilly and woody. Near the mountain mentioned was a village named Bimbina, and eastward from it, and extending to the river, is the great kingdom and city named Ghou, or Kawkaw; the name given to it by Batouta, and who describes it as the first place of importance on the Niger below Timbuctoo; and the capital, which is situated in the land of Maly, as being " *one of the finest cities in Soudan.*" More to the eastward is the place which he names Zagha, or as it is called by Sultan Bello, Segho or Sheegho, where Park, in his progress down the river, was attacked by a large party of the Tuaricks, whom he beat off with considerable slaughter. Proceeding 160 miles on the bearing above-mentioned, two large towns appear on the south bank of the river, one of which is the town of Kaffo, mentioned by Park's guide in his account of their progress down the river. High mountains bore N.E. from this point. The stream pursued its course in a S.E.

* The writer of this has had the opportunity to know, from unquestionable authority, that Sidi Hamed was a very intelligent man, and greatly superior in intelligence to most of his countrymen.

direction for thirty-two miles, with several windings in its course. At the end of this distance the river comes to a very great ridge of mountains thickly covered with trees, and so abrupt and steep, that no path remained between the stream and the mountains. "It ran against the side of the steep mountain," says Sidi Hamed. From the summit of this ridge, "a large chain of high mountains was seen to the westward." In passing through this ridge, the river forms an acute bend to the S.W. In his rude delineation of the curve of the Kowara, Sultan Bello's schoolmaster lays down in this quarter a similar acute bend or curve. After a journey of six days (about forty miles) across this chain, which is "thickly covered with trees," the river is again approached on its north bank, where it is narrow and full of rocks, "which dash the water most dreadfully." Close to this is the point where the road from the country of Alfine, situated to the eastward of Lake Dibbie, to Jekky, crosses the river. According to Dupuis' information, "the water of the river was here very great," and the traveller is landed "at the great rocks" west of Kankaw-ansa. To the eastward of Kaffo, Park's guide states that they came "to a very difficult passage, where rocks had barred the river," dividing it into three channels, through one of which they passed in safety, having been deterred from attempting one of the others on the opposite side, from the appearance of an army of natives, apparently in hostile array, assembled close to it. From this place the river pursues its course 126 miles in a S.E. direction, but with numerous windings, which indicate a more level country. "Many small streams" join the river in this space, from the eastward; a fact which shows elevated and cultivated countries to lie in that direction. Along the space, too, just mentioned, "high mountains were plainly discernible" to the westward. "The stream looked deep, but not very wide." At this point, says Sidi Hamed, Caravans rest, 432 geographical miles from Timbuctoo, where there is a ferry, and numerous canoes plying on the river. 160 miles from this point, in a south-easterly direction, the river passes Yaoori, which is clearly the Wassanah of Sidi Hamed, where the river, he states, turned and ran nearly to the south "between high mountains on both sides, though not very close

to the river" at Yaoori, facts which we know to be true, both from
Lander and Clapperton.   Yaoori has for many centuries been
one of the greatest and most powerful states in that portion of
the interior of Africa, and well-known centuries ago to the
shores of the Atlantic, around the Delta of the Niger, and
places to the westward thereof.   Batouta mentions it under the
name of Yuwi, and that it was at that time the most powerful
state in the interior.*

Yaoori is certainly the Wassanah of Sidi Hamed.   The
distance and the direction which he travelled from Timbuctoo,
(592 miles,) corresponds exactly, and with no other place in
that portion of Africa.   His account of its great magnitude,
which took him one day to go round, is confirmed by Lander;
and its great commanding and commercial importance, adverted
to by other authorities, is established by the fact in his (Sidi
Hamed's) narrative, namely, that the king's son urged him to
accompany him on a trading expedition, consisting of a great
number of boats and slaves, to "*the great water*," or sea, a
voyage of three months; and where he would meet pale people,
Christians, in great ships, and with great guns, &c. &c.   Sidi
Hamed also states that the river, at this place, turned and ran
directly south.   The following references will go to establish
that Yaoori has been for centuries, and until of late years that
its power has been broken by the Fallatahs, one of the greatest
and most important states in this portion of Africa; Batouta
thus speaks of it 500 years ago.   From Timbuctoo, he states,
the Nile or the Niger "descends to Zagha (the Sheego or Sogho
of Sultan Bello), then to Kawkaw (Ghou); next to the town of
Muli, which is the extreme district of Maly.   It then goes to
Yuwi (Yaoori), the greatest district of Soudan, and the king
of which is the most potent.   No white person can enter here;
for if you attempt to do so, they will kill them before he
reaches it."   Next in proof of its former power and extensive
connexions, Dupuis says (p. xlii.),—"Two of my informants
declared that they had performed the voyage from north to
south, under the protection of the Sultan of Yaoori, as far as
the gates of Benin;" and which informants further added, that

* Authorities for these sections of the work—Ptolemy, Batouta, Sidi Hamed,
Sultan Bello, Dupuis, Bowditch, Shabeeny, Park's guide, L'Hage, Mahommed,
Lander, Clapperton, and several native travellers.

any traveller might go from Benin, by water, to Timbuctoo and Sego, without setting his foot on shore.

Yaoori is about seventy miles north of Boussa, the intermediate space being filled by a very high chain of hills, which, on the east side, stretch away to the high mountains of Aushin; and, on the west side, are called the mountains of Fagh, which run S.W. to the Jibbel Sargha range. Through this ridge the Niger bursts, running over a very rocky bed, and expanding to the northward of Boussa to the breadth of six miles, even in the dry season. The channel, however, is in different places very deep. Sultan Bello informed Clapperton that, even in the dry season, Park could have passed down the river at Boussa in safety, had he known the proper channel. On the north side, and at a short distance above Yaoori, the Niger receives the considerable river Quarrama or Cubbie, which springs in the granite range a little to the southward of Kashna, and runs by the capitals of Zamfra, Goober, and Saccatoo, increased by several rivers on either side. To the westward of this river, the Niger receives another stream from the N.E., which runs through the kingdom of Maury; still further westward, another and more considerable stream, which comes in the same direction, and runs through the countries called Azwa and Taghzar; and still more to the westward, a large river which passes by the town called Dody. This river is a remarkable feature in Ptolemy's Geography of this part of Africa, where he brings a stream descending from Mount Usurgala to the Niger at Panagra. Dupuis' informants particularly mention this river and its position; and Sidi Hamed states pointedly, that within the distance and from the direction mentioned, several streams join the Niger. The writers in the Encyclopædia Britannica (5th edition), the Maps of Joannes Blæav, &c. have a river here coming from the same quarter, 240 miles below Timbuctoo; then considering that place to be 4 or 5 degrees more to the eastward than it really is. The country, in the parts alluded to, has both mountains and streams, and abundance of cattle, provisions, and fruits, so far as the confines of the Great Desert.*

* Authorities for this section—Leo, Sultan Bello, Dupuis, Encyclopædia Britannica (5th edition), and several native travellers.

All these countries, to the north of the Niger, from Saccatoo to Ghou, are comprehended in the great district of Africa, called Marroa, elsewhere noticed. It was described to Dupuis as nearly resembling the N.W. portion of Haoussa, and to be a very fine country. The plough is used in the countries to the north, and also in some few situated to the south of the Niger; the manufactures of cotton goods, trinkets, cutlery, and other wares in it, are not inferior to those which are made in some parts of Morocco; corn and vegetables are represented to be abundant, and also that scarcely a piece of waste land is to be seen. Dupuis' information about the general state of the districts around the central course of the Niger is very important. Besides the Niger, which runs through the heart of the greatest district of the whole, namely Fillany, and which district is bounded from Ghou to Haoussa by the Niger on the north, there are, adds Dupuis, " many other navigable streams connected with that river, both on the northern and the southern shores." Timbuctoo enjoys the supremacy amongst the cities in Fillany, although Taslima, Jinne, and Wakwari, are esteemed larger and more populous. Fillany was the first important conquest in Africa of the Moors from Morocco, as Marroa to the eastward was by the Arabs from Cairowan, at a very early period of their conquering history. The boundaries of this district have already been stated. It is of great extent, stretching eastward on the Niger from Ghou, to the borders of Haoussa, and from the Niger northwards, to the desert. "The land hereabouts," says Dupuis, (p. lxxxviii.) "is described as a sort of African Paradise, and the population is proportionally great; numerous streams intersect the plains, some of which are of great magnitude, rolling volumes of water, southerly and easterly to the Niger." Ben Ali fully confirms this, for he states that from Timbuctoo to Haoussa, the banks of the Niger are better peopled and cultivated than the banks of the Nile in Egypt—and in fact surpassed only by the cultivation in England.—(*Proceedings of the African Association,* 1791.)

With regard to Haoussa, Shabeeny states two or three curious particulars, which are worthy of notice; he says that in Haoussa the hot winds come from the east; that it is then hotter in Haoussa, than the summer is in Morocco, but that it is hotter at Timbuctoo than in Haoussa; in which country he states, at least in that part of the country where he was, that the rains are not so frequent and violent as in other parts of southern Africa. In Haoussa, he further states, that the cold winds come from the west, a fact which the position of the countries, as these have been described, fully confirms.

Yaoori, the capital of the state of that name, is situated about four miles N.E. from the north bank of the Niger, and is described by Lander as being a very large place. The walls, he states, are thirty miles in circumference, and the population within them very large. Its position can be fixed with considerable accuracy. Boussa is situated in 10° 14′ N. lat., according to a celestial observation made by Clapperton at the place. In going up the river from Boussa to Yaoori, at the close of the dry season, Lander took twenty-three to twenty-four hours to accomplish the distance. The current of the river was then very little; the canoe-men, he says, pulled at a good rate, and generally made good way; consequently, three miles per hour is a reasonable rate to allow for his progress up the river to the point where he disembarked for Yaoori, which would give sixty-nine miles, and four more for the northing made good to the position of Yaoori. In descending the river from Yaoori to Boussa, Lander took nineteen hours by water and five hours travelled by land from a point where he disembarked from the river above Boussa. When he descended the stream it was in flood, the current about three miles per hour, while the canoe-men, during the greater part of the voyage, pulled well. Four miles per hour is not an unreasonable allowance to make for the distance accomplished, with the deduction of five or six miles on account of the time occupied in stoppages at landing places, from going ashore and pushing into the middle of the stream. To the remaining distance must be added three miles, the distance due north, from Yaoori to the Cubbie river, on which Lander embarked very near its junction with the Niger. The distance thus taken by both modes of reckoning will closely agree, and make out seventy geographical miles as the difference of latitude betwixt Boussa and Yaoori, thus placing the latter in 11° 24′ N. lat., and from other computations, subsequently to be mentioned, in 5° 6′ E. long., being thus a little to the westward of both Boussa and Rabbah. Such is the position of this place, thus giving the course of the river below it to be a little to the eastward of south, as both the bearing by Clapperton, Lander, and the schoolmaster give to it.

Immediately below Yaoori the Niger divides into several branches, and runs through a dreadfully rocky channel, here again bursting through another chain of mountains, the stupendous rocks on its banks throwing a dreadful gloom over the river for the distance of several miles. The channels, however, betwixt the rocks which divide the stream, are easily navigated during the dry season, and during the rainy season the whole are covered to a great depth. Above Garnacassa there is one channel a mile broad, and shallow; but Park passed through another channel that was deeper than this. At Garnacassa the river again unites in one stream, and, for several miles downwards towards Boussa, Lander describes the stream as being six miles broad, but in many places very shallow, and in other places with deep channels.

Here we must quit the river and the account of the country adjoining this place, and turn for a moment to consider the tributaries which this great river receives from that vast space of country which stretches from near Jinne, eastward to a river at a point above mentioned, and from the Jibbel Sargha mountains to a stream on the north. We shall take the latter division first. In this portion of the subject Sultan Bello and Dupuis must be our chief guides. In his geography of this part of Africa, his description of the country stretching westward is divided into three lines. First, from Yaoori westward, through Degomba to Maly. Secondly, the countries westward from Saccatoo to Massina. Thirdly, the countries from Saccatoo westward, on the N.E. bank of the Niger, and along that river to Timbuctoo. Immediate attention is directed to the two first of these divisions: first in the list is the province or state of Gourmon. Clapperton tells us that this state is eight days' journey north from Kiama in Barghoo. This state is placed on the west side of the Niger, in a direction nearly

N.W. from Yaoori. " It is," says Sultan Bello, "extensive,
...... and contains woods, sands, and various rivers," particularly one named the " Yaly," which is clearly the " Oli" of
Clapperton and Lander, which flows eastward, near Wawa,
into the Niger. The great range of mountains called Fagh,
which are very high, stretch westward from the Niger near
Yaoori, bound the state of Gourmon on the S.E., and which
mountains run on south-westerly to the great range of Jibbel
Sargha, already mentioned, where the Rio Volta and other
rivers of Ashantee take their rise. In this space and in this
direction, according to the information obtained, both by
Ledyard and Lucas, the hills or ranges, from a little distance
S.W. of Kashna, are of a "stupendous height" all the way
to the Gold Coast. This information has been confirmed by
the accounts which Dupuis received concerning the ranges of
mountains called Fagh and Jibbel Sargha, &c. Robertson
heard that some were covered with snow; so also a seaman,
formerly belonging to the Owen Glendower frigate, who
travelled over them in his way to the Gold Coast, says, one
had "a white cap," or snow. Leo also states, that the cold in
Gago was so great during the winter, that to keep themselves
warm the inhabitants clothed themselves with the skins of
beasts.

Westward of Gourmon, according to Sultan Bello, lies the
country of Mousheer, or Moushee. " It is," says he, " extensive," and has a gold mine, that is, gold is found in that
country. It contains rivers, woods, and mountains. Asses
are very numerous in it, which animals are exported to
Ghunjah, where they are employed to carry warlike stores.
This country is specially mentioned by both Bowditch and
Dupuis, and there is no disagreement as to the position in
which both they and Sultan Bello place it. It is a country of
considerable extent, and Kaybee, a little to the westward, may
probably be included in it; in which place, according to
Bowditch, asses are exceedingly numerous. On the right of
Mooshee, that is, to the south, the great country of Assentai,
or Ashantee, is situated. In this description by Sultan Bello,
laconic as it is, we readily recognise the country of Moosee,
or Mouzee, mentioned by Dupuis and others. North of

Mousheer, says Sultan Bello, lies the country of Sanghee, which is extensive, fertile, and well peopled.   The inhabitants thereof are remnants of the Sanhaja, the wandering Arabs, and the Falatine.   Beyond Sanghee, to the west, the very extensive province of Maly is situated.   This province contains Bambarra, &c. &c.; in short, it is the great country of Maly or Melli, which extends to the east as far as the boundary of the Mandingo nations, namely, to the boundary of Sanghee, and on the west to the Atlantic ocean.   So far the accounts regarding these particular countries, furnished by Sultan Bello. There remains to notice the great country of Gago, which, from its position, there is no room to doubt, formed or included the great kingdom of Magho, mentioned by Dupuis, and also the state of Mooshee, mentioned by Sultan Bello.   Major Rennell places Gago, the capital, to the north of Degomba, and in about 12° N. lat. and 3° E. long., which is not very far from being correct.   Leo states that Gago was in his day a great kingdom, that it lay 400 Arabic miles to the southward of east from Timbuctoo, and that the merchants belonging to it were rich, and that every thing was abundant in the country. The people of Acca or Akim, on the shores of the Gulf of Guinea, carried on a great trade, according to Leyden's Africa, to Tonowa (Tonouma), Gago, and Meczara.   At that time the frontiers of Acca was said to extend to Tonouma.   When Leo visited Gago it was bounded by Melli on the west, and by Yarba or Yarribah on the S.E., which clearly points out not only its great magnitude, but its position; and that at the time mentioned by Leo, it included all the countries and states now known under the names of Magho, Mouzee, &c. Sir George Collier (see Report to House of Commons, June, 1820) states, that to this day, or rather to that time, Dahomy carries on a great trade with Gago and Meczara.   The writer in the Encyclopædia Britannica, 5th ed., states that Gago was situated to the southward of Timbuctoo and Hoaussa, and near to the north side of a chain of hills which run from east to west; from which chain issued many rivers that flow north to the Niger.   The same authority places Dahomy, as it really is, to the southward of Gago.   It has been considered necessary to be as particular as possible about these countries and places, in order to ascertain as correctly as we can their true position; as also to show both that rivers run through them, and that these rivers bend, as they must bend, their courses northward to the Niger; while the different authorities just referred to, go to confirm and to elucidate the important information which Dupuis received when at Coomassie, regarding all these matters.

Sultan Bello, in his African Geography already referred to, places to the west of the Niger, in the middle route to Jinne, different countries; the first beyond Gourmon and nearest the Niger is Bitenkoobi; the inhabitants of this country are Felans, and it abounds with mountains, plains, &c. Next and west from this is the country of Maazo-Moudi, a low mountainous country, and beyond this is the country of Yaghra, which contains woods, small mountains, and a well-known deep river called Yali; and between Yaghra and Maazo-Moudi through stony plains, is the well-known river called Sirba. Beyond Yaghra, through woody plains and low ground, is the country of Sebtako, the inhabitants of which are also Felans. This country abounds with horses and cattle, is hilly, and has a large lake called Doura. Beyond this, through desert plains, in the midst of which there is a large lake called Bookma, is the country of Jelghooji. This country is mountainous, and has a well-known lake called Jaboo, besides a great many wells; the inhabitants are Felans, and possess a great many swift horses, oxen, and other cattle. This country is placed, in the rude delineation which accompanies the narrative, in a position where it will lie to the northward of west from Magho, and to the eastward of it is Yaghra, and in the midst of the plains the well-known river called Sirba. Beyond the country of Jelghooji is the country of Hajri, already mentioned, situated seven days' journey to the eastward of Massina, and which contains the remarkable mountain Dombori, previously alluded to, situated in, or rather forming a part of, that great range of hills which Dupuis was informed lay to the eastward of Jinne. This more minute description of the portion of Africa under review, will serve to give the reader a clearer idea of the country; at the same time it conveys the information that there are many rivers in those districts, and also that the country being so moun-

tainous and woody, must in every part afford supplies to rivers.
That rivers, such as are about to be mentioned, do flow, and
very nearly in the directions stated, through this part of Africa,
the physical features of the country render certain, and at the
same time these require such drains for carrying off the springs
and the waters which are to be found in them. We are decidedly
informed by Dupuis, that the whole country from Magho to
Jinne westward, and from Magho to the Niger towards the
north and the east, is exceedingly mountainous and woody;
which is the reason given why the Moors and the Arabs have
never been able wholly to subdue the nations in those parts of
Africa; because cavalry, which is their chief force, cannot act
with the same effect as in those countries which are more open.
Secondly.—Dupuis' informants, who seem to have been well
acquainted with all the interior parts of this vast district, pointedly state that there is a great river running eastward from the
country in the neighbourhood of Jinne, almost parallel with the
course of the Niger, betwixt which river and the Gulbe of
Ghoroma there is a water communication. It is best in the
first place to give the sereferences in his own words; page xcii.
he states, "The Gulbe of Magho, after a long eastern course
inclining to the north, runs into the Nooffy river," which is
the Niger: at page xciii. he proceeds, "The Gulbe is said also
to flow easterly upon a parallel with the Kowara, which it joins,
as has been related in Haoussa. A diversity of opinion prevailed upon the topic of its source, some maintaining that its
fountain existed in the chain of mountains before mentioned
between Kong and the river Ahmar, whilst others affirmed that
the Gulbe itself was a branch separated from the Kowara by a
ridge of mountains in the vicinity of Janny, (Jinne,) and that
the navigation of this southern limb was open and unobstructed
from Janny to Ghoroma, the capital of Magho, through Kom-
boii; perhaps the latter was the prevailing opinion." We are
now so well acquainted with what the African Moors mean by
water communications from place to place, after the manner related, and which very often implies not only rivers running from a
particular portion of the country in parallel lines, but in opposite
directions, that we readily perceive the true meaning of the
above statement, and thus the account which De Caillé has given

us of the river Kowara Ba descending from the south to Jinne,
gives us clearly to perceive the meaning of the information here
conveyed to Dupuis.

We are warranted, therefore, in bringing a branch of the
Niger under the name of Gulbe, a name generally applied to great
rivers in every part of Africa, from the centre of the mountainous
range which certainly stands to the eastward of Jinne. The
source of this branch most probably is near the remarkable
mountain of Dombori; while from the nature and extent of the
country to the southward, it is extremely probable that more to
the eastward a branch may join on the southern side, flowing
from the S.W., which will explain the statement made by some
to Dupuis, that the source of the Gulbe lay towards the country
of Kong. Mr. Dupuis informs us that travellers go northward
from Magho to the heathen kingdom of Gotto, with which the
information he received led him to believe the communication
could be made by water, connected with the lake Konsagho,
situated six days' journey to the northward from Andary, where
the Gulbe is quitted on the second day after leaving Ghoroma,
in the way to the lake mentioned; and that after leaving lake
Konsagho and marching eastward, the traveller again comes to
the river Gulbe. The lake Konsagho here mentioned by Dupuis,
is as nearly as possible on the spot where Sultan Bello places the
lake Doura, and thus we find that the river which comes from the
westward communicates with this lake; and this lake, by means of a
river running from it, with the river of Ghoroma, also called Gulbe.
Whether or not the two lakes previously mentioned, called
Bookma and Jabboo, communicate with the river from the westward, there is no authority to state; but it is probable that they do,
and it may be also that the river in question passes through them,
for it must pass near or upon the positions in which they are placed.
In the notice of the mountains called Jibbel Sargha, the source of
the river Ghoroma on the north side of that chain was distinctly
pointed out, and which, joining and running through the country
of Moushee, descends to Ghoroma, where the magnitude of the
stream has become so considerable that the passage for two
days above Ghoroma may be made by water. Bending its
course to the north-eastward, this river will form a junction with
the one from the westward, which latter above the junction, or

probably even the united stream, may bear the name of Sirba, as mentioned by Sultan Bello. The designation which he gives this stream, namely, "the well-known river Sirba," points out that it is a river of no ordinary importance. Proceeding eastward, this river probably joins the Niger, about eight days' journey above Yaoori, and seven days' journey below the ferry, mentioned by Sidi Hamed, and where it must be a very considerable stream. The town of Ghoro, mentioned by one of Dupuis' informants as being in the route from Ghoroma to Kashna, and in that part of it which is to the south of the Niger, appears to stand on this river, though the exact point cannot be ascertained, and there his informants stated that "the water of the river was very broad."

That a river of great magnitude joins the Niger in this part, cannot admit of a doubt. Besides what has been already stated in proof of this, we have the comparative magnitude of the Niger at Timbuctoo and at Yaoori, taken in exactly the corresponding period of the year, as a further proof: at the latter, the stream is described to be at-least double the breadth that it is at the former, viz., as three-quarters of a mile is to above a mile and a half. Now from the N. and from the N.E., no great rivers either in number or magnitude flow to the Niger, to increase its volume to this extent. It is exceedingly probable that a river does join the Niger from the N.E., in the neighbourhood of Ghou, and somewhere near the village of Bimbina, where the mountains, as Sidi Hamed tells us, bend the Niger from its eastern course. At or near this point, certainly stood the Nigira metropolis of Ptolemy, who makes a river join the Niger at this place from the quarter mentioned; but then it is clear, from the nature of the country, and the desert being so near, that it cannot be very large. If it had been large, Sidi Hamed would probably have mentioned it. After passing the great chain of mountains so often alluded to, Sidi Hamed states that the stream "looked deep but not very wide," thus indicating his opinion that the magnitude of the stream at this place, and at Timbuctoo, was not materially different. It is below the spot where he made this observation, that the larger supplies to the Niger, both from the N.E. and from the S.W. certainly come, and which increase the magnitude of the Niger to be so much greater at Yaoori than it is at Timbuctoo. That such a river as that alluded to joins the Niger from the S.W. we have another proof, in the fact stated by Shabeeny, that at the port of Haoussa, clearly and certainly below where the junction takes place, he found the stream deeper and larger than what it was at Timbuctoo. To all these authorities and remarks it may be added, that both D'Anville and De Lisle, bring a river flowing from the S.W. to join the Niger in the same quarter.

It was at Boussa that Park, our unfortunate countryman, and the only companion of his laborious travels, Martyn, perished, four months after leaving Sansanding. They left the latter place on the 17th November, 1805, and according to Amadi Fatouma, their guide, they passed Jinne, and presented the chief with a piece of baft, and then proceeded on their voyage. It was probably three weeks after this, that they passed Cabra, as a letter was received at Mogadore in March, 1806, by a merchant there, from his correspondent at Timbuctoo, which must have been written in December; which letter stated, that a boat with some Christians had arrived from the westward at Cabra, and which after stopping part of a day and a night, went on, the inhabitants not understanding their signal of peace. According to Amadi Fatouma's account, they were here attacked, and killed one native in beating them off. Sultan Bello states that they stopped for some time above Timbuctoo, with the son of the sovereign of that place, who received and treated them kindly. After leaving Cabra, they proceeded down the river, and passing Ghourouma, they were attacked by a great number of canoes full of armed natives, at a place called Gottoijege, in the kingdom of Ghourouma, or Ghou. These however they repulsed, after, says Amadi Fatouma, killing a vast number of them. Sultan Bello confirms the fact of this engagement, and says that it was at Gharwalgao, the same as Ghou, in the country of Shego, that they were attacked by the Tuaricks, who were defeated with much loss. On the side of Park, one if not more persons were killed. They then proceeded down the river, navigating below Kaffo, through a dreadful rocky part of the stream, where it was divided by the rocks into three channels. This is clearly amidst the high ridge of mountains described by Sidi Hamed, as has already been noticed, and part of the range running westward on the south side of the Niger, called by Dupuis, the mountains of Batako.   After this they came to Carmasse; next to Gourmon, and next to Yaoori, where Park did not land, and where Amadi Fatouma left him in terms of his agreement.   No time is given betwixt these places, and therefore we are left to ascertain it by Amadi Fatouma's journal, which says it was four months after leaving Sansanding.   This is confirmed by the accounts received by Clapperton and others, that it was during the feast of the Rhamadan, or towards the end of March. From Yaoori, Park proceeded downwards, but mistaking the deepest channel of the river, he approached too close to the western side, and was there attacked by the population of Boussa; and to avoid them, and perhaps, as he considered, a worse fate, he jumped with Martyn into the water, where both were drowned : the canoe, books, and papers, and some servants became the prize of the victors.   One of the bodies was found and buried ; and, according to the account given to Bowditch by an eye-witness, the other floated down the stream to the island of Gange, probably Gongoo, where it was found and interred.   Various accounts are given by the native travellers of the causes which led to this fatal and much-to-be-lamented catastrophe; but that received by Clapperton at Saccattoo, during his second journey, is by far the most probable and reasonable, and no doubt accurate, namely, that his arrival was at a time when the Fallatahs were attempting to penetrate into these parts; that the people of Boussa, taking them to be the vanguard of these dreaded and destructive enemies, accordingly watched, and assailed them, with the fatal result which has been stated. None of Park's papers have ever been recovered, which is deeply to be regretted.   Had he escaped at Boussa, ten days more would have brought him to the sea, and to a glorious termination to all his fatigues, labours, and dangers.

From Boussa, the course of the river downwards is, by compass, from NN.W. to SS.E.; but regarding the stream at this important point, our accounts are not so clear and satisfactory as could be wished, or as they might have been. Lander has given as the great breadth of the stream, at a short distance above Boussa, to be about six miles. A short space below Boussa, at the village of Songha, Clapperton gives the breadth of the river to be three-fourths .the breadth of the Thames at Somerset House, when it is high water, and with a current of two miles and a half per hour; and at the ferry at the village of Comie, the breadth is said to be a quarter of a mile, the current two miles per hour, and the depth in the middle ten or twelve feet, in the dry season. This appears a diminutive and inconsistent account of the magnitude of a stream which, both above and below this place, is said to be, and known from the best authorities, to be so much greater. Lander and Clapperton had recourse, in order to account for this difference, to the opinion that the river at Boussa has large subterraneous passages, such as are to be found in calcareous countries.*   This, to a certain extent, may be the case ; but, after all, they may have under-estimated the breadth, and still more under-estimated the speed of the current.   On this latter point, every thing depends.   Clapperton mentions, that in going from Boussa to Comie, and when at some distance to the westward of the stream, he heard "the Quorra roaring" over its rocky bed ; and in another place, that he saw the stream dashing with great violence against the rocks which rose on its bank. These facts show that the current must have been very rapid.   Now the quantity of water discharged by any stream through any given space, is as the square of the velocity of its current. Hence, any river with a current of four miles per hour, will discharge sixteen times as much water in the same space of time, that another river will do with a current at the rate of only one mile an hour, and one hundred times as much if the current is increased to the rate of ten miles per hour; and so on in proportion, either increasing the quantity of water discharged, or narrowing the channel.   Hence we find, that the great river Congo, which is three miles broad above the cataracts, is compressed, at one of the greatest of those rapids called Sangalla, within a breadth of fifty yards.

* The bed of the Niger near Boussa, is, according to Lander, six miles broad, and composed of banks of large round stones, bare in the dry season. Amidst the vortices of these, a vast body of water would quickly disappear. Such is the case with the great river Cuanene, in Southern Africa, the mouth of which, during the dry season, appears without water from the cause alluded to.

From Boussa the Niger proceeds about SS.E. until it passes Rabbah, situated in 9° N. lat. and 5° 11′ E. long. From the junction of the Moussa the Niger flows along the northern base of the Kong mountains in a direction a little to the southward of east until it approaches the village of Cuttum Currafee, when it turns to the south and is joined by the great river Shadda, or Shaderbah, from the east. At a short distance above Egga it receives the Coodonia, and further west, near the island of Gongoo, the Kontankora river on the north side. About 20 miles above Egga, Lander passed the island of Gongoo, situated in the middle of the river. This is the island of Gongoo which Ben Ali mentions in his journey from Kashna to Yarba, or Yarribah, and where, according to him, the river was 24 feet deep, and " the width such, that even at the island of Gongoo, where the ferryman resides, the sound of the loudest voice from the northern shore is scarcely heard." This island was named by Mr. Bowditch's informant, Gangee; and on this island so named, as stated also by other travellers, the body of either Park, or Martyn, his fellow-traveller, was found, having been carried down the river from Boussa to that place. The Niger in this part of its course, according to both Lander and Oldfield, had during the rainy season a most magnificent appearance, being generally from two to three miles wide.

From Boussa to the Niger near Rakkah, that river receives three tributaries from the westward. The first is the Menai, which rises in the mountains of Fagh, and enters the Niger close to Boussa. This stream, which has but a short course, is called the water of Wada, from its passing Wada, the capital of the country called Wawa. Where it joins the Niger it is about 20 yards broad and 12 feet deep, but with a sluggish current. Thirty miles below Boussa a considerable stream, named the Oli or Yali, joins the Niger. This stream rises in the mountainous country to the N.W. of Nikky. The bed of this river is very rocky: during the rainy season it is not fordable, and the current then is very strong; at the close of the dry season it was 40 paces broad and 8 feet deep. To the southward of this is the river Moussa, which joins the Niger a little below the town of Rakkah, and to the southward of Rabbah, which latter town is situated on the east bank of the Niger. The Moussa springs in the mountains to the northward of Ghofil and to the eastward of Gamba, and flows past Nikky, the capital of Berghoo. Its bed is also very rocky. To the southward of Kiama the stream during the dry season is very narrow, but with a strong current; during the rainy season, however, it brings down a vast body of water. A short distance above Rakkah, this river is joined by a stream called the Juffie, which flows from the S.W. and the northern front of the Kong chain of hills. The Oli is called by the travelling Moors, Doodirba, and the Moussa, Kadarko. Kiama, sometimes reckoned the capital of Berghoo, or Killingha, contains 30,000 inhabitants; but Nikky is a still larger and more important commercial city. The land throughout all this district of Africa is very fertile, generally well cultivated, the population extensive, and the large towns very numerous and very populous.

THE COUNTRY FROM BADAGRY TO KATUNGAH.

Lander and Clapperton inform us, that having landed through a terrible surf near Badagry, they, soon after leaving the beach, came to the river Formosa, one mile broad, which they crossed, and then came to the town mentioned. The river here mentioned is not the river Formosa, but a branch from that river and the Lagos River, which runs along the coast at a very short distance from the sea, all the way to the Rio Volta. From Badagry, 6° 26′ N. lat. and 2° 43′ 30″ E. long., they proceeded on their route to Katungah. After passing Bidge, twenty miles from the coast, they crossed a river, which Clapperton says was a quarter of a mile broad, and full of low swampy islands and floating reeds. Lander says, that they were an hour and a half in crossing it in a canoe, owing, as it would appear, to the rapidity of the current, and that the other canoes carrying the rest of the party were equally long in effecting their passage. This stream is the Lagos River, called the Komashar, in its upper and its early course. Proceeding northward, they came to Afoora, fifty-five geographical miles from the coast in a direct line ; before reaching it, they crossed the river Akkeni, which with other streams in that quarter, flow N.W. (S.E.) to join a larger river which falls into the Lagos River. The Akkeni is full of sunken rocks. The town called Assouda beyond it contains 10,000 inhabitants; and the town of Duffoo south of it from 10,000 to 12,000. Beyond Afoora, says Clapperton, the country was beautiful, and the valleys filled with streams of water, all running from the N.W. At the town of Choco, more to the north, and about eighty-five geographical miles in a direct line from Badagry, they came to the southern base of the range of hills, generally called the Kong range, rising 2,500 feet above the level of the land to the south, and extending in breadth about seventy-five miles to the north, and running from W.N.W. to E.S.E., through Jaboo and Benin. These mountains are composed of granite; the country amongst them is exceedingly picturesque, fruitful, populous, well cultivated, and studded with towns and villages. As the travellers advanced towards the northern summits, the scenery became more grand and magnificent. Approaching the populous town of Choki, about 150 miles in a direct line from the sea, they travelled through a tremendous pass, the country northward rising hill above hill, and rock above rock, in proud magnificence, until they came to Choki, situated on the very summit of the highest ridge. There the air was cool, the atmosphere clear, and the prospect around most magnificent. From the sea-coast to the town of Choco, the land rises regularly and gently to the base of the Kong range. Entering this range, and in passing through it, the scenery is everywhere very grand. In some places the immense and lofty granite masses appear in rude and fearful positions, as if they had been torn asunder by some terrible convulsion of nature. The verdure amongst these ranges is unfading, and the trees in many places of stupendous magnitude. Choki was stated to be only one days' journey on horseback, NN.W. from the country of Berghoo; and Clapperton was told by the chief of Choki, that the mountains through which they were travelling passed through Ghunjah, thirty-five days' journey distant W.N.W.; and that they continue to the eastward, or E.S.E. through Yarribah and Benin. From the town of Layboo, near the parallel of 9°, Berghoo was represented to be only one day's journey distant; and from Namah, a walled town, a little more to the north, the capital of the country of Berghoo, was stated to be only one day's journey distant. Beyond Namah, at the distance of three quarters of an hour of travel, they crossed a stream called Juffie, which runs into the Kowara opposite Nyffe. The Juffie must be a branch of the Moussa, and probably joins that stream near Rakkah. Beyond Tschou, and one hour's travel from Anchoran, they crossed a stream which flowed into the Kowara, there only three days' journey distant. Katungah, the capital of Yarribah, is situated a little to the eastward of this stream, in N. Lat. 8° 59′, and in E. Long., from corrected notices, 4° 41′. This capital stands in a fine valley, at the base of a high range of granite-hills, which form its boundary wall on the east, while westward the valley stretches out as far as the eye can reach. Katungah is a place of considerable importance, but not so much now as it formerly was, yet it contains a large population. The walls of the town are about fifteen miles in circumference: the diameter of the city one way being six miles, and the other four miles. Cotton is abundant, and much cloth is here manufactured from it. Every evening there are seven different markets held in the town. The king of Yarribah told Clapperton that the Moussa, which was only three days' journey distant, came from the N. W.*

DELTA OF THE NIGER—CAMEROONS, &c.

The Delta of the Niger next requires our attention. The researches of Bosman and other old navigators, and latterly the voyages of Lander, Laird, &c., place this important portion of Africa with sufficient accuracy before us; and it is remarkable how the latest and most accurate of these confirm the accounts given by the old Dutch navigator, and others, who sixty years ago traded to that quarter. To commence with the Bight of Benin. Here we have first the great river Formosa, so named on account of the exceedingly beautiful scenery upon its banks. At its mouth it is nearly four British miles broad, with two bars; the outer of hard sand; the inner of mud, on which there are thirteen and fourteen feet water. Inwards it deepens to five or six fathoms, with, at all times, a considerable

---

* Authorities for these sections:—Clapperton, Lander, Dupuis, Sheeref Inhammed, Sultan Bello, Oldfield, and various native travellers.

current, but during the rains, to the velocity of five or six knots per hour.   About ten miles from its mouth, a navigable branch flows off to the westward, through what is called the Cradoo Lake to the Lagos, running within a short distance of the sea; in fact, separated only by a sand-bank, thrown up by the waves, which beat most violently on that part of the coast. About twenty miles upwards, it is joined by the Gatto Creek, a tributary, says Robertson, to the Formosa, and formed probably by some mountain streams.   About twenty miles from the Formosa, and at the head of this creek, and to which the tide extends, is situated the village of Gatto, or Agatton, and the kind of Port of Benin, or rather of the capital of Benin, called Oedo by the old Portuguese navigators, situated inland about ten or fifteen miles NN. E.   The course of the Formosa, upwards to the point where the Niger divides into branches, is nearly east to west.   " It meanders," says Robertson, p. 297, " through a fine, fertile, and numerously peopled country."

Robertson states, that at Lagos he met five Arab travellers, who, from the account which they gave him of themselves, must have been from Fezzan, and who told him they came from Lake Issebee, the point where the water separated into three streams, in five days; but " that the water," to use their own phrase, " run fast then," being in August.   In this we recognise the lake of Lander above Eboe, a large lake, when the river is in full flood, but when it subsides several feet, a bank in the middle rises above the water and forms an island. Where the Rio de Formosa branches off above Eboe,* the branch, according to Laird, (see vol. i. p. 112,) is from ten feet to six fathoms deep and 800 yards wide, with a strong current.   Lander pointedly mentions this branch, (vol. iii.

* The comparative distances between Eboe and the mouth of the Nun, and to Benin, is given by Laird, vol. i. p. 101, thus: to Benin, four days; to Brass or mouth of the Nun, seven days; others four days to the Nun, and seven from it.

Captain Beecroft surveyed the branch from the mouth of the Nun to the junction of the Shadda, and has made an excellent chart thereof.   He was sent by his employer last year to the Formosa, in order to take the preparatory steps for a mercantile expedition, to go up it into the interior this season, and in which he is at this time engaged.   In the mouth of the Formosa, he in July last writes, " this is a princely river compared to the Brass, (Nun) and I have no doubt is the great navigable outlet of the Niger."

p. 171,) exclusive of the branch at Kirree.   Oldfield, (vol. ii. p. 142,) places the point of the separation of this branch about one hour's navigation above the separation of the Bonny branch.   The next Great Benin branch, or the Rio dos Forcados, is below Eggaboo, lat. 5° 26′, and is from 600 to 700 yards wide, (*Laird*, vol. i. p. 89,) and six, seven, and eight fathoms deep, having a stronger current and being deeper than the Nun.   Oldfield, Beecroft, and Lander specifically mention this branch.*   Southward of the mouth of the

---

* But on these important points it is considered proper to give the statements of the different writers, in their own words.

" At seven A. M. we saw a small river enter the Niger from the eastward, the banks of which, as well as those of the Niger, were elevated and fertile.   Shortly after we observed a branch of the river running off to the westward, about the same size as that from the eastward.   On the right bank of this river, close also to the bank of the Niger, we observed a large market, which I was informed is Kirree; and that the river, flowing to the westward past it, runs to Benin.   A great number of canoes were lying near the bank."—*Lander*, vol. iii. p. 132.

" We soon after passed Kirree, and a fine branch of a river, supposed to run from Benin, the first reach of it lying about south-west half west.   At half-past four P.M. we passed another branch running to the north-east, which is said to lead to Fundah."—*Oldfield*, vol. ii. p. 137.

We got under weigh at six P.M., and proceeded on our course by moonlight until past eight, when it became thick and foggy, and we anchored in two fathoms water.   Between six and seven we passed a branch of a river leading to Benin.   Started next morning at six A.M., and at half-past nine came to anchor off Eboe."—*Oldfield*, p. 242.

" We now found ourselves on an immense body of water, like a lake, having gone a little out of the road, and at the mouth of a very considerable river, flowing to the westward, it being an important branch of the Niger; another branch also ran from hence to the south-east, while our course was in a south-westerly direction on the main body; the whole forming, in fact, three rivers of considerable magnitude.   The banks were all low and swampy, and completely covered with palm-trees."

" An hour or two after this, or about mid-day, one of the Eboe men in our canoe exclaimed, ' There is my country !' pointing to a clump of very high trees, which was yet at some distance before us; and, after passing a low fertile island, we quickly came to it."—*Lander*, vol. iii. p. 171.

" At eight o'clock in the evening of the 9th of November we left Eboe, and by the light of a splendid moon, threaded our way through a very intricate navigation until two o'clock in the morning of the 10th; when, being in very shoal water, we came to anchor about fifteen miles from the town.   This was the widest part of the river that we had yet seen; its breadth cannot be less than 3000 yards; and here the river throws off its great branches, the Benin and Bonny (what I presume to be these rivers).   We crossed the Benin branch, and

Formosa we have the Rio dos Escravos, called also the Brody, up which slave-trading ships penetrate to the town of Warree. Next to this is the mouth of the Rio dos Forcados, which has an island in its mouth, between which and the northern bank is two British miles, but only eight feet water. Next, and third, is the Dodo; and fourthly, a little to the westward of Cape Formosa, we have several unnamed branches.* Eastward of Cape Formosa we have the Nun branch, down which Lander first descended, and up which Laird and Oldfield ascended, and down which they afterwards descended. It is much smaller than the Formosa, and throws off such a number of branches that it becomes so narrow near the sea as to be navigable for only small vessels, having in several places only eight or nine feet water, and the breadth, in Louis Creek, from thirty to forty yards. Going eastward, there are five different outlets betwixt the Nun and the great estuary of the New Calabar and Bonny rivers, which estuary is eleven miles broad, very deep, and navigable for ships of any tonnage. The course of the New Calabar is from the N.W., and that of the Bonny from the N. E. At twenty miles from the sea, the New Calabar is six fathoms deep. The Bonny River divides, and throws off a considerable branch, the Andonny, or St. Anthony's River, and which enters the sea considerably to the eastward, thus forming an island of considerable dimensions. The current, out of the estuary of the Bonny and New Calabar River, is strong and rapid, discharging a vast volume of water into the sea. The rush of water, says Sir George Collier, in his Report to Government, that issues from the outlet in question, is so great and powerful, that it can only proceed from its being one of the embouchures of a great river. Twenty rivers of great magnitude enter the sea through this delta, all derived from the Niger; and such is the volume of fresh water which they pour into the sea, that it is stated, *vessels are found*

found it about 800 yards wide, with a depth varying from ten feet to six fathoms. The Bonny branch appeared to run out in a SS.E. direction; but as we were some distance from it, I cannot speak from personal knowledge of its size and depth."—*Laird*, vol. i. p. 111.

* The branch which flows off from the Nun, and which unquestionably forms all these rivers, the Dodo included, is, according to Oldfield, at the point of separation, 500 yards broad.

to be sailing hours together in fresh water, without the smallest mixture of the water of the ocean, even to the distance of twenty-five miles from Cape Formosa.

Eastward of Andonny River we come, first, to the estuary of Old Calabar River, and next, to the estuary of the Rio del Rey River. The former is twelve miles broad, and is, in fact, in some measure, an arm of the sea, which penetrates and widens upwards to the distance of sixty miles to the north. It is formed by the waters of Cross River, a branch of the Niger, and by Old Calabar River. In many maps Cross River is laid down as entering into the inlet from the N.E., and the Old Calabar river a little more to the south from the same quarter. The name Cross River is of itself a proof that it comes from the Niger. Robertson, who knew that coast well, asserts that it did; the late French maps and charts, constructed for the use of the French navy, lay it down in a similar manner; and these maps also lay down the tributary to Old Calabar River, as descending directly from the north, which, considering every thing, especially the very high lands to the north-westward, is extremely probable. Next, as regards Cross River, its direction and connexion with the Niger is settled by the account transmitted by Mr. Colthurst, a traveller who, a few years ago (1832), set out to explore the interior from this point, and who engaged canoes from Duke Ephraim, or rather the other engaged canoes and assistants for him, which were to carry him to Eboe and the Niger by means of the Cross River. No doubt therefore can any longer remain on this point. Mr. Colthurst unfortunately died at the capital of Duke Ephraim's country, about sixteen miles up the Old Calabar or Bongo, before he had entered upon his journey for the-interior. In his communication to the Royal Geographical Society in England, he pointedly states, that by means of the Cross River, the people about the Old Calabar inlet traded with the Niger and Eboe. The Old Calabar River does not belong to the Niger, but comes from the east and south-east. A short distance by land from it, over a hilly country, brings the traveller to Fundah. Cross River he also pointedly states communicates with the Niger.

Captain Cummins of Liverpool, who traded to these parts

during the space of fifteen years, has lately given the writer of this some valuable information regarding Old Calabar and Cross Rivers, which has been adopted in the construction of the map of those parts.   Where he quitted the Old Calabar it was one-third of a mile broad, and six fathoms deep, but the natives told him that its course from the eastward was not long, and this also is his own opinion, as there was no trade on it except for red wood.   It can have no communication with the Cameroons, because the natives around its banks, who wish to go to Cameroons, descend and proceed by the Old Calabar.   The tide rises seven feet in ordinary tides at Duke's Town, and nine feet in spring tides.   Its rise in Cross River is about the same.   He had been through the whole of the creek which runs into Cross River, and found it one quarter of a mile broad and three fathoms deep.   He had also.been in Cross River to about the parallel of 6°, with a ship of 450 tons.   The rush of water on the turn of the tide is exceedingly strong.   Below Acricock, a creek or branch enters from the west, which communicates with Egbo-shary, a great oil country, and to which canoes and traders from the Bonny resort.   At Acricock the river is 400 yards wide. Captain Cummins stated that his mate went up it in a canoe paddled actively by negroes, during the space of three days and three nights; but unfortunately, Captain Cummins cannot remember the direction or bearing which was taken; but Captain Oldfield subsequently gave the information which enabled me to place it correctly on the map.   The country to which the mate went was called Botseraen, and the people are described as a superior race.   The Bonny and Old Calabar traders meet in the Egboshary markets, and Bonny and Old Calabar canoes and traders are found in the markets of Eboe, Iddah, &c.; complete proofs that all these places are connected by water communication.   Captain Cummins saw no mountains at the highest point to which he ascended the Old Calabar.   The land there around it appeared to be of the same elevation as that about the Mersey, near Liverpool.

Robertson, who was well acquainted with the western coasts of Africa and the Bights of Benin and Biafra, and who had collected many facts regarding places in the interior, states, p. 312, that Acricock bounds the kingdom of Qua to the north; that

Acricock lies in the interior of Bannee, or Bonny, where the traders of Bannee and Calabar resort for oil, &c., (p. 310,) and at p. 314 adds, that " salt for the interior was sent from Old Calabar across what the natives called the middle river, which is in fact a creek to the eastern branch of the Bannee River, where it finds its way into the country to the westward." Rorob, a country celebrated for oil, he places N.E. from Old Calabar, and adds, p. 312, that the Bongo (Old Calabar) River in the interior, is interrupted by cataracts.

Mr. Oldfield communicates the important facts that a short distance, five miles above Acricock, there is a reach called Beaufort reach, at which the stream is seven fathoms deep, and that distant mountains, seen from thence to the N.E., run from N. to S. in the direction of the Qua mountain ; that some miles further up the river, a branch comes from the westward; the chief stream, according to the natives, coming from the north-westward, navigable and navigated for several days' journey further.

As regards the great river Niger, and the branches into which it divides on approaching the alluvial country, Laird expressly tells us that the great flow of water from the parent stem is to the westward ; that to that quarter all the large branches run, while those which flow to the eastward are all of less magnitude. The direction of the current, however, in these streams or branches, shows the source from whence they come. Oldfield, in going from the anchorage at the mouth of the Nun to Brass Town, tells us that he went eastward on the creek and branches " with the current in their favour, at the rate of three and a half miles per hour."

Concerning the course of the river through the Kong Chain, Lander (vol. iii.) gives us a few particulars worthy of notice. Below Attah the hills on the N.W. side appeared to decrease in height; those on the eastern side to change their course to the S.E. ; and soon afterwards, and above Damuggoo, the banks, especially on the south side, become low and swampy. Damuggoo market is frequented by people and canoes from Bonny, Calabar, Brass and Benin (p. 91.) The natives of Abasacco consider the Bonny branch the largest. Above Damuggoo a few miles, Lander saw a branch running off to the S.E. The N.W.

side of the river there was low, and covered with jungle; the
S.E. bank was rather higher (p. 95). Damuggoo was stated to
be eight days from the sea, (p. 98,) and also that the anchorage
of ships in Bonny River was only four or five days' journey (by
water,) from Damuggoo, (p. 100.) October 31st he found the
Niger receding rapidly; within two days fallen two feet (p. 112.)
Might reach Bonny from Damuggoo, without touching at the
chief of a great country, one day's journey down to his territories. This must be Eboe and King Obie, and the communication must take place by means of the branch about to be
mentioned. A little above Kirree, saw a river enter the Niger
from the eastward; shortly after, saw a branch running off to
the westward, about the same size, and which runs to Benin
(p. 132). The river from the eastward, is that which Laird says
is about 400 yards wide, and which Oldfield was told led to
Fundah, although he frankly acknowledges he does not believe
this to be the case, but that it runs off S.E. to Old Calabar, as
can scarcely fail to be the fact.

With regard to the river Adoo or Edoe, which the same traveller states seems to run into the Niger, above Damuggoo,
from the NN.E., such can hardly be the case, because the
Niger itself descends in that direction. At this point, Allen
lays it down, coming in at right angles, or from N.W. by W.
Oldfield is of opinion, (formed from the information given him
by his servant Lily, who was a native of the country through
which the river runs, and from which it would appear that it
takes its name) that from its point of junction with, or rather
its separation from, the Niger, it soon turns and runs W.S.W.,
and flows to the sea towards Lagos or Whydah. He grounds
this opinion on the information which he received regarding the
traffic by it, which consisted of European goods, rum, &c.,
brought from the coast in ten days. On looking into Robertson's Notes, he gives the country of Adoo as lying between
Yarribah and Benin; that is, above Benin, as Oldfield was told
it did, and to the eastward of Dahomey; and in fact Robertson
in his map seems to consider Adoo and Benin as the same.
According to the Encyclopædia Britannica, 3d ed. (Article
Guinea), the first Portuguese, &c., discoverers of Africa, gave
the name of Oedo to the capital of Great Benin, situated, as

they stated, sixty miles inland. Robertson also, p. 297, states that the river of Oedo and Lagos have the same communication with the interior; and residents at Lagos stated that the latter river came from a great lake (river) in Haoussa. It appears, then, that the country of Benin and Adoo, or Oedo, or Edoo, is the same, and that the river Adoo, mentioned by Oldfield, Allen, and Beecroft, is the river of that country, and that it flows through it from NN.E. to W.S.W. The banks of the Niger at the point of separation, are known to be low and marshy; consequently no physical difficulty occurs, and it is much more probable that this stream flows in the direction mentioned, than that it comes in from the NN.E. The nature of the trade by it, and the time occupied in communicating by the river with the coast, settles the point, it is conceived, in .a decided manner. In Dupuis' map, he has in this part of Africa a river passing westward near Quassie, and coming into lake Cradoo in the direction alluded to, and to the westward of Benin. His map seems to have been taken from old Portuguese narratives and sketches, which, though rough, give after all, not incorrectly, the general outlines of these rivers and places. At page 55 he pointedly states of this delta and the rivers in it, "it is admitted that there are channels which intersect all the Warree rivers at right angles, running within the compass of one or two days from the sea-shore, out of the Formosa river into the Forcados, Dodo, Nun, St. Nicholas, Bartholomew, Calabar, Bonny, &c."

Immediately adjoining the estuary of Old Calabar River, is the Rio del Rey. This outlet is ten miles broad; and soon afterwards, as the interior is approached, it narrows, and as the mountains are entered, the stream is found not only to become much contracted, but to descend over cataracts and rapids, all of which indicate that its course is not of great length. Such were the accounts given by Nicholls, who went to explore the interior from this point, but who perished in the attempt, after having ascended this river to some distance. Betwixt this river and Old Cameroons to the southward, is the exceeding high land of Bimbia, or Cameroons, rising in a mountain almost close to the sea, to the height of 13,000 to 14,000 feet, and very often covered with snow. It is most certainly, "The

Chariot of the Gods " described by Hanno, which he states was opposite to Carthage. It is clearly an extinct volcano now, but in his days was probably in full activity, and hence he gave it the name, " The Chariot of the Gods." It is also the termination to the westward of Ptolemy's Mount Arualtes. Beyond are seen peaks certainly still higher, because, seen from the sea, the most distant appears to be of equal height with the one nearest the sea. To the N. and NN.W. of the Elrei River, is the high land of Rumby; and beyond the river the mountains of Qua, in peaks which seem almost to rival the other.

The appearance of the great delta of the Niger marks clearly to the eye of the observer the nature and means of its formation. Below Damuggoo the alluvial country commences. All the land from a point to the southward of that place, has unquestionably been formed since the deluge, by the mud and sand, &c., brought down by the great rivers from the interior. The very strong current which in the ocean sets from the south, along the coast of Africa, from the equinoctial northwards, would necessarily meet; first, the estuaries of the Rio del Rey, Old Calabar and Cross rivers, and which rivers, pressed from the south, would throw back part of the mud which they brought down first, northward and north westward. This again would be met by the great volume of the water of the Niger, issuing from the Kong mountains, which would throw the mud and sand of the whole back in a circular form, yearly increasing, and narrowing the space forming the great inlet of the sea at Old Calabar, as we now see it. The vast sediment brought down by the Niger, the Shadda, &c., would also extend by degrees southward and westward, and form the whole delta of the Niger in a manner the most natural, and in the direction and situation which we now find it. Met in its progress southwards from the Kong chain, the stream of the Niger would, by the greater force of the ocean current, which came from the southward as before mentioned, than that which came in the sea from the Gold Coast to the west, naturally throw the greatest flow of the waters to the westward: consequently all the greatest branches or outlets of the Niger would flow in that direction, as we find them, and as Mr. Laird expressly tells us is the fact. The two opposing ocean currents would, with the mud brought down by the vast river Niger, place the delta and the alluvial land in these parts, exactly as we find them. The yearly increase of this delta must be very considerable, and in the course of 4,000 years there is ample time given for the formation of the whole. Within the memory of African traders now living, a bank consisting of mud and sand at the mouth of the Bonny river, formerly only dry at low water, is now firm land, and excellent pasture for cattle. This shows how rapidly the land gains, and must gain on the sea in that quarter. Hence the appearance of this coast must have been very different in the days of Hanno, the celebrated Carthaginian navigator, who visited it, (for it was this point he certainly did visit, and at this point where he turned back in sight of the Chariot of the Gods, and nearly opposite to Carthage, as he pointedly states,) to that which it now bears. The appearance also of this delta must, 800 years ago, have been very different to the early Arabian conquerors, to that which it now bears, and hence the discrepancy which appears in their accounts, and the accounts of modern navigators, concerning it and the rivers and lakes therein. That the great eastern and western arms or branches of the Niger should in early times have formed an island, and that in this island there should have been found a lake, as Hanno says there was, is extremely probable. That lake, moreover, would necessarily be gradually lessened and filled up, till it became like that one which Lander found covered during the inundation, at the separation of the great branches of the river.

Immediately adjoining the high land in question, and to the south, is the Old Cameroons, or Jamoor river, in lat. 3° 40'. This river is about two miles broad, and navigable for vessels drawing eighteen feet water. About 3° 20' lat. we have the estuary of the Cameroons and Malemba rivers. The extreme breadth is twelve miles, and it communicates with Old Cameroons by means of Bimbia Creek. In an old map of Africa, I find the course of this river laid down to the distance, and on the bearings, it has been placed, and also the other three rivers adjoining are placed according to the same authority.

The Jamoor, or Old Cameroons river, is clearly only a branch of the Cameroons. The course of the latter river, there is every reason to believe, is not very long, and has probably been extended too far into the interior, in the map accompanying this work. This opinion is grounded upon the information which has lately been received from traders who have frequented it, who generally state their opinion that it cannot have a very long course, because there is little or no trading intercourse or articles with the population on its banks upwards ; a proof not only that its course does not extend very far, but also that it comes from a rugged and mountainous country. The Malemba River they describe as by far the largest, and in proof that it has the longest course, there is a very considerable trade by it with countries in the interior. Its course is from the S.E. or S.E. by E., while that of the Cameroons is from the N.E., or N.E. by E. Around the mouths of these rivers the land is low and marshy ; in fact, a delta resembling the delta round the mouths of the Niger, though by no means equal to the latter in extent. This delta, or alluvial land, round the mouth of the Malemba and the Cameroons, has been formed in the same manner as the delta, of the Niger, and produced from the same acting cause namely, the strong current setting in from the SS.W., which in the lapse of ages has extended westward the alluvial deposits, and driven, as it were, the great outlet of these rivers against the base of the volcanic peaks of Bimbia, or the Cameroons, " The Chariot of the Gods" of Hanno, and the Arualtes of Ptolemy. The courses of all the rivers in this portion of Africa, that is, from the high land of Cameroons to the Nazareth, is in my opinion extended one degree too far to the eastward.

Southward of this river the coast rises into a table land extremely beautiful and healthy. Passing Cape Clara in 1º 10′ N. lat., we have Moohnda, or Danger River, a deep and powerful stream, navigable for vessels of any burden. The island of Corisco, or Thunder, is situated in its mouth, which renders the passages on each side narrow, and, from the strong current and tides, rather dangerous ; but when once in, it is a very safe anchorage. Its banks abound with the finest timber, fit for ship-building and other useful purposes. Forty miles south, along a low swampy coast, in fact, almost a

morass, the entrance to the Rio de Gaboon is found, in N. lat.
0° 30'. Its extreme breadth is thirty miles, but a short distance
inwards it contracts to twelve miles. Forty-five miles from the
sea the river separates into two branches, one flowing from the
N.E. and the other coming from the S.E. The S.E. branch
is formed by the union of a number of small streams, at about
sixty miles inwards from its entrance. The northern branch
stretches N.E., in a deep stream, until, as the natives say, it
comes from the Moohnda, which flows from the same direction.
While this account is by no means improbable, still we are now
so well acquainted with what native Africans mean by their
information regarding rivers coming from the same sources, or
from one stream, that these rivers may after all be different
streams flowing into the same estuary. The source of the
Moohnda is represented to be forty-eight days' journey distant
from the mouth of the river, which, at a reasonable computation for each day's journey, will place its sources in about
14° 15' E. long., and about 2° N. lat. Near its sources, or
rather around them, is situated the countries of Paamway and
Sheybee. On their northern frontier is the kingdom of Key-
bee, through which the river Wole flows to the eastward.
This river is described by the people of these parts as the
largest river that they know, and they add that it runs to an
immense distance,—to India, and farther, in the usual African
mode of expression; and that the Moohnda, and all the rivers
in that quarter of Africa, proceed from the Wole. To the
south of the Rio de Gaboon, is a large river called by the
natives Oggawai, which forms all the rivers which enter the
sea in the neighbourhood of Cape Lopez. The distances from
the Gaboon to the sources of this river, in about an E.N.E.
direction, is thirty-nine days' journey by land and by water, and
which, by a reasonable computation, will place the same in
nearly the same meridian as the sources of the Gaboon. The
natives state that the Oggawai is a broader and deeper river,
and that it has a great number of turnings and windings in its
upward course. Near the sources of this river on the east, is
the negro kingdom of Okandee, described as the greatest state
known in these parts. The capital is very clean, and the law
forbids any native to be sold as a slave. Eastward from this

state the river Wole and its tributaries are found flowing to the eastward, which river Wole we shall by and by find, is one of the greatest northern branches of the great river Zaire, or Congo.   The high lands which give birth to these rivers will be found to run south from the Mount Arualtes of Ptolemy, or the great ridge which stretches eastward from Cameroons, southwards, or a little to the eastward of south, to that rocky ridge through which, according to Tuckey, the Zaire forces its passage.   From the Cameroons to the Moohnda, is a distance of 200 geographical miles, throughout which space the shore is bold and abrupt, and where there neither are nor can be any rivers.   There is therefore abundance of room in the space alluded to, for the formation of all the rivers mentioned ; and considering every point, the information which has been gleaned regarding these rivers and their different courses, not only do not depict any thing that is geographically | improbable, but every thing that is geographically correct.   Moreover, it will be a remarkable feature in African geography, that in this part of the west coast of Africa, we have almost the exact counterpart of the courses of the rivers which are found in the farthest parts of western Africa, where we find the Rio Grande, the Gambia, &c , flowing westward, and the Joliba, like the Wole, flowing to the eastward.*

THE LOWER NIGER, AND THE SHADDA, OR SHADERBAH.†

Turning to the northward and the interior, it is first necessary to observe, as regards the great delta of the Niger, that it is extremely unhealthy.   The whole, to a vast extent, is nearly flooded during the inundation, to a distance of from forty to fifty miles up the branches of the river.   The tide runs full fifty miles up the Nun, which shows how level the surrounding country must be.   The coasts of the sea and the banks of the rivers are thickly covered with mangroves ; and the whole space being thinly inhabited, and where inhabited, occupied by the most idle, the most ignorant, and the most

* Authorities for these sections of the work :—Bowditch, Robertson, African Pilot, Bosman, Laird, Lander, Oldfield, and various British, French, and Portuguese navigators, also Nicholls, Colthurst, and Sir George Collier.

† In several manuscripts by Moors it is written simply " Shad," or " Shadda."

profligate of all the population of Africa, the country consequently remains uncleared, uncultivated, and not drained,
and therefore becomes one nest of pestilence and disease.
Beyond the Rio de Formosa, however, to the north, and at a
short distance above the separation of the branches of the
river, the country from the former rises gently and uniformly
all the way to the Kong range, and is dry, the soil most excellent, and the country free from the malaria generated in the
delta. Were it not for the malaria, proceeding from the causes
mentioned, and the sickness which it occasions, the Rio de
Formosa, says Bosman, "is a very desirable place of trade by
reason of the pleasantness of the rivers and adjacent country,
which is very even ground without hills, and yet rises by
gentle degrees, affording the most agreeable prospects in the
world, and is yet improved by the multitude of trees which
stand so regular as if they were designedly planted in that
order." Further, as regards the country about the capital
itself, he adds, "the circumjacent country is as pleasant as
could be wished, where no interposing hill or wood rudely
intercepts the agreeable prospect of thousands of charming
trees, which by their wide-spreading branches, full of leaves,
seem to invite mankind to repose under their shade."

The journeys of Laird, Lander, Oldfield, &c. have put us in
possession of accurate information regarding the course and
magnitude of the Niger in its lower course, and also of the
junction of its last and its greatest tributary—the Shadda.
About ninety miles above Eboe the river is found for the
space of upwards of thirty-five miles, some distance below the
influx of the Shadda, flowing through the range, or rather
ridge of mountains generally designated Kong, which rise like
a wall on each hand close to the river to the height of 2000
to 3000 feet; the chasm or opening appearing as if it had
been burst asunder by some great convulsion of nature, in
order to afford a passage to the river. Upwards from Eboe,
the river is in one stream studded with islands, confined even
during the highest flood within its banks, and from a mile and
half to two miles broad; the current, five or six knots per
hour, and the depth from five to twelve fathoms. What an
immense body of water must here flow downwards! Clothed

with torrid vegetation, the granite hills seen from the bosom of this mighty stream, present views at once sublime and beautiful. At 120 miles above Eboe the Niger receives from the east the powerful tributary named the Shadda, or Shaderbah. This river was explored above its junction,* to the distance only of 104 miles, when want of provisions, and the inhospitable and dreary appearance of the country, obliged Oldfield to turn back. The course of the river is therefore no further certainly or accurately known, but its magnitude shows that the source must be at a considerable distance. Oldfield and Captain Allen were told the customary negro stories, that this river came from the Lake Shad, and that they could reach Bornou by water in ten or twelve days. That they could reach the territory of Bornou in that time, and which was really all that their negro informants meant, is certain, because we find that at Dogbah, where they turned back, they were within a few days' journey of the Bornou territory, the messenger whom they had despatched to Domah, about two days' journey distant, having been turned back by some of the king of Bornou's troops, which sovereign was then at war with the king of Domah.

Captain Oldfield plainly tells us, that at the point where they turned back they could obtain no information, such as could enable them to form any certain opinion as to the source and the upward course of this river; but from all appearances his opinion is, that it rises amongst the hills to the S.E. He also tells us, that the range of hills which rose from the Niger at the junction of the rivers, and bent east at about eight miles from the Shadda on its south side, gradually sunk and disappeared into a plain about forty miles upwards from the junction. In order to form, therefore, some accurate idea of the source and the course of this stream above Dogbah, we must have recourse to different data and information, scanty as that is. The first is the magnitude of the river itself; and the second is the appearance and nature of the country in this portion of Africa. Whoever inspects the map will perceive that there is abundance of room for the formation of such a river as the Shadda in these parts is found to be, together with all the rivers which we know of in the adjoining portions

* Junction in lat. N. 7° 55', and long. E. 6° 55'.

of Southern and of Central Africa. From the N. and the
N.E. where there is a very large space of country, and all very
mountainous and abounding in water,* many streams undoubtedly flow from the southern side to join the Shadda, as
we find them flowing from the western face of the mountains
to form the Coodonia, &c.

Let us look a little more closely at this matter. Oldfield,
vol. i. p. 445, at Dogbah says, " I was in hopes of reaching
Beeshle and Jacoba, places of great trade, eight or ten days up
the river," &c. The distance here given would be the space
up the Shadda so far, and then by the Sharra to Jacoba, (the
scale here adverted to is that which has been taken for the
delineation of the Sharra on the accompanying map) beyond
which, on the north, is the country of Beeshle. Lander,
vol. ii. p. 126, heard that by means of the Sharra " canoes
could be paddled to the Niger at any season of the year," from
lake Shad. Lieutenant Allen, in the article which he inserted
in the Journal of the Royal Geographical Society, 1838,
p. 15, states thus : " I was myself informed at Dogbah on the
Shadda, that Jacoba was *seven* days higher up the river, and
that the city of Kouka in Bornou is said to be only six days for
canoes, *above* Jacoba, on the *same river*." Lander, vol. iii.
p. 109, says he was told by a Nouffie man at Damuggoo, that
Jacoba and Bornou being at peace, " a person can travel from
Jacoba to Bornou by land, in *seventeen* days, but that to travel
by water up the Shadda to Kuku would be a journey of
nineteen days." These extracts will strongly show the utter
recklessness and carelessness with which accounts regarding
places and countries in Africa are sought, and given and
received, and the almost inextricable confusion which such
recklessness and carelessness create, and are calculated to
create, regarding subjects and matters otherwise obvious and
plain. The errors and contradictions above stated and quoted
are obvious, namely, that the Sharra and the Shadda are taken
as the same river, and that the asserted water communication
between Jacoba and Kouka (Bornou), is like other asserted
African water communications, which have been heard of, con-

* See Leo Africanus—his great river bounded by Temian on the south, which
is clearly the Shadda.

sidered, and explained, to be neither more nor less than the probable near approach of the sources or branches of the Sharra and the Yeou to each other. Whoever looks at the map will readily perceive this. The distance given by Lander for the land journey is not far from being correct, but if travelled along by the rivers alluded to, it would take two or three days more. Moreover, it may be here remarked, that Lander's account that at Dunrora he saw to the east a very high hill, at the foot of which, and evidently by the side thereof, stood, as he was told, the city of Jacoba, a mile or two from the Shar, or Sharra, is an account which may embrace a greater space than may be generally taken and supposed. The hill alluded to might be the high peak of a range, the eastern base of which and Jacoba, and consequently the Sharra, may be still farther to the east than has been represented, and which it is more than probable is actually the case.

The magnitude of the Shadda itself will enable us, when that is contrasted with the magnitude of other rivers, to ascertain with considerable accuracy the probable length of its course. Laird tells us, that in April the Shadda, at its junction with the Niger, was three quarters of a mile wide, two fathoms deep, and the current from two to three miles per hour. On the 23d of June, after it had begun to rise, the width at the same place was a mile and a half, but broken by sand banks and islands into three channels. Oldfield informs us, that the width at the junction during the height of the flood, in August, was half a mile, the depth from one to three fathoms, and the current two to three knots per hour; but the account given by Laird of the magnitude of the stream in the dry season, is that on which the comparison to be made is founded. According to De Caillé, the main branch of the Niger at Cabra was three quarters of a mile wide, the depth twelve feet or more, and though the current was not quite so strong, about one and a half to two miles per hour, yet the addition of the waters of the deep, though narrow, N.E. branch of the Niger, would bring the body of water in both streams, at the points mentioned, to be nearly equal, though giving a considerable preponderance to the Shadda, in the quantity of water discharged at the points alluded to, nearly treble in fact, taking the current of the Niger at a mile and a half, and the current of the Shadda at two miles and a half per hour.* To Timbuctoo, the course of the Niger on its general bearings along its bed, cannot be more than 1,000 geographical miles. In its upper course, it runs through countries as near as possible the same as those countries we may reasonably suppose are through which the Shadda runs; and although the Shadda in its course can hardly receive more tributaries than the Niger is known to receive in its course above Timbuctoo, yet it can scarcely be supposed that it receives fewer, or, in other words, smaller supplies of water; for although the tributary streams which join the Shadda in its upper course may not be so long in their courses as some of those which join the Niger, yet it may fairly be presumed that they are equally, if not more numerous, and from the general nature of the country, even stronger, compared to their length of course, than some of the others.

Considering these facts, and others still to be adduced, there cannot remain a doubt that the Bahr Kulla of Rennel, laid down by him in about 9° N. lat., and from 18° to 20° E. long., and the Shadda, or rather the Shaderbah, are one and the same river. Various authorities state that Africa, in these parts, is very populous, and abounds with rivers, as must naturally be the case when that part is, we may say, in the . midst of those mountainous ranges which give birth to so many rivers, which flow in different directions and to other quarters. Browne states, that the rivers which flowed to the westward and south-westward of Darfur, in the places beyond the copper mines, all run, as nearly as he could learn, westward. We shall soon see their termination; and the Bahr Kulla, or Shadda, fills up the blank with a river running from the western face of the Mountains of the Moon, to the north-westward. The distance from Cobbe to this point, according to the distance given by African calculation, will be 600 geographical miles. Westward of Darfur, the whole road lay amongst rivers. Dar Kulla and the country around it are, says Buckhardt, "throughout mountainous, and several very large rivers flowed through them, which were never dry"—a strong metaphorical and Arab

* 1½ square = 2.25 : 2½ square = 6.25.

expression, used to denote large rivers, and countries certainly well watered. From the point mentioned, to the junction of the Shadda with the Niger, the distance on the general bearing is 720 miles, so that the sources of the Bahr Kulla, or Shadda, may still be placed further to the eastward, as they ought to be; and probably are; because the Bahr Kulla, in the place mentioned by Rennel, is described as a large stream, and its course thence will be north-westerly to the south of the Mount Thala of Ptolemy, the Mendify Peaks of Denham, and to the north of the Mount Arualtes range of Ptolemy, in 3° N. lat., this latter range extending from the high land of Cameroons already alluded to. Mr. Oldfield clearly points out the opening, when he informs us, that the ridge running parallel with the Shadda from its junction eastward, had completely disappeared; and that, at the point where he turned back, " the river has taken an ample sweep to the southward" (vol. i. p. 450); with which course, moreover, we have a fine elucidation of Ptolemy's statement, that the Niger receives to the rising sun one branch " above" or to the south of the Lybian lake (Lake Shad), and that it also joins together Mount Mandrus and Mount Thala; in other words, that all the waters which flow from them, though running in opposite directions, run to one common termination.

Further, and in reference to the Shadda, the account which the native of Mandara gave to Denham will turn out to be correct. This man stated, that a journey of twenty days south from Mandara brought him to a district or country where the mountains were *ten times* higher than those in Mandara, and where he found and crossed before he came to the capital of Adamowa (Ghorin) a large river running between two ridges of mountains, which river, he said, was the same as the great river in Nyffe, and that it had no connexion with the Kano river (Yeou), nor with the Shary river, both of which entered Lake Shad. The fact stated, namely, that he met a large river running between two ridges of mountains, twenty days' journey to the south of Mandara; and that that river communicated with the Nyffe river, or the Niger; clearly establishes the point, that the river in question could be no other than the Shadda. The distance, twenty days' journey

south from Mandara, would certainly bring the extreme point
of his journey beyond the parallel of that country through
which the Shadda flows to the westward.   By a proper and
corrected scale of estimating distances, the position of Mora will
be in about 10° 30′ N. lat., Musafeia, a little to the southward
of the parallel of 10°, and the high Peak of Mendify in about
9° 30′ N. lat.   This brings the Mandara range and these high
peaks to the very parallel where Ptolemy places his Mount
Thala, namely, in 10° N. lat.; and when his longitudes are
corrected from known points, also in the same meridian.   The
termination of the journey of Denham's informant, namely, at
the capital of Adamowa, called Ghorin, would be to the south
of, but not far from, the parallel of 8° N.   His informant does
not say how far the "great river" which he crossed lay to the
north of the capital, but merely that he did cross such a river
before he came to that place.   The expression, "great river,"
clearly indicates a stream of that magnitude which must
previously have had a very considerable course from the eastward.   This man's account is wonderfully corroborated by
Sultan Bello.   The Mandara traveller states, that part of the
population of the capital of Adamowa were Fallatahs, and
another part Pagans; but that the hilly or country people
were all Kerdies or Pagans.   Sultan Bello tells us exactly the
same thing, and states that one-third of the population were
Mahommedan Fellans, and the remainder Pagans.   All the
districts in these interior parts of Africa, though mountainous,
are nevertheless well peopled.   The rivers in them are very
numerous; and the proof that these rivers are of considerable
magnitude, is furnished by the fact, that the natives use large
canoes to cross them.   To the south of Mandara, Denham
moreover states, that there are many lakes in the country, that
fish is very abundant in these lakes, and that the numerous
natives which inhabit these countries eagerly seek cotton goods
and other manufactured articles.

Dupuis, in his account of the rivers of the interior of Southern
and Central Africa, mentions, amongst other things, that of the
number which run to the sea at Benin, there is one called the
Shaderbah, which, from its position, is clearly the Shadda;
and of these rivers, he further states that one of them, he was

informed, afforded a communication between Benin and a tribe
of people at a great distance, called Gangori. This tribe, he
was told, lived in tents; that they were not black, but had red
skins, yet were not Arabs. The best mules and horses, he
was told, came from thence. Let us attend to the following
account, given by Browne (p. 159). The people of Kulla,
he says, were represented as partly negroes, and partly of a
red or copper colour; their language was nasal. They had
ferry-boats on the river, which were impelled partly by double
oars like our canoes. Water was very abundant, the trees very
large, and the pimento-tree in particular very abundant. Into
this country, the inhabitants of Dar Bargoo, or Dar Saley, make
war by sudden incursions into the country of Kulla, laying
waste a large space in a short time, and carrying off the
inhabitants into slavery. It would appear, that the population
which Browne describes are actually the tribe named Gangori
by Dupuis' informants, and who have a communication by
water with Benin. Further, as regards this country of Kulla,
Horneman was informed, that the Niger runs to the river of
Kulla, or, as he thus describes it, " the Niger flowed from
Haoussa south till it joined the Bahr Kulla." Park also had
obtained similar information in his first journey; and in his
memorial to Lord Camden, he urges the fact, that the Bahr
Kulla and Niger communicated with each other. Bowditch
establishes the same fact; for in his last published volume, he
gives the distance from the island of Gange, or Gongoo, by
water, down the Niger by Attagara, thence on the Shadda
through Kowara Raba (Fundah and places to the eastward)
to Lake Caudee, to be sixty-five days' navigation, and not
sixty-five days' journey, as he had previously stated.

In vol. ii. p. 6, of Laird's, &c. Travels, Oldfield remarks,
that the Shadda, on the 18th of August, to their surprise, fell
nearly ten inches, which fall they concluded to be the commencement of the general annual decrease, which it was not;
and accordingly, on the 16th of October, when they returned
down the Niger, they remarked that the Shadda appeared to
be then even much larger than when they were in it during the
month of August. The phenomenon they observed, however,
is a curious but common one in every river of Northern

Africa, either near its sources, or near any point where it receives numerous supplies from several tributaries which join it from sources not very remote. Park gives us a beautiful illustration of the cause of this, in his Second Journey, when within a short distance of Bammakoo. At p. 252 (4to edition), he observes:—" It is a common observation of the negroes, that when the Indian corn is in blossom, the rain stops for eleven days. The stopping of the rain evidently depends on the sun approaching the zenith of the place, the sun, by this day's observation, lat. 12° 57' (Park took 15th declination for 14th—corrected to 14th, lat. 13° 16' 29''), being only seventy-one miles north of us; and it is a wonderful institution of Providence, that at this time the maize (Indian corn) here is in full blossom; and on passing through the fields, one is like to be blinded with the pollen of the male flowers." In his passage to this point, Mr. Park found the mountain streams had subsided; and the fall in the Shadda, at this time mentioned, proceeded from the same natural cause, and proves that it receives many supplies not far from this part of its course, or numerous tributaries issuing from mountainous ranges, which tributaries have no great length of courses, and are consequently soon influenced by the continuance or the discontinuance of the rains. The causes here mentioned, go, moreover, to clear up the important facts mentioned by Laird (p. 233), namely, that "the waters of the Shadda were colder than the waters of the Niger," and that the former " *rose sooner and more suddenly*" than the latter.

YACOBA, ADAMOWA, ETC.

The large space of country betwixt Kano and Kattagum on the north, and the river Shadda on the south, and betwixt the sources of the Coodonia on the west, to the borders of the Shary on the east, next requires consideration. This large space comprehends a number of districts and states known under different names, such as Kurrykurry, Yacoba, Kornorfa, and part of Bornou, which includes Mandara and Adamowa. According both to Sultan Bello and Clapperton, this country, or a very large portion of this country, particularly the western division thereof, is comprehended under the general name of

" Boushy," so called by the Mahommedans because the
inhabitants thereof are Pagans. Sultan Bello particularly
states, that Yacoba forms one of the districts of Boushy; and
he places the capital thereof twelve days' journey south of
Kano. Other authorities give the distance ten days' journey,
which will no doubt depend upon the season of the year, and
the mode by which the distance is travelled. Sultan Bello's
authority, however, for the correct distance, is certainly the
most to be relied on. Boushy, Boushee, and Boucheer, designate the same place. The whole of the extent of Africa under
consideration is exceedingly hilly. From Kattagum, the
country to the S.W. Clapperton tells us, began to rise into
hills, and westward the hills of Dull rose to the height of 600
or 700 feet to the south; and from the mountain of Nora,
near the source of the Sockwa, a lofty ridge of blue mountains
extended thence from north to south, which the inhabitants
informed Lander ran in that direction to the salt water, and
which he, in his journey to the south, saw for several days
bounding the horizon to his left. Both Sultan Bello and
Clapperton pointedly inform us, that the whole of the country
under our consideration is extremely hilly. Clapperton states,
that the hills in some places consist of lime-stone, and that
they are said to yield antimony and silver. Sultan Bello
states, that there is a gold mine among them, or, in other
words, that the country produces gold. Abou Beker, a native
of Kouka, and who was long on board the British ship of
war, the *Little Belt*, states, that at the distance of fifteen days'
journey to the southward of Kashna, the mountains were so
high that some of them were capped with perpetual snow, and
that they resembled in appearance the boldest peaks of the
Cape Verde Islands, (*Quarterly Review, May*, 1820.) In the
country of Yacoba is included the districts inhabited by people
known all over Africa by the name of Yem Yems, or Yum
Yums, whom all accounts represent to be cannibals. Lander,
according to the account he received from the king of Yacoba,
the sovereign of these people, places them to the eastward of
the capital, for he states, that in the contest which the king of
Yacoba had with Bornou, these people assisted him, and were
in fact the first in the contest. This sovereign affirmed to

Lander, from his own knowledge, that these people were cannibals. Both Lander and Clapperton were told this at other places, and from other authorities. Browne was told the same thing in Darfur. Buckhardt was told this at Shendy. Dupuis was told this at Coomassie. Lyon was told this in Mourzook; and he states that the country of Zegzeg was four or five days' journey S.W. of Kano; and that six days' journey south of it lay Yagooba, the country inhabited by cannibals. He further questioned a boy from that country as to the fact, who not only admitted the truth of the statement, but minutely described the parts of the human body which were considered to be the most delicious to eat. Every Moor and Arab traveller repeats the same account regarding these people. They are certainly pagans, and seem at all times to have maintained their independence against all the efforts of the neighbouring states, Bornou, Sultan Bello, &c.; and from this courageous spirit, they may, in the customary African metaphorical mode of expression, be designated cannibals; in other words, the destroyers or the devourers of their enemies. Still, the testimony against them in their worst character, it must be admitted, is universal, and stands as yet uncontradicted.

Amongst the countries in this great district of Africa, and in the S.W. portion thereof, is the great country of Kororofa, as found in old African maps; and by De Lisle and by Beaufoy is stated to be situated to the westward of Bagherme. Sultan Bello gives the proper name of this country; namely, Kornorfa, which, he says, embraces about twenty divisions. In his fourth, fifth, sixth, and seventh divisions, and in the province Boucheer, or Boushee, he places Yhass, Codoor, Kotoo, Aadam, no doubt the Domah of Oldfield, as these places lie in rotation to the S.E. of Rar-wee, or the Rary of Lander. In his eighth division, he places another, Kotoo, which contains a *copper-mine* and one of alum. Laird, be it observed, states that up the Shadda, there was a copper-mine. The positions of these countries are sufficiently ascertained, for Sultan Bello gives us the position of Attaghar, or Attagara, the Iddah of Laird, a great province, which, the former states, reaches to the sea where the ships of Christians come to trade; east of this, or, as he says, to the right, lies the province of Nafra (or as it is better known to Europeans by the name of

Biafra,) and upon a river larger than what the Kowara was in its middle course. Northward of this province lie the districts mentioned, and north-east Kornorfa, which he states contains a gold mine, and also one of antimony. When he states that Kornorfa contains no fewer than twenty divisions or districts, he clearly indicates the great magnitude of the country which stretches eastward to the borders of Adamowa. The whole of these districts are in what is called the country of Boushy, and consequently to the north of the Shadda. This district of Africa also seems to be that mentioned by Leo under the name of Temian, abounding with "wild woody mountains, containing many springs of water," and inhabited by a wild, savage people, who are represented as cannibals. This country was also stated to be bounded by the Niger on the south, for every river that was found in Africa, Leo, like others, seems to have considered as the same. Bowditch also mentions both this country and the Shadda, the latter under the name of the Quolla-raba, the supposed continuation of the Niger eastward to the lake Caudee or Shad. His informants stated that the kingdom adjoining it, called also Quolla-raba, or Koara-raba, was a very great kingdom, that it lay next to Atagher, or Attagara, and comprehended the whole of the countries of Canno, Dull, and the Yem-Yems. It is exactly in the position where we now find the celebrated state of Fundah. Sultan Bello, in his map, gives it the position mentioned, but calls the country Quorra-raba, which means the same thing as the name given by Bowditch, and, as regards the river, means only a tributary to the Niger.* Sultan Bello further informs us regarding the great district of Kornorfa, that it was "ruled by one king, who often sallied forth upon Kanoo and Barnoo, and caused much desolation," thus distinctly intimating both its power and its position. Bowditch states that this country, through which the river flowed, was thirty days' navigation" from Attagara, or the territory of Attagara, Atta, or Iddah. The dominions of Atta, it is here necessary to observe, commence to the westward of Yimmahah: That six days' navigation beyond the boundary of this country (Quorra-raba), the river passed Mafeegoodoo, from whence to

* Thus the Arab travellers designated to Dupuis the Quarrama, which passes Saccatoo as the Koara raba, or a tributary branch to the Kowara.

lake Cadce, or Caudee, or Shad, was thirteen days' journey; and he further adds, p. 203, the very important and curious fact, that " a very high mountain was spoken of at an equal distance between the Lake Caudee (Shad) and the Quolla," or the rvier which we now know to be the Shadda.

In the high mountain just alluded to we distinctly and clearly recognise the Mandara chain which intervenes between the river Shadda and the great lake Shad in Bornou. The Mandara mountains, as Denham informs us, run, one chain E.S.E. towards the sources of the Bahr-el-Abiad; one S.W. towards the high peaks at Cameroons; and one westward to the country of Yacoba. The mountainous range which gives birth to the Yeou, &c., flowing eastward and northerly, and to the Makkamee, Accra, and Coodonia, flowing westward, proceeds, as Lander has shown us, some distance to the south, and thence bending their range south-east, reach the mountains of Mandara. Approaching the sources of the Coodonia, they recede easterly, in order to leave, as it would appear, a valley from Fundah, to a certain distance eastward and along the Shadda. Whoever looks at the map will perceive, that from Kano and Fundah, to Mandara, a very large space intervenes, and which large space is, as has been shown, a very mountainous country; it is, therefore, plain that many streams must rise in the hills and flow to the south, to the south-west, and to the west, as the direction given by the ranges allow; while on the north-east from the source of the river, which is called " the Little River," which enters the Yeou near Old Birnie, to the sources of the streams a little to the southward of Mora, no river of any importance flows from the ranges in question through the territories of Bornou, either to the north-east or to the east. The province of Bobyra, belonging to Bornou, which lies in the direction of the ranges alluded to, abounds, we are told, with water, which could not be the case if it was destitute of rivers; and amongst other productions which Leo mentions as abundant in this district, designated Temian, in which Bobyra is certainly situated, he particularly enumerates the wild citron and the lemon, torrid clime fruits, which are only to be found in countries where water is abundant.

The next district of importance in this portion is the great district of Adamowa, situated to the eastward of Kororofa, or

Kornorfa. The true position of this place becomes of considerable importance in fixing several points connected with the geography of the interior of Africa. Fortunately it can be fixed with, it may be said, perfect accuracy. Sultan Bello states that it is twenty days' journey south of Bornou, and further, that it is immediately to the south of Mandara. Clapperton, in his first voyage, (see p. 261,) tells us that, at his interview with Sultan Bello, after having reached Saccatoo, that chief pointedly reproached him, and also the Dey of Tripoli, as being his enemies, because, while approaching him with the voice of friendship, Clapperton's friend, Major Denham, and Bhoo kalloom, a military officer from Tripoli, had, in a wanton and unprovoked manner, attacked his (Bello's) territories and subjects in Adamowa. There, it will be recollected, it was that Major Denham lost nearly all his baggage in his flight after the defeat of Bhoo kalloom and his party. This baggage was carried to Saccatoo as one of the trophies and the prizes of victory; and at Saccatoo what remained of this baggage was restored to Clapperton, in order to carry it back to his fellow-traveller, Denham, at Kouka. There can be no mistake about this, therefore, nor the position of Adamowa. Clapperton also, in his second voyage, during his passage from Boussa to Kano, fell in with one of Bello's officers, who spoke of the engagement at Adamowa as a victory obtained over the Christians, making Denham the chief of the party. Further, a route is given from Kano eastward by the Bahr-el-Abiad to Senaar, as travelled by pilgrims, in which the first country of importance mentioned beyond Kano in that route is, first Adamowa, next Bagherme, &c. The position, therefore, of Adamowa may thus be considered as being clearly and satisfactorily established. Buckhardt tells us that Mandara, an eastern province of Bornou, is inhabited by an Arab tribe, called Dar Mandara, and that the country is subject to the sovereign of Bornou, and near the Shary.

THE RIVERS AND COUNTRIES EASTWARD FROM BOUSSA TO BORNOU.

The very interesting and important portion of Africa which we have here approached, naturally draws the attention to the countries and places from Comie and Boussa, east of the

Niger; more especially as to the east of these places, there is found elevated lands, which separate the waters that bend their course westward to the Niger, and eastward so far to the great inland lake of Bornou called the Shad, or more properly Zad. This is more particularly necessary, because doubts have been stated regarding the information so lately received, and the accounts generally credited, and theories in consequence advanced, which go to plunge (could they be successful) the geography of Africa, just emerging from darkness, into confusion and obscurity. To clear up the point fully and satisfactorily it is necessary to begin with the Niger at Comie, and consider the country between that place and Kano, Saccatoo, and Kashna on the west, and Bornou, Jacoba, and Adamowa, &c., on the S. and S.W.

The theory above alluded to is that advanced by Lieut. Allen, and published in the journal of the Royal Geographical Society, vol. viii. 1838; namely, that the Yeou, instead of running into Lake Shad, runs out of it, and proceeds westward beyond Kano, by "the Little River," or the Yeou, (for which string to the bow is taken by the writer does not clearly appear,) and that from its western bed beyond Kano, it proceeds first S., and then from Cuttup, S.E., by Jacoba to the Shadda; that it is, in fact, the Shadda; that all the rivers which Denham crossed from Kouka to Farinoce, running eastward, all those Lander crossed, running, as he says, westward, were still the same stream which issued from Lake Shad; and finally, that Lander, Clapperton, and Denham, were altogether mistaken in what they saw, in what they visited repeatedly, and in all the information which they had received. This is in substance the contents of the bold doctrine advanced, and, in a manner unsatisfactory to any African geographer, maintained. The respectability and geographical authority of the high channel through which the speculation has been conveyed to the public, alone entitles it to notice or consideration.*

* Lieut. Allen speaks of this great discovery as his "Closet" work. There is, however, nothing new in it. Misled by the account which Buckhardt gave of the course of the Shary, namely, from N.E. to S.W., I was led into the same error twenty years ago, and accordingly brought the river from Lake Shad to the Niger, through the same districts of Africa.—See *Map and Geography of Northern Central Africa. Blackwood, Eding.* 1821.

First, on the southward or westward, we begin with the
route from the Niger at Comie to Kano. Clapperton crossed
the river at Comie, and thence proceeded eastward. The first
place they reached was Tabra, situated, as he expressly states,
on the *north* bank of the stream called Mayyarrow; there, says
Lander, "serpentine and of irregular breadth; in some places
so narrow, that a person may easily jump across, and at others
widening from twenty to thirty yards; its depth generally
fluctuating between eight and twelve feet." (Vol. i. p. 177.)
From Tabra they proceeded to Koolfu, a considerable town,
and at a short distance to the eastward. Previous to reaching
Koolfu they "crossed a stream coming from the north" (Clapperton, p. 129). Lander, p. 181, calls it "a broad but shallow
stream." This was at the close of the dry season. Koolfu
contains about 15,000 or 16,000 resident inhabitants, and is a
place of considerable trade and importance, being in the great
road between the central countries of Haoussa, and also
Ghunjah, Ashantee, &c., and Bornou. Eastward of Koolfu, at
the town of Waza, or Wazawa, the province of Kontankora
commences. The next place of importance is the considerable
town of Womba, in the province of Kontankora, the capital of
which has the same name, and is situated thirty miles *to the
north* of Womba. All the caravans from the west and from
the east halt at this town. It is in 10° 35' N. lat., and 7° 04'
E. long. A small stream of water runs past the western gate,
from which the city is supplied. The population is about
12,000. The country around is well cultivated, and both to
the east and to the west very fertile, populous, and beautiful,
but towards the east it is hilly and woody. From Womba they
proceeded to Guari, passing in their route the town of Curijie
and Guber in Dushie. Close to the east of the former runs
"a small stream, which was then full and deep." (July 2d.)
Guari is situated in 10° 54' N. lat. and 8° 25' E. long. The
country around is hilly. The town is built partly on a hill
and partly in a valley, through which a muddy stream runs,
and which is dry in the summer, but during the rains it is so
large, that Lander, on his return, was detained a whole day
before he could ford it. It rises to the north of Guari, runs
through part of Zamfra, dividing in one part the states of

Kontankora and Guari, and flowing south, enters the Kudonia
in Nyffe. (Clapperton, p. 155.) The next place of importance that he came to was Zaria, situated in 10° 59' N. lat.,
and 9° 31' E. long. Though the adjacent parts are all hilly,
yet, says Clapperton, "the country at present on this side of
Zaria looks like some of the finest in England about the latter
end of the month of August; all around is green and beautiful,
with only trees here and there." Dunchow, to the east, is the
first town in the province of Kano, after which they reached
Baebaejie, a town about twenty-two or twenty-three miles SS.W.
of Kano. The country everywhere around Baebaejie looked
beautiful, the grain just being high enough to wave with the
wind. The hills of Nora bore east ten miles distant, those of
Surem south twenty-five miles distant, and the top of one of
the high hills of Aushin was seen in the west. North of
Baebaejie, about six miles, is the river Gora, running east to
the Girkwa, and next, about eight miles further, and nearer
Kano, is the river which Lander calls the Kogie, a considerable
stream which rises in the hills of Aushin to the west, and flows
east till it joins the Sockwa, one of the tributaries of the Yeou.

It has been considered proper to be thus particular about
these streams, both as showing the physical features of the
country, and as tending to elucidate the geography of this
portion of Africa, and also as tending to clear up a portion
about to be alluded to. About half way between Guari and
Womba, Lander, on his return, which was in the rainy season,
passed a large river, and about ten miles to the west of
Womba he crossed to the south side of another large river,
which I consider to be the same, and to be the chief stream
of the Mayyarrow. It must now be observed, that both he
and Clapperton state, that they passed in the dry weather
to the west of Koolfu, "a broad but a shallow stream,"
which came from the north; this I take to be a river which
comes from Kontankora, the capital of the province of that
name, situated to the north of Womba, and I do so, because
Lander on his return says, that he crossed, and with considerable
difficulty, "the large river Quontankora" about fourteen miles
from the Niger, to the east of a hill or ridge which lies between
it and the Niger. This can be no other than a river from the

quarter mentioned, and the united stream of it and the May-yarrow. Where this river joins the Niger we have no certain account, but it is remarkable, that in his rude map, delineating this portion of Africa so near himself, Sultan Bello lays down a very considerable river flowing for a considerable space at a short distance on the east side of the Niger, in its course below Boussa, before it joins the latter river. This may fairly be taken as the river just noticed, and which joins the Niger, above the junction of the Coodonia with that mighty stream. This position agrees too with the rude delineation which Sultan Bello has given of these rivers.

The next and most interesting point to consider, is Lander's journey from Kano to Dunrora. At a short distance to the west of Baebaejie, he left the Nyffe, and took the Fundah road. This journey, be it remembered, was performed during the rains, and immediately after they had commenced. His course on the first day was a little to the eastward of south. After-wards, until he passed Damoy, his course was south a little westerly; and to the eastward, bounding the horizon on that quarter, were observed, day after day, for four days in succes-sion, very high mountains, stretching south from the hills of Nora and Dull, which former mountains extend, as the inha-bitants asserted, to the salt water. After leaving Damoy, his course was generally S.W., and the last day SS.W. On the 3d of June, between Cookie and Carifo, he crossed one large and then two small streams, all running to the westward, and during the next two days he passed several other small streams flowing in the same direction. The large river here mentioned is readily recognised as that which he crossed close to Egge-bee, on his return northward to Zaria. About twelve miles beyond Damoy, he crossed a large river called Accra, its course then N.W. This river is also readily recognised as that which Lander crossed on his return north near Mammaleek, and called the Makkamie. North of Fullandushie he crossed another large river, also running westward, and which, as we shall presently see from undeniable data, joins the Coodonia below Cuttup. The next he came to, was the Coodonia, or Kadania, and from the manner in which he speaks of it, it is clear that it was the largest of any that he had passed in his

present journey.   He calls it "the large river Coodonia,"
which term gives us a scale to estimate what he means by the
word "large," as applied to others.   On the 11th of June, it
was too deep to cross, but next day they forded it, "*the water
reaching to our chins*," the stream running N.W.   The information here conveyed, shows that all these rivers, though
much swollen, were still fordable, and this, with the fact, that
in a few hours, from being unfordable, they decreased so as to
become fordable, shows that their sources cannot be very far
distant.   Proceeding onwards S.W. by Cuttup, he, between
Coogie and Dungoora, passed a large river called the "Rary,"
running to the S.E.   In his short journal, published along with
Clapperton's, he calls this "a large river," (p. 296,) but in his
narrative published separately, he, p. 124, calls it merely "a
stream or river called Rary," without stating how it flowed.
The expression here used, "stream or river," and the easy
way he got across it, though it was then much swollen, shows
that it was here only a mountain stream, and much inferior
to the Coodonia, the magnitude of which near Cuttup we
have been able to ascertain with some accuracy.

It is probable that this river passes near Jacoba, or rather
the capital of the country known under the name of Yacoba,
which Clapperton was informed at Kattagum was so named
after the sovereign.   This city stood, as Lander was informed,
at the foot of a large hill, which hill was half a day's journey
to the east of Dunrora, where Lander was compelled to turn
back.   Half a mile from the town, (Jacoba) as his guide Mahommet informed him, there flowed "a river called Shar, or
Sharra, deriving its source from Lake Shad, and that canoes
can be paddled from the said lake to the Niger at any season
of the year.   The Sharra enters the latter river, or Niger, at
Fundah," after which the Niger flows south to the salt water.

It is not difficult to perceive, amidst the errors of this African
narrative, what Mahommet means by the Lake Shad, &c.,
which is neither more nor less, than that the small river which
runs by Jacoba, flows into the Shadda in the kingdom of
Fundah, by which means canoes may indeed be *paddled* thence
to the Niger, but certainly not to or from the Lake Shad in
Bornou.   In eight or nine days indeed, they might paddle a

canoe to the river Shad, and also to Bornou, that is, the
territories of Bornou; for we learn from Oldfield's Journal,
that at the point where they turned back, Dogbah on the river
Shad, they were within two days' journey of the dominions of
Bornou. But to paddle a canoe from the capital of Jacoba, to
the Lake Shad in Bornou, a distance by the supposed water
course of 480 miles, would be quite a different thing, and
could not be accomplished, even if a water communication
existed, as there certainly does not, in fewer than thirty days.

From the Rary, Lander proceeded S.W. to the paltry town
of Dungoora, and afterwards SS.W. to Dunrora. Between
Dungoora and Dunrora, he passed a hilly country, and amongst
frightful precipices, the road by the edge of which was hardly
wide enough for the foot of man or beast to pass. He mentions one 700 or 800 feet high, over which one of his asses
tumbled, and was extricated with great difficulty. This shows
the high mountainous country hereabouts, which moreover two
other important facts go to confirm more fully. Before he
came to the Rary, the rain fell in torrents, and the water, roaring down the sides of the mountains, rolled in one mighty
stream into the valleys, and carried every thing before it in its
progress. " This continued for hours," (vol. ii. p. 124.) Yet
after all this, how little was the Rary! Moreover, we learn
from Sultan Bello's Memoirs, that there is. in this part of
Bousheer, or Boushee, a district called " Raree," which probably gives the name to this mountain stream. Next at Dunrora he stood upon an eminence so high, that he clearly
discerned every part of the lower country southward, to the
distance of eight days' journey. These facts establish the
mountainous nature of this district, and prove that the streams
were mere mountain torrents, swollen at that time considerably
by the violent rains.

From Dunrora Lander was turned back, and set off to
Zaria, with the king of Zegzeg's messengers. They returned
to Cuttup first, and thence taking a different road from that
which Lander had travelled, they proceeded about fifty miles
westward, where they again came to the Coodonia, which, says
Lander, was " larger, deeper, and more rapid than it was at
Cuttup," insomuch that it was dangerous to cross it (vol. ii.

p. 132). He accordingly refused to try, and remained in the neighbourhood two weeks. Again he set out, and again came " to the banks of the Coodonia, but found the river still too deep to ford," and over which the party was at last ferried on temporary rude bamboo rafts.* The obvious reason why the stream here was deeper and broader than it was near Cuttup, is, because it must have received on its north side the large river, which Lander mentioned he crossed to the north of Fullandushie, because on his return northward he crossed only two considerable rivers, the Makkamie, or Accra, at Makkamee, the town of the former name, and another at Eggebee, to the south of Zaria, both at these points running southward, which would bring them to fall into the Coodonia below the point where he crossed it. In his progress south from Baebaejie to the Coodonia, Lander crossed three considerable streams, but in his progress from the Coodonia north to Zaria, he crossed only two, and at the places last mentioned.

It is very clear that all the streams just alluded to, the Rary perhaps excepted, come from the eastward, and from the bosom of that high range of hills stretching south from Nora and Dull. They join, and must from the nature of the country join, the Kudania, which Lander says he was expressly told entered the Niger, and he states, in his second journey, when running down the latter stream, that he passed the mouth of the Coodonia at some distance, about three hours and a half, say fifteen miles, above Egga. Clapperton, p. 116, tells us, that below Comie the Niger runs more to the eastward, until joined by the river Kadania flowing from the eastward, after which, &c. Lander further says, that the Coodonia forms the northern boundary of the province of Bouchee; so also says Sultan Bello, and farther that it comes from the east, and enters the Niger, or Kowara, in Nyffe. In his map of this portion of

* His words demand attention. In his Journal, published with Clapperton's, he says he found the Coodonia at this point "much too deep to walk through," and in his Journal published separately, (vol. ii. p. 134,) he says, " found the river still too deep to ford;" thus clearly intimating that its magnitude was such, that at any other period of the year, and even at intervals during the rainy season, it could be forded, and could be " walked through," as be it here observed, he had, even at this time of the year, *walked through* all the other rivers which he had found in this part of his journey.

Africa, he has delineated the course of this river with considerable accuracy, and, what is more remarkable, he lays down exactly the number of considerable branches or tributaries, namely, three, coming also from the eastward, south of Kano, and north of the river, all joining it; while these branches again, at least the most northern of them, are joined by some small streams represented as flowing south, from the countries to the south of Saccatoo; and although we are not to look in Sultan Bello for the geographical accuracy of an Arrowsmith, yet it may be readily allowed and supposed, that he had some geographical and general knowledge of his own dominions.

The observations made about the view from the eminence at Dunrora, shows beyond dispute the greatly elevated nature of the country around it. The hills here form, no doubt, a portion of that range through which the Niger bursts, near Egga, and above Cuttum Currafee. But elevated as the country about Dunrora is, we have unquestionable data to show that it is still more elevated towards the north. After quitting the banks of the Coodonia, Lander found that both the palm and the plantain trees disappeared, and were not again seen till he came to Yarribah. These trees, it is well known, will not grow at a great elevation above the sea in the Torrid Zone. Lander describes the country through which he travelled, in all these parts, to be exceedingly populous, well cultivated, fertile, and in many places exceedingly beautiful. Around Eggebee, which contains about 7,000 inhabitants, it is particularly so—abundant cultivation, lofty trees, the whole appearance of it bringing to Lander's mind the description given of the Garden of Eden.

The inhabitants are principally pagans, and though living in a state of comparative happiness, they seem to be thickly enveloped in African superstition, and all its attendant evil consequences. Slavery and the slave-trade are universal, and nothing regarded; and in conformity to the general African law, parents have it in their power to sell their own children. The following extract from Lander's Travels will show us how deeply rooted the evil is, and to what an extent in want of feeling this evil gives rise amongst them :—

" The Bowchee people appear to have no affection for their offspring—the gentle appeals of nature are unknown to them—parental

tenderness dwells not in their bosoms; and they sell their children
as slaves to the greatest strangers in the world, with no greater re-
morse of conscience than if they had been common articles of merchandise."—*Lander*, vol. ii. p. 114.

"A travelling slave-dealer passing through the place, had purchased
several of their children, of both sexes, from the inhabitants; and
amongst others, a middle-aged woman had an only daughter, whom
she parted with for a necklace of beads. The unhappy girl, who
might have been about thirteen or fourteen years of age, on being
dragged away from the threshold of her parents' hut, clung distract-
edly, like a shipwrecked mariner to a floating mast, round the knees
of her unfeeling mother, and looking up wistfully in her countenance,
burst into a flood of tears, exclaiming with vehemence and passion:
'O mother! do not sell me; what will become of me? what will
become of yourself in your old age, if you suffer me to desert you?
Who will fetch your corn and milk? Who will pity you when you
die? Have I been unkind to you? O mother! do not sell your
only daughter. I will take you in my arms when you are feeble, and
carry you under the shade of trees. As a hen watches over her
chicken, so will I watch over you, my dear mother. I will repay
the kindness you showed me in my infant years. When you are
weary, I will fan you to sleep; and whilst you are sleeping, I will
drive away flies from you. I will attend on you when you are in
pain; and when you die, I will shed rivers of sorrow over your grave.
O mother! my dear mother! do not push me away from you; do
not sell your only daughter to be the slave of a stranger!' Useless
tears! vain remonstrance! The unnatural, relentless parent, shaking
the beads in the face of her only child, thrust her from her embraces;
and the slave-dealer drove the agonized girl from the place of her
nativity, which she was to behold no more."—Pp. 114—116.

With regard to the positions of these places and rivers, as they
have been placed in the map, they have been so placed after the
strictest research, and the greatest consideration. The number
of days and hours that Lander occupied in travelling from Kâno
to Dunrora, have been collected, and after allowing nearly two
geographical miles to each hour, the distance was protracted
according to the bearings given. The result is as stated, and
which corresponds very exactly indeed with the position of other
places calculated from the same and other authorities. Lander
was seventeen days travelling over the space mentioned. No

one at all acquainted with African travelling in any country south of the Desert, but especially during the rainy season, will allow more than ten geographical miles made good each day on the general bearing.   This will give 170 miles, which, with the circuitous nature of the general route, would considerably lessen the latitude, and bring Dunrora to be not more than 2° 45' S. of Kano, or in N. lat. 9° 15', and E. long. 9° 44', or 116 miles, at least twelve days' journey from Fundah, even according to the position in which different observations place the junction of the Shadda with the Niger, and from it, of the town mentioned.   Besides, we have another check to the accuracy of these calculations, namely, the authority of Sultan Bello, who, in his Geographical Memoir, pointedly states that Yacobah, that is, the capital of the country, is twelve days' journey south of Kano. This corresponds well with the positions of the places given from Lander's narrative, and forms a check upon them. Even taking these at dry season and open country journeys, but which they certainly are not, they could not extend beyond 180 geographical miles. There are also authorities which make the distance between Kano and Jacoba only ten days, but Sultan Bello is the safest authority to take for our guide.   The roads during the latter part of Lander's journey were dreadfully bad— we have seen what they were from Coogie to Dunrora; and from Cuttup to Coogie, they were so bad that he and his guide travelled often in water up to their waists, and were sometimes obliged to carry the baggage over precipices. It is here necessary to remark that Lander states Fundah lay due west from Dunrora, and he supposed twelve days' journey distant. At the same rate he travelled from Kano to Dunrora, that would be the distance, and if he spoke, as it is presumed he did, of the bearing by compass, he is very nearly correct.

In attending to the above narratives, it is clear that the highest land is to the westward of Kano, extending from the mountains of Aushin, north of Zaria and west of Baebaejie along towards Duncammee, in this space dividing the waters which flow to the Yeou on the east, from those which flow west to the Niger; while at the point mentioned this elevated land meets and joins the very high ridge which extends from the Niger between Boussa, or rather Engaskie (a continuation of the Fagh range to the S.W. of the Niger), and Yaoori N.E. to Kashna, and which separates the waters which flow north-westward into the Quarrama, and south-westward into the Coodonia, the river of Kontankora and that called Mayyarrow. All accounts agree in stating that the land in these parts is greatly elevated. The fruits and produce show this in a very convincing manner, and we have the authority of Leo to state that fires are used by the inhabitants both night and day. Clapperton also tells us that at Kano, in the middle of February, he felt the weather very cold; in fact it was so much so, that a fire all day was necessary, and that the practice of the natives was to have fires all the year round.

From Kano, Clapperton pursued his way to Saccatoo. As he travelled over this space both in the dry season and in the rainy season, we have the features of the country, and streams which intersect it, placed before us under opposite circumstances. From Kano to a short distance beyond Farinoce, the bed of several rivers and streams were passed, all shaping their course to the eastward, but at the time of his first journey they were dry. In the wet season, a few miles from Kano, he passed a stream *one quarter of a mile wide,* and so deep that the horses in crossing were at times swimming. *It ran eastward.* From Kano to Gadania the country is woody, and the trees higher than those which are found in Bornou. Beyond Gongode and Gadania, he passed in the wet season one small river and several streams, the courses of all which were to the eastward. A little to the east of Duncammee passed the bed of the river, which divides Kano from Kashna, and which rises amongst the granite hills to the southward of the latter place. The channel is twenty feet broad. From Duncammee the stream pursues its course about W.N.W. After passing Zirmee, the capital of Zamfra, it breaks through a ridge a few miles to the east of Quarrie, near which it is joined first by a small river from the south, and a little below it a small stream which comes from the south-west, and on the north-west bank of which that town is situated. Below it, the junction of the two streams mentioned, with the Duncammee river, thence downwards, called the Quarrama, takes place; and soon after, it receives the river Fulche, which passes midway between Quarrie and Burderawa, and comes from the southward and flows into the Quarrama, half a days' journey to the northward. The channel of the river, during the dry season, was from thirty to forty yards broad. During the rainy season, it was found 100 yards broad, full of water, the current two and a half to three miles per hour. The banks were low, and country adjoining woody. From Duncammee to Kutah the country is well wooded. Around Bershee and Kagaria it is delightful and well cultivated. The land rises gently into hill and dale, with numerous verdant valleys, and beautiful and clear springs of water are found running amongst the granite ridges. From Kagaria to Bobagim, the country is eminently fertile and beautiful, like an ornamental park in England shaded with luxuriant trees. Betwixt Bobagim and Quarrie, the country continues to be highly cultivated, and the roads thronged with passengers and bullocks loaded for the market of Zirmie, the environs of which are populous, and also well cultivated. The view from the opening in the ridge above-mentioned, westward along the bed of the Quarrama, is represented as exceedingly fine. The banks of the river were planted with onions, melons, citrons, indigo, cotton, and some wheat, and watered during the dry weather by means of a bucket and lever out of holes dug about two feet deep in the bed of the river, in which water is always found in abundance. On the east bank of the Quarrama is situate the large and populous town of Kutri, which has numerous dye pots in its outskirts. Zirmie is situated in 13° 7′ 14″ N. lat., and 8° 40′ E. long. Quarri contains from 5000 to 6000 inhabitants.

. From Burderawa to lake Gondamie and Kaimoon, the country is woody, and during the wet season, swampy and uncultivated. It forms what is called the dreaded Guber bush, a wild country, on the confines of Saccatoo, east, and between Goober and Zamfra. It occupies more than two good days' journey to cross, during which time travellers hurry forward at the utmost possible speed, night and day, in order to escape the attacks of the numerous and merciless banditti which constantly frequent this sad spot, and who frequently plunder and murder the people composing the caravans. Even when the main body escapes the fangs of these robbers, the toil, thirst, and excessive fatigue, cut off numbers, especially of the slaves, who seem to perish unlamented.

The following extract from Lander will show the true nature of this dismal spot, and the great dangers and fatigues of African travelling, even near populous districts in Africa :—

"At eleven o'clock in the morning of the 4th of May, a signal to depart was made by a loud blast from a thousand horns, producing a frightfully discordant noise ; and in about an hour afterwards, the whole party was in motion. On entering the dreaded " Goober Bush," a wild and uncultivated tract of ground, covered with stunted trees, we were obliged to double our pace, in order to escape the fangs of the merciless Towayahs. Boussa Jack (a horse, so called from having been made me a present of by the king of Boussa) I rode myself, on account of his swiftness and agility; but being unused to so violent an exertion, the little animal became much fatigued, and began to lag behind the others. The weather was at this time intolerably hot; vegetation shrank before the piercing rays of the sun ; and the dust, raised by the hoofs of the horses, &c., arose in huge volumes in every direction, entering my eyes, my mouth, my nostrils, and penetrating even the pores of my skin. Not a breath of air fanned the leaves of the trees ; I was almost suffocated for want of it, but snuffed up only sand and dust. The camels were far a-head : I was faint and exhausted, and ordered Pasko to fly to them for a drop of water. The horse would, or rather could, proceed no further; I was obliged to dismount, and seat myself under a tree ; there, holding the bridle of the poor animal in my hand, I begged, I prayed the thousands of Falatahs and Tuaricks that were passing, for a mouthful of water to quench my parching thirst, but the unfeeling, iron-hearted wretches mocked my misery, and scoffed at my piteous entreaties, observing one to another, ' He is a Kafir ; let him die !'

" This cruel disappointment almost choked me ; I was so hoarse that I could no longer be heard ; and falling flat on my back, let the bridle slip from my fingers, and covering my face with my hands, tears came involuntarily into my eyes. At length, a young Falatah, from Foota Toora, accidentally seeing me lying along the earth with a horse standing listlessly by, came to the spot, and exclaimed in a tone of kindness, ' Christian, Çhristian, why don't you go on ?' On hearing him, I again sat up, and answered, ' I am faint and sick for want of water ; no one will relieve me ; and how can I go on ?' "—*Lander*, vol. ii. pp. 91—93.

"I, as well as the horse, was greatly refreshed with the small quantity of water thus taken, but soon becoming again weak and dispirited, I was nearly reduced to as bad a condition as before. A few hours afterwards, my legs were swollen so prodigiously, that my boots split into fragments, and fell from my feet; and I experienced the most acute pain in every part of my body."—P. 94.

" The young Falatah to whom I owe my life, came to me on the 7th, and informed me that the whole of the slaves of the king of Jacoba being missing, a party of horsemen had been sent in quest of them, and were just returned with the shocking intelligence of having seen thirty-five of their dead bodies lying along the road ; and that hundreds of vultures were already hovering over them. The other fifteen could not be found; but were strongly suspected of having shared the same fate. These unfortunate creatures had the task of carrying loads on their heads the day before ; but being unable to keep up with the rapid pace of the camels, were necessarily obliged to be left behind, and thus perished miserably of thirst and fatigue. I congratulated myself on my own good fortune, in having so narrowly escaped a fate so peculiarly frightful ; and thanked the Almighty with fervour and sincerity for having snatched me from the very jaws of death. On his leaving me, I gave the Falatah a pair of scissors and twenty gun-flints, as a small recompense for the eminent service he had so cheerfully rendered me."— Pp. 95, 96.

Lake Gondamie is the first of a series of lakes which are formed by the Quarrama, or river of Goober, and which stretch to Saccatoo by Megaria, where the river is again confined to its customary channel ; and in the neighbourhood, and to the east of Saccatoo, the river was found to run in a narrow, winding bed, within sandy banks, and to be sixty yards broad and twelve deep in February, and the current two and a half miles an hour. The country from Lake Gondamie is very marshy, but it rises on the south into hills, the ridges of which run from NN.E. to SS.W. Megaria is accounted very unhealthy, because the N.E. winds drive the vapours from the swamps adjoining the lakes upon it. The ridges open into more extended valleys as Saccatoo is approached.

The position of Saccatoo is known with considerable accuracy; but after examining the distances travelled with the greatest care, my decided opinion is, that it is at least forty miles more to the eastward than the position which Clapperton

has given it. It is distant from Yaoori seven days' journey
N.E. by the most accurate accounts.*

From Zirmie to Kashna Clapperton passed through a very
fine country, intersected by granite ridges, all running from
NN.E. to SS.W. It being in the dry season, he found no
rivers, but crossed repeatedly, between Yanducka and Kashna,
the dry bed of a river, through which, no doubt, a large body
of water is conveyed to the Quarrama during the rains. Kashna
is situated in 12° 59' N. lat., and 9° 10' E. long., and was at
one time known by the name of Sangrass, and afterwards by
that of Geshna. It is a place well known throughout all the
interior of Africa. It is built on the top of one of the many
ridges which are found in these parts, and which run from
N.E. to S.W. Melons, figs, and pomegranates, are abundant,
and formerly grapes were to be had in plenty, until the vines
were rooted up and destroyed by the Fallatahs. From Kashna
to Duncammee the country is of a similar description to that
which we have been considering, and from Kashna northward
to Agadez the country continues to be fertile, as it also is to
the eastward, towards Bornou.

KASHNA, GHANA, OONGAROO, ETC.

The important town of Ghana, and the position where it
stood, next require a moment's attention. Some centuries ago
it was the chief seat of the Arabian power in Africa, then a
mighty empire, the authority of which extended over a very
considerable portion of central Africa. According to Edrisi,
the province of Ghana was bounded to the north " with the
broadest desert, lying out between the countries of the Blacks
and Barbary, and on the south it joins the infidel's country, to
wit, Lamlam and other inhabitants." It is, according to him,
distant from the old town of Germa, by way of Agadez, 37
caravan journeys. That Ghana and Kano (the G and the K
being used indiscriminately) are the same, can scarcely admit of
a doubt. To the east the empire of Ghana was bounded by
the Mahommedan states comprehended in the extensive country

* Clapperton's private opinion, I know from good authority, was, that a correct
observation would place Saccatoo in 7° E. long.

named Kanem, which we know is situated to the north of the Yeou, and to the north and to the east of Lake Shad; for the empire of Bornou, which has since risen amidst the ruins of both countries, was then wholly unknown. To the west it was bounded by the great Negro kingdom of Kuku, Kawkaw, (a place far distant from the Kuku, in the land of Kanem,) which, according to Batouta, as has previously been shown, is the first place on the Niger to the east of Timbuctoo, and within the limits of the land of Maly, or Melli. According to a note, in the translation of Batouta, by Professor Lee (see p. 238), extracted from Abulfeda, Ghana, the metropolis of the empire mentioned, must have been situated where Kano now stands, because he states that the river of Ghana, or the branch of the Nile, as the Arabs then denominated every interior African river on which the city stood, flowed into the ocean or lake in lat. 14° N., and 4° distant from Ghana. There is no other ocean or lake so near Ghana as Lake Shad, therefore it must be the ocean or sea here alluded to: the latitude is correct, and the longitude very nearly so.

Ghana was represented as being placed upon both sides of a fresh-water river, and one part was said to be inhabited by Mahommedans, and the other by infidels. This seems to be the case with the town of Kano at this day. It is divided into two towns by a marsh in the dry season, which is, no doubt, full of water in the wet season. In the days of its former splendour the marsh might have been a small clear stream, though now absorbed in, and spread into a marsh, since the decay of the city. It still contains 30,000 inhabitants; and to the southward, that is, amongst the hills of Yacoba, we find it is still bounded by infidels or pagans, exceedingly rude and savage. In ancient times the sovereign of Ghana was repre-sented to be exceedingly rich and powerful, and to have had in his possession a remarkable piece of gold, weighing 30lbs., which, on great occasions, he used as a throne. Abulfeda says, that Ghana was fifty days' journey distant from Segelmessa in Tafilet (Edrisi gives the distance the same), through dread-ful deserts, and that the merchants which traded between the two places brought back chiefly red gold, stated to be very abundant in Ghana. Much of this gold, however, it is now known, was produced in other countries, and brought to Ghana in the course of trade, though some of it may have been obtained in the mountainous countries to the south of Kano, in which pagan countries Sultan Bello's narrative informs us there is a gold mine, or, in the African acceptation of the word, a country which produces gold.

So much for Ghana, formerly so greatly celebrated, and which clearly stood where modern Kano now stands. While on this point, regarding the great interior divisions of Africa, it will be proper here to allude to a name frequently mentioned by modern travellers in Africa, namely Afnoo. According to Lyon, the term Afnoo designates an immense district of Central Africa extending from Kano and the meridian of Kano on the east, westward along the northern bank of the Niger to Timbuctoo, and the meridian of that place. According to the same authority, Agadez is without the boundary of Soudan proper, and so also is the country of the Yemyems, or Yacoba on the south. This account agrees with the information which Dupuis received at Coomassie regarding the southern portion of the latter country, which was placed by his informants in Soudan Dakhlata, or Lower Ethiopia.

Much has been written, and many grievous errors have been committed, by confounding the names Owencara, Guangara, &c., with the modern Wangara, and from not attending to the facts related, regarding the countries to the east of Kashna, north of the Yeou, and to the west of Bornou. The position of Wangara, see p. 18, has been sufficiently and accurately ascertained. By attending to this, and to the facts stated concerning the other, we obtain from undoubted authority the solution of many doubts, and the explanation of some most important portions of African geography, particularly as these are given to us by Arabian, and still adhered to by some modern, geographers. The province of Oongooroo, as the natives of these parts pronounce the name, lies to the east of Kano and Zamfra, &c., the very position in which Leo places his Guangara, and some Arabian geographers Owencara. There can be no doubt about the identity of the names and places. The existence of such a place as Oongooroo was denied and ridiculed, because it destroyed, if it did exist, many

N

fine theories advanced regarding the geography of interior Africa. The existence of this place, however, has lately been established beyond cavil or dispute. At Bershee, a town a little to the west of Duncamee, Clapperton met the king of Oongooroo on his way from Saccatoo to his kingdom, situated to the eastward of that place. Bowditch states, that from Kano to Oongooroo, through the large towns of Madagee and Adaga (perhaps Hadega,) the distance was nine days' journey, but seven days if travelled on a camel. Oongooroo, he further states, was fifteen days' journey west of Bornou, and that it was subject to the latter state; he also adds, p. 483, that Oongooroo " was skirted by a river on the south." Hutchison was told at Coomassie (see Bowditch, p. 206) that Oongooroo lay to the east of Kashna, and that at one time its power extended to Goober on the west, (Sultan Bello confirms this,) while at the time Hutchison wrote, it was bounded by Bornou on the east. Lyon gives this country under the name of Ongornou, and states that it is fourteen days' journey (p. 127,) E. by S. of Bornou. The bearing, by a customary mistake, is wrong; it should be N. by W. Sultan Bello, who in this instance ought to be the best authority, calls it in his geographical narrative, p. 7, " Oonghor," and places it to the eastward of south of Kashna. Horneman heard of this country under the name of " Ungura." All dispute about the existence of the place is therefore at an end. The word Oongooroo is the negro pronunciation and corruption by them and by the travelling Moors of the word Oonghor, clearly the Oongooroo of Bowditch, Clapperton, &c.; the Ungura of Horneman; the Guangara of Leo, and the Vancara or Owencara of Edrisi and others. This appears quite obvious, even if the position of the place did not invincibly fix the point. It is quite a different place from the Wangara now known in Africa, and stands moreover in a very different and a very distant part of Africa from the latter remarkable country.

Whoever looks at the map, and examines the course of the rivers and the country to the north of Kano, which is situated betwixt them, and a considerable portion of which is to this day known by a name similar to that which the old Arabian geographers gave it, will perceive, first, that in the Arabian acceptation of the term it is an island; its length, from the eastern side of Lake Shad and the Shary inclusive on the east, to eight days' journey to the east of Kano, the boundary given by Edrisi on the west, is at least 300 Arabic or geographic miles; and its breadth, from a little to the eastward of Kashna on the north, to the mountains of Dull on the south, or rather from the northern shores of Lake Shad to the Shary above Loggun, about 150 miles, and which is the extent Ibn al Vardi gives this country of Vancara, and says it extends "in the form of an isle or peninsula." Further we are assured, from excellent authority, that the whole of this country is deeply flooded during the rainy season, particularly during the month of August, and in former times it is extremely probable that, after the numerous rivers subsided, the inhabitants around them collected, as Edrisi said they did collect, gold in considerable quantities in the sands and banks brought down by the rivers from the hills during the inundation.

Meczara, or Meczarat-el-Soudan, or Maghrara, lay to the west of Vancara, and south of the land of Ghana. It was through it that a Nile ran to the sea, at the island of Ulil, from which to Gana was forty days' journey or caravan stations distant. Part of this was in boats up this Nile. Sir George Collier (see Report to the House of Commons, 1820,) shows, further, the position of Meczara, namely, to the east of Gago, and to the north of Dahomey; in other words, the country from about Nikky on the west to the country of Yacoba on the east, and through which the Niger, or the other Nile, flows which is mentioned by Edrisi and Ibn al Vardi. To this day, the number of journeys from Benin to Kano is reckoned forty journeys, (see Dupuis,) the number which Edrisi gives as the distance between the sea-coast opposite the Isle of Ulil and Kano or Ghana. Ibn al Vardi calls the water on which the country of Owencara is situated " the Great Bahr," by way of eminence, it is presumed, and consequently can relate only to Lake Shad. Edrisi states, that Vancara lay to the east, and commenced at the distance of eight days' journey from Ghana, and that Caugha was one month and a half's journey east from Ghana; and also that it was subject to the empire of Vancara: but he adds, that some negroes stated it to be subject to Kanem. Mackrisi states that it was subject to Kanem, and that it was the last place in that country to the south, and three months' journey distant from Zeilah, in Fezzan, the first town in the country of Kanem to the north. Ibn Said places it as far south as 10° N. lat., and says that it had a river of the same name, and further, that the place was situated to the eastward of this its river. (Lee's Batouta, p. 237.) Browne places Caugha, or Cooka, for the place is the same, three and a half days' journey S.E. by E. of Fittre. Lyon states that Fittre is fifteen days' journey easterly of New Birnie, and Caugha sixteen days' journey E. by S. Bowditch and Buckhardt place it in the same position. The position, therefore, of Caugha, and the extent of Vancara this way, as also its true position, is, from the consideration and collation of these authorities, very clearly ascertained. Ibn Said has, perhaps, placed it too far to the south; but the excellent and particular account which Mackrisi gives of the very extensive country of Kanem, the manners, customs, &c., of its people and rulers, the same as we find these to be in Bornou and places around Lake Shad at this day, enables us, joined to the authority of Browne, Lyon, Buckhardt, &c., to correct that error.

Lamlam, according to Edrisi, was bounded on the west by Meczara, on the north by Ghana, and on the east by Vancara, and south by a desert or unknown country. Ibn al Vardi calls Meczara, Maghrara, and says that Lamlam was included in it. Owencara, he says, is situated to the east of Maghrara. The capital of Maghrara, he adds, is "Oulili, situated on the shore of the sea; there are salt pits, and a great trade in salt." It was through Maghrara, or Meczara, that the Nile or river ran which Edrisi said had the Isle of "Ulil not far distant from the continent, (one day's sail,) and in it are those famous salt pits, the only ones we know in all the country of the negroes, whence they are everywhere supplied with salt," &c.

Further, in reference to the rivers westward, from Kashna to Yaoori, it is necessary to state more particularly that these flow first westward from Kashna through Goober, thence west to Saccatoo, and from thence S.W. to the junction of the Niger above Yaoori, having betwixt the two latter places been joined by two rivers, one from the N.W., and one from the S.E., springing in the mountainous country of Abbi. The state of Goober lies on both banks of the Quarrama, and is represented as being a very fine country, and its inhabitants as descendants of the Kopts from Egypt. They are all free, and both sexes are as fair in complexion as the Gypsy tribes seen in England. They have been able to maintain their independence against all the power of Sultan Bello. This state seems to have two principal towns, one called Kalawawa, situated on the south side of the river, and the other Coonia, on the north side of the river, each about four days' journey from Saccatoo. Bowditch states, that fifteen journeys from Gamhadi, which is two days' journey from the Niger in the route from Degomba to Kashna, and nine days' journey from Gamhadi, that travellers pass a large river; and in another place he tells us, that Goober is the first place of importance westward from Kashna, at eight days' journey distant, and " across a great river," which can be no other than that mentioned under the name of Quarrama: the travelling Moors call this river the Koara Raba.

Next, we come to the river which descends from the northward and eastward of Kashna, and which forms one of the tributaries to the Yeou. The following authorities are adduced for this. First, Ptolemy, who brings a river from his Usargala mountains to the Gir. His words are express and remarkable, that his river Gir joins together or unites the Garamantican and Usargala range; in other words, that the rivers which flow from these ranges have one common receptacle and termination. The Usurgala mountains, the middle of them in 4° west of his Gira metropolis, and 1° west of the meridian of his Mount Arualtes, the one falling where Gambaroo, formerly the capital of Central Africa, and the other where we now find the lofty range terminating on the Atlantic in the high land of Cameroons. This Usargala range Ptolemy places in 20° 31′ N. lat., very nearly indeed in the place where, according to Dupuis, we find the Jibbel Twarick mountains and the Megran mountains mentioned in Arrowsmith's map. Secondly, D'Anville, who had excellent information regarding the interior of Africa, places a river in this quarter springing still

more remote to the north, and which he calls Wad-el-
Mazzeran, and adds, that the caravans from the north to
Agadez and Soudan travelled during the space of seven days'
journey along its banks before coming to the town mentioned.
Thirdly, Mr. Dupuis places in his map a river called Bahar
(Beiram), descending from the north, passing to the east of
Kashna, and forming the boundary betwixt the country of
Haoussa in that quarter and Bornou, and flowing eastward to
the Yeou. For this, he says, he had very clear authority,
repeated unto him, too, after he had exhibited to his informants
his delineation of it on the map.   Fourthly, we have the
information which Lyon received about this river, which he was
told was called Ringhem, and was found at the distance of
seven days' journey east from Kashna, though in another place
he gives the route from Kashna to this river to the northward
as being only three or four days.   Both he and Dupuis add,
in their customary African phraseology, that this river comes out
of Bornou.   Fifthly, Wargee, a travelling Moor, or Twarick,
stated at the British settlement on the Gold Coast, about sixteen or seventeen years ago, as follows :—" That one day's
journey south of Agadez, a large river is crossed, about four
hundred yards broad ; and that, though this took place in the
middle of the dry season, still the depth was so great that it
came up to the shoulders of the camels when crossing it.
This river, he further stated, ran through the Twarick country."
(*Gold Coast Correspondent*).   Sixthly, That there are rivers
here we have an invincible proof in the known nature of the
country itself.   " Agadez," says Lyon, and whose description
of it is amply confirmed by various other authorities, " is a
large district having a town of the same name.   It is thirty-six
days' from Mourzook in summer, and in winter is sometimes
forty-five.   It is fifteen or twenty days' from Kashna; twenty
from Bornou; thirty in summer, and thirty-five or forty in
winter, from Ghraat; and forty from Tuat.   The inhabitants
are Twarick, of the tribe of Kellewi.   It is a larger town than
Mourzook : the houses are of mud, and are built in the same
style and of the same size as in Fezzan : some have a kind
of second story.   It is surrounded by a wall of mud and stone,
of sufficient strength to protect it.   There is a very high

mouadden, or minaret, to the principal mosque, which the Twarick affect to consider higher than any in Egypt. The country is independent, and is governed by a sheikh, who is a mulatto, and of middle age, Yusuffah. He is considered as great a man as the Sultan of Fezzan. Dome dates are in great plenty: the common ones are scarce, and never arrive at any degree of perfection. The soil of the country is earth, not sand, and *is quite covered with grass*. There are large trees, chiefly the Talkh. Corn and vegetables are in plenty, and animal food is very cheap. The people are rigid Moslems." (*Lyon's Travels*, p. 131.) It is scarcely necessary to observe, that neither this part of Africa, nor any other, could be in such a state without water and without rivers.

Sheref Inhammed's account of the route from Mourzook to Kashna is interesting, as giving to the inquirer a pretty correct idea of the nature of the country between these two places. From Mourzook to the province of Hiatts, is a journey of fourteen days SS.W., five of which are through a sandy desert. From the province of Hiatts, they cross the mountains of Eyre, from which there flows a small river that speedily loses itself in the sands. This river is left on the right side of the road. The sixth day brings them to Gannatt. From Gannatt it is nineteen days' journey to Assouda, during six of which they pass a thirsty desert. From Assouda to Agadez, is a journey of eight days, through a delightful country, as fertile as it is numerously peopled. Indian corn is abundant, and herds of cattle are frequently met with. From Mourzook to Agadez, are forty-seven days of active travelling. From Agadez to Begzam, is three days' journey, through a country where there is a luxuriant growth of Indian corn, and in the pastures multitudes of cows and flocks of sheep. From Begzam to Tegomah, is a journey of two days, through a country of herdsmen. From Tegomah to Kashna, is a journey of twelve days, the first two of which are over desolate hills; the third day comes to scorching sands; and on the evening of the fifth day, the traveller reaches a fine country, beautifully diversified with hill and dale, and covered with rich rewards of the husbandman and shepherd's toil. It is remarkable that grapes do not grow to the westward of the meridian of Kashna.

The position of Kouka, the capital of Bornou, has been ascertained by various travellers with sufficient accuracy, namely, 12° 56' N. lat. according to Denham, and by various authorities in 14° 28' E. long., and nearly S. of Mourzook. This agrees with the account given by all native travellers that Bornou is south of Mourzook, and it also agrees in a very curious and remarkable manner with the itineraries collected by Buckhardt and others regarding the distances and countries eastward from Bornou to the Nile, and also with the journeys and distances given both by native and British travellers regarding the countries to the westward and northward. That the Shad is a lake, and has no outlet, will be more particularly noticed and clearly established in another place. To one of its tributaries, the Yeou, attention is in the first instance directed; but before doing this, it is necessary to remark that in adverting to tropical African rivers, the season of the year under which they are considered, and any thing relating to them stated, must always and particularly be borne in mind.

Towards the close of the dry season, Denham and the party with him visited the banks of the Yeou in order to examine and survey the ruins of Old Birnie and Gambarou. On the 24th of May they reached the Yeou at Lada, seventy miles from Kouka. There the river makes a bend like an S; it was extremely shallow, and had a dry path over the bed; they followed to some distance the easterly course of the stream. Next day they proceeded westward along its banks towards Birnie, and in their route passed several lakes, the remains of rainy-season streams. From the top of one of the ruins " they obtained a sight of the Gambarou, running nearly east, notwithstanding its windings, and only a few miles distant." From Old Birnie they visited Gambarou, the former country residence of the sovereigns of Bornou. It is situated on the south bank of the river, at a short distance from Old Birnie and Lake Muggabee. " It came from Soudan; here a very noble stream, nearly a quarter of a mile in breadth, and situated between two high banks, thickly overgrown with jungle, bushes, and bamboo. We endeavoured to ascertain if there was any current, but the water appeared perfectly stationary. Omar Gana, however, and the Showaas who had accompanied us, were unanimous in declaring that after the rains a very strong current from west to east constantly flowed."—P. 155.

On the 26th of May the party followed the course of the river to the eastward nearly three miles, and at length came to an open dry shoal of sand, the bed of the river extending more than 200 yards; and from that point the stream was here again called Yeou. Next afternoon they moved and crossed about two miles distant to the north bank of the river. " On the following day proceed on our course, winding with the river, nearly as broad as the Thames at Richmond;" recrossed the Yeou to the eastward at a very dry spot, and then came to Damasak. Subsequently the party went with the army of the sheik, and again crossed the Yeou at Kabshary, a town on its north bank to the westward of Gambarou. Again saw the river four miles from Bassecour, &c. On the 19th of June again visited Kabshary; saw and bathed in the river Gambarou at the former place.

All the parts around Old Birnie to the south and the west were particularly examined, and were then quite dry, except small lakes here and there, the remains of the flooding of the river, and of what is called a rainy-season stream, which will presently be specially attended to.

Captain Clapperton proceeded on his journey from Kouka to Saccatoo on the 14th December following, soon after the rains had ceased. On the 16th they came to the Yeou, to the east of Damasak. Where they approached to it, it was one quarter of a mile distant. It had fallen six feet, but was running at the rate of three miles per hour. Along its banks westward there was a chain of lakes. The country from Damasak to Lake Muggabee was then inundated by waters, the junction of streams formed in the wet season, and which flow to the Yeou, (p. 3, &c.) The travellers were consequently obliged to take a circuit from the river, that is, towards the S.W., in order to avoid the waters and the marshes; and in order to regain what is called the lower road, or that by the river side, they had " at noon to halt on the banks of one of these *temporary rivers* which are formed during the wet season: it still contained a considerable body of water, which was running at the rate of two miles an hour." They were ferried over on temporary rafts, formed with long reeds, which grow on the borders of the current. "They proceeded two or three miles *up* (that is, to the W.S.W.) the banks of the river, which last summer did *not contain a drop of water;* but nobody, from merely seeing it in that state, could suppose that for nearly one half the year it is a broad sheet of water; or, that the upper road itself is traversed for the same period by several large streams falling into the Yeou."

Here it is proper to remark, that the fact of there being no canoes, which are always to be found at all permanent rivers, in order to transport passengers, is of itself a proof that this, as the travellers stated, was merely a rainy-season stream, as regarded the low country; while the magnitude of the stream at this period showed that its sources must be at a considerable distance, and in a very elevated, woody, and mountainous country, where the effects of the dry season had as yet been little felt.

On the 20th of December, the party travelled over the upper grounds on account of the inundation, and on the 22d, again came to the Yeou, and crossed over a neck of land formed by the river, when they came to Dungamee. "The banks of the river are everywhere studded with towns and villages. On the 23d of December they marched and followed a winding path, nearly due west, and reached Deltago." Having passed several towns and villages they came to one called Kukabonee, also on the bank of the Yeou. "The country to the west of Old Birnie rises in gentle undulations of hill and dale," but "there are very few trees, except on the banks of the Yeou." December 25th, they "left Deltago, and winding along the banks of the river, or occasionally cutting off a bend by a cross path, they reached Bedeckarfee." Here they quitted the Yeou and crossed the Bede, a woody country to Bedeguma. Near Lake Zumbum, in its neghbourhood, the country westward and southward at that time appeared a dismal swamp. At Bedeguma "I inquired of the governor about the course of the swollen river we crossed on a raft between Gataramaram and Old Birnie, which *again* presented itself close to our present encampment. He told me that it rose in the *country* of Jacoba among the rocky hills, and running to the eastward of Old Birnie, soon afterwards entered the Yeou. The river," he said, " was distinguished by the name of the *Little River*, and in these parts did not dry up the whole year." The country to the S.E. and S.W. then appeared to be an entire swamp, from the overflowings occasioned by the tropical rains. Bedeguma was about twelve miles SS.W. of Lake Zumbum. The *Little* River suddenly breaks off to the southward at a town called Gobeer, a short distance west of Bedeguma.

Before quitting this part of the country, it will be best to notice what Clapperton says about it and the Yeou on his return from Saccatoo, just at the termination of the dry season. On the 26th of June, he reached Guba, a small town on the south bank of the Yeou, within the dominions of Bornou, and N.E. of the Bede country. On the 27th of June, he crossed to the north bank of the river, which was then almost dry, and travelled E. by S. by it to Muznee. On June 28th, travelled eastward along a crooked path to the town of Redwa. On the 29th, travelled E. by N., and, crossing the river, came to Kukabonee, formerly mentioned on the south bank. Thence, June 30th, to Dungamee, and July 1st, to Lake Muggabee. July 3d, passed on by Lake Muggabee; thence to Gataramaram, and thence, July 4th, eastward on the banks of the Yeou, when, quitting the river, he proceeded by the nearest road to Kouka.

But the evidence obtained from facts relating to the upper part of the course of the Yeou, and its early tributaries, is equally strong and conclusive as to its easterly course. Proceeding westward from Bedeguma, Clapperton came on the 1st of January to the little village of Obenda, not above one quarter of a mile from the Yeou. Near the river were large fields of wheat; the population were then busy in sowing their second crop. The appearance of wheat shows the elevation of the country. Besides, the thermometer, on the 26th of December, after sunrise, stood at 49$_{\circ}$; on the 28th, at 45°; December 31st at 42°; but on the 27th, in the Bede country, the cold was so great " that the water in the skins was covered with thin flakes of ice; the water skins were frozen as hard as a board, and the horses and camels stood shivering under it." Clapperton, in his letter dated Kano, February 2d, 1824, announcing the death of Dr. Oudney, states, "that the water was frozen in the dishes." This indicates a very high elevation indeed of the country in this part, and, moreover, proves that the country to the northward must be very high also. In lat. 12° N. it could scarcely be less than 10,000 feet above the level of the sea.

At mid-day on the 2d of January, they crossed the Yeou. Its channel here, close to Kattagum, was about 150 yards broad, but the stream of water was not above one-third the breadth of the channel, and in some places it was almost dry. The Dushee hills or rocks began to the S.W. of Kattagum, and run in the direction of S.W. About one day's journey north of Kattagum, and at a town called Hadega, the Yeou, according to Clapperton, is joined by the Shassum, and, of course, the other rivers from the west, and at no great distance. South of Zangeia, and thence westward towards Kano, arise high blue mountains, the hills of Dull, 600 or 700 feet high. All the country to the S. and S.W. between Kattagum and Kano is very hilly. Soon after passing the town of Murmur, where Dr. Oudney died, Clapperton crossed "a narrow stream called the Shassum," and between Boogawah and Katungwa, the first town in the country of Haoussa, he crossed another stream, which he names the Shassum, but it is quite obvious, that from the course he travelled, E. to W., and the course of this stream, "running nearly north," that it could not be the Shassum, but another and a distinct river coming like the other from the south. The Yeou he was told at Kattagum rose on the hills south of that place, and between Jacoba and Adamowa. The two streams mentioned, like that which pass Girkwa, come in the same direction, and from the mountains of Dull, while the Sockwa, which passes Duakie, flows from the hill of Nora, situated ten or twelve miles to the east of Bae-baejie; and to the south of Duakie is joined by a larger stream, which flows east from the hills of Aushin, and passing eight miles to the south of Kano, where Lander crossed it, and calls it the Kogie; and which stream again is, to the westward of Duakie, or rather to the S.W., joined by another stream, which Lander calls the Gora, and which comes from the same quarter as the other, and flows eastward about eight miles north of

Baebaejie to the Kogie. Baebaejie is, as clearly stated by Clapperton, the highest point in the road from Zaria to Kano, and the hills in the directions mentioned clearly form the elevated ranges which, on their respective sides, turn the waters westward to the Niger, and eastward and northward to the Yeou. Moreover, the Girkwa is the stream which a Sheeref wanted on a preceding day to make Clapperton believe formed the water communication always talked of between the Quorra and the Yeou, but which ocular demonstration showed him to be false.

Katungwa, as has been stated, is the first town in the country of Haoussa. The country here is thickly wooded. About Zangeia and Nansarina, it is highly cultivated. Cotton is very abundant, and the females are very generally employed in spinning it into yarn, from which cloth to a considerable extent is made. Betwixt Nansarina and Girkwa the country is very beautiful. A small stream is crossed a little to the east of Girkwa, but the name of it is not stated. The channel of the river Girkwa is extremely shallow, and only from sixty to seventy yards broad. In the channel of the Sockwa, the water was only " ancle deep," and at that period not above one-twentieth part of its breadth was covered.

In their progress from Mourzook, and after having passed the desert, Denham and his party came to the Shad, or Zad, on its north-west point, and afterwards going south, near its western borders, they came, on the 13th of February, " to a very considerable stream called Yeou." "It had a hard sandy bottom," and " banks perpendicular." In some parts it was more than fifty yards broad; the current strong, about three miles and a half per hour. It flowed to the eastward. At times it was stated to be double the breadth just mentioned. The inhabitants around, " were *unanimous* that it came from Soudan," (p. 59.) This was early in the dry season, and before the river was at its lowest ebb. When on his return to Tripoli, Denham again crossed the stream, on the 23d of August, during the height of the wet season. The Yeou was then in flood, a considerable stream full of water, and running towards the Shad at the rate of three miles an hour. " In the afternoon, Bellal," the guide, " accompanied me down the river about nine miles, where, increasing in width to about 100 yards, it flows into the Shad with a strong and deep current of water."

Let us next proceed to Lake Shad itself, in order to show that it is a lake without any outlet. Denham travelled along the whole of its southern and western shores, and found the Yeou running into it in the former quarter, and the Shary, with two smaller streams, on the other. On the north shore he travelled two days, but was obliged to turn back when he was only four days' journey from Tangalia. It had no outlet there, nor could it have any, and every one informed him that it had none. To the north and north-east there is even no permanent supplies received, as is proved, not only by what the natives relate, but by the fact, that the caravans which traverse the country between Dar Saley, and Mourzook, and which pass at no great distance from its northern and eastern shores, cross no rivers or streams, but are obliged to have recourse to wells for water to drink on the journey. Barca Gana, whom Denham met returning from his expedition around its northern, or north-eastern shores, met with no rivers there. But Sheikh el Kanemy, the ruler of these parts, who knows the country well, and who had repeatedly gone round the lake, settles the point, completely and satisfactorily, in the letter which he wrote to Major Denham from Bornou, after the Major had reached England. In this letter he says, " with regard to the desire which you expressed to us, to know the source of the inundation which divides our country, we have to inform you that this sea (river) of ours, is a *great and extensive lake*, the circumference of which is about twenty days' journey, and into which various rivers empty themselves, from the part of the land of Soudan, and from the right and EAST of our country."—*Appendix*, p. 152, dated 20th of March, 1825.

The great extent of this lake is sufficient in such a climate, and in such a country, to account for the absorption of its waters by evaporation; and another proof that it has no outlet is, that it overflows its shores to a great distance during the rainy season, and sometimes very suddenly, as Denham and his fellow-travellers witnessed immediately after reaching its banks; where in the month of February it rose several feet in one night, extending its waters above a mile from their former bounds. Denham's words are remarkable. Near Lari, " the soil of the lake was a dark, firm mud; and in proof of the great overflowings and recedings in the water, even in this advanced dry season, the stalks of the gussub of the preceding year were standing in the lake more than forty yards from the shore. (Denham, p. 47, February 5th.) If it had any outlet it would not thus overflow its banks.

The course of the Yeou and its tributary streams, together with the principal streams and their tributaries, which run in an opposite direction, have thus been very fully examined and determined. Nothing can be more specific than the accounts which we have of the nature, the magnitude, and the course of the Yeou and its tributaries, during both the wet and the dry season. Again and again were its banks visited, its course and current and its termination witnessed and examined. Were every river in Africa as well known, we should have little to desire in African geography.

It remains only to sum up, as shortly as possible, the facts, the authorities, and the evidence given from the course of these streams, and more especially of the Yeou, of its course east, and termination in Lake Shad. First, then, we have the authority and positive testimony of both Denham and Clapperton, given after repeated ocular demonstrations, that the Yeou and its tributaries run east, and terminate in the Lake Shad. Secondly, we have the positive testimony of both Clapperton and Lander, after repeated personal examinations, that the rivers to the west of the sources of the Yeou, the Coodonia included, are all separate streams from the Yeou, and run west and join the Niger. Also, we have their testimony given from information repeatedly received while on the spot, that the Coodonia, or Kadania, flowed from the east, and entered the Niger in Nyffe. Fourthly, with regard to the Coodonia, we have the positive testimony of Sultan Bello to the same effect, and that the river is named Kaduna as well as Kadania and Coodonia. Fifthly, we have the authority of Lander to state, that in descending the Niger on his second voyage, he passed some distance above Egga, but during the night, the mouth of the Coodonia on the eastern side of the Niger. Sixthly, as regards the Yeou, we have the clear testimony of Dupuis,

who, under the name of Gulbe Kerba, lays down this river as
flowing from the west, and after its junction with other
tributaries flowing into the Lake Shad, similar to the way
that Denham and Clapperton represented it to do.   Seventhly,
Abdal Gassam, the son of a Fallatah chief, at Jinne, a man
who could repeat the whole of the Koran by heart, and who
had travelled the whole way from that place to Timbuctoo,
along the whole course of the middle Niger, and thence on
from Kano to Bornou, told Denham there, that the river
Yeou was a distinct and separate stream from the river of
Timbuctoo.   Eighthly, the Mandara traveller, whom Denham
met with in Mandara, and who had travelled and crossed the
great river to the south of that place in Adamowa, assured
him, that while the great river he alluded to was connected
with the river of Nyffe, yet that neither of them had any connexion with either the Yeou or the Shary, each of which,
while they were distinct rivers, flowed into the Lake Shad.
Ninthly, Lyon's informants told him, (see p. 142) that at
Kattagum, the Nil or Gulbe passes from behind Kashna. " It
runs N.E. at this place, and must be crossed;" and again,
(p. 127) his informants state, a river, called Nil by the natives,
flows across the road from Bornou to Kashna, to the N.E.;
further, (at p. 129) another set of informants told him, that " in
Kanem, and within one day of Maoo, the capital is a very
large river, which comes from the S.W. to the N.E.; it is
called by the people of the country Yaoo, but by the Moorish
travellers Nil;" the informants here making both the Yeou
and the Lake Shad, as one.   Tenthly, we have the positive
testimony of Sheikh El Kanemy, that the Shad is a lake,
and that it has no outlet, but that the Yeou, from the west or
Soudan, and the Shary, with other rivers from the south, run
into it.   To his authority also, we must add that of the old
Dugganah chief, Tahir, who had lived all his days upon its
borders, and who told Denham, at Tangalia, on its S.E. shore,
that it was a lake, and had no outlet.   Eleventh, and to turn
to very ancient authority, we have first the testimony of
Ptolemy, that all the rivers in that quarter of Africa were
distinct, and had no connexion with the Niger.   Twelfth, we
have the positive testimony of Shceabeddin, the old Arabian

geographer that the Nile, as the eastern river was called, " did not run to the sea" *i. e.* to the Atlantic Ocean ; " but only to the end of the inhabited part of the land of Ghana." Lastly, we have the fact of the great elevation of the country itself westward to Kano, &c. Other authorities might be adduced to the same effect, but it is considered unnecessary.

After this, after the clear and satisfactory information which has been received ; after ocular demonstration by men acknowledged to be sane, and with their eye-sight perfect, and chosen to explore Africa because they were sane, and had their eye-sight perfect ; and which information goes to establish ancient authorities, and enables us to correct the errors of others, and also our own ; the question might have been considered as completely set at rest. The Egyptian Nile theory was reason ; and that of Sir Rufane Donkin, that the Niger ran from Wangara about Bornou through the mountains of Tibeste and the deserts of Africa to the Mediterranean Sea near the Syrtes, were sanity when compared to Captain Allen's speculations. The Quarterly Review, in support of its Nile theory, might have asserted with as much justice, that Laird, Lander, Oldfield and Allen, were wholly mistaken in what they saw, and that the Kowara or Niger, and the Shadda ran out of the sea, and from the alluvial country, instead of running through the one and into the other, N.E. and then east to the Bahr el Abiad.

It has been objected, and it may yet be objected, that Lake Shad being, as it confessedly is, fresh water, must have an outlet, because it is uncommon or unknown in any other quarters of the world that any lakes, except salt water lakes, are without such outlets. This reasoning and argument come with an ill grace from those who assert and admit that Lake Fittre, a fresh water lake, has no outlet. The reason, however, is at once refuted and silenced by a reference to the fact, that the " Sea of Durrah," as it is called, the receptacle of the river Helmund, in Western Asia, is fresh water, and yet has no outlet. The authority of Ebn Haukal, the most accurate of all the Arabian geographers, is decisive on this point ; especially as it is universally acknowledged that he witnessed personally all he relates. At p. 206, Ouseley's Translation, he

o

says this lake or sea of Durrah "is in length about *thirty* FARSANG (120 miles), and in breadth about one *Merhileh* (30 miles); ITS WATERS ARE SWEET AND WHOLESOME, and afford abundance of fish."

Bornou is a very extensive country, extending from 10° to 16° N. lat., and from about 11° to 18° E. long. The country all around the Lake Shad, and for a considerable distance to the W. S.W., and the south, is all alluvial and marshy, and by no means cultivated in any part to the extent that it might be. This, however, may in part be accounted for by the constant wars in which the sovereign has been engaged, he having only of late years rescued the country from the destructive power of the Fallatahs, who had overrun the whole of it, and shattered to pieces the former great empire of Kanem, on the ruins of which and of Ghana and Vancara the modern empire of Bornou has arisen. Sheikh Kanemy, the ruler, is a man of superior judgment and enterprise; he is most anxious to have a communication with Europeans, and could he only establish one certain and secure, as might without much difficulty be done, he would speedily change the face of affairs for the better in the whole interior of Africa.

Kouka, the capital of Bornou, as already stated, has been fixed, as regards its position in Africa, with considerable precision by the concurrent testimony derived from the distances given by all African travellers. In order to shew that the positions of the other places are fairly placed, it may not be improper to lay before the reader, in a tabular shape, the time and distances occupied and traversed by the different travellers in their respective routes, taking that distance only at two geographical miles per hour; the utmost which, on the general bearings, can be made good, even in the dry season, in any country south of the Great Desert. The African period of travelling from Kouka to Kano, is thirty days; and Lander informs us, that the distance from Kano to Saccatoo occupies twenty regular journeys to get over; and on his return we find that he left Saccatoo on the 4th, and reached Kano on the 25th of May. Lyon was informed, that Nyffle was twenty days' journey from Kano.

Kouka, Bornou, to Kano.

	Days.	Hours.	Geo. Miles.
Kouka to Bedekerfee	10	72	144
Bedekerfee to Kattagum	7	68	136
Kattagum to Kano	10	83	166
Total . .	27	223	446

This journey was performed in the dry season, and the course was nearly due west; but fifty miles of the journey was taken up in travelling about N.W. from Kouka to the Yeou, during which time only about thirty-five miles of westing could be made good. Still, with what remains, and after making a reasonable allowance, Kano cannot be farther west than where it is placed.

Next let us turn to the journey from Kano to Saccatoo. This journey was also, in the first trip by Clapperton, performed in the dry season, and early in it.

	Days.	Hours.	Geo. Miles.
Kano to Duncammee	5	34	68
Duncammee to Quarrie	5	39	78
Quarrie to Saccatoo	4	44	88
Total . .	14	117	234

The latter days were partly occupied in long and hurried marches through the dreaded Goober Bush, which spot sets at defiance all accurate geographical calculations. Lander, in following his master, took seventeen days, $121\frac{1}{2}$ hours, to perform the journey. In returning, Lander took twenty-one days; but during some of these he halted, without particularizing the number. Clapperton, returning towards the close of the dry season, took only thirteen days, about 100 hours; but then he travelled unusually quick.

Quarrie to Kashna, &c.

	Days.	Hours.	Geo. Miles.
Quarrie to Kashna*	4	34	68
Kashna to Duncammee	3	$22\frac{1}{2}$	45

* Quarrie to Zirmie was eight hours of this.

Kano to the Niger at Comie.

	Days.	Hours.	Geo. Miles.
Kano to Baebaejie	1	11	22
Baebaejie to Zaria*	5	32	64
Zaria to Guari	5	44	88
Guari to Womba	5	$39\frac{1}{2}$	79
Womba to Koolfu, by Beari . . .	6	50	100
Koolfu to Niger	4	$27\frac{1}{2}$	55
Total . .	26	204	408

Lander, from Kano to Dunrora, &c.

	Days.	Hours.	Geo. Miles.
Kano to Cuttup, by Baebaejie, &c. .	14	88	176
Cuttup to Dunrora	3	28	56
Total . .	17	116	232

The last day, from Dungoora to Dunrora, the longest day's journey in point of time of the whole; but little progress was made, owing to the dreadfully mountainous, rocky, and inundated state of the roads. The whole journey was performed during the very worst part of the wet season. Under the particular circumstances he could not make good, on the general bearings, above ten geographical miles per day, or, in all, 170.

Dunrora to Zaria.

	Days.	Hours.	Geo. Miles.
Dunrora to Cuttup, northerly . . .	3	28	56
Cuttup to Coodonia, westerly . .	4	28	56
Coodonia to Zaria, northerly . . .	8	$60\frac{1}{2}$	121
Total . .	12	$88\frac{1}{2}$	177

* The two first numbers are taken from Clapperton's advance just at the commencement of the rainy season, but before the rains materially impeded travelling; the remaining numbers are taken from Lander's return journey from Zaria to the Niger, during the rainy season, when travelling is slower and generally much impeded.

From Womba to the Niger.

	Days.	Hours.	Geo. Miles.
Clapperton, Second Journey from Niger to Womba, was	12	80	160
Lander, returning from Womba to the Niger, was	9	74½	149

THE RIVER .SHARY, &c.

The River Shary* and the country adjacent next demand our attention. A little to the east of Angernou, which is one day's journey from New Birnie, Denham tells us there is a little river called Molee, which enters Lake Shad in its S.W. quarter. The expression " little" shows that its magnitude cannot be great, although we are not told what that magnitude is, nor from what quarter it flowed; but, every thing considered, the stream must come from the S.W. Beyond this, and more to the eastward, about half way between this river and the River Shary, we are told by the same authority, flows the river called Gambularam. Bowditch mentions this river under the name of the Gabooa, about ten days' journey from Old Birnie. We have no definite idea given of the magnitude of this river, but it must be considerable from the facts stated by Denham, namely, first, that when he came to it on his return from Loggun, he found it near Filla not fordable; and, secondly, that when the army of Bagherme was defeated by Sheikh Kanemy on its western bank, a great number of the fugitives were drowned in its waters in their hurry endeavouring to escape across it. The course of the Shary shows us that this river also must come from the south-west, and most probably from the north-east corner of the Mandara range. In marching to Mandara, Denham says that they ascended the whole way; that near Degoa, on the north, they passed a broad dry river-course, and which, it appears, was the first they had reached in their progress from Kouka to this point. Advancing south, they crossed its bed on the following day, then without water. As they approached Dolou, to the south of Mora, the

* The manuscripts of travelling Moors write this word " Shar," " Sher," " Shavr," " Shary," or " Sharree."

country rose rapidly, and the Mandara chain, a primitive granite range, stood before them.   In the neighbourhood, and south-west of Mora, Denham found many springs, and after passing through the beautiful pass of Horza, to the south of Mora, they came, first, to a small stream, the Mikwa, and, fifteen geographical miles further, to another stream, called Makkeray, the water in which, when crossing it, came up to the hips. These springs and streams are most probably the sources, either of the Gambularam, or the western branch of the Shary, and most likely, I think, the sources of the former.   In his route from Bornou, Denham crossed no rivers, and conse-quently he must have passed to the westward of the branches of the Gambularam.   The course which he has given the Shary, its short distance from the route to Mandara, as laid down in the map constructed for his work, when taken in con-nexion with the fact of the existence of such a river as the River Gambularam, all go to prove that his route to Mandara must have been to the westward of south considerably, perhaps SS.W., and not due south, as the constructor of the map has made it. He himself does not give us the bearing of his route, except the stage from Angernou, which was south ; and if the journey was made, as I presume it was made, by compass, then in that quarter the variation being about two points would give a SS.W. course, and consequently the direction just stated. That the route was by compass we are warranted in concluding, because he tells us that he had one with him.   From the first perusal of his journey, my impression, every thing considered, was, that Denham's route from Kouka to Mandara lay con-siderably to the westward of south, and subsequent researches, and a deeper consideration of the subject, tend more and more to confirm that opinion. This admitted will leave suffi-cient room, and no more, for the positions of the sources and the courses of the Gambularam and the western branches of the Shary. The distances which Denham has given us as travelled over, namely, thirty miles per day, 180 miles in six days, from Mora to Kouka, have already been adverted to, and a more reasonable distance taken, and the position of Mora regulated and fixed accordingly, namely, in 10° 30′ N. lat.

Fifteen miles beyond the Makkary is the strong Fellatah

town of Musafeia, where the marauding expedition with which Denham travelled was beaten back. Thirty-five miles more to the south rose the alpine peak of Mendify, around which and from which masses or ranges of hills spread themselves in every picturesque form and direction, more especially southward, while the Mandara range ran, as he states, in interminable ranges E.S.E., S.W. and W., and W.N.W. The valley of Horza is about 2500 feet above the level of the sea. The nearest and surrounding peaks rose 2500 feet above that valley, and the more distant to the south again rose several thousand feet above these. Denham speaks with rapture of the beauty of the country to the south of Mora; it would seem to be very populous. Degoa contains 30,000 inhabitants; Mora a great number. S.E. of Mora is the pagan town and country of Musgou, and S.W. (in another place he says W.) is the town and country of Karowa, where iron abounds, and from whence that used in Mandara is brought. Buckhardt mentions, in his enumeration of the population of Bornou, the tribe of Mandara or the Arab tribe, called Dar Mandara, as dwelling in these parts, and that they were subject to Bornou. This country and people, we learn from Sultan Bello and his schoolmaster, are situated to the north of the great district of Adamowa, sometimes also called Foobena, which is mountainous, and " contains vales, hills, and rivers." The capital is Ghorin, an d two-thirds of its people are infidels, and the other third Mahommedan Felans.

The Shary, as stated, enters the Shad from the south. At Showey it is 650 yards broad in the dry season, and this after having thrown off three branches, one branch towards the north-east and two to the north-westward. Denham speaks of it as deep, descending from Showey to the Shad. When united in one stream it must be a considerable body of water; yet Denham states, that at Dugheia, below the first and a north-western branch, it is fordable in the dry season, the water reaching up to the neck. The north-western branch at Maffetai, where forded in the dry season, was so deep that the water came up to the body of the horse, and south-west of it, to some distance, the country is marshy, intersected with arms of the river, in one of which, where crossed, the water came up to the saddle of the horse. Quitting Showey and passing

Maffetai and the branch there, Denham travelled through the country to the west of the Shary, by Aflatai, Kola, and Alph, to the Shary, at Kussery, where the river, he says, is " a wide and handsome stream," and sweeps thence, first to the SS.W., and next S.W. to Kernuck, the capital of the province, or country of Loggun, where the river, he adds, flows with great beauty and majesty past the high walls of this capital, which contains 15,000 people, " the cleverest and most immoral in all Africa," says Denham, and is situated in lat. 11° 7′ N. The river here is, however, only 400 yards broad ; scarcely more than one-half the width, when the branches thrown off below are considered, that it is at Showey.

In order to prove that a river of considerable magnitude must join the Shary from the eastward, and most probably below Kussery, let us attend to the following facts. At Showey, the Shary, after having thrown off three very considerable branches, was, in the main stream, still 650 yards broad in the dry season, and so deep as to require the canoes to be propelled by oars instead of poles. At the ford of the western branch of the Shary, at Maffetai, the water came up to the neck in crossing it, and more to the westward divergents of considerable depth were also crossed. At Kernuck, the capital of Loggun, the united stream of the Shary was only 400 yards broad, the current about the same as it was at Showey, and though the depth at the former place is not stated, still there is the best reason to believe that it was not materially different. Denham, in his progress from Showey southward, passed at some distance westward from the Shary, until he came to Kussery, about twenty-five geographical miles above Loggun.   He has not given us the magnitude of the river at Kussery ; otherwise we should have been enabled to judge whether the junction of any river from the eastward took place above Kussery or below it ; but as he travelled from Kussery to Loggun, near the Shary, it is reasonable to suppose, that had any river joined it on the opposite side for that distance, he would have heard of it, and therefore it is probable, or indeed we may say certain, that the junction of the Bahr el Fittre, or the Bahr el Feydh, with the Shary, takes place below Kussery.   In the Quarterly Review, No. 58, it is stated, on the authority of accounts then received from Denham and Clapperton, after their arrival at Bornou, that in the African mode of expression, the Shary sent off a branch, which falls into Lake Fittre, and again, specifically and plainly, that "the Shary was said to receive *large supplies* from Lake Fittre, twelve days' journey to the east of the mouths of the Shary." This gives the distance correctly, and proves the water communication alluded to. Edrisi also, (see Rennell's map and dissertation in Park's Travels) particularly mentions the communication between the rivers in this part of Africa, as we shall afterwards have occasion to advert to.

Denham gives us no idea of its depth at Loggun, but states that the current was two miles and a half per hour, and that it came from the S.W., and that above Loggun it received a large branch, which came from the mountainous countries situated to the S.E. Sultan Bello's geographical memoir calls the branch alluded to above Loggun, an extensive fresh-water sea or river, named "Asoor or Ashoo," and that it lies between Lughwi and Bagherme. Clapperton, in his second journey, obtained further information about this river, from a traveller who had passed that way to Senaar, in his pilgrimage to Mecca. The route he gave was from Kano to Adamowa, then to Bagherme, then to Runza (perhaps the country of Runga or Roogha, of Sultan Bello, which lies between Baghermi and Waddai, and which is stony, but abounding with rivers—the people infidels), then Raffins, then Darfur, and then Kordofan. The river Ashoo, he states, joins the Shary above Loggun—it comes from the S.E., through the country of Bagherme. Till joined by this river, the Shary is fordable, and the Ashoo, he states, is the only river in the route not fordable during the summer, between the Quorra and the Bahr el Azreek. This river comes certainly from the N.W. corner of what is called the Mountains of the Moon. The pilgrims who come from Dar Saley to Senaar, and other places eastward, on their route to Mecca, state that the Bahr el Abiad comes from a country called Bahr el Lessee, from which country the waters on the other side of the hills at its source flow in the direction of Marok or Marocco. The direction, therefore, given to this branch in the map, cannot be materially wrong.

The confusion with regard to the positions of the countries
to the north-eastward, to the eastward, and to the south-eastward of Lake Shad, and the rivers which are found in the
latter, is very great; but part of the confusion alluded to arises
from the errors in the bearings given, and a want of a strict
attention to these, and to the details of these matters, as given
to us by different authorities.   Much, if not the whole of the
mass of confusion in which this portion of Africa has hitherto
been presented to us, may be unravelled by patience and
labour.   To elucidate it, however, in the clearest and most
correct manner possible, it is necessary to commence the investigation from Mourzook, the capital of Fezzan, a position which
has been correctly ascertained.   This city is situated in 25°
54′ N. lat., and 15° 50′ E. long.   From hence, the journey
across the desert to Kouka, the capital of Bornou, is a journey
of from forty-two to forty-five days.   There are a few facts and
points connected with places in this desert, which are of considerable importance in the inquiry at present in hand.   According to Denham's narrative, at Karsowa, a town about fifteen
miles to the north of Teggery, or Tegerby, the road branches
off for Waday and Kanem, in a direction of S.E.; the separation of this road is in 24° 24′ N. lat.   Denham states that this
road, according to his informants, was the nearest route to
Bornou, but that the reason why it was not generally taken,
was because it was more destitute of water than the one to the
westward, by which he travelled.   Between Omah and Mesh-
roo, in about 24° N. lat., he says that he saw Alowere Seghria,
a range of hills bearing E. by S.   Alowere el Kabir, a still
higher ridge, lay more to the east, but was not visible.   The
latter are the highest mountains in the Tibboo country, except
Escherdat Erner.   The road to Kanem from Mourzook lay
through the Alowere range.   From this point, viz., near the
parallel of 24°, the country to the south is very mountainous,
and more to the south the inhabitants are called Tibboo Irchad,
or Tibboo of the rock.   Two days' journey beyond Meshroo,
in about 23° N. lat., is the Hermat-el-wahr range of hills, the
highest seen from the time of leaving Mourzook.   The highest
peak rose about 600 feet, and formed part of a ridge which
stretches away eastward to Tibeste, or Tiberts, where the hills

are still higher and bolder. Six days' journey farther south, Denham came to Yaat, or Izhya, in about 20° 45' N. lat., to the east of which was a plain extending as far as the eye could reach, and to the west the high circular range of Tiggeren-duma, stretching westward five days' journey. Lyon, in the route given him from Tegerry to the Tibboo of Borgoo, gives, first, six and a half days' journey south, and then four days S.E. to Abo or Aboo, a well in the country of Tibeste. Buck-hardt, in a very accurate itinerary which was given him of the road from Waday to Mourzook, has this well in the very same position, counting the journeys from south to north; and he more-over states that it is in the district of Tiberts, and on the north side of the great ranges of mountains which extend thence to Dirky on the south, and denominated by him the Dirky ranges. The well Abo lies in about 22° N. lat. Twelve days' journey to the southward of it, the traveller crosses the mountains called *Hedjir-es-soud*, or the Black Rocks, so called from their colour, and which are part of the Dirky range. At the entrance of the Hedjir-es-soud, is the well called Byr-el-Assoad, where the caravans rest a few days. This ridge will lie in about 19° 30' N. lat. To the eastward, and betwixt the parallels of 19° and 22°, the country, as we learn from Lyon and others, is ex-ceedingly mountainous, and of volcanic origin. Lyon's in-formants told him that " in Tibesty, there is a large spring of hot water, which appears to boil as over a fire. The soil on which this spring is situated is composed entirely of sulphur, in many places quite pure." The taste is acid. The inhabitants use it medicinally; and people come from other countries to use it for the same purpose. The country, in these parts also, we learn, is by no means a barren waste; for we are told, that the inhabitants have a great number of camels, sheep, goats, and cattle, and that dates are so abundant that considerable armies might be supplied with them. In fact, from these, their ruthless invaders and destroyers from Fezzan draw their supplies, during their destructive inroads, and also for their journey homewards through their own barren wastes. The vales are fertile in corn, and its mountains afford excellent pasturage, and abound with innumerable springs. It is in this part of Africa, be it observed, a short distance to the eastward

of Izhyat, that Ptolemy places his Mount Girgires and the
springs of the two branches of the river Cinips, in 21° N. lat.,
which range of mountains corresponds exactly with the ranges
of mountains which are found in the country of Tibesty,
and the Tibboo of Borgoo, or the Tibboo of the rocks.

The country in this part of Africa, to the southward of
Ghatrone, and about Tegerby, is unquestionably very elevated.
Denham, during the early part of December, felt the cold very
severe in passing through these districts.   One day's journey
south of Izhya, Denham states, " January 31st, cold shivering
morning, thermometer, 49°;" and one day's journey south of
Anay, the thermometer, at 7 A.M., was down to 42°; but Lyon
gives us a more definite notion of its severity.   A little to
the north of Wudakaire, in about 24° N. lat., and on the 14th
of January, he states thus (p. 256) :—" Thermometer, 2° 30'
below zero,—water which we had left in a bowl over-night,
became ice of the thickness of half an inch, and the gerbas
(water skins) were so completely frozen up at the necks, that
we were obliged to melt them over a fire."   The Negro slaves,
fresh from Soudan, suffered severely from this degree of cold,
as they were without clothing, and obliged to sleep in the open
air without any covering.   This degree of cold, though in the
middle of winter, certainly almost under the tropic, could not
be felt but in a country, the elevation of which above the level
of the sea must be considerable ; and it is much to be
regretted that we have not a scientific estimate of what that
elevation is.*   The degree of cold felt in this place will also
help to account for the frost which Denham met with in the
Bede country, in the parallel of 13° N., very nearly in the
same season of the year (December), at which time, he states,
the wind was a little to the eastward of north.

From Yaat, or Izhyat, Denham and his party proceeded to
Bilma, situated in about 18° 40' N. lat., the capital of the

* Doubtless the adjoining country, and the country to the north, so strongly,
so deeply, and widely impregnated with saline particles as it is, would tend
greatly to increase the degree of cold felt at this place ; but still, after making
every allowance on this account, the degree of cold thus felt, almost under the
Tropic of Cancer, and so near the burning deserts of Africa, would argue a
country very elevated.

Tibboo, and a place of considerable importance, in the great road from Bornou to Mourzook. For a small space around it there is a little vegetation, and some springs of good water. Around it, to the S.W., the W., and the N.W., at a distance of a few miles, are, says Denham, "several lakes, in which are great quantities of very pure crystallized salt: some was brought to us for sale, in baskets, beautifully white, and of an excellent flavour. The time for gathering the salt was at the end of the dry season, when it was taken in large masses from the borders of the lake. This transparent kind they put into bags, and send it to Bornou and Soudan ; a coarser salt is also formed into hard pillars, and for which a ready market is found. In Soudan, a single pillar, weighing eleven pounds, brings four or five dollars. The Twaricks supply themselves with salt entirely from the Wadeys of the Tibboos. Twenty thousand bags of salt were said to have been carried off during the last year by the Twaricks alone." The inhabitants of Kashna and Agadez are said to have employed a thousand camels in this trade. The Twaricks inhabit the whole of the Great Desert, from the meridian of Mourzook westward to the meridian of Lake Dibbie.

The lakes here mentioned, and this place, are, no doubt, the salt lake of Domboo mentioned by Rennell and other geographers. The distance, viz., forty days' journey N.E. from Kashna, corresponds exactly. The district of Africa also, in which Bilma is situated, is, we learn from Lyon, called Kowar or Kour; in fact, Kowar and Bilma are the same place ; and we learn from the early Arabian geographers, that Kawar or Kour bounded the land of Kanem to the north.

South from Bilma, the country for the space of seven days' journey is a complete desert, and scarcely anything is to be seen but moving billows of burning sands. Immediately beyond this point, the country for a day's journey assumes the appearance of the heaths in England, with plenty of cattle ; and three days' farther south, the travellers came to Kanemani, where the country, even at that time (January 31st), was found to be verdant, and covered with flowery grasses ; and during the next day's journey, they travelled through herbage resembling wild corn, which came up to the horses' knees.

Kanemani is about sixty-two miles to the north of Lari, which town is situated on the N.W. borders of Lake Shad, in 14° 14′ N. lat., in the country of Kanem. To the north and to the N.E , the country is inhabited by different tribes of Tibboos.

The next point of importance, and it is one of great importance, concerning the geography of this part of Africa to consider, is the position of the land of Kanem. The following authorities will enable us to do this with considerable accuracy. Lyon (p. 123) pointedly informs us, that Kanem is the northern boundary of Bornou; and at p. 129, he further clearly establishes the position of the S.W. part of this country. In one of the inroads made into this country by Mukni, the merciless ruler of Fezzan, Lyon states, that "he made an attack on the defenceless people of Kanem, Moslem as well as Kaffir, and having first burnt their town, pursued them to the banks of the river (Yaoo): many were drowned in attempting to cross it, others were taken out of the water, and the women and children who had not the power of escaping were caught on the banks; the number of captives made on that day amounting to 1800." " The Shiekh of Kanem, whom I have already mentioned, was fortunate enough, on this dreadful occasion, to escape to Birnie, many of his family having fallen sacrifices to Mukni's barbarity." Denham confirms the account given of this part of Kanem. At p. 283, he mentions, when on his return to the north, that five considerable Kanemboo villages, viz. Ittagoni, Betagana, Asaden, Yeouganee, and Boro, were on the banks of the Yeou. At pp. 284, 289, he mentions that Barka-Gana, who had gone on an expedition to the N.E. shores of Lake Shad beyond Tangalia, had been worsted in that expedition, and compelled to return home through Kanem; and as he further states, down on Kanem to Woodie, &c., for supplies, at which town he met him. Again, he states (p. 288), that the country of Kanem is in a most wretched state, and that the population thereof depends alternately for protection from the sovereigns of Bornou and Waday; but that the protection afforded by either party is not effectual; while self-interest makes each of the powers long to annex it to their own dominions. It is accordingly subjected to perpetual and destructive inroads by the Arabs from Fezzan, who every year desolate a large portion of the country, and carry away thousands of the helpless inhabitants into a state of slavery. In another place also, wherein he describes his expedition to the eastern shores of Lake Shad, he gives an account of another expedition which had been sent by the Sheikh of Bornou against Mendoo and Mapo, the capital of Kanem, on the N.E. shores of Lake Shad; the latter town about fifty miles from Tangalia. Also, he further states, of his penetrating from Lari eastward along the lake through Kanemboo villages; and that on his arrival at Lari from Mourzook, some slaves who had been liberated at the latter place, and who belonged to Kanem, went eastward from Lari to their native place. Sheeref Inhammed, a very great traveller in the interior of Africa, also places the country of Kanem north of Bornou, and on the road to Mourzook.

Kanem was formerly a very extensive and very powerful country, though now broken to pieces and reduced to the most wretched state. The old Egyptian historian, Makrisi, gives us the following account of this country —" On the borders of the Nile, lies also Kanem, the king of which is a Mahommedan. It is at a very great distance from the country of Maly. The residence of the king is in the town called Heymy. The first town, on the side towards Egypt, is called Zela (Zeilah in Fezzan, 26° 11′ 48″ N. lat., and 16° 42′ E. long.), and the last, reckoning lengthways, is called Kaka, about three months' journey distant from the other. The people of this country go veiled (that is, as the original means, they cover their faces with a handkerchief); their king is hidden behind curtains, and sees nobody, except on the two feast-days, in the morning, at the time of the Aszeer. During the whole of the year, nobody speaks to him, except behind the curtain. Their main food is rice, which grows there without being sown ; they have wheat, dhourra, figs, lemons, badenjons, turnips, and dates. Their currency is cotton-stuffs, woven in the country, and called Dandy, or Wandy: every piece is ten peeks in length; and they make purchases with pieces of it of one quarter and more. They use also as a currency, shells (*i.e.* cowries), glass beads, broken copper, all of which have their fixed value

in the cotton stuffs. To the south of them are forests and
deserts, inhabited by wild creatures." .... " The gourds grow
to a large size : they make ships of them, upon which they
cross the Nile." The inhabitants "are of the sect of the Imam
Malek Ibn Anes. It is said they are descended from the
Berbers." The description, thus given by Makrisi, of Kanem
in the early days of its renown, corresponds in every respect
with the present state of the country, and the customs of the
population round the shores of Lake Shad. The produce
of the country, especially rice, the customs adhered to by
the sovereigns of Bornou and their people, and the currency
in the country, are, as we learn from both Lyon and Denham
and others, the exact state of things in Bornou at this
day. And a last and perhaps the strongest proof of the
whole, regarding the position of Kanem and the identity of
these countries, is that stated by Burkhardt, viz. that the
religion of the people of Kanem, on the east shores of the lake
Shad, is of the " sect of Imam Malek Ibn Anes;" which Ibn
al Vardi, the old Arabian geographer or historiographer, also
states, thus :—" Konem, or Kanem, is a large country situated
along the Nile : the inhabitants were all Mussulmen, of the sect
of Imam Malek." Edrisi states, that Kanem was a large
district; and adds, "some Negroes stated, that Kaugha (the
Kaka mentioned by Makrisi, for the word is the same) was subject to it." Abulfeda, on the authority of Ibn Said, says of this
place,—" Kawkaw is the residence of the Sultan of these parts,
and that he is an infidel. 'Opposite to him, on the west, are the
Moslems of Ghana, and on the east, those of El Kanem. This
place has a river named after itself, but the place is to the eastward of this its river. It is said in the Kanun, that Kawkaw
is situated between the equinoctial line and the beginning of
the first climate. It is said in the Azzizi, that Kawkaw is in
the latitude of 10°, and that its inhabitants are Moslems."

There can be no longer any doubt, therefore, about the position
of Kanem. It formerly comprehended all the country from
Zeilah in the north, to Bagherme on the south, and from a
portion of the country west of Lake Shad on the west, to the
borders of Dongola on the east; and included the whole country
then known under the name of Kawar, or Kouar, or the modern

country of Bilma and the Tibboos, which country of Kour or Kawar, the early Arabian geographers state was bounded north by the Desert, which separated Egypt from Fezzan, adding, that the country mentioned, extended eastward to Al Wahat. In its reduced state, the land of Kanem will extend from the borders of the Bahr el Ghazelle on the east, around the northern shores of Lake Shad, to near Gambarou, on the west, and stretching north from the lake to about the parallel of 16° N. lat. Kaugha or Kawkaw, which was said to be formerly subject to Kanem, we readily recognise in Caugha or Kooka, to the southward and eastward of Lake Fittre.

With regard to Lake Shad itself, the extent of it, as given by Sheikh el Kanemy, viz. twenty days' journey in circumference, or 300 miles, is certainly the most correct. The extent given to it by the constructor of the map with Denham's work, considerably exceeds that given to it by Denham himself. From Kooka to Angernou, he gives one day's journey south; Angernou to Angala, two days' journey S.E.; Angala to Showey one day's journey east; Showey to the ford over the Shary, one day's journey S.E. From the Shary to Tangalia he gives the distance travelled east, about fifty-two miles. From Tangalia to Woodie, by Lari, he states the distance to be eight days' journey, and from Woodie to Kouka, the distance, according to him and to other authorities, is four days' journey. These distances taken together, would, even including the turnings and windings of those to the south, give just twenty days' journey as the circumference of the lake, which Sheikh el Kanemy states it to be, say 300 geographical miles; whereas, the circumference of the lake in the map alluded to is rather more than seven degrees, or, in the general bearings, about 430 miles. The lake is clearly extended nearly a degree too much to the east, and the course of the river Shary, very nearly as much too far in an easterly direction. Its course to the lake will thus be confined to within the meridian of 16° E. long., and which other facts, about to be stated, go to establish: or rather, as it should be stated, while the course of the Shary is more direct from the south, the point of its entering the lake, and the centre of the lake itself, should be removed one degree more to the eastward. Bornou, whether Kouka, the

present, or New Birnie, the late capital, is due south from
Fezzan and Tegerby; both Lyon and others distinctly state this.
The former, in particular, gives the route from Tegerby to
Kanem twenty days' journey south by east, and fifteen days'
journey from Kanem to Bornou south by west. This most
clearly places Bornou a little to the eastward of Tegerby, and
Kouka, the capital, at least a degree more to the eastward than
the point where it has been hitherto placed. Denham and his
party most certainly travelled to the eastward of south in all
the southern part of their journey. The distances given to
the districts of Tibeste, some tribes of the Tibboo, and more
especially of the road from Mourzook to Waday, clearly
establish this. Where that road leaves the path by which
they travelled to Bornou in a S.E. direction, they distinctly
state, that it was the nearest and the shortest road to Bornou.
Taking the whole of these facts into consideration, Kouka and
Lake Shad have hitherto been placed at least one degree too
much to the west, and removing them, as they ought to be,
one degree more to the east, will correspond very exactly
indeed with the distances which Clapperton travelled southward from Mourzook to Bornou, westward from Kouka, by
Kano, to Saccatoo and to the Niger; and, moreover, to the
longitudes where Ptolemy places both his Lybian Lake and
his Lake Nuba, and also with all the distances which are
given regarding the extent and the positions of the countries
from the Shary eastward to the Nile.

The elevation of Lake Tschad above the level of the sea is
differently estimated; from the observations by Clapperton, it
is calculated to be about 1300 feet. A French writer reduces
it to about 900. Looking, however, carefully at every circumstance connected with it, the very high lands which the degree
of cold felt in the countries to the north, to the west, and to the
south, give us to see exist in that part of Africa, the elevation
must be a great deal more than even the highest of the estimates
given. The country all around, more especially to the south
and to the east, is evidently a very singular country. The soil
around it, to a great distance, is all alluvial, and to the eastward, and to the S.E., and to the N.E., the country is not
only alluvial and level, but the beds of what have formerly

been large rivers are in more than one place found, and also other considerable lakes are found in these places. Some of these are probably the remains of mighty rivers which are formed during the tropical rains, the deep pools of which, (when these streams in the middle and lower portion of their courses are dried up, and thus cut off in the dry season,) remain as lakes, and continue full throughout the dry season, as Burkhardt distinctly informs us are the facts.

The next points to consider are, the positions of the countries called Bagherme, the Bahr el Ghazelle, Dar Saley, or, as the latter is also called, Waday and Bergoo, with the other countries to the eastward of them, together with the rivers which are found to flow through them. First, as regards Bagherme, Sultan Bello informs us that next, and east to Adamowa, is the province Lughwi or Loggun, and that from this country to the territory of Bagherme is two days' journey "through mountains and rivers." Mr. Beaufoy states that Bagherme lies twenty days' journey S.E. of Bornou, meaning, of course, this distance from Old Birnie, the former capital. Denham pointedly states 'that Bagherme lies to the south of Bornou, and that the river Shary divides Bornou from that kingdom; the province of Loggun on the Shary thus bounding Bagherme on the S.W., and Bornou on the S.E., to which latter empire, however, Loggun belongs. The territory of Bornou, he states, stretches south to the parallel of 10° N. and E. to the Shary, and even, as he states, to 18° E. long., but which of course must be wrong, as that will extend beyond the Shary. Lyon also informs us that Bornou is bounded on the east by Bagherme, and that from New Birnie to Bagherme is ten long days' journey S.E.; Loggun, which belongs to Bornou, being just half way betwixt the two points. Denham gives the distance to Loggun as nearly, or it may be said exactly the same. Bowditch mentions, that the capital of Bagherme is five days to the east of the Shary; and Browne gives the extent of the kingdom of Bagherme to be twelve days from east to west, and fifteen days' journey from north to south. Sultan Bello gives the former distance ten days' journey, and the latter as being greater than that. The information which Dupuis received was to the effect that Bagherme, Dar Saley, and Darfur lay east, and in rotation from Bornou, and that Bagherme was twenty days to the east of Bornou, the distance probably being taken from Old Birnie in place of New Birnie. To the south of Bagherme the country is mountainous, and inhabited by Pagans, into which, particularly Battah and Mulqui, (Mosgou,) the people of Bagherme make frequent inroads, in order to procure slaves. Denham heard that a branch of the Shary came from the eastward amongst these mountains. Mesna was the former capital of Bagherme, but Denham mentions Kernuk as the capital, which having been destroyed by the forces of Bornou, the Sultan, at the time he was at Bornou, was proposing to build it again. From Buckhardt we learn that the three Arab tribes which dwell in the principal districts of Katakou, and which seem to comprehend the eastern frontier of Bornou, are Beni Hassan, &c. in the districts of Dar Mandara; Dar Makkary, and Dar Ankala or Angala, Dar Afady, and Dar Kolfey, the Gulphy of Denham. The tribe of Beni Hassan also inhabit a part of the Bahr el Ghazelle. Browne informs us that, from the capital of Bagherme to Kattacum or Kattakou, the bearing is N. $\frac{1}{4}$ W., and, from Kattakou to the capital of Bornou, the bearing is the same, and that the total distance is eighteen days' journey; and to show further the southern position of Bagherme, Clapperton's informants, who gave him the route from Kano to Senaar, by the Bahr el Abiad, enumerates the states thus: from Kano, first, Adamowa; second, Bagherme; third, Runza; fourth, Raffins; fifth, Darfur; sixth, Kordofan. Cotton is produced in Bagherme in great abundance, and large quantities of cloth are manufactured from it by the women, both for home consumption and for exportation. It is engaged in perpetual wars with its neighbours, and was some time ago overrun and conquered by its powerful eastern neighbour of Waday.

The position and extent of Bagherme, therefore, is thus distinctly ascertained, viz: to the east of Bornou and the Shary, and considerably to the south of Lake Shad. The next place to consider, is the celebrated district called Bahr el Ghazelle. According to Burkhardt, this district bears from Bornou in the direction of the Kebly "Mecca". Lyon is most specific: the south part of it, he says, bears E.N.E. distant ten days' journey from New Birnie, Bornou; and he adds, it "runs N.E. and S.W. to a great distance." The bearing given by Lyon is exactly the same as that given by Burkhardt, and brings us to the S.E. corner of Lake Shad, nearly, but to the north of Tangalia. Near this place, Denham informs us that the army of Sheikh Kanemy met their allies, the Shouaas, of the tribe Dugganah, under their chieftain Tahir. This tribe, we learn from Burkhardt, the Dugganah or Degganah, dwell in the Bahr el Ghazelle, in that portion thereof which is nearest to the land of Kanem; and he also states, that it is in the country inhabited by this tribe that the fresh water lake named Hadeba, ten days' journey from Fittre and eight from Kanem, is situated. Burkhardt mentions a curious fact with regard to the Arabs of the tribe of Beni Hassan, who dwell in the Bahr el Ghazelle, and more to the south, namely, that, when they pray, they turn their faces to Dar Saley, which points out that the latter country lies from them in the same bearing as Mecca. The population of the Bahr el Ghazelle, says Burkhardt, retire in the dry season towards the limits of Kattakou, Bagherme, and Dar Saley, and that they intermarry with the people of these countries. The Bahr el Ghazelle is an immense wadey or valley, full of trees, and having many inhabitants, who are wanderers; a considerable portion of them are pagans. The people are a fine race, well made, and very active. The general dress is leather. The cattle are in such numbers, that parts of the country appear literally covered with them; there are also vast numbers of camels, and large herds of sheep. Elephants, rhinoceroses, lions, buffaloes, and cameleopards, are also very numerous. Elephants' teeth are found in great numbers, without any to carry them away. Rice grows wild. All accounts agree, that in ancient times there was a river of great magnitude which flowed through it. It is a great extent of low grounds thickly covered with trees, and inhabited by pastoral Arabs and negro tribes. Immense bones of unknown animals and fish are frequently found here in a state of petrifaction. By the description which the natives give of the bones and vertebræ, some of the fish must have been ten or twelve feet in length. FIVE days' journey N.W. lays another great wadey or valley, called Bahr Battali, in every respect the same as the Bahr el Ghazelle. Some state that it is part of the Bahr el Ghazelle: they may certainly be reckoned districts in every part of a similar description. It is also asserted to have been formerly the bed of a great river, and petrified bones are stated to have been found in it. Burkhardt, in the itinerary which he gives from Dar Saley to Mourzook states, that at fourteen days' journey from the former country, the traveller comes to a place called Bahr, a low ground, where, by digging pits in the sand, good water is found in great plenty; it is called Bahr, because in the rainy season the ground is overflowed. The position of this place will agree with the position of the Bahr Battali, and the latter is probably a continuation of the former, both being either the bed of a rainy-season stream, or else the former bed of a river issuing from a lake formed by some rivers to the eastward. Still farther to the N.E., and placed as correctly as the bearing and distance given will enable us, is the considerable fresh-water lake called Boushashem, which is said to overflow its banks much during the rains.

Between Kanem and the Shary is the district called Dar Karka, which district, says Buckhardt, forms no part of the Bahr el Ghazelle, and is inhabited by the Bedouins named Kory. These people pasture their cattle on the banks of a large river called Bahr el Feydh, or inundating river, from its periodical risings, and which river empties itself into the Shary. The district of country here mentioned, appears to be that situated on the S.E. shores of Lake Shad, and betwixt it and the kingdom of Bagherme. The position of both it and the Bahr el Ghazelle is thus clearly and satisfactorily ascertained; the Bahr el Ghazelle stretching from the eastern shores of Lake Shad, north-eastward to the territory of Dar Saley, and more northward to the lakes Bahr Ma Halou, &c. &c. and south-westward from the land of Kanem to the borders of the Kory, who dwell next to Bagherme, which latter country, or rather the N.E. quarter thereof, Buckhardt informs us is four or five days distant from the Bahr el Ghazelle.

Lyon in his travels, (p. 266,) gives a singular account of two countries or districts in eastern Africa, which he calls Wajunga.

He states that they are ten days' journey to the north of
Waday, and to the east and to the south of the Tibboo of
Borgoo. That Kanem lies twelve days S.W. of Borgoo ;
the Bahr el Ghazelle five days south, and Waday fourteen
days SS.E. This district of Wajunga, he states, "has two
large towns or districts one day E. and W. of each other.
The eastern one has a very large river running N. and S.
through it, 500 or 600 yards in breadth, and of great depth.
The water is brackish, and in it are abundance of very fine
fish. The whole of this country is very mountainous, having
large rocky tracks of perfectly black stone." " Some of the
rocks here, as well as in Borgoo, are so perpendicular and
high, that, to use an Arab expression, you could not see their
tops without losing your tagaia or red cap. The western
Wajunga has three rivers running through it, two of which are
sweet as honey, and one salt. The largest, which the Arabs
say is the Nile, is of great breadth, and very deep, and runs
from west to east. Dates are very plentiful here, and the cattle
very numerous. There are also elephants in this country,
and multitudes of ostriches. The people of both sexes are
clothed in skins; some, however, wear a curious leather gown.
They are a fine race of people, and are swift runners, but the
Arabs consider them in the light of Caffirs, asserting that they
were not made by God, but that they came by chance."

This account given by Lyon opens up an almost new and
very remarkable feature in African geography. If it is correct,
the country and rivers which he mentions will lie in about
16° to 17° of N. lat., and 21° to 22° E. long. The country of
the Tibboo of Borgoo, lies one month's journey in a bearing
about S.E. from Mourzook. From Borgoo to Waday he
gives fourteen days' journey SS.E. From the Borgoo of
Yen he gives nine and a half days' journey to Werda, but
without the bearing, but that bearing was probably south ;
which, taken together with some allowance for the extent of
the country of Wajunga, or considering the distance from Wajunga to Werda to be only to the confines of the latter country,
would certainly make up the distance on the different bearings,
between Mourzook and Werda. But how shall we then
account for so many and such large rivers in this portion of

Africa, and the almost total silence of writers and travellers about them? A river 1800 feet broad, in eastern Wajunga, and running from N. to S., must have had its sources at a great distance to the north, even considerably into the interior of the range Girgires of Ptolemy. The country which produces such a stream, and the tributaries which it must necessarily receive, must, as a matter of course, be fertile, and if so, then surely, through this country would have been the nearest and best road from Waday and Bornou to Egypt. The distance from one cultivated country to the other could not be above 600 miles, yet there is no account of any caravans passing by such a route. Both Lyon and Burkhardt were very explicitly informed, that, betwixt Mourzook and Waday, the traveller did not pass a single river, although there were abundance of excellent wells, which afford very good water. From Dirky to Abo, a distance of 400 miles, the country is certainly exceedingly mountainous, and to the eastward of that line of road still more so, while the great quantity of dates which the country of the Tibboo of Borgoo produces, and the great number of sheep, goats, and cattle, which the natives possess, show that, although the country is mountainous and bare, yet, that it is not altogether barren. Still, had the southern part thereof given rise to such rivers as Lyon mentions, the probability is, that they would have been more and better known.

Ptolemy no doubt lays down his river Cinips as issuing from Mount Girgires, and running in a direction directly opposite to the greatest river of Wajunga, and when his longitudes are corrected in the same meridians, or very nearly so. He makes the sources of the Cinips to spring in Mount Girgires in lat. 21° 30′ N., the eastern branch in 45°, the western in 40° E. long. from Ferro, and to unite in 25° N. lat. and 42° E. long. from the point just mentioned.

Having thus examined the positions of the countries situated to the eastward of Lake Shad, let us next attend, as far as the information in our possession will enable us, to the positions of the rivers which run through them. We have already considered the Shary and its tributaries. That branch, which is represented as coming from the eastward through a mountainous country, which is situated to the south of Bagherme, will

fall in with the Junchor of Rennell's map. Denham's information on this point is very specific; and beyond this large river
to the south of Bagherme is a pagan country, represented to
be very populous. Denham adds, that the Shary was stated
to come from a Kirdy country, called Bosso. Clapperton's
informant told him that the river Asoo came from the S.E.,
through Bagherme, and fell into the Shary above Loggun.
Lyon states, that a large river runs through Bagherme called
Kamadakoo, and that to the eastward of Bagherme there is
another large river, from which fish are taken and carried to
the Wara market. Denham clearly intimates that there is a
river to the eastward of Loggun, which runs through Bagherme, for just as he had begun to explore the river above
Kernuck, he was compelled to desist and to fly from Loggun,
because "the Baghermies were again on the Medba, and
coming towards Loggun." This river will answer to the
Terruge of Rennell's map. Regarding the Shary itself,
Denham found its course to be from S. to N. Burkhardt's
informants gave him the geographical line of the river for the
current of the stream, viz, from N.E. to S.W., although one
informant, who was the most correct, gave the course of the
stream to be from S.W. to N.E. Lyon was also told that the
Shary ran from S.W. to N.E., and that the natives around
it said the river ran past Fur. Browne's informants stated,
that on the road from Bagherme to Bornou, two rivers are
crossed by travellers, one of which is called Kitchena, which
runs from S.W. to N.E.; in this we recognise the Shary:
and the other river must be the Gambularam, or more probably the Bahr el Feydh.

Buckhardt gives us the name and the source of the Gir or
Om Teymam, the same as the Bahr Misselad of Browne.
Browne informs us that the Bahr Misselad is crossed three
days' journey west of Wara; and he further states that the town
or village of Batta, two and a quarter days' journey west from
Wara, is situated on a small river which flows from the south,
and then turns west and falls into the Bahr el Fittre. Batta
belongs to the country of Dar Misselad. In the small river
here mentioned, we readily find a stream formed by the Ouled
Rashed and the Abou Redjeyle of Buckhardt, small streams

which he states are found from Wara eastward on the route
(evidently a southern route) to Darfur; the other river which
he mentions, the Om Ettymam, being clearly a different river
from his Om Teymam, or Gir, which he informs us is the principal river that runs near the western boundaries of Darfur.
The three rivers just mentioned, having formed a junction, pursue
their course westward, by Batta, to the Bahr el Fittre, where
at the point alluded to there is said to be a lake of some magnitude, variously reported to be four or more days' journey in
circumference. Tahir, the Degganah chief, who was born on
its banks, pointedly stated that a river entered the lake from the
S.W. or by the customary African mode of expression, that a
river flowed from the lake in the direction mentioned; for that
such was his meaning is clear, when he stated that Lake Fittre
and Lake Shad were different, because the former had an
outlet, whereas the other had none. A water communication
from this lake unto a lake or river considerably to the westward
was said by Edrisi to exist, and is marked by Rennell in his
map accordingly. There can be no doubt that this river is
the Bahr el Feydh, or inundating river of Buckhardt, which he
says empties itself into the Shary, and on the northern bank of
which is the country called Dar Karka, where the Bedouin
Arabs, called Kory, dwell between Bagherme and the Bahr el
Ghazelle and Kanem. The junction of this river with the
Shary accounts, as has been stated, for the lessened magnitude
of that stream at Kernuck, compared to what it is at Showey,
connected with its other branches.

Sultan Bello and other authorities enable us clearly to know
that Bagherme and the countries immediately adjoining it are
intersected by many rivers. There is yet another to be noticed,
an important point mentioned both by ancient and modern authority. This is the country, or district, or village, named Dar
Kooka, or Kaugha. This place is eight and a half days' journey
west of Wara, and according to Lyon, sixteen days' journey E.
by S. of New Birnie in Bornou. Bowditch gives the distance
from the boundary of Bornou to this place, which he names
Caugha, to be fifteen days' journey; and he gives the distance
to Fittre to be the same, which is nearly correct, for Lyon gives
it fifteen days easterly from New Birnie. From Kooka to

Budagho, or the district of high mountains of black stone, is two days' journey west, and from Budagho or Mudagho to Lake Fittre is one and a half day's journey N.W. Burkhardt calls this place Kauka. Edrisi calls it Kaugha, and says that it is situated " on the north bank of the fresh water from which its inhabitants draw to drink. This city is subject to the empire of Vancara; nevertheless some of the negroes reckon it under the dominion of Kanem. It is a populous city, without walls, famous for business, and useful arts for the advantage of its people." He adds that it is one and a half month's journey from Ghana, and one month's journey from Damocla, or the king-dom of Old Dongola on the Egyptian Nile.* It is clear, then, that Kooka or Kaugha, (for the name has the same meaning,) is situated upon a river, which river must come from the south, and is probably the river running to the east of Bagherme, alluded to by Lyon. It will answer to the Miri, mentioned by Arabian travellers, and alluded to in Rennell's and other maps. This river will naturally join the Misselad or Gir, a little to the eastward of the Bahr el Fittre, and whether that be a river or a small lake is not of much consequence to the inquiry in hand. Browne states that " the people on the banks of the Bahr el Fittre are called Abu-Semmim, and are Mahommedans. They use little boats for the purpose of passing from one place to another on-the river." Burkhardt gives the Arab tribes around Fittre to be the Belale, who inhabit nearest to the Bahr el Ghazelle, Djaathene, El Heleylat, and El Khozar.

From Kanem to Fittre, according to Buckhardt, is a journey of eight days. From Tangalia, according to Tahir, to Fittre, is a journey of four days; and from the Bahr el Ghazelle to Fittre, according to Burkhardt, is a journey of five days. The Degganah chief, already mentioned, states a curious and im-portant fact regarding the country to the S.E. of Tangalia. He informed Denham that, in travelling both to Fittre and to Waday, they passed over a " high country where there were but few wells," &c., on which account he was exceedingly anxious to. purchase Denham's water-skins, being able to obtain none like them in that part of Africa. Ten days' journey from Fittre is a place named Mezrag, near which is a fresh-water lake, Bahr

* See p. 208, for Ibn Said's particular description and position of this place.

Ma Halou, two days' journey long and half a day's journey broad, in what is called Wady Hadeba, and represented to be always filled with water. The position of this lake we are enabled to ascertain with accuracy, because Buckhardt informs us that it is in the country occupied by the Arab tribes Dagganah, who inhabit the country in the Bahr el Ghazelle, close to Kanem. From the Bahr el Ghazelle to Bagherme, Burkhardt informs us that it is a journey of five days.

There is another point and place in this quarter of Africa that requires to be noticed. This is the city of Kuku, mentioned by Edrisi. The passage we must take in his own words, according to the translation of the abridgment of his work, which only has reached Europe. " From Caugha to the city of Kuku, is twenty days' journey towards the north at the rate of the camel's travelling. The city Kuku is famous among the negroes for magnitude ; it is situated on the bank of a river, which, flowing from the north part, washes it, and affords drink to the inhabitants ; and although many negroes relate that the city Kuku is situated on the bank of the Nile, others place it near a river flowing into the Nile. It is, however, I apprehend, the true opinion, that this river glides along till it passes for many days beyond Kuku, and then pours itself out into the desert, through sands and plains, in the same manner as the river Euphrates doth in Mesopotamia." After giving a splendid account of the court and the power of the king, he says : " With respect to the clothing of this country, the common people cover their nakedness with the skins of beasts, but the merchants clothe themselves with vests and tunics, wear caps on their heads, and adorn themselves with gold, &c."

If this account of Edrisi's could be relied on, and there seems no reason to doubt its general accuracy, we should have a clear solution of the rivers of Wajunga, mentioned by Lyon ; for the distance which Edrisi gives between Caugha and Kuku, twenty days' journey N., would place the latter town in 17° N. lat., near the point where the town of eastern Wajunga, and the great river coming from the north, is stated to be. It is also curious, that when the great error in Ptolemy's longitude between the Canary Isles and Alexandria is corrected, that the sources of the rivers mentioned will be in the mountains of Tibeste.

The information which D'Anville in his latter days received regarding the interior of Northern Africa is on all hands acknowledged to have been excellent. That celebrated geographer had received information that a river ran in the Bahr el Ghazelle, or, as it is otherwise called, Wad, or Wady el Ghazelle—the Arabic word used to denote a river—and joined the Nile, or the lake Zad during the inundation (*Mem. Inscrip.* vol. xxvi. p. 6). Nothing is more probable than this; and, in fact, other accounts go to confirm it. All accounts agree in stating clearly, that large districts to the eastward of the lake are flooded during the rains; but which are found in extensive cultivation during the dry season. The river, therefore, in the Bahr el Ghazelle is no doubt a continuation of the river of the Kuku of Edrisi, descending from Lake Boushashem, and that of Bahr Ma Halou. The fact that the beds of many rivers in Africa are dry during the dry season is well known. Take, for example, what Clapperton states regarding the Quarrama in that part of its course at and above Kutri; likewise, also, the small river near Timbuctoo. The course of the river also from the north or the north-west, as stated by Lyon's informants, is countenanced by the accounts received by Beaufoy, namely, that a branch of the Nile, erroneously called the Egyptian Nile, runs into the desert of Bilma, (*African Association*, 4to, p. 138;) and, at p. 142, he states, that the river of Bornou runs north-west into the desert of Bilma, though, it may be observed, that Lake Shad runs from Birnie in that direction, and may therefore really be the river alluded to by Beaufoy. The junction of a stream through the Bahr el Ghazelle with Lake Shad, or Zad, or Zadi, however, is fully confirmed by the information and express statement made by Sheikh el Kanemy, in his letter to Denham, already alluded to, namely, that Lake Shad was joined by rivers flowing from "*the right*" (that is the south), "and EAST of our country." Thus, the account of the celebrated French geographer and others, previously doubted and lately set aside, is amply and satisfactorily confirmed; as is also the report given by Edrisi, that the river of Kuku runs south, and expends itself in the sands of the desert, like the Tigris in Mesopotamia; in other words, was temporarily absorbed and cut off in the

dry season. Ptolemy places a river in this quarter of Africa
(11° W. of Alexandria), descending from Mount Girgires, and
unquestionably the river of Kuku of Edrisi, as forming two
lakes, and in the intermediate space sinking under ground,
and again appearing; in other words, in a portion of its course,
dry, except during the rainy season.

The accounts received by the African Association from Sheeref
Inhammed regarding the mountainous district of Tibeste, is
extremely interesting, and bears out the accounts received by
Lyon. From Mourzook to the frontiers of that kingdom is one
hundred and fifty miles; and next comes a desert, two hundred
miles broad. After this, the district of Tibeste is entered, bearing
S.E. from Mourzook. The western portion of the mountains
is crossed on the eastern route to Bornou. In two days the
travellers pass vast hills, when they come to a fertile and beautifully diversified country, four days' journey broad, well
peopled, and abounding with cows and sheep. Ben Ali, who
travelled over the centre of these mountains, states, that on
the twenty-sixth day's travelling, after leaving Mourzook, he
came to the part named Waddan, or the Rivers, where the
land was very prolific, and the people had dates, tobacco, and
multitudes of sheep, and goats, and camels, and horses. They
traded with Bornou, and exported, amongst other things, *wheat*
to that kingdom. Bornou was twenty days' forced marches
distant; though the road was chiefly through a sandy desert,
yet there were some places well watered. Kanem, five days'
journey south of the desert of Bilma, he says, contained multitudes of camels and horses. The capital was ten days' journey
from Bornou, and the capital of the latter place was seven days'
journey from the northern frontier.

The warlike movements of the nations, and the slave-catching expeditions to this part of Africa, occasionally enable us to
ascertain and to fix the positions of towns and countries.
Thus, in addition to other passages which have been quoted
from Denham, regarding the position of Bagherme, he says,
(p. 214,) " the Baghermies had once more come down the
south side of the Shary, and induced the people of Loggun to
declare for them," &c. Lyon, (p. 231,) tells us that the slaves
which come to Fezzan, from Waday, are procured from Kooka

or Kaugha, Kota, Tama, Runga, and various petty states in their vicinity. According to Browne, the infidel nations nearest to Darfur, from which slaves are brought, is, first, Dar Kulla; second, Benda; next, Djenke, or Donke, or Donga; fourth, the Yem-Yems, whose country we know; and lastly, Olla, which is in the neighbourhood of Ashantee. Tahir, the Daghana chief, stated a curious fact to Denham, viz., that Bahr Fittre was always known to the people around it as the Darfur and Shilluk water. This lake appears to be the Nuba Palus of Ptolemy, which lake is placed by him about one degree and a half to the south of his Lybia Palus, and ten degrees and a half to the westward of the meridian of Alexandria. The rivers to the westward of Wara are shown to be of considerable magnitude, by the facts that they abound with crocodiles and hippopotami, and are crossed in canoes by the inhabitants. Mr. Seetzen was informed at Cairo, that the river near Wara was as broad as the Nile at the latter place; and Ritchie heard that the river, after issuing from Lake Fittre, was a mile broad. The accounts we have of other rivers in the neighbourhood enable us to reduce this mode of African amplification; but still sufficient will remain to show that they are considerable streams.

There is one bearing and distance given by Browne which has created much confusion in the geography of this part of Africa. It is the bearing and distance from Dar Ruma to Wara, eight and a half days' journey N.E. The true bearing should be S.W. Such mistakes are quite common in the information given by African travellers. The informant was looking from Wara to Dar Ruma, instead of looking from Dar Ruma to Wara, which was the distance and the bearing which he really had under consideration. Pages might be filled with examples of similar errors in other places.

Bornou is, as has been stated, a very extensive country: Dar Saley is next to it in importance. Ten different languages, it is said, are spoken by the nations comprehended in the empire of Bornou. Bagherme ranks next to Dar Saley. The Mahommedan religion has the sway in all these countries, but a considerable portion of the population, comprehended within the territory of each, is still pagan. The interminable wars which are carried on betwixt the states mentioned, and also betwixt these states and their pagan neighbours, destroy all security, render all improvement impossible, and reduce countries, which otherwise would be most productive, to general scenes of ruin and desolation; nor will it, nor can it be otherwise, until a better order of things arise in this part of Africa, and, indeed, it may be said, in every part of Africa, when security and industry will prevail, and capital by labour be created in, or introduced into, all these countries.

Amongst other countries in this quarter deserving of notice there is one named Runza, which appears to be situated to the S.E., or on the S.E. quarter of Bagherme, and on the S.W. quarter of Waday.   In the route from Kano to Senaar, which Clapperton obtained from a native traveller, he gives the countries from Kano eastward in their order thus:—first Adamowa, second Bagherme, third Runza, fourth Raffins, fifth Darfur, sixth Kordofan; from which it would appear that this great route, which takes the Bahr el Abiad in a very early part of its course, passes close upon the southern limits of Waday. Browne has a country named Rugna, no doubt the same as Runga or Runza, which country he states has a king of its own, but that it is more dependent upon Waday than Darfur. Sultan Bello shows us this country under another name, viz., Dar Rooga, which he says is next to Bagherme in the road eastward; three days' journey beyond which country, he. states, the traveller reaches the territory of Waday.   This country of Runga or Runza, Sultan Bello states, "is stony, abounding with rivers, and inhabited by infidels."   This state may therefore be placed in about 10° 30′ N. lat., and 20° 30′ E. long.

The next country requiring notice is that named Waday, Bergoo, or Dar Saley. Next to Bornou, this is the most extensive and most important country in this part of eastern Africa. It extends from 10° to 15° N. lat.; twenty days' journey from north to south, and fifteen days' journey from east to west; bounded east by Darfur, north by the Lybian Desert, west by Kanem and Bagherme, and south by Runza and other pagan countries, stretching towards Donga and the sources of the Bahr el Abiad, into which infidel countries, situated at the distance of fifteen days' journey, according to Burkhardt, and

south south-westward from the limits of Waday, the people
of the latter country make frequent and furious inroads for the
purpose of procuring slaves. A portion of these slaves are
exported to Fezzan, Egypt, and other places, but the greater
portion are retained in Waday itself. To the south of Waday
the country becomes very mountainous, and abounds with
rivers, but to the north it becomes arid and more level. The
territory of Waday itself is described as being in general level,
with but few rivers, except such as are formed during the rainy
season, and which in several places leave large receptacles for
water, or lakes, which retain large bodies of water throughout
the dry season. Sultan Bello states that the inhabitants of this
country are principally supplied with water from wells. The
position of this country is ascertained with sufficient accuracy.
Sultan Bello states, that from Sira, a town on the eastern confines of Bornou, to Bergoo, is a distance of twenty days'
journey. Buckhardt was informed that the distance from
Bornou to Waday was, by one roundabout road, thirty days'
journey, but by a shorter road, twenty days. The distances
given by Browne from Darfur westward, to Wara and Fittre,
correspond exactly with the distances given by Lyon, Bowditch, Buckhardt, Sultan Bello, and others, from Bornou to the
former places. The territory of Waday extends further to the
north than Bāgherme, which latter is bounded on the N.E. by
the country called Kory, and Kanem on the Bahr el Ghazelle.
Denham (p. 216) gives us the position of the northern, or
rather north-western point of Waday, when he states that "a
party of Showaas had once indeed, since our residence at Kouka,
come from the borders of the Waday country beyond Kanem,
to sell a few camels, &c.," and in another place, (p. 215,) he
states that bad news had reached Kouka, "both from the Bagherme side and the Kanem—from the S.E. and the E." In
fact, at that time, a war of extermination raged between Bornou
and Waday, for the possession of Kanem. Lyon (p. 3,) states
that Waday lay southward and eastward of Fezzan, and when
the different bearings and distances which had been given by
him and by Buckhardt of the positions of different places on the
road are considered, the bearing to Wara comes out nearly S.E.
by S. The exact distances, bearings, and positions, given by

Q

different authorities, it is difficult at times exactly to ascertain, because sometimes these are given to the confines of a country, at other times to a province of a country, and at other times to the capital of the country, or of a particular province therein. Waday, according to Buckhardt, is divided into several provinces, one named Djyr, or Gir, from the river of that name, which passes about three days' journey to the westward of Wara; this is on the S.E. There is also the province of Runga; and also, on the S.W., Munkary, or Mungari. There are also the provinces of Sila, Dar Tama, Gimur, (the Gimer of Browne) Modjo, supposed by Buckhardt to be the same as the Muddago of Browne, and the Metko of Mr. Seetzen. Lastly, there is Wara, which is a very large province, and in which the capital, Wara, or, as Sultan Bello calls it, Hoowara, is situated. Although the country is in general level, yet there are several mountains in it, some of which are in the neighbourhood of Wara, and there appears to be a large mountainous district betwixt the province of Wara and Darfur. Muddago, or Buddago, according to Lyon, consists " of some high mountains of black stone." The Waday traders state, " that several very large rivers, which are never dry," flow through the pagan countries which are situated to the south-westward of their country. The ruling population of Waday are Mahommedans. Throughout Waday the number of slaves is very great; in every house and family there are several. These manufacture copper, and make earthenware and pipe heads. They work also in leather, copper, &c. Silver is said to be very abundant in these pagan countries.

Next to Waday, and east therefrom, is the country of Darfur, the position of which is so well known from Browne's travels, that little need be said of it here. It is a very extensive country, "hilly, sandy, and droughty," so much so, says Sultan Bello, "that, notwithstanding the great many deep wells they have, the people are obliged to preserve their water within the trunks of trees. They possess plenty of swift horses, camels, oxen, and sheep. The capital is called Nantalti, through which a river runs during the rainy season, but in winter the people are obliged to dig wells in the bed of that river for water. They live upon the Dokhun and Dura, and they have some date gardens." The territories of Darfur

stretch southward to the banks of the Bahr el Abiad, and as
these approach to the latter, and its tributary streams on the
north side, the country becomes more hilly and fruitful, and is
thickly intersected with streams of water. To the S.E., and
immediately on the frontiers of the kingdom, is the district of
Sheibon, so renowned for its gold mines. The people are all
black; the younger and the unmarried go quite naked. The
population in this part are independent of the Arabs, and subject only to their own numerous petty chiefs. A vast number
of slaves are brought from this district, most of whom are
prisoners of war. Wars amongst them, as amongst other
nations in Africa, are very frequent, and slavery is the doom of
the conquered. The number of slaves annually exported from
Darfur is supposed to be from 9,000 to 10,000. The caravan
with which Browne returned to Egypt carried with it 5,000
slaves. To the south of Cobbe, the capital of Darfur, according to Browne, twenty-three days' journey, are the much talked
of copper mines of Fertit, situated in a very mountainous
country. Near these, and to the N.W., is the source of the
Bahr Misselad of Browne, the Om Teymam, or Djyr of Buckhardt, and the Gir of Ptolemy. Three days' journey to the
east of Fertit is the Bahr Taisha, one of the north-side tributaries of the Bahr el Abiad ; and four and a half days' journey
east from thence is Tendermi, where the Bahr Taisha joins
the Bahr el Abiad. Donga, a large district, in which the principal western sources of the Bahr el Abiad are said to be, is
south from Abou Talfain. The country around Donga is represented to be very hilly. The distance from thence to Shilluk is
stated to be forty days' journey, and the extreme western point
of Donga to be only twenty days' journey from the S.E. limits
of Bornou. Every kind of labour, both in Kordofan and in
Darfur, but especially in the latter, is performed by the women.
The manners of the whole population are exceedingly licentious, and the intercourse betwixt the sexes, open, profligate,
and disgusting in the extreme. The population is not large,
and consists of various Arab tribes, who are all Mahommedans.*

* The authorities for the preceding sections are, Edrisi, Makrisi, Ibn Said,
Abulfeda, Browne, Buckhardt, Denham, Clapperton, Sultan Bello, Sheikh el
Kanemy, Lyon, Dupuis, Bowditch, Horneman, Ptolemy, Leo, and several native
African travellers.

The next country betwixt Darfur and the Nile, or rather the Bahr el Abiad, is Kordofan. Buckhardt gives the distance from Dar Essoltane, the residence of the sovereigns of Darfur, to the confines of Kordofan, to be twelve days' journey, and thirteen by another road; and from thence to Obeydh, the capital, is three days' journey. This place was named by Bruce, Ibeit; Sultan Bello calls it Loobi. From Obeydh to Shendy, on the Bahr el Abiad, is, according to Buckhardt, a journey of thirteen to fourteen days. From Menkarah, on the same river, to the same place, is, according to Dr. Holroyd, sixty-seven hours forty-five minutes' travelling, or 170 miles S.W. Sultan Bello says of Kordofan, that " it is very fertile, and has small mountains, hills and sands; as also it contains fine horses, and plenty of cattle and asses." The Arab tribes, Beni Tadhel and Maaly, live on the route from Obeydh to Shilluk, on the way to Senaar. They supply the best gum, liban, or incense. Kordofan is a complete oasis, being separated on all sides from the neighbouring countries by deserts of six days' extent, except that of Shilluk, which is only four. The Bahr el Abiad may be considered as the boundary of Kordofan on the east; and on the north, its territories are said to extend to within six days' journey of Old Dongola, on the Nile. Obeydh, according to Dr. Holroyd, contains 30,000 inhabitants.

One of the countries mentioned by Edrisi, and other old Arabian writers, as situated in these parts, and mentioned also by Browne, is that named Zagawa. It lies to the north of Darfur. According to the Arabian writers alluded to, it lies twenty days' journey S.W. from Old Dongola, which would bring its position to be in about 26° 30′ E. long., and 16° N. lat. According to Ibn Said, who places this country in about 5° long. W. of the meridian of Alexandria, Zagawa in early days was subject to Kanem. Zagawa was a large district, and the capital of the same name stood in the southern part thereof. The towns and villages of this district, and those of Taju, its northern neighbour, extend along to the borders of the Egyptian Nile.

Before adverting to the Egyptian Nile, its early tributaries, and the countries situated around them, it is proper to take a

glance at Nubia, a country once well known in the history of
the world, but now reduced to the lowest possible state of im-
potence and decay. It extends from the confines of Egypt to
about the lat. of 11° N., a distance of 780 geographical miles,
and its breadth, from the Red Sea to what may be termed the
line of the Great Libyan Desert, is about 500 miles. With
the exception, however, of the banks of the Nile, the whole of
the space to the north of 15° may be considered a desert, the
cultivated land extending along on each bank of the river from
a distance of one half mile to two and a half miles, but very
seldom going beyond the distance of one mile. All beyond
this, but more especially to the westward, is barren sands, and
utterly waste and worthless. The towns and population,
which are numerous and considerable, are confined to the
narrow strip of cultivated land laying along both banks of the
Nile, already mentioned; but the cultivation is only maintained
by water drawn from the bed of the Nile to moisten the soil,
and sustain vegetation. The Nile, in no part of its course
through Nubia,—which, including the great and remarkable
winding of its stream in this country, is nearly 1000 miles,—
does not overflow its banks. Betwixt the Nile and the Red
Sea, but more especially adjoining the shores of that sea, the
country is mountainous, and a considerable belt of bare and
barren hills extend along the whole western coast of that remarkable inlet of the ocean. There are but very few ports or
harbours on the Nubian coast of the Red Sea. The principal is
the ancient Berenice, on the very limits of Egypt and Nubia;
and more to the south, Suakem, through which the principal
intercourse with central Africa and Arabia is carried on. This
port is the greatest slave-trading port in all the Red Sea, and
a very great number of slaves are yearly carried through it and
embarked for Arabia. It may here be remarked, that the
Nile of Egypt may, as a river, in reference to its magnitude,
be considered to terminate at El Mekheir, a little below the
junction of the Atbara, in about 17° N. lat.; because, from
thence downwards, it not only receives no supplies, but is even
diminished in magnitude, through the waste of its waters in
passing through such a vast burning desert country, and by
the quantity of water which is drawn from it to enliven the

cultivated land of Nubia. Nubia may be at present considered as being subject to the Pasha of Egypt.

THE BAHR EL ABIAD, ETC.

The next points which deserve consideration are the early tributaries of the Egyptian Nile, and the sources and the courses of the chief of these, namely, the Bahr el Abiad and the Bahr el Azreek. The former is a much larger river than the other. Bruce, in fact, states that the Bahr el Abiad carries in its stream three times as much water as the Bahr el Azreek, and that without the vast tribute of the latter, the stream of the Bahr el Azreek would not in the dry season reach the land of Egypt. The junction of these rivers has been accurately determined by Linant to be in 15° 34′ N. lat., and 32° 31′ 58″ E. long. Above this junction he sailed up the river, during the month of April, about 160 geographical miles. An officer, named Ibrahim, belonging to the Pasha of Egypt, marched upward from the junction with a military force, on a slave-catching expedition; part of the force marching on the one side of the river, and part on the other, to a distance of thirty-five days' journey; which would bring the point of its termination to about 10° N. lat. and 29° E. long. In this marauding expedition they marched through the territory of the Shilluks, extending fifteen days' journey; and penetrated six days' journey into the territories of Denke, or Donga, when they were obliged to turn back unsuccessful. Linant, in the month of April, found the river at its junction 1800 feet broad, and a little higher up one mile and a half wide, and the depth from three to four fathoms. The regular banks were four miles separate; still higher up the river expanded to a greater width, resembling, in fact, a great lake; and during the rains and the floods the breadth was stated to extend to twenty-one miles. At Shilluk the river is considerably contracted, but in the country of Denke it again expands, and where the Egyptian officer turned back, he describes the width to be equal to six hours' passage. At this point he saw no mountains in any direction. The land on both sides of the river upward is, in general, alluvial, and in some places densely peopled. The elevation of the country must be considerable. Linant, in April, felt the cold very keen with a strong north wind. The mountainous districts, where the river takes its rise, must therefore be, as they really are, at a considerable distance both to the south and to the west; and from the south, there is every reason to believe, the most important branches come. Sultan Bello, Clapperton's informants, and the people about Senaar, state that travellers and pilgrims from Dar Saley, and from Kano, through Adamowa to Senaar, travel, after leaving Adamowa, first up another river, and reach the Bahr el Abiad at a point so high that they can wade across it in the dry season, and that from thence they travel two months along its banks in their journey to Senaar. This shows the great distance of its sources to the west, and which is further confirmed by the following facts. Twenty-three and a half days' journey from Cobbe W. by S. is the country of the copper-mines, called Fertit; from thence three and a half days' journey east is the Bahr Taisha, a tributary to the Bahr el Abiad; and four days further east this river joins the Bahr el Abiad itself at Tendermi, which shows that the course of the river from Aleis upwards is, as the Turkish officer states, from west to east. From the junction of the Bahr Taisha the direction of the main bed of the river runs, probably, considerably to the southward of west, because, as has already been stated, from the confines of Waday and Bagherme to the country around its sources, is about fifteen days' journey to the westward of soùth. From the confines of Bornou to the country of Donga, where the westernmost sources of the river are said to lie, is twenty days' journey; and from Shilluk to the sources is stated to be a journey of forty days. Ledyard was told, by slave-traders and slaves who had come from the countries around the sources of the Bahr el Abiad, that these sources (western) lay fifty-five days' journey west of Senaar. Dr. Holroyd tells us that Khursched Pasha had gone up the Bahr el Abiad twenty-one days' journey, or rather navigation, above Aleis; and after passing the country of the Shilluks, he entered the country of Denke, or Donga. Above Aleis there were several rocks in the river.

All these points show that the sources of one branch of the

Bahr el Abiad is far to the west. The truth is, that the river
for such a distance spreading out like a great lake, proves that
its sources must be very remote, and in woody, mountainous
countries, which produce powerful streams; otherwise the great
evaporation which must take place from these lakes in the dry
season, would not leave a river of the magnitude which Linant
has described it to be in that season. Another point mentioned by Linant is, that after the flood in the river had begun,
it brought down with its waters enormous multitudes of fishes,
which he takes as a proof that the river is formed by a succession of lakes. The truth is, this fact shows that the
river is supplied by a very great number of streams from mountainous districts, and of considerable length; which streams
falling very low in the dry season, the fish seek refuge and
breed in multitudes in the deep pools, from which they are dis-
lodged when the currents become strong after the rains. Park
found this to be the case in the tributaries of the Senegal,
which he passed during the dry season. Another proof of
the length of course of the Bahr el Abiad is its magnitude
at the junction with the Blue river, as compared to the
magnitude of other rivers; thus, it is as wide at the point
mentioned as the Niger is near Jinnie, after a course of
700 miles, and very much larger indeed than the Bahr el
Azreek, after a course of an equal distance. During the
dry season, where Buckhardt crossed the Atbara, the principal
branch of the Blue river, not far from Shendy, he forded it
easily, the water scarcely reaching above the knees; the
current very slow, scarcely perceptible; the banks were twenty
feet high, and from 400 to 500 paces distant from each other;
yet the course of the Atbara to this point is nearly 500 geographical miles.

. From the height of the mountains near Mandara, from the
immense peaks rising to the limits of snow adjoining the
Bight of Biafra, and from the very high land which is found
about the sources of the Bahr el Azreek, which Bruce calculated, and most probably correctly calculated, to be 10,400 feet
above the level of the sea, while the Peak of Samen, in the
neighbourhood of Antalow, covered with perpetual snow,
rises to a still greater elevation, we may reasonably conclude

that the hills in the neighbourhood of, or around the sources
of the Bahr el Abiad, rise equally high, and give birth, as it is
clearly evident they do, to numerous mighty streams flowing
in different directions. It is also exceedingly probable, that
the range which bounds and gives rise to the tributaries of the
Bahr el Abiad to the south is at a considerable distance from
the positions of the rivers as now placed. The accounts given
by the Egyptian officer referred to, which state that he perceived no mountains in sight on the upper course of the river
where he had travelled, go to confirm this supposition; and it is
almost certain that the ridge which bounds the bed of the Abiad
on the north, is, at least to the meridian of Wara, of no great
height; and which, together with the position in which we find
it, can afford no supplies of any great importance to the
Abiad from that quarter. This we really find, so far as the
country is known, is actually the case.

"In the country of the Shilluks it is certain," says Linant,
"that there are other rivers which come from the west, and
the following is a list of them, in the order in which they are
met in *ascending* the stream:—First, the *Ned-el-Nil*, or feast
of the Nile, which passes close under the mountain of Guebel
Dahir, or *Mountain of the Round*, so called because it is
ascended spirally. It is covered with negro villages, is situated
in the country of *Taggalla*, and the river which passes to the
south of it is said to flow from a great lake, to which I heard
several names given, none of which I shall therefore cite;
several other rivers are reported to fall into it, one called the
Bahr Soudan. Second, the Suar. Third, the Hou el Kame.
Fourth, the Serat. Fifth, the Hor el Nahal, besides some
others." A clue to the position of the main western stream
may, it is presumed, be found in the river called "the Bahr
Soudan;" which, coming from the westward, naturally assumes,
amongst the natives to the eastward, the name of the river
Soudan; and this is confirmed by Sultan Bello's memoir, which
designates all the pagan nations to the southward of Darfur
"tribes of Soodans." The "Bahr Soudan," therefore, thus
mentioned by Linant, is very probably the great western
branch of the Bahr el Abiad, in its early course; which, coming
from the westward, and from amongst those tribes of Soudans,

is, of course, denominated by the Arab population, not improperly, " the Bahr Soudan."

Further, and in proof that the Bahr el Abiad must come
from a point considerably more to the westward than it has
hitherto been supposed to do, and from at least 23°E. long, when
its course will be 900 geographical miles; take the fact, that the
Bahr el Azreek, from its source to the junction with the Bahr
el Abiad, runs over a space of nearly 700 geographical miles.
On either hand it receives numerous and important tributaries;
some of them of a great length of course, and running through
very mountainous countries. Now, the Bahr el Abiad can
scarcely receive a greater number of important tributaries.
Its chief supplies must come from the south; for it is not only
evident, but certain, that on its northern side it receives but
few supplies, and that these supplies cannot be of any great
magnitude. To form a river of a magnitude so much greater
than the Bahr el Azreek, it must be allowed a considerably
longer course, even admitting that it receives supplies from the
southward, as it certainly does, equal to, or even greater than
those which the Bahr el Azreek receives on every hand.
Placing its sources, therefore, at the point mentioned, we shall
have the curious and important culminating point of Central
Africa, where the land is probably the highest, and from which
points flow the waters of the Bahr el Abiad east, the waters
probably of the chief branches of the Congo to the S.W.,
the waters of the Shadda to the W.N.W., the waters of the
Asoo, the chief branch of the Shary, to the N.W., and the Gir
of Ptolemy from the very point where he has placed it; and we
shall have the further important fact disclosed of his eastern
branch to the Niger from Mount Thala, and certainly " above"
that is to the southward of his Lybian lake, or Lake
Shad.

Here it may be necessary to observe, that the map accompanying this work has been constructed upon the accounts
generally given by travellers, and received by travellers, and
also the opinions of geographers, formed from travels and
writings, several of which have already been referred to, and
especially Linant, one of the latest. It must be observed,
however, that the latter, as regards the swelling of the different

rivers, from the effects of the tropical rains, reported chiefly what he heard and was told on this very important point. Instead of the Bahr el Azreek flooding before the Bahr el Abiad, other authorities, equally good, and better, inasmuch as they describe, as regards this matter, what came under their actual observation, pointedly state that the Bahr el Abiad floods before the Bahr el Azreek, even so much as a month earlier; which fact establishes, from incontrovertible data, that the main stream of the Bahr el Abiad comes from a very distant part in the south of Africa, and at no great distance from the equator, as in fact the two important authorities about to be referred to state that it really does.

The superior magnitude of the Bahr el Abiad is indisputable. Bruce says, that it is three times the breadth of the Bahr el Azreek, (half a mile at Senaar,) and also that it carries in its stream three times as much water as the Azreek, and, moreover, that without the supply which the White River brings, the Bahr el Azreek would never reach the land of Egypt, but be evaporated in its passage through the Nubian desert. In Bruce's Original Journals, which have been printed in the last edition, (Edinburgh, 1805,) Mr. Bruce has the following remark (vii. 91,) —"The Tacazze, or Atbara, joins the Nile four days on the other side of Shendy, or three days on the side of Berber. The place is called Magiran, which in Arabic signifies the junction. In summer it is so shallow you pass it on foot, the water taking you up only mid-leg. All the rivers in these countries fail when the sun goes south of the line, however abundant and full these were before; and were it not for the Abiad, which rises near the line, and whose inundation is perpetual, from its enjoying the rains of both rainy seasons, the Nile itself would be eight months in the year dry, and at no time arrive across the desert in so much fulness, as to answer any purpose of agriculture in Egypt. The Abiad river is three times as big as the Nile." And (p. 92,) "the Nile would fail, were it not for the never-failing Abiad, or Bahr el Aice; this rising near the line, considerably south of the sources of the Nile, in the latitudes where fall perpetual rains, it never decreases, but is always full." These passages are, from some cause unknown, but unaccountable, suppressed in Bruce's narrative, and also the course of the Bahr el Abiad expunged from, or not laid down in his map, although the points stated are of the greatest geographical importance, more especially as the accounts given are confirmed by later and specific authority.

Mr. Inglish, who accompanied the army of the present Pasha of Egypt in his campaign against Senaar and the countries adjacent, and who penetrated to Singue, to the south of the place mentioned, most pointedly states, from a personal know-ledge, and even ocular demonstration of the fact, that the Bahr el Abiad began (23d April) to rise one month before the Bahr el Azreek; that the stream is formed by one important branch coming from the south-westward, and besides others, there is one still more important, coming in its middle course from the southward. He pointedly also states, that the rise of the Bahr el Abiad at its junction with the Blue river commences in the month of April. This, and the rise being one month earlier than the rise of the Bahr el Azreek, at once establishes the fact, that its most distant source must be far to the southward, and at no great distance from the equator, where the rains, in the eastern half of that portion of the continent of Africa, com-mence in March. The rains in the very high lands precede the sun nearly one month, so that when the sun approaches within 3° of the equator, on the south side thereof, which is in the beginning of March, the rains commence in about 4° N. lat., and increase as the sun approaches these parallels. The dis-tance from this point, say 4° N. lat., and 26° or 27° of E. long., would agree well, and bring the commencement of the flood in the Bahr el Abiad, at its junction with the Bahr el Azreek, to be about, or after the middle of April, as Mr. Inglish says. Linant did not see the Bahr el Abiad at the beginning of its rise. Mr. Inglish did, and therefore his account must be admitted to be correct, or at any rate that which is the most to be relied on; and taking it to be so, it establishes, on invincible evidence, the great distance to the south of the chief springs of the Bahr el Abiad. One mile above its junction with the Blue river, Mr. Inglish says it is one mile and a half broad. This is an immense river, then too just at the commencement of its rise, and is another proof of its remote sources.

This view of the matter also brings before us other curious

points relating to tropical Africa. While the rains precede
the sun on the high lands in the eastern division of that continent, that is, to the eastward of the central high lands, which,
in about 26° E. long., divide the waters which flow eastward
into the Indian Ocean from those which flow westward into
the Atlantic, the rains are found to follow the sun, or rather
the sun precedes them above 6°, or one month, in all the less
elevated parts of Africa, whether to the east or to the west of
the central chain; but as in the mountainous districts to the
east, so in the mountainous districts to the west, as in Ashantee,
the rains commence early in March. This gives a fine elucidation of the different periods for the flooding of the African
rivers, and goes to determine, with considerable accuracy, the
positions of their respective sources. On the return of the
sun to the southward, the phenomenon mentioned is reversed,
and the rains precede him in the western parts of central
Africa, and hence the rise of the Congo in September (the
7th), as Tuckey found it about 280 miles from its mouth.
Hence also the continuance of the Shadda in flood longer than
the Niger, as Oldfield found and states in his narrative; because
its chief sources are considerably to the southward. Thus,
while one great branch of the Bahr el Abiad comes from the
W.S.W., a greater, and the main branch, in all probability,
comes from the SS.W. or S. by W., and in the longitude and
latitude above-mentioned, from a point to the eastward of some
of the branches of the Congo, and to the westward of some of
the branches, or rather of the chief branch, of the Quilimancy.

Mr. Inglish's words are very pointed: after stating that the
source of the Adit, or Blue River, is at the distance of sixty
camel days' journey south from Senaar, he adds, (see *Quarterly
Review*, No. 55, pp. 89, 90,) from information received, that the
course of the Bahr el Abiad " was nearly parallel with that of
the Adit, but that its source was much further off among the
Gebel el Gumera; that it is augmented by the junction of
three other rivers, one from the south-west, and two others
from the east, running from the mountains south of Senaar.
The source cannot be in the same range of mountains as the
Adit, or Bahr el Azreek, as, notwithstanding it is stated to be
further off, the *inundation precedes that of the Azreek nearly a*

whole month." The rise took place on the 23d of the month Shaban. Dr. Holroyd tells us, on the authority of Khursched Pasha, that the Bahr el Abiad divided at a considerable distance above Khartoum, which division, probably, forms the eastern branch alluded to by Inglish.

The Bahr el Azreek takes its rise in the province of Gojam in lat. 11° N., and about 37° E. long. It springs from two powerful sources, and pursues its course due north, when, entering, and passing through Lake Dambea, it continues its course first S.E., then S., then S.W. and N.W., until, passing the country of the Gongas, it pursues a course, being joined by several streams on both sides, by Senaar to its junction with the Bahr el Abiad. Its sources are about two miles above the level of the sea. Below Lake Dambea, it is already a considerable stream, and falls over the cataract called Alata, about 40 feet high, with a terrific noise and rapidity; its course downwards from thence is nearly circular and very rapid. In passing the country of the Gongas, it bursts through a chain of mountains in which there is a cataract 280 feet high. In these parts it is occasionally fordable, but generally so deep that the savage tribes of the Galla, in their inroads into Abyssinia, pass it on rafts supported by inflated skins. Abyssinia is a country exceedingly mountainous, rising in all the picturesque and singular forms imaginable. The air on these mountains is cool, but in the valleys it is very hot. These valleys are very fertile, and the population is considerable. Another branch of the Egyptian Nile is the Atbara, or Tacazze. It rises in the beautiful province of Angot, 200 miles to the S.E. of Gondar, 11° 30' N. lat., and 41° 30' E. long.; and passing northwards, at a considerable distance west from Antalow, and by the eastern base of the snowy Peak of Samen, it continues a N.W. course, joined by several streams from both sides, until it joins the Nile, about twenty miles above El Mekheir. To the south of Sire, where Bruce crossed the stream in his advance during the dry season, he found the bed of the river 200 yards wide, and the stream three feet deep. It bears, he states, in its bed one-third of all the waters in the empire of Abyssinia. The range of hills which thus give it birth, will approach within seventy-five miles of the sea at

Zeilah. Abyssinia was once a very powerful empire, and extended its sway over a great portion of the great eastern Horn of Africa. But intestine wars and attacks on the part of its savage neighbours the Galla, and also of the Arabs from the south and from the north, have greatly reduced its power, and deeply injured and destroyed the population of the country. It is still, however, a considerable state, extending about 500 miles from north to south, and as many from east to west, and is situated betwixt 8° and 16° N. lat., and 35° and 43½° E. long. The climate, from the great and general elevation of the land, is in many places moderate, and very fine. The tropical rains are exceedingly violent from April to August, which cause all the rivers to swell to a very great height—from eighteen to twenty feet above their customary level—and bear down to the north that immense flood of waters which inundates and fertilizes all the land of Egypt. The capital of Abyssinia is Gondar, but the residence of the court of late years has been principally at Antalow. Its best ports on the Red Sea are Arkeeko and Massouah, to the west of the Isle of Dhallac; but the mountains which run along the whole coast of the Red Sea, beyond the straits of Babelmandeb, rise to great height, and leave no roads for any general communication, except, perhaps, from the Bay of Assâb. Abyssinia has been from early times a Christian country, of the tenets of the Alexandrian Greek church. They are surrounded on all sides by tribes of the most savage character; and from the frequent inroads of these tribes they are, in many things, descended to their level; amongst which is the barbarous practice of eating raw flesh—of even cutting it out of the living animal. Still Abyssinia is an interesting country; and a connexion with a strong civilized European power may even yet make that state the means of spreading knowledge and civilization through the hitherto most unknown and most impenetrable portion of Central Africa.*

* Authorities for these sections of the work:—Bruce, Portuguese Missionaries, Linant, Ibrahim Pasha, Rennell, Browne, Buckhardt, &c. &c.

AFRICAN RIVERS WHICH FLOW TO THE SOUTHWARD.

The African rivers which flow southward and south-eastward from the great central range of mountains, generally denominated the Mountains of the Moon, remain next to be considered. This great range of mountains extends from the high land of Cameroons, in lat. 3° 40′ N. along in an E. by N. direction, by the sources of the Bahr el Abiad, in about 4° N. lat. eastward to the sources of the southern tributaries of the Egyptian Nile, in 7° N. lat., and thence eastward again in an E.N.E. direction to the Indian Ocean, in from 10° to 11° N. lat., from Cape Ras Halfoon to Cape Guardafui, or Guardefan, and Cape Asser; the latter the most eastern point of the continent of Africa. The highest land in this eastern portion of Africa is the mountain called Samen, to the west of Antalow, and on the west side of the Tacazze.

Part of the range to the north-west is denominated Lamalmon, on which Bruce, in the middle of winter, found the thermometer 32°, attended with hoar-frost. To the southward of these parallels, the whole country of Abyssinia, to the parallel of 6° or 5° N. lat., is one vast collection of mountains, of the most abrupt and fantastic shapes, intersected with deep valleys, through which flow numerous deep and rapid streams, chiefly to the Bahr el Azreek. The lofty peak of Samen is covered with perpetual snow. In the centre, or rather beyond the centre of the province of Shoa and Effat, to the east, the mountains are very high, and run on the bearing of north to south. The part of the province called Effat is enclosed within high and craggy mountains; crossing and descending which Bermudez and his companions represent the path, in metaphorical language, like descending into hell. The valley at their foot is very fertile, and much cotton cloth is manufactured in this country. In the south-east of this province rises the river Hawash, which flows about N. by E. from Ancobar, and is lost in salt lakes or sands, near the south-west corner of the Gulf of Zeilah. Neither at Tadjoura, nor at Zeilah, nor between these places, do travellers notice or state that there are any rivers; which proves, in the most convincing manner, that the dividing ridge approaches very near the sea, in the environs of Zeilah, because in the province of Angot, on the opposite side of the chain, springs and rivers are exceedingly numerous. This part or province of Abyssinia is covered with perpetual verdure, which shows that its elevation must be considerable, and that, consequently, the streams are not dried up from the severity of the drought in the dry season. To the east of Angot, and south-west from the Strait of Babelmandeb, is situated in 11° 16′ N. lat. and 42° 49′ E. long., the capital of Adel or Adaiel, named Zeilah, at the bottom of a small bay, formed by a promontory extending a short distance into the sea. It has some trade with Aden and Mocha. It is low and hot, and the country around is destitute of vegetation. The population only obtain water from wells. It is carried from the wells by camels. Between Zeilah and the isles Eybad, the channel has only five feet water. The countries or states of Bali and Doara or Dowara, border on Adel to the south; and to the south-west lies a Christian state, called Ogge. This is by far the best and the nearest point to penetrate into Abyssinia, and to those interesting countries, for interesting they must be, which are situated around the sources of the Zebee, and the extreme southern branches of the Bahr el Abiad.

The capital of Shoa and Effat is named Ancobar, and is situated in about 40° 3′ E. long. and 9° N. lat. to the southward (for such is its position, from the following important information) of the river Hawash. This town is clearly more to the south than it has appeared in modern maps, and is more, probably, to the southward of the parallel of 9° N. than to the north of that parallel. A strict attention to the subject, and close research, make it appear, from every account which we have of these parts, that the dividing range which separates, to the S. W. of Ancobar, the waters which flow north into the Bahr el Azreek from those which flow south into the Zebee, &c. is farther south than has hitherto been supposed, and probably lies and runs in the parallel of 7° 30′ to 8° N. lat.

Just as these sheets were about to be put to press, D. Coates, Esq., of the Church Missionary Society, kindly favoured me with the perusal of some letters written by worthy missionaries despatched by that Society to preach the gospel in the Abyssynian province of Shoa or Effat, where no European has ever

been since the days of Alvarez, in 1520. The last letter is
dated June 1st, 1839, at Farry, a town only half a day's journey from Ancobar. They landed at Zeilah, from which place
they proceeded first to Tadjoura, which is quite wrongly laid
down in our present maps. With a good breeze it took them
about thirteen hours to go from Zeilah to Tadjoura. At the
latter place, they found a merchant vessel from the Mauritius,
which gave them the latitude of the place, 11° 58' N. The
principal exports of Tadjoura are slaves. Its commercial
communications and intercourse is with the African country
called Aousa, peopled by Habashah Christians. From Tadjoura they set out, on the 26th of April, on their journey to
Ancobar. They travelled several days (four) along the Gulf
of Tadjoura, which is stated to be much deeper than represented on the best maps. On the fifth day they lost sight of
the Gulf, and began to cross a *very high* mountain; and on
the sixth day came again in sight of the Gulf, which is much
deeper in that part than what is given on any maps. On that
day they passed the salt-place, from whence the people of the
interior, especially the people of Shoa, are supplied with salt,
and which article they obtain in exchange for *wheat* and other
articles. This salt-place is eight miles long and three broad,
having salt on the one (west) side, and salt water on the other
(east) side, which salt water, the natives affirm, has a communication with the Gulf by subterraneous canals.

From this spot the missionaries proceeded on their journey,
and at the end of sixteen days they came to Mulloo. They
travelled about four hours each day. The heat was very great,
the thermometer generally at 100; and being in the height of
the dry season, the country was very bare, though they met
with water daily, and some trees, under the shade of which
they could rest during their halts. The population was very
scanty, the inhabitants having gone, with their cattle, to other
places where pasture could be found, until the rainy season
arrived, when they again return. In the neighbourhood of
the salt lake the missionaries saw the mouths of many extinct
volcanoes. The country through which they passed during
the period mentioned, was alternately valleys and hills, ascending, as they state, in this part of the journey; but none of

these hills were so high as those in Abyssinia: therefore camels could traverse all that part of Africa, from Tadjoura to Shoa. From Mulloo they set out, on the 21st of May; on the 29th of that month they crossed the river Hawash; and on the 31st they arrived at Fary or Farry, half a day's journey from Ancobar, the residence of the king, who was at that time at Angallalla, a town about a day's journey S. W. of Ancobar, to which latter place he was expected to return in a few days.

Such is a general sketch of this interesting journey, through this remarkable, and, we may almost say, unknown portion of Africa. General, and not very specific as it is, it nevertheless supplies us with some facts of importance. The high mountain which they crossed on the sixth day after leaving Tadjoura, must have been of a very considerable elevation, because they felt the air pure and keen, compared to the valleys below. The point of the harbour of Zeilah is probably the termination of this mountain. They passed, in their route westward, near Errur, or Hurrur, as it is called in our present maps. It is to be regretted that the bearings are not given, nor the magnitude and the direction in which the river Hawash ran, stated; but as they only crossed it once in their journey, this would indicate that it passes to the north instead of the south of Ancobar, and that the termination thereof is in some of the salt lakes, which, from the preceding accounts, are situated to the S.W. of Zeilah, and south of the point where the travellers alluded to quitted the environs of the Gulf of Zeilah and Berbera. The allusion also made at Mulloo about Errur or Hurrur shows that they were then near that place, and stating that they saw the mountains of the Galla, clearly means that they saw these mountains to the south of their intended route; as in proceeding from Mulloo to Ancobar they knew they had to pass through the northern frontiers of the Galla country, during the space of five days' journey. Being at Mulloo to the north of the river Hawash, it is therefore probable the ridge or high lands which divide the rivers that run into the Indian Ocean, from those which flow into the Hawash and the Nile, run from Capes Guardafui and Ras Halfoon, in 10° to 11°, in a direction of W.S.W. to about 8° N. lat. in the meridian of Bosham.

Moreover, from the preceding information, the following

very important facts are deduced. First, that there are no rivers entering the sea between Tadjoura and Zeilah ; thus proving that the high mountains approach very near the sea in that quarter ; and which high mountains, or dividing range, most probably run from the capes at Babelmandeb, in a south-west direction, to the sources of the Hawash and the chain previously alluded to, north of Bosham, separating the waters which flow into the Nile, from those which flow into the Hawash ; but proving, at the same time, that from the point whence the preceding informants crossed the Hawash, namely two and a half days' journey to the east of Ancobar, that the Hawash receives no rivers from the north or north-west; thus establishing the extension and the position of the province of Angot, in the south-east part of Abyssinia ; and that the rivers in that province flow north to the Tacazze, and not south-east to the Hawash or the Indian Ocean. Further, the informatoin received, shows and proves that Mr. Bruce is wrong in his theory and general information, namely, that the rains preceded the sun, on the eastern portions of Africa, one month ; because here we find that the travellers alluded to, crossed the country between Zeilah and Ancobar, in a period of time from the 26th of April to the 1st of June, and met with no rain. In fact, the country was every where dried up, and the rainy season had not commenced. At the same time we know that the rains do commence in the high lands in Abyssinia, 3° more to the north, in March, the same as we find they commence in Ashantee, and the high mountains and woody countries in that portion of Africa. Hence it appears that the rains commence more than two months sooner in the high, mountainous, woody, and culminating points of Africa, than they do in countries and places low or less elevated, though placed further to the south on the northern torrid zone ; and hence, with the commencement of the swelling of the rivers in any given place, we have the elevated countries and culminating points from which these rivers flow, with a great degree of accuracy.

One hundred and fifty miles S.E. by E. of Zeilah, is situated the town of Berbera on the coast of this part of the Indian Ocean : it carries on a considerable trade with Mocha. The exports from this town to Arabia consist of horses, mules, asses, gum-arabic, myrrh and frankincense, and slaves. The incense is of the finest quality, and comes from the neighbourhood of Guardafui, and along the whole coast westward to the Straits of Babelmandeb. Berbera also supplies Mocha with a considerable quantity of provisions, which proves that the country around it is fertile. A caravan goes regularly from a country called Kunun, twenty days' journey west of Berbera, to the latter place, in order to purchase Indian goods, &c.; and the place first mentioned carries on a considerable trade with the country, as far to the westward as the Mountains of the Moon. A caravan also goes regularly from Gondar to Berbera with slaves, horses, ivory, &c. The trade of Berbera is chiefly in the hands of the Arab tribes called Somaulis, and one part, where much of the trade is carried on, is called Bunder-cassim; near Jibbeel-Feel, called by the English, Cape Felix. The S.E. winds which blow during eight months in the year over Africa to the eastward of the Straits of Babelmandeb, are felt exceedingly hot at Mocha, though by no means so hot as the N.W. winds which blow over the desert and the Red Sea to the south of Egypt. A small river enters the sea at Berbera; and another called the Mete in the meridian of 39°. This river was known about 2,000 years ago by the name of the Akanai or Daphnon. To the eastward another small stream enters the sea at Elephant Point, which is the name, Elephant River, that it bore at the early period just mentioned. Cape Guardafui was known to the ancients under the name of Aromata, and Ras Halfoon, under the name of Cape Tabai, the bay between them being then named Bellia or Beyla. South of Ras Halfoon was the ancient port of Opone. The whole shore south-westward to à little beyond the parallel of 5° N. is an iron-bound coast, without anchorage or water, to a short distance to the north of Cape Baxas, where there is an anchorage anciently known under the name of Serapion, and a small stream formerly called Bendal de Agoa. Proceeding southward we come to a stream called Doara, anciently known under the name of Bendal Veijo, and at the mouth of which there was an anchorage anciently known under the name of Nicon. The river here mentioned is not of very great magnitude, and was denominated by the author of the Periplus of the Red Sea as an " obscure stream." It is a curious fact, that the commerce carried on with all this great eastern horn of Africa, is the same that it was 2,000 years ago, with the exception that it is not now so great as it then was. Then, as now, however, slaves were a principal article of export.*

In the parallel of 2° 1' 8" N., and in the meridian of 45° 19' 5" E., we come to Magdosha or Mugdoxa, as it has been denominated by the Portuguese, which has a very large river known also under the name of Webbe, and Yass as it is denominated by Bruce, which enters the sea at this point. Abulfeda, on the authority of Ibn Said, calls the city from which the river takes its name Makdishu, and in the customary eastern phraseology he states that it is a branch of the Egyptian Nile; and that it annually floods and overflows like that river. He further states, that the river rises in a lake called Kaura, a lake supposed to give birth to the Nile, and in fact to all the rivers in this quarter of Africa ; but the true meaning of which we now know to be merely that these rivers take their rise in the same district or quarter of Africa. The branches of the river mentioned, spring on the south side of the range of mountains, which give birth to some of the tributaries of the Nile ; and others of its branches rise to the eastward of Hurrur, and to the south of Zeilah in the parallel of 10° N. lat. The different branches unite below Gunana, and thence pursue a S.E. course to the sea, in the words of Abulfeda, " NEAR MAGDUSHA." The length of this river will be about 550 geographical miles. Immediately under the Equator we have the town of Jubah, at the mouth of a very large river, which here enters the sea, and comes from the N.W. This is the Zebee or Kibbee, (the Acco of Bruce,) so called in the early part of its course from its colour resembling that of melted butter. The only account that we have of the upper part of this stream, is from some Portuguese ambassadors from the court of Abyssinia to that of Lisbon. They left Gondar in 1613, intending to proceed southward to the Port of Melinda, on the Indian Ocean. They crossed the Nile south-west from Gojam, in the parallel of 10° N., and in the meridian of 36½° E. long. From this point they proceeded nearly south, crossing the river Maleg in its upper course, and the great central ridge which divides

* Authorities for these sections—Bruce, Lord Valentia, Periplus, Red Sea, &c.

the African waters that flow in opposite directions, when they came to Narea or Enarea in about 7° 10′ N. lat., and one of the most southern provinces of the Abyssinian empire. This province is very damp and marshy, being a wide extent of plain or table land, betwixt immense chains of mountains. At this point, secret enemies to their mission, instead of helping them forward to the south, and to Melinda, as was intended, got their journey directed eastward towards Cape Guardafui, in which intermediate space there being several Mahommedan States all very hostile to Roman Catholics, which they were, it was calculated that the ambassadors might be cut off. From Narea they accordingly proceeded in a direction about S.E. by E. to the kingdom of Gingiro. Five or six days' journey from Narea, and after crossing in the latter part thereof a very high mountain, they came to the river Zebee or Kibbee, as above mentioned. It ran with fearful rapidity betwixt high banks of solid rock, bearing in its stream a *larger volume of water* than the Egyptian Nile at the point where they crossed that river. The period, be it observed, when the passage of the river was effected was in the month of March, at the very close of the dry season in this part of Africa. This shows that the source of the Kibbee must be nearly 250 miles distant; for the Egyptian Nile had flowed through a greater length of course at the point where they had crossed it. The colour of the river, as has been stated, resembled melted butter. This is a curious and important fact, as it brings to our knowledge very distinctly the nature of the country in this portion of Africa. It must be all calcareous, and the river flowing over white calcareous and flinty rocks, with white sand, and constantly in a turbid state from the rapidity of the stream, will thus attain the appearance mentioned. This appearance is to be seen in many streams running through calcareous tropical countries. From Gingiro the travellers proceeded in an E.N.E. direction towards the kingdom of Bali. A day or two after leaving Gingiro they again crossed the Zebee, running with great rapidity, but not with such force as at the point where they first crossed it. Here they crossed the stream by means of cow hides inflated like bladders. After this, they came to the kingdom of Cambat, an-other of the most southern provinces of Abyssinia, and situated to the southward of the great dividing central ridge. From hence they proceeded to the Arab kingdom of Alaba, where they met with such a harsh reception that they were compelled to relinquish their journey and return into Abyssinia. From the point where the travellers last crossed the stream, the Zebee pursues its course S.E. to the Indian Ocean at the town of Jubah, above mentioned. The extreme length of the stream on the general bearing will be 700 geographical miles, which gives a river of great magnitude, and accordingly the people at Jubah report that the stream rises in Abyssinia, and is navigable for canoes to the distance of three months' journey.

With regard to the nature of the country through which all the last-mentioned rivers run we know but little. It is inhabited throughout the courses of the Zebee and Webbe by the wild, and savage tribes of the Galla, which, during the last century, have overrun and ruined some of the finest provinces of the Abyssinian empire. Their country throughout is exceedingly mountainous; but, at the same time, fertile and fruitful wherever it is cultivated. Beyond the Abyssinian province of Damot is the territory of Conche, which is separated from Abyssinia by a broad and rapid river. The sovereign of this state is said to be rich and powerful, and capable of bringing into the field an army of 20,000 foot, and 10,000 horse. The country of Narea is situated beyond Gongas, and is represented as a large plain or table-land, surrounded on all sides by high mountains. The country produces corn and cattle in abundance; and gold in large quantities is found, and also brought from countries to the westward. Narea is amongst the most elevated countries in Africa. The separation of the waters to the north and to the south takes place in it. To the eastward of these people, nearly the whole of the great eastern horn of Africa is covered with Arab states, which, some centuries ago, were much more powerful and wealthy than they now are; the power of these people everywhere decaying rapidly. One of the most important of these states was the kingdom of Adel. Betwixt this state and Abyssinia, in former times, were severe and numerous wars; but the power of both has been so much weakened, that each of them is reduced to such a state of

weakness as not to be able to withstand the power of the
Gallas. This portion of Africa is a very interesting country,
both as regards its climate, the soil, and the productions
thereof. In ancient times, it was still more so, when it
supplied myrrh and frankincense to the most civilized parts
of the world. According to the author of the Periplus, one
of the exports from it was sugar, made from the cane, and
it was probably from this quarter that the " sweet cane,"
mentioned by the prophet Isaiah and also by Jeremiah (chap.
vi. 20—" sweet cane from a far country"), was brought.

The kingdom of Angot, in Abyssinia, is described as being
a very fine country, very fertile, and intersected by numerous
beautiful streams, and having, from its great elevation, a
very fine climate. It is reported that about the end of the
twelfth, or the beginning of the thirteenth century, Lalibela,
then sovereign of Abyssinia, attempted to dry up the Egyptian
Nile, by turning the waters of its southern tributaries into
other channels, and that he so far effected his purpose as to
turn the course of two streams, which from that period have
continued to flow into the Indian Ocean. His object was to
destroy by this the Mahommedan power in Egypt, which at
that time was harassing greatly the Abyssinian territories from
the shores of the Red Sea. At what point this project was
attempted, is not stated; but the probability is, that it was made
on the Nile itself on the south-east corner of the province of
Damot. The general courses of the Nile to the north, and of
the Zebee, &c. to the southward, were well known to the
Egyptians 3,000 years ago. The sacristan of the temple of
Minerva at Thebes, in Egypt, told Herodotus that half the
waters of the Nile ran to the north, and the other half to the
south, and that they were produced by the tropical rains. The
course and sources of the Bahr el Abiad appear to have been
better known at that time than they are at this day. Ptolemy.
Euergetes, when sovereign of Egypt, penetrated into the southern
parts of Abyssinia, or, as it was then called, Ethiopia, which he
conquered; and he describes his passage in some places to have
been effected over mountains deeply covered with snow. At
the sources of the Nile the barometer, according to Bruce, stood
at twenty and a half inches, which gives a very great elevation.

He in fact estimates the elevation to be two British miles above the level of the sea. The rains in the southern and very mountainous parts of Abyssinia commence in April, cease about the 8th of September, recommence about the 20th of October, and are constant but moderate till the first week of November, when they terminate. From the lat. of 4° N. to the lat. of 4° S., the rain falls throughout the year, but it is heaviest to the south when the sun becomes the second time vertical.[*]

Proceeding southward from Jubah, we find, betwixt the parallels of 2° to 3½° S., that is, between Malemba and Patta, a large delta thickly intersected by streams, the estuaries of a large river, which, according to the authority of the Portuguese, as searched out by that excellent geographer D'Anville, are the mouths of the great river Quilimancy. This river, from the nature of the country and from the course represented by some maps on the authority of the Arabs, appears to take its rise to the south of the central chain of the Mountains of the Moon in about 3° N. lat., and 27° to 30° E. long. From this point it bends its course about S.E. by E. to the sea at the places mentioned, in its upper course no doubt augmented by numerous streams flowing from the northward and the north-westward, and probably also some from the south-westward. Its extreme length will be about 900 miles, and flowing as it does through such a large portion of central Africa, all very mountainous, it must necessarily bring, as it is known that it does bring, to the sea a vast body of water. But of the countries throughout its course we have scarcely any knowledge. All accounts agree that, in about the meridian of 25° E. long., an elevated range runs south from 5° N. lat. to 24° S. lat., near the springs of the Orange River, and that this great range, called the spine of the world, divides the waters throughout the space mentioned, which flow west into the Atlantic from those which flow east into the Indian Ocean. It is in the northern portion of this great range, and no doubt forming part thereof, that Ptolemy places Mount Arangas, 14½° to the eastward of the middle of his Mount Araultes, which being unquestionably the high land to the eastward of the Cameroons, and taking the middle thereof to be in 11° E. long., will place Mount Arangas in 25½° E.

[*] Authorities for these sections—Bruce, Portuguese Travellers, Periplus of the Red Sea, &c.

long., on the very meridian that the spine of the world is by all reported to be, and running directly north to the very centre of the El Komri range. This chain, therefore, and this point separates the .waters. which flow S.E. and S.W., or to the Quilimancy River on the one hand, and to the great river Zaire or Congo on the other.

The Bulletin of the Geographical Society of Paris (Nos. 67 and 68, of July, 1839) contains, from the pen of Mr. Jomard, some important information regarding several rivers in a portion of Africa situated considerably to the S.W. of Gingiro. The curious facts, about to be stated, have been furnished by a young Galla, named Ouare, a native of Limmou, and the son of an enterprising chief named Kilho, the sovereign of a country about W.N.W. from Limmou, called Dangab. About twenty years ago this chief conquered. Limmou. In 1835, young Ouare left Limmou with a considerable trading caravan, consisting, as is customary in these parts, of a number of slaves; and entering Abyssinia, and crossing the Blue River in Damot, and again recrossing it near the south end of Lake Dambea, they proceeded on their journey betwixt Lake Dambea and Gondar, and thence in the ordinary route came to Khartoum, the place of his destination. The time occupied on this journey was four months, including ninety days (540 hours) of active travelling. In the days on which the caravan travelled, they made out from five to six hours daily, and sometimes more, which Mr. Jomard calculates, on an average from each day's journey, at 325 leagues; and separately at 210 leagues, fifty-seven days from Gooderoo to Khartoum, and 115 leagues, thirty-three days, from Limmou to Gooderoo. The first part, however, of the journey would necessarily be more rapid than the last, because the parties would be less fatigued; therefore a greater distance must be allowed in an equal space of time, between Limmou and Gooderoo, than between Gooderoo and Khartoum, which will consequently place Limmou farther to the S. and W. than Mr. Jomard has placed it; and as, from the position of Gingiro, it certainly is. Averaging the distance travelled each day at ten geographical miles, would give in all 900, and the proportion of this between Limmou and Gooderoo would be 330 geographical miles,

which will place Sobitche, the capital of Limmou, in the latitude and longitude after mentioned, even after a proper allowance is made for the considerable detour which, after crossing
the river Wouelma, Ouare and the caravan took towards the
east, before they began to proceed to the northward. The
eastern detour taken in the space mentioned was to avoid
obstacles in their way arising most probably from a range of
hills to the northward of their route. The length of the route
taken by Ouare from Gooderoo to Khartoum on the general
bearing is 9° 50′, or 590 miles. Now if this space was travelled
over, as it was, in fifty-seven days, when all with the caravan
were become excessively fatigued, more than a proportionable
space must have been travelled over in the first thirty-three
days, when all were comparatively fresh; but even a proportional equal space will give 360 geographical miles nearly between Gooderoo and Limmou, which will place Sobitche in 5,
10′ N. lat., and 32° 30′ E. long.

To the westward of Sobitche, the capital of Limmou, is the
great river Habahia, running from the north to the south
betwixt a chain of mountains; and still farther west is the
country of Wambar, north of which is Dangab; and still more
to the north another country, called also Gooderoo, all on the
west side of the Habahia. These countries are very woody and
mountainous, and the banks of the river are covered with very
large bamboos, while the mountains produce cotton trees from
ten to fifteen feet high. S.W. of Wambar, and also of Limmou, commences the country of the Shankallas, a nation of
Blacks, considerably different from, and more rude than the
Gallas. Proceeding from Sobitche to Gooderoo, Ouare first
crossed the river Tchandi, next the Bowou; and at a greater
distance to the north, the river Wouelma. The near approach
of these rivers to each other shows that they are as yet only in
the early part of their courses, and the same also may be said
of the Habahia. Proceeding eastward, Ouare traversed the
country of Djedda, and then, towards the north, the great
countries of Amourou, next that of Horro, next Gouma or
Djima, next Kobbo, and then Gooderoo. Gingiro he knew, as
he had been sent there to stop some mines. It lay to the right
of his early route, that is, to the east of Limmou. Many rivers

rise in these parts, and flow to the Indian Ocean. In his route northwards through Djedda, &c., to Gooderoo, Ouare passed one large river, (this must be the Zebee) and some others, but he nowhere makes mention of having had to cross any very high mountains.

The other countries mentioned by Ouare in the neighbourhood of Limmou, to the E., S.E. and S., are laid down in the accompanying map, on the bearings and at the proportional distances in which Mr. Jomard has placed them. The mountainous country on the east bank of Habahia is peopled by a race of men called Gammodjis. The people of the plains are called *Baddas*.

The Gallas of Limmou and the adjacent parts, are a brave set of men, with agreeable countenances. Their arms are a corset and a crooked sabre, a lance, &c., the former resembling the representations of those which are found in the ancient monuments of Egypt and Nubia. The dress of the men is a long piece of cotton cloth wrapped round the whole body, with a girdle and waistcoat, and a jacket *à la romaine*, extending down to the knee. They are all pagans; the females have a special protectress, of the feminine gender; and besides her, the male sex invoke a deity named Lambata, the females one named Marina, female children one named Gorobbe, and both sexes a superior divinity named *Ouack*. A year is termed *bara* and a month *dj̃a*.

The difficulties in Ouare's route were many and great, and the fatigues and privations experienced by the travellers in the caravan so severe, that *one third* of the slaves accompanying it died during the journey, showing a much greater mortality amongst the slaves in a portion only of what may be called the middle passage of this internal African, slave trade than Mr. Buxton makes out on the middle passage of the European African slave trade.

Between Amourou and Horro is a town named Daga, and to the right a mountain named Gambela.

The next point for consideration is the great river Zaire or Congo. This important stream carries to the ocean a greater body of water than any other river, the Niger not excepted; although, from the tremendous rocks and cataracts

throughout a space of forty miles, commencing at the distance
of 140 miles from its mouth, it is rendered wholly unavailable
for any purpose of internal navigation as connected with external trade. The magnitude of the stream shows that it must
have numerous tributaries, and that the sources of these must
be very remote. According to Tuckey (see p. 84), the true
mouth of the river is at Fathomless Point. There " it is not
three miles in breadth," the mean depth forty fathoms, and the
mean velocity four and a half miles per hour. The proper
breadth of the stream, however, may be reduced to two miles.
The magnitude of the river, as stated by Tuckey, be it observed,
was the magnitude of the stream at its very lowest, nearly at
the close of the dry season.   Here then is a river of a breadth
at least equal, and a depth almost double, and with a current very
nearly equal to, that of the united stream of the Niger between
Iddah and Damuggoo, in the very height of the flood. Such
is the force of the water of the Congo, that in the centre of its
stream the current near its mouth forces its way for a considerable distance against the whole strength of the tide of the
ocean. The rise of the Zaire at its highest flood is, towards
its mouth, about twelve feet, which is considerably less than
the rise of the Niger (Laird, we believe, estimates this at
eighteen feet), which may however be accounted for in this
way, namely, because it does not sink so low from the effects
of the dry season, having some of its tributaries to a considerable distance within the southern torrid zone, which will
continue to supply its stream with a large quantity of water,
while its more remote and powerful tributaries, situated in the
northern torrid zone, are reduced from the effects of the dry
season. Every third or fourth year, the river is stated to rise
to a greater height than it does in the intermediate years. The
river begins to rise about a month before the rains commence ;
and, above the cataracts, Tuckey first perceived the beginning
of its rise, which was slow, gentle, and gradual, on the 7th of
September. This fact is an invincible proof that the chief
source of the river is at least 4° or 5° to the N. of the equator,
where the rains commence before the sun becomes vertical the
second time; the rains preceding his march generally about
one month. In the course of a fortnight the river, near its

mouth, had risen about seven feet. The slow and gradual rise of the river which Tuckey observed led him to form the opinion that the river issued from a lake; but while this may partly be true, the gradual rise of the stream can be accounted for on generally more correct principles, namely, its very remote sources. Its early tributaries, becoming flooded a considerable time before any rain moves its lower tributaries, or is felt in its lower course, will by degrees extend, and, from various causes, lose their strength as they proceed, and, gradually and more gently merging in the stream, tend, as they are further increased by additional rains and additional tributaries, to produce the gradual rise of the river, witnessed in its lower course. Moreover, it is well known that water every where tends to work itself clear, and that, where not defiled by a constant introduction of muddy particles, it gradually becomes clear. Throughout the distance of forty miles, as above stated, the cataracts and rapids extend. At Casan Yellala, the lowest and the first, the river is half a mile broad, and rocks stretch from the north side two-thirds of the whole width across the river. The channel on the south side is smooth, but the current is very rapid in it; and immediately below this rapid the current breaks furiously on a ledge of rocks. (Tuckey, p. 145.) At the great fall of Yellala, a slate island in the middle divides the stream into two channels. The channel on the north side, when Tuckey saw it, was nearly dry. That on the south side held the whole river, and in which " the torrent rushes with great fury and noise over rocks. By marks on the slate island alluded to, the river must rise during the rains twelve feet; then the whole of the island is covered, except the top of the rock, which is fifteen feet above the level of the stream when it is at its lowest point. When the river is in flood, the agitation of the river is dreadful at this point. (Tuckey, p. 147.) At ten miles above Mavoonda, and at a place named Sangalla, the river is compressed within the smallest space. It is here crossed by a great ledge of rocks, leaving only a passage close to the foot of the hill on the left bank, about fifty yards wide, through which the stream runs at least eight miles an hour, forming whirlpools in the middle, whose vortices occupy at least half of the channel," &c. Above, the river shews a broad

expanse, but below, it is a rocky ledge. At the point where
Tuckey turned back, about forty miles above this place, the river
again expanded to the breadth of from two and a half to four
miles, without any further obstruction in its course upwards; and
the scenery around its banks, from having been below wild and
barren, had become exceedingly fine and beautiful. The
current, at the point where Tuckey quitted the river and turned
back, was from two and a half to three miles per hour.

The accounts which he received regarding the river upwards
were that, at ten days' journey in a canoe above Mavoonda, there
was a large sandy island, above which the river divided into two
branches, one coming from the N.W. and the other from the N.E.
Above this separation, there was no obstruction in the navigation of the north-east branch, except at one place, where there
were some rocks in its bed, but which, nevertheless, canoes
could pass safely with proper precaution. At twenty days'
journey N.E. from the island mentioned, the river was reported
to issue by several streams from a large lake of mud ; and
beyond this Tuckey could hear nothing further about it. The
idea of a large river issuing from a lake of mud by several
streams is so ridiculous as to be unworthy of attention. That
there is a lake in that part—that the country around it is
marshy—and that several streams run into the lake, instead of
the river issuing from the lake in several streams, is all
extremely probable ; and, in fact, is the true meaning of the
accounts which the natives of Congo gave to Tuckey regarding
the northern branches of this important river. We have,
however, in these accounts, the facts of a north-eastern and a
north-western branch. The Wole, which we learn from other
authority is a large river, and flows to the eastward past the
state of Kaybee, is another, a higher, and more important
north-west branch, and which there is every reason to believe
runs into the lake in question. Next, there is another branch
from the N.W. which rises and runs to the east of the state of
Okandee, and which must, from the direction it takes, join the
river below the lake mentioned. According to maps of Africa,
constructed upon the authority of other natives from these
interior parts, there is another branch coming from the N.E.,
on the most south-western point of the Mountains of the Moon,

and also a branch from the eastward, descending from the northern part of the Mount Arangas of Ptolemy. The features of the country render the accounts about these rivers not only probable but certain. From the south-east also, the Zaire, we know, receives several very powerful tributaries; namely, first, that called the Barbela, which is represented by Portuguese writers to be as large as the Po of Italy in its lower course; and next the Coango, a river of great magnitude, which comes from the south-east, and has its sources at a great distance, but its course is not accurately known. Beyond it, and from the eastward, the Zaire certainly receives some important branches; but there is no accurate account to be had, either of their courses or of their magnitude. The whole of the rivers alluded to join to form the mighty river Zaire; and yet after all, and viewing the space of Africa in which they are said to take their rise, and through which they flow, there appears no more than sufficient, in fact scarcely a sufficient space or number of tributaries to form this important stream. In truth, there is reason to suppose that the sources of all these tributaries, whether on the south or on the north, are still more remote than in the positions in which they are at present laid down; in which case, as regards the northern ones, the most western branch of the Bahr el Abiad will, as is elsewhere stated, be shortened to the west, and more to the eastward extended to the south. The rocky ridge through which the Zaire, as Tuckey describes it, forces its way, rises to the elevation of about 2000 feet on each hand, in this point resembling the chain of hills through which the Niger bursts below the junction of the Shadda; but without any rocky interruptions in its bed, such as are found in the Zaire. The country around the Zaire, so far as Tuckey ascended it,—a distance of about 280 miles from its mouth,— was thinly peopled, and barren and unproductive.

Except at the points above-mentioned, the breadth of the Zaire through the cataracts and rapids extends generally from 200 to 300 yards. The great volume of water, both above and below these cataracts, compared to the apparent volume which ran through the most contracted points in them, natu- rally excited surprise in the minds of Tuckey and his com- panions, and led them to conjecture that a great portion of

the water found its way through subterraneous passages under
these rocks. This is by no means improbable. The tremendous
whirlpools which they found in the river where it began to
expand beyond and to the westward of the rocky ridge, go in
some measure to confirm this opinion. But there is another
and still stronger reason to think that Tuckey's opinion is the
fact. This is, that to the westward of this range of hills
through which the Zaire forces its way, and generally throughout the interior of the country extending through Loango to
the Atlantic, the whole surface of the earth seems to be
placed over and to be moved by volumes of water, which
frequently burst out and carry off large portions of the surface
of the land. Still, however, the rapidity of the stream through
these cataracts may account for the apparent difference; for
by the rule already stated, a stream running at the rate of
ten miles an hour through a passage double the depth of the
ordinary bed of the river will reduce a river three miles
broad, and with a current of three knots an hour, into very
narrow limits indeed; and, accordingly, this may actually
occasion the apparent reduction of the breadth of the Zaire at
the points mentioned.

To the south of the Congo, or Zaire, the western coast of
Africa is deeply intersected with rivers, the names of which at
their mouths are only known to Europeans: some of them are
of considerable magnitude, but none of them have courses of
any great length, except the Coanza, the Cuanene, and the
Orange River, which latter may be said to form the northern
boundary of the British colony of the Cape of Good Hope.
The Coanza is the largest of the three rivers mentioned. It
has its sources at a considerable distance, and to the south-
east of Cassange, in about 24° E. long., and 12° S. lat. The
course is first north-west and then west into the Atlantic, nearly
under the parallel of 9° S. lat. It has a great number of
considerable tributaries, but the courses of the whole, as well
as the countries around them, are imperfectly known. The
geographical knowledge which the Portuguese had of these
extensive countries was kept secret as much as possible, and
has been in a great measure lost to the world. Their settlements in Angola, Congo, and Benguela, were, at one time,

flourishing and extensive; but, unfortunately for themselves, and unfortunately for Africa, the discovery of the Brazils withdrew their attention from Africa and fixed it on South America; after which, the labour which should have cultivated, and which would have, to a certain extent, civilized Africa, was withdrawn, at an enormous loss to Africa, and placed in America. The course of the Coanza has been traced to the distance of fifteen days' journey from the islands of Quindango in that river, and in the district of Mattemba, from which islands to Cabasa, the ancient capital of Ginga, is four days' journey north-east, and from that place to a branch of the Coanza is a journey of three and a half days in the same direction. The great kingdom of Moropooa lies between Cassange on the west and Cassembe in the east, and about the very middle of Southern Africa, under the parallel of 10° to 12° S. lat. This state is represented as being very populous and powerful, and the people to be clothed in European manufactures brought from the Portuguese settlements on the east coast of Africa, about Mozambique. The capital is large, with regular streets, which are watered daily and kept very clean. There are regular markets. The country is governed by a king and by a queen, who live at a considerable distance from each other, and only visit once in fifteen days. The name they bear is Muata; and each sacrifice fifteen negroes daily at their respective residences. The river Lucala, which runs near this country, is stated to be a branch of the Coanza, and farther that canoes from Angola navigate up, first, the Coanza, and next the Lucala. The districts in these parts of Africa, and Mattemba and Cassange, were at one time overrun and subjected by a ferocious and savage people, called Jagas, or Giagas, who some centuries ago came from the neighbourhood of Sierra Leone and spread over Africa, carrying desolation in their progress. They seem to be a people of the same warlike and desolating disposition as the Tartars and Huns, which formerly desolated both Europe and Asia, but more brutal and more savage, inasmuch as they are stated to eat the captives they take in battle. They neither sow nor reap. Their women destroy their children as soon as they are born, that they may not be encumbered with them, and the army is recruited by the youths of the nations which they subdue. Their power, once so formidable—in fact, irresistible in Africa, is now greatly decayed; like every power of a similar description, it becomes exhausted by its own ferocity, and folly, and mischief.

The Coanza has a course on the general bearings of about 600 geographical miles. The countries around it are generally very fine, fruitful, and populous, and abound with minerals of various descriptions, and, under the direction of an enlightened and powerful country, the productions of this portion of Africa would add immensely to the wealth and the happiness of the human race.

The Cuanene has its sources between the meridians of 16° and 18° E. long., and in the parallels of 12° 30′ and 14° S. lat. It enters the sea under the name of Nouries River under the parallel of 17° 20′ S. lat. It is a considerable stream, but the greater part of its course is unknown. During the dry season, the bed of the river at its mouth, though very broad, is almost dry. The waters that remain sink amidst and under the large bank of round stones and pebbles which are in it : thus many rivers sink in Africa. The country around it, but more especially between it and the sea, is very mountainous, and it is fair to presume that the land, on its eastern banks, is of a similar description. At some distance from its western bank, and in 14° S. lat., and in the meridian of 15° E. long., the Portuguese have a settlement called Caconda, which, from its considerable elevation above the level of the sea, is very healthy, and the country around very pleasant and fruitful, yielding ready and large returns to the industrious cultivator.

From the mouth of the Cuanene to the Fish River, in 26° 30′ S. Lat., the coast of Africa is very little known; but the presumption is, that beyond the southern tropic the country in general is more destitute of rivers than it is to the north, and that the soil also is inferior. In the latitude of 28° 30′ S. there is the mouth of the Orange River, about one mile broad, but upwards it soon ceases to be navigable, although, from its extreme source, the course of the river is nearly 700 geographical miles, and the course nearly from east to west. The source of its principal branch is about 220 miles S.W. by W. of Delagoa Bay. The object of the present inquiry, however, being the tropical rivers and countries of Africa, it is considered foreign to the subject to introduce anything concerning the Cape of Good Hope and Africa to the south of the Orange River, more especially as almost every thing that could be stated regarding these parts is already well known to the public.

The eastern coast of Africa beyond the Cape of Good Hope, has also numerous rivers, but the courses of all of these, with the exception of that one which enters the sea in Delagoa Bay, probably the Moriqua of the interior, are certainly short, and also scarcely at all known to Europeans. The first of importance and in magnitude is the Zambeze, which enters the Indian Ocean by several mouths, between the parallels of 17° 30′, and 18° 30′ S. lat. This is a large river, and has its principal sources in the centre of Africa, in about 27° E. long., some of them most probably adjoining those of the Coanza. From both the north and south sides it receives many tributaries, which run through interesting countries; at least, from the little that we have heard concerning them, they must be so. One branch, the northern, or the Quilimane, is about one mile broad near the town, but upwards, and at the distance of about thirty-two miles in a straight line, it narrows to about twenty to thirty yards, and three days' journey from that point is the separation of the stream from the branch called the Luabo. The banks of this river are twenty feet high, yet they are all overflowed during the rainy season, which lasts from November till March: then the deep water channel extends one mile and a half broad. This river, above the separation of the Quilimane, is full of sand banks, or little islands, twenty feet high in the dry season, but all flooded during the rains. The current amongst them is exceedingly rapid during the dry season; so much so, that a canoe can only make one mile and a half per hour against it. In this part of its course the bed is about one mile broad. Towards Senna, the country to the N.W. is very hilly. Below Senna, a river called the Shirry enters the Zambeze from the north, which river is said to be navigable for canoes to the distance of thirty days' journey. It is deep and rapid. Tete is sixty leagues beyond Senna—the passage to it occupies six weeks; the town is built on a high ground near the Zambeze, and the country around it is said to be very fine, healthy, and fertile. The whole navigation of the Zambeze is said to extend to 300 leagues upwards. The Portuguese settlements in these parts, once very considerable and flourishing, are now in a most deplorable state of decay; yet an energetic government would soon bring them round, and make them more flourishing and wealthy than ever, as they have all the elements of tropical commerce and agriculture within them. Senna is in 17° 30' S. lat., and 35° 38' 8" E. long.

Beyond the Zambeze, to the north, the coast of Africa is thickly intersected with rivers, but they are all probably of little magnitude, until we pass Cape Delgado. There, almost under the parallel of 10° S. lat., the river Mongalla enters the sea, which river it is generally supposed flows from the great lake called Maravi, although there can be little doubt that considerable supplies also join it from the N.W. A considerable river enters the sea at Kulwa, or Quiloa, called the Cuaro, but scarcely any thing is known of its interior course. The next point of importance on the east coast is the island of Zanzibar, extending between 6° and 7° S. lat. It is forty-five miles long and fifteen broad; very fertile and populous, containing several towns and about 200,000 inhabitants. It is subject to the Imaum of Muschat, and has a considerable trade, both with India and Arabia. Opposite to it, and on the shores of the continent, several rivers enter the sea, which are in every probability the mouths of one great river, the great drain of all that vast portion of Africa which may be said to extend from the branches of the Zambeze on the south to the branches of the Quilimancy on the north, and from the sources of the tributaries of the Congo or Zaire, and the Coanza on the west. An inspection of the map will show what a large space is here, as it were, empty, but which, from the scanty reports which have reached us, is most certainly studded with high mountains, and intersected by numerous powerful rivers; but we have no accounts that can enable us to lay them down with anything like geographical accuracy. At Port Dunford a large river enters the sea, but of its upward course scarcely anything is at present known.

The population of almost all Southern Africa is sunk, if possible, into a lower depth of ignorance, superstition, and barbarity, than their brethren in the northern central parts.

The little knowledge planted among them about three centuries ago by the Portuguese, after the first discovery of the western coasts, has continued to decay with the decay of the power of Portugal, and is now in their remaining settlements almost extinguished, even amongst the native population, and utterly gone in its effects on the native states which adjoin them. So also it may be said it is with regard to the Arab states on the east coast. The comparative civilization, and it was but comparative, which they spread in the days of their strength, from the Straits of Babelmandeb to the boundaries of Sofala, is now decreased with their power, till it has become as weak and enfeebled, as the civilization spread by the Portuguese around and in their African settlements; but the elements for a better order of things remain, requiring only energetic, prudent, judicious, and powerful hands, to collect and call them forth. Nature has done every thing for Africa; man nothing. Yet there is no other quarter of the world which abounds more with vegetable and mineral wealth than tropical Africa does; no, not the most celebrated countries in either Asia or America. In southern Africa there are, moreover, several powerful native kingdoms and chiefs, which might, under prudent instruction and advice, be made the instruments of spreading cultivation, commerce, and civilization, in all these portions of Africa; nor have they ever shown any indisposition to be thus instructed, when honestly and fairly treated, and their customs, and manners, and institutions, touched with a forbearing, a gentle, and a friendly hand. The religion which Europeans profess, teaches them that this is the course which they ought to pursue with respect to all mankind; and with untaught and ignorant savages, in particular, this should be their course and their conduct; yet in almost every instance it has been the reverse. Like as in the northern parts, slavery as a domestic institution, and a foreign slave-trade, are universal. Some of the states, such as Cassembe, Moropooa, Cassange, &c. &c., have, however, the rudiments of order to a certain and to a considerable extent established, and in operation amongst them. One dreadful evil afflicts Africa; it is this—not one of her people seems to have the slightest idea of the value of time, and till they learn to appreciate this, they will never be brought to understand the sacred right of property, or the propriety of acquiring it by means of honest industry.

The southern portion of Africa, extending south from the Mountains of the Moon, abounds with large fresh-water lakes. Besides that named Maravi, which is of great extent, and situate in that part of Africa to the north of the middle course of the Zambeze, there is one in about 20° S. lat. and 23° E. long., which, according to every account, is very large. There is said to be another in the course of one of the branches of the Zaire, and named Aquilunda, near the country of Matamba. Besides that lake through which the north-east branch of the Congo flows, and situated almost immediately under the equator, there is another, said to be of great magnitude, sixty days' journey due east of Pombo, a district in about 4° N. lat., and on the west side of the Congo, or Zaire. This distance would bring the position of the lake in question to be in 4° S. lat., and about 28° E. long. The interior of Southern Africa, there also is every reason to believe, is very mountainous, with large districts of what is called table-land, such as are met with in different parts of South America. In all these table-lands the climate is necessarily good, and there can be no doubt that the population in them is very considerable.

CONCLUDING REMARKS.

It is a curious fact, and one well deserving notice and attention, that the general rise of all rivers in Africa, from the tropical rains, is in every place equal and uniform. Thus, in Abyssinia, Bruce pointedly observes, that the marks on the banks of all the rivers, great or small, indicated the rise at the height of the flood to be twenty feet. Dr. Holroyd clearly states that the average rise of the Blue River is twenty feet. Laird states this as the height of the flood in the Niger. Park found this to be the height of the flood in the Senegal and its numerous tributaries. De Caillé found this to be the height of the flood in the Mandingo tributaries to the Joliba. The British officers who lately visited the Zambeze found that the height of the flood was the same in it, namely, twenty feet. There are occasionally remarkable seasons and extraordinary natural causes operating, which produce larger floods, but it is clear that these are not frequent, and that they are exceptions to the general rule, namely, that the fall of water yearly throughout Africa is uniform. Excessive floods recur every four years.

Many nations in the interior parts are exceedingly anxious to open up a commercial communication and intercourse with the kingdoms and states of Europe, and especially with England. Dupuis (p. li.) assures us that this was the anxious wish of the sovereigns of Dagomba, Ghunjah, and Zogho. The Sultan of Sackatoo, the chief of Bornou, &c., expressed themselves in a similar manner. The price of various descriptions of human food in Africa is exceedingly favourable for procuring labour at a low rate. De Caillé, when at Jinne, could purchase as much butcher's meat for forty cowries (*twopence*) as would dine four persons; and Laing tells us that, when in the countries to the eastward of Sierra Leone, he could live like a prince for four-pence sterling per day! By means of the Niger and its tributaries, Africa may be penetrated to its deepest recesses: westward from Benin to Courouassa, by the Niger itself; eastward, by means of the Shadda, the territory of Bornou could be readily reached; and by the same channel the extreme sources of the Bahr el Abiad, the Shary and the Congo could be gained. From the bay of Howakil and Zeilah the interior parts of Abyssinia could be reached without difficulty; from Berbera the eastern horn of Africa could be deeply penetrated; and by means of the Zebee and the Quillimancy, the extreme sources of these rivers, and the Bahr el 'Abiad and others; the countries of Gingiro, Enarea, and Limmou could easily be gained. The population in all those quarters is very great, and metals and minerals are abundant. To the south of the Congo large deep rivers, such as the Coanza and Cuanene, penetrate deeply into tropical Africa on the west; and to the south of the Quillimancy, on the east coast the Zambeze, and other very large streams, lay open the African continent to an immense extent. Why is it that European nations do not take advantage of these numerous and extensive channels in order to extend their trade and commerce, and with these industry, knowledge, civilization—Christianity in Africa?

There is a good deal of confusion in De Caillé's narrative

about the true position of Jinne. He states that, after crossing the river at Cougalia, and travelling about six miles
W.N.W., he crossed one stream, and soon after another
stream, both fordable, the first the deepest, and then entered
Jinne, situated on the bank of the second. The Joliba, he says,
appeared at ten miles distance to the west. On leaving Jinne
in the canoe, they went, it would appear, by the arm last mentioned, westward to the Joliba, and thence by an arm or
branch to Cougalia. In their progress, he says expressly that
they were aided by the current, which clearly establishes the
point, that the arm or branch by which he went to Cougalia
flowed from the Niger to the Kowara Ba. There is no other
way of making out, in a satisfactory manner, what is the true
meaning of his narrative, except the view which has been here
taken. The fact, that he went, first to the Joliba, and next
from the Joliba with the current of the branch alluded to,
enables us to ascertain and to determine this point.

According as Ptolemy's geography has come to us, there is
an error of no less than 12° 52′ 33″ between Ferro and Alexandria, his first meridian. Alexandria he places, or is made
to place, in 60° 30′ E. from Ferro. Now, Ferro is in 17° 44′
(west point) W. long., and Alexandria in 29° 53′ 27″ E. long.,
together 47° 37′ 27″; thus showing an error as above
stated of 12° 52′ 33″. The points where this error is obvious
are in his positions of Cape Verde, lying in 10° E. long.
from Ferro, whereas it is only 3°. This makes his space
between Mount Mandrus and Cuphæ, the position of modern
Timbuctoo, 7° wrong, while his position of the Nigrites Palus,
clearly Lake Dibbie, is wonderfully correct in longitude, .
namely, 15° east of Ferro, (2° 44′ W. of Greenwich,) and in
lat. 18° N., not very far wrong. His accuracy also in the
position of Mount Mandrus, clearly the high mountains south
of Walet, namely 14° E. long., or 1° W. of the Lake Nigrites,
is equally, or still more remarkable. His space again between
the Nigira metropolis, 17° 45′ lat. N., and 25° 20′ E. long.,
and his Gira metropolis, 18° 20′ N. lat., and 36° E. long.,
10° 40′, is exceedingly correct. The remaining portion of the
general error, 12° 52′ 33″, or 5° 52′ 33″, is found to be between
his Gira metropolis, the Lybian Lake, and thence eastward to

Alexandria; in other words, he makes the desert between Lake Lybia and Lake Nuba and the Nile 5° 52′ 33″ too broad, otherwise his positions are, in some instances, wonderfully correct.

In his geography, Ptolemy lays down different places thus:

	Lat.	Long.
Garamantican Rampart . .	10° N.	50° E. from Ferro.
Mount Thala	10° N.	38° E. ,,
Mount Arualtes	3° N.	33° E. ,,
Mount Arangas	2° N.	47° E. ,,
Mount Usurgala	20° 20′ N.	33° E. ,,
Gira Metropolis	18° N.	36° E. ,,

In order to give these places their true positions, and to correct the error in Ptolemy's longitudes; besides the positions of the places already adverted to, which the natural features enable us to ascertain clearly, we have two other points which enable us to correct the positions of different places. The one is by Ptolemy himself, which places his Gira metropolis one hour and one-eighth in time, 16° 52′, west of Alexandria; or, as regards the longitude, as nearly as possible in the place where Gamberou, or Old Birnie, now stands. A river which runs to the Niger, near Panagra, has its source in the Usurgala mountains, in 3° west of this place, and above, and a little to the west of Agadez. Secondly, we have the correct position (centre) of the high land of Cameroons, clearly his Mount Arualtes, viz. 11° E. long. His Mount Thala is 5° east of this, which brings it exactly to the Mandara range. Next, his Garamantican rampart is in 50° long., or 17° east of Mount Arualtes, which will bring the former to 28° E. long., which we find is very correct; and lastly, his Mount Arangas is 14½° east of Mount Arualtes, which will bring its true position to be 1° 30′ N. lat., and 25½° E. long., the determination of which positions and points is highly satisfactory. If we take the distance of Mount Thala from his Gira metropolis, or Gamberou, or Old Birnie, we have just two degrees corresponding with the other; and if we take the position of Mount Arangas from the position of his Gira metropolis, or Old Birnie, we have 12° of difference, bringing Mount Arangas also to the same point as by the former calculation, proceeding from the fixed point of the high land at Cameroons.

CONSTRUCTION OF THE MAP.

THE narrative is accompanied by a map, drawn first upon a large scale, forty-five geographical miles to one inch; subsequently reduced to its present size, and next engraved and published under the hand of one of the best geographers in Europe, Mr. John Arrowsmith. It may here be necessary to state, shortly, the manner in which the map was constructed. My mind was made up to judge for myself; and whatever labour it might cost, to be satisfied on every point. The labours and speculations of geographers, or writers on African matters previous to this day, were brought into aid. The accounts of travellers, ancient or modern, that were known, or that came in my way, were carefully and separately examined; their statements retained or rejected, according as these agreed with themselves as a whole; or, as they stood the test of rigid examination when contrasted with others. The bearings and distances given in each were all carefully considered, as these were found to be given when travelling from different points in Africa to other points in Africa. Every one of these journeys were then protracted upon a large scale, and afterwards reduced, combined, and connected, by which means, with the aid of one or two fixed points, and a few more stated positions in which there could be no great error, one traveller and writer was made to check the other, and sometimes themselves. Great care has been taken to point out what the native travellers really did state, or intended to state, and not that which they have been in too many instances made to state. In this way the true meaning of many apparently confused narratives, the erroneous speculations and conclusions of others, and the wrong positions taken by nearly all, were clearly demonstrated and ascertained. The day's journey and the day's travelling are two different things; and differing still more according as these relate to the countries in the mountainous and cultivated parts; or, to the Great Desert; and also to the dry season or to the wet season. These important points were minutely attended to, and the correct meaning of the travellers or writers in these points also ascertained, by comparing them with others. Much care was taken to find out whether the journey under consideration was undertaken with a caravan, or by an isolated traveller, or by a small party of travellers, on foot or on horseback; and whether the time taken on the whole was the time actually travelled, or the time travelled including also that devoted to rest. Thus, three months' journey from one place to another gives quite a different distance to ninety days actually travelled, because the former often includes the time the traveller takes to rest on his journey, which is on an average perhaps from one-third to one-fourth of the whole. In like manner the estimated ninety days' journey gives a very different distance made good to the space actually travelled during that space of time. Sometimes the time from place to place is given without stating that in that period is included the time in which the traveller rests, and sometimes the distance is given to the capital of the state or country, and at other times only to the frontiers of the state. A day's journey by Arab and Moor estimation of distance is about 15½ geographical miles made good on the general bearing, whereas the space actually travelled, especially in the mountainous, uncleared, and uncultivated and river countries, does not, particularly in the rainy season, exceed ten geographical miles on the general bearing, and frequently much less. In stating, by narrative, the distance from place to place, the Moor and African traveller frequently or generally uses the former calculation, namely, fifteen to sixteen geographical miles, and it consequently becomes of great importance to ascertain whether in such narratives it is this scale, and the time allowed for resting, or the time, not including stoppages, which is intended; or if it is the rate and time actually travelled from place to place which is meant; and, further, if it is the time taken to travel to the capital of any country, or only to the frontiers of any country, that ought to be taken as the meaning of the informant, or the correct information obtained from them. Want of proper attention to these points has led into numerous and great errors in African geography, and which preconceived opinions, obstinate theories, and prejudices, tended still further to distort and confound.

Lander, in the following passage, places this point properly before us: " The reports of the natives, whether owing to the difficulty of expressing themselves so as to be understood by a stranger, or from other causes, vary considerably. I should conceive that the former is the chief reason of this difficulty so often complained of; and that, in their relations of rivers and streams, the natives do not designedly deceive, but the inter-rogator, taking no pains to obtain a clear idea of their meaning, forms an opinion of his own, which he fancies approaches nearest to that which his informants themselves entertain."—*Lander*, vol. ii. p. 146.

All these important points, however, have in the present in-stance been very carefully attended to, and the result has been not only eminently satisfactory, but such as never was at the outset anticipated it could be. The repeated journeys of Park, that of Laing, De Caillé, Mollien, and the itineraries obtained by Bowditch and Dupuis, &c., were severally protracted in the manner alluded to, and the positions of places and the courses of rivers thus clearly and satisfactorily found; although, as re-gards the western rivers of Africa, and the positions of places to Timbuctoo, I found, when I had finished my inquiries, that the vast labour might have been spared by taking Mr. Arrow-smith's last map, so far as it relates to the western rivers, the Senegal, Gambia, &c., and also to the great space between the Atlantic and Timbuctoo, especially in the position of that celebrated town; for I found, after the closest investigation, that there was not more than thirty miles difference in longitude; while the palm of accuracy is readily yielded to his researches in preference to my own; thus placing Timbuctoo in 17° 10′ N. lat., and 3° W. long. instead of 2° 30′ W. long. and 17° 40′ N. lat. The Nile, with the exception of some of its most remote tributaries, and also the coasts of the Mediterranean, are also from Mr. Arrowsmith.

There is another point which, in considering the narratives and statements of Moor and Arab travellers and writers, requires to be most carefully attended to, and corrected by different references and narratives; and that is the bearings which they give, or which the European ear or narrator gives, to the information drawn from them. These, in very many, and in most important cases, are just the reverse; that is, we shall say S.W. instead of N.E.: pages might be filled with these errors. But take the following:—Lyon was told (see page 127,) that Oonghor, or Oongooroo, was fourteen days' journey E. by S. of Bornou (New Birnie), whereas it is W. by N. He was also told that Guber was three days S.W. of Saccatoo, whereas it is three days to the N.E. Browne was told that Wara lay N.E. from Dar Ruma, whereas it is S.W. So also, Mesna, the capital of Bagherme; it is S.W. from Fittre, instead of being N.E. By not detecting these errors, proved by subsequent travellers to be so, Major Rennell carried Bornou to 24° N. lat., whereas, taken as it is stated with the distance and bearing from Mesna to Dar Kattakou, the frontier Province of Bornou to the west of the Shary, five or six days west, and next, thirteen north (the remainder of the time given by Browne,) to old Birnie, we find the whole exactly as Denham, &c. found them. As regards one Kuku, Caugha, or Cooka (not the Kuku of Edrisi, situated twenty days' journey north,) it is found on the river, and in a position far to the south, as Ibn Said had stated it to be, namely, 10° N. lat. It is, in all probability, still further south than it has been placed in the map accompanying this work. Ibn Said is probably nearest the truth.

It is also customary with Arab travellers and writers to describe as islands countries situated within or at the forks of rivers, or that are nearly encompassed by rivers. Another important point is that, unless checked, and specially questioned in their narratives and relations, they put the geographical bearing of the bed of the river for the course of the current, which reverses our manner of stating the fact. Thus, they say, that the Egyptian Nile goes to Abyssinia; we know that it comes from that country. They, moreover, often in their narratives, oppose right and left banks of a river, &c. to what we would state these to be. Thus, in describing the right, they always speak of the right hand, or what is to the right hand of their position, in reference to their face being turned towards Mecca. Attention to all these points will tend to elucidate many apparently irreconcilable statements in the information given by these people; and attention to them would also have prevented many errors into which geographers have fallen in their African geographical dissertations and speculations. This

mode of reversing positions and courses of rivers is not confined to Moors and Arabs. We find it in many European
books, where, describing the bearing of one place from another,
the writer, in his mind, is walking to, or starting from, the
wrong point. Oldfield says of Kirree, that it is 6° 6′ lat.
south of the equator instead of north, and of the branch of
the Niger above Eboe which runs to Benin; he says, p. 137,
"supposed to run *from* Benin." So Clapperton, p. 155, says
of the river of Guari, it "rises a day's journey in the mountains and hills *south* of Guari, runs through part of Zamfra,
&c., and enters into the Koodonia in Nyffe," whereas the
course is just the reverse; so also with the river Akkeni,
he states it to run N.W. to the Lagos river, whereas it
must be S.E. Of the river which flows from the Niger on
the east side above Kirree, Laird and Oldfield were told
that it *went* to Fundah; whereas, could it possibly be connected with that place, it must come from it.

It is only necessary to observe further, that complete
geographical accuracy is not pretended to in the map accompanying the subsequent narrative. In the present state of
our African knowledge, and with days' journeys as the only
means of fixing the positions of countries, places, and rivers,
perfect accuracy is unattainable. The object held in view
was to present to the public a rational, and as nearly as
possible, a correct delineation of the great physical features
of Africa; this it is presumed and hoped has been done, with no
material error in the general delineation of her great rivers and
ranges of mountains, &c. &c. Considering the confused materials
which could only be obtained to work with; a survey, so perfect
as that now produced, was not calculated upon; but labour,
thought, and patience, have done more than was anticipated,
and completed a delineation of Africa, which it is hoped future
accurate researches, and future information, may probably look
at with advantage.

In no portion of the work were there more difficulties to
encounter in constructing the map, than in that portion thereof
which had to delineate the course of the Niger above the Delta,
and from thence to Rabba. There was little or no agreement
amongst the different authorities. It therefore became neces-

sary to collate and check the whole. For this purpose, the general delineation of the river is taken from Captain Beecroft's Minute Survey, extending from the mouth of the Nun, to the junction of the Shadda; but the longitudes and latitudes are, as regards the latter, taken from his and other accounts; and as regards the former, from the accounts of native travellers, but especially from the bearings given, and distances calculated, according to the time occupied by Lander and Oldfield, and all of which a strict inquiry shows to be generally correct. Subsequent to the construction of the map, the kindness of Captain Beaufort of the Admiralty, put into my hands the chart, constructed by Lieutenant Allen, of the Niger, from the sea to Rabba. In this such a great disagreement from Beecroft, Oldfield, and others appears, as satisfies me that the course pursued has been the safest and the best. Thus, Captain Beecroft lays down Eboe in 6° E. long., and the junction of the Shadda in 6° 15'; whereas Lieutenant Allen places the former in 6° 25', and the latter in 7° 8'; but he states, in an article inserted in the journal of the Royal Geographical Society, already specially alluded to, that his observations as to the longitude of Stirling, varied from 3' to 16'. Mr. Hill's journal places Kirree in 6° 1' N. lat. Captain Oldfield's journal has it in 6° 6'; which, he says, he obtained from Lieutenant Allen on the spot. This has been retained as the most correct. In Lieutenant Allen's chart, already alluded to, he places Kirree in 6° 12' 30" N. lat. In this chart, however, I was pleased to observe the "mouths of the Coodonia" laid down joining the Niger above Egga, instead of coming from Lake Shad, and running to swell the Shadda by Jacoba; thus showing that the theory promulgated in England, is quite different from the accounts which appear to have been collected in Africa. In this chart, moreover, there appears to be no branch above Eboe laid down running to the westward. The mouths of the Niger and the Delta have been taken—the coast, from the late survey by Captain Owen, and the rivers, or rather branches, and their numerous intersections, have been copied from excellent charts, constructed from actual surveys of that portion of Africa by the following navigators; viz. Bosman, 1702; Matthews, 1776; Clemmisson, Norris,

Woodville, and T. Clarke, 1780; Fairweather and Latham, 1790; Penny, &c.; and also from the written and oral communications of various individuals, who have, within the last thirty years, been in that quarter. While these sheets were in the press, and the map under engraving, I have had the pleasure to learn from Mr. Oldfield, who has but lately arrived from that coast, that the delineation of the New Calabar, and the intersections or creeks between it and the Nun, through most of which he had actually been in his last visit to these parts, are correct; and moreover, as I had stated from other authorities, that the whole space between the Bonny and the Old Calabar, is a delta, through which various branches or creeks run from the one to the other.

On reviewing and reconsidering the whole work, it is conceived probable, that the day's journey in Ashantee and the adjoining districts may have been too much restricted, say to the extent of one mile daily, which if it has been so, will so far proportionately alter the positions in these quarters of Africa, and carry the Jibbel Sargha mountains and sources of the Rio Volta, &c. &c. about thirty miles more to the north. But this is the utmost that can be allowed, and even this is perhaps unnecessary, or too much. The chain of which the high land of Cameroons is the termination, will be found to run in a zig-zag direction in about the same parallel eastward by the sources of the Cameroons, the Congo, the Shadda, the Bahr el Abiad, &c. to about 30° E. long., whence it will run along north-easterly by the sources of the Habahia, the Zebee, and branches of the Bahr el Azreek, to the sources of the Hawash; from whence it will branch off in one direction to Cape Babelmandeb, and another to the Capes Guardafui and Ras Halfoon.

APPENDIX.

HERE it may be proper and useful to give, from various authorities, the distances, and the bearings, where these are given, betwixt one place and another, in Central, Eastern, and Northern Africa.

NORTH OF THE NIGER, ETC.

Morocco to Cairo, 6 months caravan, 4 months special messenger.

Morocco to Tripoli	40 days' journey.
Asben to Cairo	3 months' ,,
Jekky to ditto	100 days' ,,
Akom to Bedawa...	33 ,, ,,
Akom to Waday	50 ,, ,,
Bedawa to Cairo	2 months' ,,
Bornou to ditto..	3 ,, ,,
Waday, or Dar Saley, to Egypt	53 days' ,,
Kashna to Darfur..	2 months' ,,
Benin to Cairo, special messenger	5 ,, ,,
Benin to Bornou, by land and water	75 days' ,,
Benin to Abyssinia, ditto............................	100 ,, ,,
Bedawa to Gulf Sydra	1 month's ,,
Asben to Tripoli	50 days' ,,
Mourzook to Gulf Sidra	18 ,, ,,
Mourzook to Tripoli..	25 ,, ,,
Asben to Tunis	2 months' ,,
Agadez to Timbuctoo (Ben Ali)........................	55 days' ,,
Agadez to Salt Lake Domboo (Casav.)	45 ,, ,,
Bornou, old Birnie, to Bagherme (Beaufoy) S.E. ...	20 ,, ,,
Cubcabea to Bornou by Wara, (Browne)	60 ,, ,,
Mourzook to Bornou (Ledyard)........................	660 geographical miles.
Mourzook to Agadez (ditto)	479 ,,
Agadez to Kashna (ditto)	17 days' journey.
Mourzook to Agadez (by other authorities)	47 ,, ,,
Mourzook to Bornou (Burkhardt)	50 ,, ,,
Mourzook to Bornou (other authorities)..............	52 ,, ,,
Tripoli to Timbuctoo (Ritchie) 1260 geog. miles ...	80 ,, ,,
Senegal, Kaignu above Gallam, to Timbuctoo, (Le Brue)	34 ,, ,,

Senegal, Kaignu, to Timbuctoo by Labat ....   32 days' journey.
Fort St. Joseph to Timbuctoo, by Tisheet & el Arroan   48   „   „
Santa Cruz to Wednoon, by Mogadore (Park)   20   „   „
Wednoon to Benown (Benown from Tisheet 10) ...   30   „   „
Mourzook to Timbuctoo (by Ben Ali)   64   „   „
Agadez to Kano (Leo and Joanes Bleav) ....   160 leagues.
Timbuctoo to Kashna, east (Rees' Encyclopædia)...   690 miles.
Lake Fittre to Shary (Bowditch).......................   12 days' journey.
Kashna to Zegzeg (Leo, &c.) ....   150 miles.
Bornou to Kano ....   30 days' journey.
Kano to Saccatoo (Lander).............................   20   „   „
Arguin to Hoden, easterly   7   „   „
Tegazza to Timbuctoo (Leo) ....   500 A. miles.
Baderma to Segelmessa (Batouta) ....   70 days' journey.
Fezzan to Timbuctoo   90   „   „
Ghadames to Agadez   48   „   „
Mourzook to Gannat   14   „   „
Gannat to Assouda   17   „   „
Assouda to Agadez   17   „   „
Agadez to Kashna ....   255 miles.
Ghadames to Twat (Rennell) S.W. ....   20 days' journey.
Kano to Kashna (Bowditch)   10   „   „
Yaoora to Kano (ditto)   28   „   „
Yaoora to Bornou (ditto)................................   52   „   „
Yaoora to Goober (ditto) N...............................   10   „   „
Kashna to Nyffe, by Saccatoo (Lyon)   17   „   „
Kashna to Nyffe, by another road (ditto)   20   „   „
Kashna to Asben (Dupuis)...............................   40   „   „
Asben to Mourzook (ditto)   40   „   „
Taudeny to Tarudent, Morocco (ditto)   50   „   „
Taudeny to Taffilet, ditto (ditto)........................   50   „   „
Old Germa to Agadez (Edrisi, bearing by Beaufoy,
    SS.W.)   37   „   „
Dar Saley to Mourzook (Burkhardt)   52   „   „
Benown to Morocco (Park)................................   50   „   „
Kashna to Fittre (Rennell, but wrong)   40   „   „
Oongoroo to Bornou, 9 on horseback, (Bowditch)...   15   „   „
Obeidh to Shendy (Burkhardt)   14   „   „
Saccatoo to Adia (Clapperton) N.   6   „   „
Nikky to Gamberou......................................   42   „   „
Mourzook to Cairo (Browne)   50   „   „
Dongola to Zagawa (Abulfeda) S.W...................   30   „   „
Zagawa to Angimi (Edrisi) W.   6   „   „
Anay to Bornou (Denham)................................   27   „   „
Agadez to Salt Lake, Bornou (Rennell)   40   „   „
Cobbe to Dar Kulla (Rennell, &c.)...............   40 to 45   „   „

Wara to Bahr el Ghazelle (Lyon) .... 7 days' journey S.W.
Wara to Fittre   (ditto)..................... 5 or 6   ,,   ,, S.
Wara to Caugha   (ditto) .... 6, 7, or 8   ,,   ,, S.W.
Tegerby to Bilma   (ditto) 20   ,,   ,, S.
Mourzook to Kashna   (ditto)....................... 56   ,,   ,,
Gago to Goober (Leo)..................................... 100 leagues.
Senaar to sources of Bahr el Abiad (Ledyard) ...... 55 days' journey.
Dongola to Ghana, country (Edrisi) 66   ,,   ,,

PLACES SOUTH OF THE NIGER, ETC.

Timbuctoo to Melli (Cadamosto) S.W. .... 30 days' journey.
Woolli to Sego (Rennell, Park, p. 400) 36   ,,   ,,
Ghonjah to Kashna (Sheerif Inhammed) 97   ,,   ,,
Ghonjah to Sea Coast, through Tonouma (ditto) ... 46   ,,   ,,
Yarribah to Ghonjah, N.W. 38   ,,   ,,
Inta or Tonouma, to Timbuctoo (Bowditch) 42   ,,   ,,
Kong to Jinne   (ditto) 42   ,,   ,,
Coomassie to Yakua or Yakoo (Dupuis) 70   ,,   ,,
Nikky to Gambaroo   (ditto)................... 42   ,,   ,,
Benin to Yaoori   (ditto)...................: 36   ,,   ,,
Benin to Kashna   (ditto)................... 40   ,,   ,,
Coomassie to great fair at Gd. Hamed Mousa, in
   Suse Morocco (Dupuis) 130   ,,   ,,
Yaoori to Kashna, 1st Konbash country ... 7 days
Ditto   2d Gharanti............... 5   ”
Ditto   3d Yantoro 5   ”
(Dupuis, p. 136) 4th Kashna 7   ”
                                          ——— 24   ,,   ,,
Greghwee to Fillanee, Province (Robertson)......... 40   ,,   ,,
Yaoori to Ghoroma, Magho, W. by S. (Dupuis) ... 30   ,,   ,,
Salagha to Ghoroma, to right of north (ditto) 24   ,,   ,,
Deboia, capital, Gobago to Yaoori (ditto) 40   ,,   ,,
Magho to the mountains of Fagh (ditto) 34   ,,   ,,
Salagha, through Nikky to Niger near Yaoori 38   ,,   ,,
   (thus:—Salagha to Nikky 26 journeys.
   Nikky to Niger, 12 or 13.)
Niger at Yaoori, through that state to Goober
   (Bowditch) 10   ,,   ,,
Goober to Kassina, cross a large river, and skirting
   Zamfra (Bowditch) 8   ,,   ,,
Timbuctoo to Bitoo (Le Hadge Mahommed) 46   ,,   ,,
Sego to Jinne, 4 by water, by land (Dupuis)......... 10   ,,   ,,
Yandi to Abomey   (ditto) 13   ,,   ,,
Yandi to Benin   (ditto) 28   ,,   ,,

Coomassie to Soko Aila, N.W. cap. of Enkassi
    (Dupuis) .... 16 days' journey.
Soko Aila to Kong (Dupuis) .... 6 „   „
Yarribah to Ghonjah (Inhammed) .... 18 or 20 „   „
Kong to Rio Pongos, across a great river (Bowditch) 2 months' journey.
Dahomey to Nikky .... 15 days'   „
Coomassie to Aughgoa cap. Moushee (Dupuis)...... 25 „   „
Abomy to Niger, or Benin river, east (ditto)......... 14 „   „
Dagwumba to Yaoori (Bowditch, p. 200) .... 42 „   „
Silla to Timbuctoo (Park) .... 14 caravan journeys.
Timbuctoo to Jinne (Wargee)......................... 25 journeys.
Sego to Jabowa (Bowditch) .... 40 days' journey.
Sego to Bambook (ditto) .... 43 „   „

PARK'S JOURNEYS.

FIRST JOURNEY.—DRY SEASON.

	Days.	Hours.	Miles.	Bearings.	Lat.
Pisania to Jondey	2	6	12	S.E. by E.	13° 35′
Jondey to Roolacienda	1	5	10	E.	
Fabujang	1	2½	5	E. ½ N.	
Medina	1	5½	11	ditto	13° 49′
Kenjorer.....................	1	3	6	E. ½ S.	
Mallaing.....................	1	2	11	E. by S.	
Kola	1	5	10	E.N.E.	
Tambakunda	1	5½	11	S.E. by E.	
Tambakunda to Kooniakary	1	5	10	E. by N.	
Kooniakary to Koojar	1	3	6	E. ½ N.	
Koojar to a Well	1	13	26	E. by N.	
Well to Fallica	1	4	8	E.	
Fallica to Ganada	1	4	8	E. ½ N.	
Ganada to Koorkoorany ...	1	4½	9	E.S.E.	13° 53′
Koorkoorany to Dooggi......	1	1	2	E. by N.	
Dooggi to Buggel	1	4½	9	E. ½ N.	
Buggel to Soobroodka	1	7	14	E. by N.	
Soobroodka to Naye*........	1	7	14	E.N.E.	
Naye to Fattecunda	1	3½	7	ditto	
Fattecunda to Kemmoo......	1	4½	9	ditto	
Kemmoo to Joag	1	6	12	E. by N.	14° 25′
Total.........	22	101½	203		

N.B.—The variation of 17° west was allowed on these bearings
by compass.

* Ba Faleme, rapid, rocky; water up to knees crossing it on horseback;
went north three miles on its banks, December 20th.

FIRST JOURNEY, CONTINUED.

	Days.	Hours.	Miles.	Bearings.	Lat.
Joag to Sammee..............	1	7	14	E. by N.	
Sammee to Kayee *	1	3½	7	ditto	
Kayee to Teesee..............	1	7½	15	N.E. by N.	
Teesee to Medina	1	6	12	S.E. by E.	
Medina to Jumbo.............	1	6	12	ditto	
Jumbo to Kooniakary	1	1½	3	E. by S.	14° 34′
Kooniakary to Soomo	1	8	16	S.E. ½ E.	
Soomo to Kanjee	1	7	14	ditto	14° 10′
Kanjee to Leeharago.........	1	7	14	Easterly	
Leeharago to Fezurah	1	7	14	E. by S.	14° 5′
Fezurah to Karancalla	1	10	20	Easterly	
Karancalla to Kemmoo......	1	15	30	E. by N.	
Kemmoo to Marina	1	8	16	Northerly	
Marina to Toordah	1	6	12	ditto	
Toordah to Funningkeddy...	1	7	14	N. by E. ½ E.	
Funningkeddy to Sembing .	1	8	16	N. by E.	
Sembing to Jarra	1	6	12	NN.E.	15° 5′
Total	17	120½	241		

	Days.	Hours.	Miles.	Bearings.	
Jarra to Waura, say	4	38	76 ⎫		
Waura to Dengyee............	1	6	12 ⎬ about S.E. by E.		
Dengyee to Wassiboo	1	6	12 ⎭		
Wassiboo to Satile, very quick	1	12	24	S.E. by E.	
Satile to Galloo	1	8	16	E.S.E.	
Galloo to Moorja	1	9	8	E. by N.	
Moorja to Datiliboo	1	12	24	S.E. by E.	
Datiliboo to Fanamboo	1	14	28	E.S.E.	
Fanamboo to Giosora.........	1	14	28	ditto	
Giosora to Doolinkiaboo ...	1	10	20	S.E. by E.	
Doolinkiaboo to the Lions...	1	10	20	ditto	
The Lions Village to Diganne, near Sego	1	4	8	S.	
Total	15	143	286		

* Bafing, beautiful but shallow river, runs with considerable force; banks, forty feet high; bottom, sand and gravel; crossed by canoes; about size Tweed at Melross. December.

MEMORANDUM.

Boubaker to Jarra	3 days.	19 hours.	38 miles.			
Samee to Benowm, journey back Deena .	5 ,,	30 ,,	60 ,,			
Deena to Benowm	1 ,,	10 ,,	20 ,,			
Jarra to Deena, Feb. 27th to 1st March .	4 ,,	28 ,,	56 ,,			
Deena to Samee	4 ,,	24 ,,	48 ,,			

No variation is allowed on the bearings in this last list from
Jarra to Sego. The exact time and bearing from Jarra to Waura
(that is, hours,) is uncertain; but there cannot be any material error
as it is taken.

Sego to Silla .... 6 days. 47 hours. 94 miles.

But this was in the middle of the wet season, when travelling
was almost impracticable, and when the distance made good could
scarcely reach one and a quarter geographical miles per hour. About
one-eighth also may be deducted from the distance on the general
bearing in all the former part of the journey.

Silla, by dead reckoning, was 13° 22' N. lat. Sego being in
13° 4' by the same.

Silla to Sego, returning...................... 13 days.
Sego to Bammakoo .... 11 days, say 110 miles.

This in the wet season :—

Bammakoo to Sibideloo .... 2 days, say 20 miles.
Sibideloo to Kammalia .... 9½ „   72 „
Silla to Sansanding .... 1½ „   15 „

N.B.—Jarra, said to be ten days' journey distant from Kammalia,
bearing about N.W.

FIRST JOURNEY—KAMMALIA TO PISANIA.

	Days.	Hours.	Miles.
Kammalia to Kongtakoro*	3	17 say	40
Kongtakoro to River Wonda†	2	16½	33
River Commeissang to River Boki	3	28½	51
River Boki to Bafing, at Manna‡	2	15	30
Total......	10	77	154
Bafing to Balee ....{	5	36 3	72 6
Balee to Ba Faleme§.................................	3	8	16
Total......	18	124	248

* Before reaching Kongtakoro, crossed the River Kokoro, a small stream such
as would turn a mill. Had risen twenty feet in the rainy season.

† Wonda, a small stream; fifty to sixty miles from Wonda, crossed the Fur-
komah as large as Wonda; about sixteen miles west of Wonda, crossed the
Commeissang.

‡ Bafing smooth and deep; little current. Temporary bridge made by bending
two trees together from opposite banks. Yearly swept away.

§ Stream easily forded, only two feet deep; flows rapidly over a bed of sand.

It must be remarked that the preceding journey was made during the best of the dry season, and the travelling was sometimes quicker than customary, but the caravan was numerous.

SECOND JOURNEY—PISANIA TO BAMMAKOO, ETC.

	Days.	Hours.	Miles.
Pisania to Medina, lat. 13° 49′.....................	5	28½	57
Medina to Teelee Corra Banks, Gambia	4	15½	31
Teelee Corra to Nerico, lat. 14° 4′ 51″............	3	16	32 ·
Nerico to Tembeco, lat. 13° 53′	2	5½	11
Tembeco to Mansassra, * lat. 13° 33′	3	15	30
Mansassra to Badoo †	4	24	48
Badoo to Faleme ‡.....................................	7	48	96
Total......	28	152½	305 ▪
Ba Faleme to Ba Lee, lat. 13° 35′	8	42½	85
Ba Lee to Bafing,§ lat. 13° 27′......................	5	27	54
Bafing to Ba Wonda ‖	5	32	64
Ba Wonda to Kokoro,¶ lat. 14° 1′	2	13	26
Ba Kokoro to Ba Woolima,** lat. 13° 41′	5	32	64
Ba Woolima to Ba Woolli,†† lat. 13° 16′	9	49	98
Ba Woolli to Bammakoo ‡‡	6	38	76
Total	40	233½	467

Regarding the former part of his journey, namely, from Pisania to the Ba Faleme, it is to be remarked that it was performed towards the close of the dry season; and the body of men composing the party being considerable, their progress, under these peculiar circum-

* Nikkidora, on banks of Gambia, is eight miles distant south.

† Badoo; Gambia, only four miles distant south.

‡ Ba Faleme, a little discoloured by rain, June 8th. Current four knots per hour. Came from S.E. sources, distant six days' journey.

§ Bafing, risen about two feet, June 26th; navigable; large river; current three knots per hour.

The Ba Lee not sensibly swelled; stepped across from rock to rock without wetting the feet.

‖ Going two days rather to westward of north.

¶ Wonda cannot be called a large river—risen two feet July 4th; shallow and rocky, called near its source Baqui.

** Ba Woolima fifty to sixty feet broad, swelled 20 feet deep.

†† This river the same as the Ba Woolima in magnitude.

‡‡ Eight hours climbing the ridge from Toniba—descended in three hours to Bammakoo.

stances, was slower than the customary rate of travelling in the same season.

As regards the latter portion thereof, namely, that from the Ba Faleme to the Bammakoo, it was performed under dreadful rains, with rivers swelled to the highest pitch, with roads become almost impassable, and with their progress constantly interrupted by the soldiers, and almost every one of the party getting sick or dying daily. No stronger instance of the slowness of their progress and of the difficulties they had to contend with, can be adduced, than the following facts, taken from the journal kept by Park himself. On the 27th of July they reached Bangazi, a short distance from the banks of the Ba Woolima, which they had crossed on the 19th, and from which point they beheld the Blue Mountains, past the eastern base of which the Niger swept his course ; yet although the distance was probably not more than 110 miles, they did not reach its banks until the evening of the 19th of August, a period of twenty-three days, during which time they were thirteen days actively engaged travelling. Under these circumstances very great deductions, as the latitudes given will prove, must be made from the course and distance made good. During the latter part the distance travelled could not exceed one and a quarter geographical mile per hour. Bammakoo is distant from Pisania, in a direct line, 450 geographical miles ; and the distance on the general bearings in the route which Park took, would be increased at least 100 miles ; together 550 miles ; or, at the rate of two geographical miles per hour for the first part of the journey, (this however is too great, one mile and seven-eighths is the utmost that can be allowed,) and about one and one-eighth of a mile per hour for the latter part of the journey, or, on the average, one and a half geographical mile per hour for the whole journey ; while some portion of the time stated in hours should be deducted on account of stoppages, &c.

CUBA—POPULATION, &c.

When in the West Indies in 1833, a commercial friend and relative connected with the trade of Cuba, Porto Rico, &c., presented me with a copy of Don Ramon de la Sagra's work, shortly referred to in my letter addressed to Lord John Russell, see p. 26. This work contains the returns of the population of Cuba to 1827 ; and also returns of the commerce of that island to 1829. Along with, and in the printed copy of the book mentioned, there was added, in manuscript, the subsequent returns of the slave population for 1829 and 1830. I now have before me another copy of that work, which continues, in manuscript, the returns of the exports and imports, &c. for the different ports in Cuba, from 1830 to 1834; but there is, unfortunately, no returns given of the population for these latter years.

Years.	1774.	1792.	1817.	1827.	1828.	1830.
Whites ...	96,440	133,559	239,830	307,051		311,051
Free Mulattoes..	30,847	54,152	114,058	106,496		195,000
Slaves ...	44,333	84,590	199,145	286,942	301,000	479,000

Since 1829, the exports of Cuba have increased above 50 per cent., which gives, as a matter of course, a proportional increase to the number of the slave population, and also a proportional increase on the number annually imported. The increase of the population since the year mentioned, applies equally to the towns that it does to the country districts. The greatest increase in exportable articles is in sugar, coffee, molasses, tobacco, &c. &c. The internal consumption of Cuba, also, bears a large proportion to the export trade—greater there than in any other European colony. Take, for example—the export of sugar for 1827, was 5,878,924 arrobas; of Coffee, 2,001,583 arrobas; but the production was sugar, 8,173,382 arrobas, (of which 8,091,837 arrobas was white, or clayed); and coffee, 2,883,528 arrobas. The slave population of Cuba, unless the export has been very considerable, and decrease by death enormous, can scarcely be less at this moment than 600,000. The importation of such articles as form almost exclusively their food, appears, from some of the latest annual returns, to have increased, since 1829, above 40 per cent.

The decrease of the slave population of Cuba from natural causes, independent of any other, must necessarily be very great, arising from the great disproportion that there ever has been between the sexes. Thus, according to Don Ramon de la Sagra, p. 7, the numbers were—

	Male.	Female.
1774	28,771	15,562
1792	47,424	37,166
1817	124,324	74,821
1827	183,290	103,652

Of late years, it is well known that, in the numbers imported, the disproportion is still greater. To make up the great decrease arising from this cause, must necessarily occasion a greater importation. The numbers enfranchised in Cuba are also very considerable.

Thus, in 1774, the free coloured population were in number 30,847 ; in 1792, it was 54,152 ; in 1817, it was 114,058 ; in 1827, it was 106,494 ; and in 1830, it was 195,000 ; of these numbers, the free blacks in 1828, were 49,000 ; and in 1830, they were 74,000. It s also stated, that there has been a very considerable exportation of slaves of late years from Cuba to the adjacent parts of the North American continent.

The returns given in the different enumerations, are, after all, only an approximation to the truth ; the numbers are well known to be still greater. Thus, though the number of slaves, in 1817, is stated to be 199,145, it is said on other authority that the number was above 220,000. Accurate returns of the number imported for a series of years cannot be obtained ; in some years they are more, and others less, according to circumstances. Various scattered notices in Don Ramon's book, show us that it must have been very great. Thus, p. 10, we have the account as given by Humboldt, that, into the Havannah alone, from 1791 to 1805, there were legally imported 91,211 ; and from 1806 to 1820, there were 131,829. At p. 258, we are told that the tax of 6 ps. imposed upon the African negroes brought into the port of the Havannah alone in 1817–1818, produced 194,017 ps., or 32,336 slaves yearly. At p. 234, we are likewise told, that the tax of 4 ps. imposed for the same purpose, for the same port in 1819, produced 160,177 ps. (40,044 slaves yearly.) At p. 148, we are informed that, of the imports (1811) into the same port, 28,361,883 ps., 7,356,800 ps. were for the value of negroes imported from Africa, which, at the customary rate of the custom's valuation, gives 52,000 slaves for that year. The number imported in 1816, was 17,733, their value 2,659,950 ps. ; and from 1815 to 1819, four years, the number imported into the same port, (see same page), was 87,534. By the same scale (see p. 156), the imports were 14,900 in 1810 ; 13,482 in 1811 ; 13,459 in 1812 ; 10,812 in 1813 ; and 10,080 in 1814. These were what were called legal importations ; but besides these, there were a great number illegally imported. Thus, into the eastern part of the island, the number illicitly imported from 1790 to 1820, was calculated to be 56,000, or at the rate of 3,000 yearly. This portion of the traffic, moreover, increased greatly during subsequent years. The Slave trade was carried on to an enormous extent during the years 1828, 1829, and 1830. The Slave Commissioners, in reference to 1830 (see Par. Pap. 1831), emphatically observe "*the extraordinary number brought to market,*" into the Havannah, during that year.

POSTSCRIPT.

AFTER all the sheets of the present work were thrown off, and the map proceeding to completion, the great kindness and attention of Mr. Coates placed in my hands the Journal of the Rev. Mr. Isenberg, from Zeilah and Tadjoura to Ancobar, just received in this country. The document is exceedingly valuable. Besides the time occupied in travelling being corrected on the spot, the bearings in almost every day's journey are given; and also the magnitude and course of the river Hawash, where the caravan with which Mr. Isenberg travelled crossed it. These important matters were wanting in the letters previously received. There is also a variety of interesting particulars given in the Journal regarding the physical features of the country through which they journeyed, which enables us to place the geography of this remarkable portion of Africa in a pretty clear and satisfactory light before the public. It, moreover, enables me to correct a material error regarding the course and termination of the river Hawash, as stated in the general body of the work, p. 243. The course of the river where Mr. Isenberg crossed it not having been given in his letters, and being anxious to adhere to the best maps previously known, the mistake alluded to was naturally committed. Except this, however, there is no material error in that portion of the work where this part of Africa is briefly noticed, and to which, from the Journal alluded to, the following more ample details are with pleasure and satisfaction added.

Zeilah is a decayed town, containing only eight stone houses, and about 100 straw huts, together occupied by about 800 inhabitants, mean and poor. Their food consists of maize, dates, milk, rice, and occasionally flesh. It may, however, shortly become an important place, from affording the readiest means of penetrating into a most interesting portion of Africa. The harbour is very bad, having many sandbanks, and several small islands, near it towards the north. The men of Zeilah dye their hair red: the women go un-

veiled, and wrap a piece of blue cloth round their heads. The
native inhabitants are quite different from the Abyssinians
and Arabs, and seem allied in language and features to the
population of Shoa, and some of the Galla tribes. Zeilah is
surrounded with walls, and has on the land side seven pieces
of ordnance, pointed to the country of the Somaulis, with
which people, dwelling to the S. and S. E., the town has a
considerable intercourse; but feuds and jealousies very frequently prevail between them. Zeilah, also, has a good deal
of intercourse with Goror, and the districts adjoining, from
which considerable quantities of coffee are brought, which is
subsequently exported to Mocha.

Regarding Tadjoura, Mr. Isenberg repeatedly and emphatically states, that the Bay is much deeper than it is marked
on any existing map; in other words, that it extends westward considerably around the base of the high lands which
stretch in that direction from Cape Ras Bir. The pointed
manner in which he states the fact, and from his having sailed
from Zeilah to Tadjoura, at a good rate, with the wind at
N. E., leads me to believe that Tadjoura is to the west of the
meridian of Zeilah. This town is still smaller, poorer, and
less populous than Zeilah, and contains only about 300 people. It is, however, the nearest road to get into the southern
parts of Abyssinia. The country to the north and west is
clearly high, hilly, and rugged, and is no doubt part of the base
of the great elevated chain which extends westward and south
westward from the Cape above mentioned, and the Straits of
Babel Mandeb, to the sources of the Hawash, and some
branches of the Bahr el Azreek, and of the Mugdosha river,
and also the Zebee. Water is readily found: Tadjoura has a
walled cistern for preserving it. Much game and sea-fowl are
found near Sukla, to the north of Sagalle, and also leopards
in the mountains adjoining that place. The inhabitants of
Berbera send to Tadjoura for water, which appears to be
readily found in its vicinity.

Passing Sagalle, the coast, for a short distance, runs due
west, when it becomes rugged, precipitous, and impassable.
The traveller takes a course N. W. through a narrow defile,
when he comes to a table-land called Wardeliham, considera-

bly elevated above the sea, as is proven by the air becoming comparatively cool and pure. From this table-land the road descends south, through a deep ravine, between mountains, to the west end of the Bay of Tadjoura, which here forms a second bay of considerable depth. From the west end of this bay, the road runs over a hill to the eminence and encampment named Muja, situated to the north of the Salt Lake, elsewhere adverted to, and called Assal. Near Muja, the ground is full of chasms and gulfs, the remains of volcanoes. Mountains bound the lake on the S. E. and S. It is distant from the Bay of Tadjoura, in a direct line, about six miles. The lake appears to have at one time extended more to the south and the west than it now does; but this appearance probably arose from Mr. Isenberg seeing it at the height of the dry season, when its magnitude may be considerably reduced. A dale, or valley, extends from the lake, first W., then S. W., through which the road runs to Guagnal; around and to the east of which both verdure and water were found, even at that period of the year. Passing Guagnal, they came to the valley of Kallu, where there was plenty of water and vegetation. This place resembled the valley of Simhara, in Abyssinia, only the mountains round the former were not so high as those seen around the latter. Here the traveller is in the country of the Arab tribe, called Mudaites, the most powerful in these parts. Their chief residence, or capital, is called Aussa, where several Ulemas and learned Mahommedans reside. This tribe spreads itself northward as far as Massowah. Aussa lies due west from Karanta, but the distance between these places is, unfortunately, not stated. It cannot, however, be very great.

The mountains south of Karanta are volcanic. In the vales are found grass, and brushwood, and also ashes. Arabdera is a vast elevated plain covered with volcanic stones. Mari is an high eminence, the air on which is so pure and fresh, that Mr. Isenberg felt rather refreshed than fatigued from the journey. Proceeding forwards a short distance, the descent to the valley S.W. is precipitous and dangerous. Between Ahuli and Lukki, is a plain running S.E. and N.W. Lukki is an eminence covered with volcanic stones, flat on the top, as most mountains passed in the route also were. From Lukki, the prospect S.W. and W. was very extensive over a country chiefly level, but here and there studded with low hills. In the distance towards the west appeared several high hills, considered to be Mount Argobba and some of the hills of Shoa. The plain beyond Lukki was full of grass, and here the travellers saw a hyena.

Here it may be proper to remark while the mountains to the N.W. side of the Hawash approach near the river, forming the S.E. barrier of the province of Angot; that on the S.E. side also another chain, of less elevation, forms the barrier, and gives the course to the river on the side mentioned. From this latter barrier, the ridges and valleys, it appears, extend from N.W. to S.E., to the boundary of the great plain or valley which is stated to run from the borders of the Hawash on the east of Ancobar towards Berbera. Beyond Barrudega there is a range of mountains extending S.E. and N.W. A short distance west of Barrudega is the village of Gaiel, the chief place of the Dannakil Warma, the chief of which was the uncle of Mohr Ali, their guide. From Hasnadera the mountains of Goror were seen to the S.W., "covered with clouds." The town of Goror was stated to be only two and a half days' journey distant. The Alla Gallas had expelled the father of the guide from Errur, or Hurrur. From this it would appear, that Goror and Errur are different places. From Kudaite the mountains of Baaden and Aialu, the latter of considerable height, were distinctly seen to the N.W. On the latter mountains a bloody battle had been fought in the preceding year, between the Mudaites and the Warma tribe, in which the latter were defeated. S.W. of Kudaite lay the mountain of Gebel Ahmar at no great distance, and more distant the mountains of the Alla Galla, between which and Kudaite lies a vast plain, which was stated to extend from the banks or borders of the Hawash, as far as Berbera. Kudaite is the last place in that quarter belonging to the Dannakil Warma tribe.

A few miles beyond Kumi, the travellers came to a deserted village, between which spot and Gamessa, they saw to their left, and at a short distance, Mount Afraba, peopled by Issa Gallas, which tribe league themselves with the Mudaites against the Dannakil Warma. To the right of the spot mentioned they saw distinctly the high land of Shoa and Effat. At Little Mulloo they found the grass in the level ground so high, that it rose above the head of a man on horseback, which indicates a good soil. At a distance on the plain they perceived a large fire. On making inquiries how it was produced, they were answered that it came by chance, which would indicate that it might proceed from some volcanic action; or it might have proceeded from accident, owing to the burning of grass and brushwood, which takes place in many parts of Africa towards the close of the dry season. From an eminence beyond Galakdiggi, they saw very clearly the mountains of Shoa. As they approached the Hawash, they crossed a considerable ridge of hills, which skirt the eastern side of the valley of the Hawash, and descending this ridge they came to Dobhille. Proceeding thence over the fine plain covered with trees, they came to the river Hawash, which they crossed on the 29th of May, at the close of the dry season. They found the stream 60 feet broad; from two to four feet deep; and the banks from 15 to 20 feet high. The course thence through the plain of the Hawash, which is of considerable breadth, is first N., and then N.E. to Aussa, near which it spreads itself into a large lake situated in a vast plain, where it terminates, being carried off by evaporation or subterranean passages, but more probably by the former. The waters of this lake are stated to be putrid, and to emit an offensive smell, and to have a disagreeable taste, which latter may proceed from some mephitic quality, and the former from swamps and marshes around its immediate shores. The magnitude of the Hawash at the point where the travellers crossed the stream, shows that the source cannot be far distant to the SS.W., while the lake wherein it terminates may be placed at the distance of 70 miles W.S.W. of Tadjoura. The right bank of the Hawash below the point where Mr. Isenberg crossed it, is in the lower part of its course inhabited by the Mudaites tribe, and the left bank by the Orgubbassin tribe, and higher up and towards the point where crossed, the right bank of the river is inhabited by the Dannakil Warma; south of them and of the route, the Abarras dwell, and still further south the Alla Gallas.

The village or town of Mulkukuji is situated on the left bank of the river, near which is a small lake, wherein there were many crocodiles and hippopotami. This region is very prolific for a naturalist. Beyond this there is another lake, the waters of which are of a disagreeable taste, and have a sulphureous smell, but which are of a remarkable cleansing quality, and are therefore much used for washing clothes. West of this, and a little to the east of Assabobe, is another and still larger lake, called La Adu, or *far distant water*, in which there are many hippopotami. The district is called Dofar, and has numerous forests abounding with game and a great variety of birds, which by their warblings rendered the roads lively. Beyond Akonti they crossed the fine valley of Kokai, abounding with lofty trees, excellent water, abundance of cattle, and a great variety of birds; and next, crossing several hills, the prominences of the high lands of Abyssinia, which extend from the south far northward, they reached Dinomali, the frontier station of Shoa, where revenue officers are stationed, and immediately adjoining which is the village of Fary, or Ferri, where the travellers rested.

From Tadjoura, the route of Mr. Isenberg and his companions lay through a country constantly rising, and studded with minor hills, eminences, and ranges; but still none of these were of any very great elevation. To the south, and to the west, in the distance, and before approaching the Hawash, mountains were seen on both hands which clearly had a great elevation. In the district passed through, from the sea to the Hawash, there was, with the exception of a few places, no spot where water was not readily found, even at that period of the year when every thing is dried up to the very utmost. In many places also the verdure and the appearance of the surface of the country indicated a climate favourable to vegetation, and a soil of a productive quality. Hyenas, leopards, and elephants, were numerous from the lowest part of the route forwards; beasts of prey which are never found in deserts or utterly barren countries and districts. To the westward of Ahuli, the air, from the great elevation of the country, became fresh and cool. The journeys, moreover, were in general performed very early in the morning, or else late in the afternoon, which enabled the

travellers to make greater progress, in any given period of
time, than they could have done if they had travelled during
the extreme heat of the day, and in African districts of a low
level.

From Fary, or Ferri, Mr. Isenberg and his companions
advanced on their way to Ancobar, the capital of Shoa.
Leaving Ferri, they crossed a few promontories and valleys,
and also first the small river Hatshani, and secondly the river
Metka Zebdu, when they commenced ascending the high
land of Shoa. Soon after, they reached a village named
Aliu Amba, situated on the top of a steep rock, where they
met the first christian governor whom they had seen in that
distant portion of Africa. From the village mentioned, they
proceeded forward to Ancobar, which is built on the summit
of a high conical hill, from whence they had an extensive
and commanding prospect—to the west, Shoa, to a great
distance ; and to the east, the Hawash and the valley through
which they had travelled. The king's house stands in the
upper or the highest part of the town, and is built of stone
and mortar, with a thatched roof. The other houses are
chiefly built of wood, with thatched roofs, generally surrounded
with a garden, and disposed around the cone in a spiral form.
" The situation, the rich vegetation in a cool vernal, or almost
autumnal, atmosphere," says Mr. Isenberg, " almost put us
in an ecstasy." The king being at Anpollalla, they proceeded
forwards to meet him, passing through only a part of Ancobar.
They marched on stony roads, and on the side of some
mountains. Crossing an elevated valley, through which a
crystal rivulet purled, which was to set a mill in motion,
then erecting by a Greek mechanic named Demetrius, "they
breathed," says Mr. Isenberg, " alpine air, and drank alpine
water." They next ascended another high mountain, abounding
with camomile, penny-royal, and numerous alpine plants.
The top of the mountain was covered with *barley fields*, then
(June 8th) almost ready for the harvest. The thermometer,
during the night, could not have exceeded 40°, which, in that
parallel of latitude, and in the middle of the northern summer,
gives a great elevation. They slept at a small village called
Metakui, and next day proceeded westward over an undulating

table-land, when, after a few hours' journey, they reached the village of Islam Amba, where they met the king of Shoa.

After protracting very carefully the route which Mr. Isenberg took from Tadjoura to Ancobar and Anpollalla, from the time and bearings given, and after making the allowances in general, which he allows in particular instances, and after giving the subject the most attentive consideration, Ancobar is placed in 8° 54′ N. lat. and 39° 17′ E. long. The positions of other places will be found by an inspection of the map.

The great elevation of Ancobar has already been adverted to, and which is further proved by the verdure and fertility of the country at this period of the year (June 8th), the very close of the dry season, and to which period no rain, or at least no rain of any consequence, had fallen. Two months before this period, however, it is well known that the rains commence in the very high lands of Abyssinia, 4° more to the north. These circumstances, here adverted to, go to prove in a satisfactory manner, the much greater, the very great elevation of the more interior parts of Africa, where the chief branches of the Bahr el Abiad take their rise, and around which the rains certainly commence about the end of March. The fact also mentioned by Mr. Isenberg, namely, that Zeilah is supplied with coffee from Goror, proves the fertility and the cultivation of the soil in that district, two things which could not be found where water is wanting. Therefore the maps by the late Mr. Arrowsmith, which represent a river running east from the quarter alluded to, and sinking or disappearing (probably from evaporation) to the west of Berbera, may fairly be taken to be correct. The river in question, no doubt, springs from the north side of the Hurrur and Alla Galla mountains, and, traversing the great plain which Mr. Isenberg says runs on the north side of these mountains eastward from the borders of the Hawash to Berbera, finally disappears in the volcanic country to the westward of the latter place.

The country from the sea coast at Zeilah and Tadjoura to Shoa is inhabited by the following Arab tribes : the Mudaites ; the Dabanik Warma ; the Ado Alli, and the Brucharts. The two first are the most powerful of the whole. The Mudaites are, however, more numerous and powerful than the Warma.

The Shohas and the Dankali are much the same in language, and figure, and features, but the latter are all rigid Mahommedans. *Adaiel* is a general Arabic name, used to denote all the Dankali tribes in this portion of Africa. Hence the name Adel was given, not only to the portion of Africa under our immediate consideration, but to a large extent of country stretching south to the Indian Ocean about Doaro. The following brief account of the character and manners of the people in the neighbourhood of Little Marha, extracted from Mr. Isenberg's Journal, may suffice for all the rest :—

"A chief occupation of the Dankils, particularly of the women, more especially when they travel, is the plaiting of mats and baskets for salt and corn, from the branches of the palm tree. The women are the most industrious. They dress very slovenly, and frequently wear nothing but a piece of cloth, of a grey, blue, or variegated colour, tied round their hips, reaching down to the knees, sometimes bound round with a fancifully wrought leathern belt. Notwithstanding, they are vain, and fond of wearing bracelets and foot ornaments, ear and nose-rings, coral strings on their neck, &c."

The Slave Trade is at present carried on to a considerable extent throughout all the districts of this portion of Africa. Great jealousy, and great fears also, are entertained by the population of any communications with the English, who are generally understood to have in view the suppression, not merely of the Slave Trade, but of personal slavery also. It is clear, from these feelings being thus spread and entertained, that great caution will for a time be necessary in order to secure a quiet and permanent footing in Eastern Africa. A premature step or word may throw back the advance of a friendly intercourse and of proper ideas and principles to a very distant period.

At Anpollalla,* (not Angollalla, as written p. 243,) Mr. Isenberg and his companions met the king of Shoa, the christian sovereign of a christian people, whose tenets are those of the Alexandrian church, but greatly corrupted from the principles professed by that church in former times, owing

* Mr. Isenberg writes this name "Anpollalla;" Mr. Kraaf writes it "Angollalla."

to their long separation from the christian world, and to the
inroads of their barbarous pagan neighbours. By this sovereign they were received and welcomed with the greatest
respect, attention, and cordiality. He made particular inquiries of them about their journey and their object, and was
especially inquisitive regarding geographical knowledge and
information. This, of itself, would augur a mind of a superior
order, and under the protection of such a sovereign it is incalculable what good such excellent men may do in Africa. So
pleased have they been with their reception, and prospects for
preaching the gospel in that portion of Africa, that Mr. Isenberg has left his colleague, Mr. Kraaf, at Ancobar, and is on
his way to Europe to solicit from the Church Missionary
Society, and through them I hope this christian country, aid
to procure an additional number of labourers for that interesting field. They will not—they cannot solicit in vain. The
judicious conduct and proceedings of the two missionaries
already sent show that their instructions have been judicious,
and the selection made by the Society equally so. May every
success attend them. Theirs is the noblest of all causes, and
the noblest and the highest pursuit in which any human being
can be engaged. The world is interested in their future labours
and future proceedings. These will render more essential
service to Africa, and confer on her more lasting benefits, than
the exertions of the whole navy of England, stationed round
her coasts for the purpose of catching a few straggling slave-
traders, ever has done, or ever can do. The former will teach
Africans those christian principles, and that industry and
honesty, which will go to increase her real wealth, security, and
independence, and which will farther go to tear up at the roots
not merely an external and internal Slave Trade, but also internal slavery, war, bloodshed, and oppression, in that portion
of Africa, as indeed wherever real Christianity spreads itself and
fixes itself in any portion of Africa, it will always do. It is a
pleasing reflection to think that through a route never before attempted by any European, a christian population in that distant
and once very important, and still interesting, portion of Africa,
can be so soon reached by Christians from Europe, and that the
road in question is now safe, and comparatively free from

danger. The impression made will, it is most earnestly hoped, be steadily and energetically followed up by the Church Missionary Society; and if the people of England, and the government of England, are wise and prudent; and if both wish, as I believe both really wish, to do permanent good to Africa; let them cordially unite, and support the efforts of the Society in question with their strength, means, power, and influence, as may be necessary.

Besides the above cheering prospect for the spread of true christian knowledge and principles in Eastern Africa, the information given by Mr. Isenberg shows that a considerable field for commercial enterprise may be opened up to the British merchant in this same quarter. The countries to the west of Ancobar are populous, with some industry and cultivation. Gold is found in considerable quantities in all the districts round the sources of the various rivers in the quarter alluded to. The coffee received from Mocha has long been known for its superior quality, although it is but little, if at all, known, that a considerable portion of the quantity which is exported from that place is received from the interior portions of Africa, at present under consideration. The calcareous ridges in the mountains of Hurrur, those around the sources of the Zebee and the Habahia, &c. are the most proper places for the growth of coffee of the finest quality, exactly as we find superior descriptions of that valuable article produced most freely on the calcareous ridges of Jamaica, Cuba, Porto Rico, and Hayti.

The journal of Mr. Isenberg gives us no specific intelligence of any other states or places except those parts in his immediate route. The journal of Mr. Kraaf, however, supplies, to a great extent, this deficiency. By the kindness and attention of Mr. Coates, this journal was put into my hands at the moment the preceding pages were about to be sent to the press. Mr. Kraaf takes up the narrative of occurrences and information from the 7th of June, the time when Mr. Isenberg's journal closes, till the 2d of October following. From this journal the following important geographical information is selected, and put in a shape as condensed and clear as possible.

Aliu Amba is about six miles to the east of Ancobar. Effat

is divided into Upper and Lower Effat.   Aliu Amba is in
Lower Effat; and Muckfood (called Marfood in our maps)
belongs to the upper district, The latter portion of Effat has
a great elevation, compared to Aliu Amba, and its neighbourhood.   Argobba is situated to the north of Ancobar, and
about due west from Lukki.   The capital city is named
Aincha, situated upon the river Tshaffa, which comes from
the westward, and bending its course N. E., joins the Hawash
in the country of Adel.   The river mentioned, separates Shoa
from the northern Gallas.   The country of Argobba is ruled
by a governor, named Bekoo, and is dependent upon Gondar.
In the neighbourhood of this district is another river, called
the Berkona, which is stated, also, to flow to the Hawash,
having, by some accounts, first formed a junction with the
Tshaffa.   The large lake, called Tehuladera, is eight days'
journey north of Ancobar.   In it is a considerable island,
called Haig, or Haik, containing a monastery, and about 100
houses, inhabited by christian monks.   It is dependent upon
the chief of Gondar.   The people in the neighbourhood are
called Deblera.   Mount Argobba appears to be from seventy
to eighty miles to the north of Ancobar, and to the E. or
E. S. E. of Lake Tehuladera.

The Chatka mountain extends to the west from Ancobar,
which city appears to be built on the eastern extremity of the
ridge.   One mile from Ancobar, and on the bank of the river
Airara, at the foot of the mountain mentioned, the market of
Ancobar is held every Saturday.   The village of Mitatet is
situated on the top of Mount Chatka, and about five miles
west of Ancobar, on the road to Dobra Berhan. The population of these parts live together with the domestic animals
in one abode, much, it would appear, after the manner that
we find the population in some districts of Ireland living at
this day.   Dobra Berhan is a place where a great market is
regularly held every week.   It is situated about twenty to
twenty-five miles W., or rather W. S. W. of Ancobar.   From
this place the best and greatest number of horses and mules
are brought.   A good mule at Ancobar costs ten to twelve
dollars, and a good horse from eight to nine dollars.   Gold is
nine dollars per ounce in southern Abyssinia.

From Islam Amba to Anpollalla, the way is over a plain, intersected by hills and rivulets. The most distinguished river crossed is that named Beresa, which, during the rains, is a considerable stream. It rises in the Galla country, and runs first to the N. E., then N. W. and next to the W., in the neighbourhood of Tegulet, the ancient capital of Shoa, where it forms several cataracts, from sixty to seventy feet in height. In every direction many villages were seen, indicating a large population, arising, no doubt, from the peace and security from civil war and discord which the people of Shoa enjoyed. Amongst the villages mentioned in the neighbourhood of Anpollalla, were Tsherkos to the W., Tophis to the N., Daletska to the N. E., &c. Tegulet, the ancient capital of Shoa, now almost in ruins, stood on the top of a steep mountain, situated on the south side of the river Daletska, which here runs in a deep dale between two mountains. The place, it appears, is about half a day's journey E. S. E. from Dobra Berhan. Mr. Kraaf says his road to it from Dobra Berhan lay in an eastern direction. The site of Tegulet is now occupied by a village called Etake. The river Tshalsha, which separates Shoa from the territory of the Galla in that direction, passes about four miles from Anpollalla. On this river is situated the village of Tsherkos, already mentioned. Mr. Kraaf saw in it one cataract seventy feet in height. The Tshalsha runs in a deep dale, between mountains. Both it and the Beresa were stated to run to the Nile. This is a curious and important fact, as it brings to our knowledge the point where the waters take different directions, from one of those numerous great culminating points which lie in the northern equatorial regions of Africa.

Bulga is the capital of Fattigar, a considerable district on the southern frontier of Shoa. The capital is distant from Ancobar about one and a half day's journey. A considerable river, named Kassam, runs in the neighbourhood of Bulga, and flows into the Hawash. In the route between Ancobar and the country of Garague, or Garagua, three rivers, the Akake, the Gurasha, and the Furri, are crossed before reaching the Hawash. The governor of Bulga resides in a town,

called Morfata. Fattigar has many mountains, some of which
are of great height. In the neighbourhood of Bulga there is
Mount Magusas, very high; another called Tantalle, and another
Woute. From Bulga to Garague, is a journey of from five to
eight days, through a country inhabited by ten tribes of the
Galla. The fifth tribe in order on the route is the Abboo;
in the district belonging to which the Hawash is crossed.
Having crossed the river, the traveller comes, after several
days' journey, to a large lake, called Suai, in which there is
an island, peopled by monks. Five rivers run into this lake.
In the country of the Abboo, there is one lake called Killole,
and another called Arsud. This country of Abboo is governed
by two chiefs, called, the one Kerroo, and the other Aminoo.
The former resides in Waleko; both are tributary to Shoa.
In Garague the inhabitants are chiefly Christians, together
with some Mahommedans, and some heathens. The
current money in Garague is salt; dollars do not pass.
Knives, scissars, needles, &c. are well received, Much coffee
and wine are produced in Garague. Tasma honey, (of the most
precious kind) is found in the province of Abamada. Their
houses are better in Garague than in Shoa. There are thirty-
nine monasteries in this country. In the neighbourhood of
Garague is the country of Sinshero, where there are a great
many Christians and Mahommedans. The Galla tribes beyond
Garague are—the Maroko; the Lake; the Lani; the Damo;
and the Endegan. Eight days' journey beyond the country
of Sinshero is the country of Mager, the king of which is
called Degaie. He is represented to be a very powerful
monarch. There is another country, called Kootshassi, in the
neighbourhood of Garague. In that country, which is surrounded by Gallas\ on every side, all the inhabitants are
Christians.

The places inhabited by Christians in Garague are:—
Aimelellelle; Narreno; Belantshooboo; Manes; Malekdamo;
Wogoram; Buijana; Jondamo; Dalshi; Fettane; Aretshat;
Heberrer; Arogamane; Dobi; Fawilui; Fatabona; Sera; San-
gania; Mohor. The places where Someai, or heathens, reside,
are:—Mascan; Aborrat; Fakedar; Warub; Mars; Sabolas;

Faderek; Wamnan; Attakiro; Duhahes; Endagach; Masmas; Magar; Ener; Asha; Tshaka; Wollane. The distinguishing mountains in Garague are:—Karra; Koffalite; Jafersa; Attakaf; Make; Feru; Engedokoffo; Bodegabab; Denekoli; Enokater; Sert. The great rivers are:—the Wiser, in the district of Damo; the Dersat; the Asas; the Sherbany; the Meke; and the Famarakodio. Most of these rivers run into the lake Suai, certainly the Zawajah of the present maps.

The Galla tribes, in their religious views, are Pagans of the lowest grade. Amongst them, there are no ministers of religion of any description. They worship a superior being under the name of Waake. This is the Ouack of Ouare, (the Galla mentioned, p. 253), the deity which is worshipped by the Gallas on the banks of the Habahia; and the account here given by Mr. Kraaf bears out, so far, the truth of Ouare's narrative. The Gallas dislike the Christian religion, because, they say, the people of Shoa who profess it, are, notwithstanding, no better than themselves.

Simaha is not the name of a country; but a word used to designate Christians, who are numerous in the countries between Shoa and Enarea. The king of Shoa is on friendly terms with the chief of Damot. From Gondar to Bosso on the Nile, is said to be ten days' journey; and from Bosso to Enarea is fifteen days' journey. Coffee is brought from Kaffa, and civet from Enarea. Shells, corals, and pieces of silk, are the current money in these places. Enarea is beyond the country of Adrina.

The king of Shoa's name is Sahala Salassie. He is only thirty-nine years old. He has reigned twenty-seven years, having succeeded to the throne when he was only twelve years of age. He has conquered an extent of country equal to thirty times the original size of Shoa. Nine Galla tribes are subject to him. Mr. Kraaf had obtained the names of forty different tribes of the Gallas who inhabit the surrounding portions of Africa. The following are the names of some of them, and the positions in which they live, as relative to Ancobar and other places:—Abedtshoo, (separated from Shoa, near Anpollalla, by the river Tshalsha), Adai, Soddo, Abboo, Lebaa, Tshedda, Assàta. Quolan, Metta, and Maitsha, all subject to the king of Shoa. The tribes Belsho and Ferrer, in the south, are not subject to him. To the north and east of Shoa, are the following tribes:—Dane, Wollo, Wara, Gaffra, Wolshate, Sako, Battoko, Tehulavera, Jellè, Aptsallo, Assabo, Layagora, Gama, Sagambo, Kallota, Jetshoo, Ittoo, Karaiu, Arresi, Tsherker; the last four tribes are on the east of Shoa. The tribes on the road from Ancobar to Garague, are :— Ferrer, Roggi, Endote, Adai, Abba, Woretshersa, Tshedda, Abado, Soddo, Liban, and Gumbetshoo. The tribes to the south of Garague, are :—Wadast, Mae, Abboso, Abosetsho, Masso, Lellon, Imer, Fallo, Banojo, Falaadoso, and Mirrer.

The people of Shoa and other countries adjoining, which profess to be Christians, reckon in their chronology 5,500 years before Christ; some Abyssinians reckon 7,332 since the creation. The male children of the king are kept in prison at Quantsho, in the province of Shoa, to the east, in the neighbourhood of the country of Adel. As soon as the king is dead, the eldest son is taken out of the prison, and introduced as king by the Shalafra Agassri, the first door-keeper, whose duty it is to crown the king. Then, the new king puts his brethren in prison, lest, being left at liberty, they should raise disturbances in the kingdom.

Amongst the Galla tribes to the south of Garague, is one named Damo, through the district belonging to which a considerable river named the Wiser, runs. From the position which Mr. Kraaf gives to this tribe, and considering that, of the six rivers which he enumerates as belonging to Garague, " most of these," or five, are said to run into Lake Suai; the remaining one, or the Wiser, no doubt flows from it southward, forming the great western branch of the river which enters the sea near Mugdosha. This is the more certain, first, because the magnitude of the Hawash, to the eastward of Ancobar, is so small, that the waters collected in Lake Suai cannot join it from the southward. Secondly, because Lake Suai is on the northern side of the country of Garague; and thirdly, because the tribe of Damo is the fourth in order south of Garague, through which tribe the Wiser, particularly alluded to, certainly flows. Sinshero, stated to be in the neighbourhood of Garague, is certainly the Gingiro of our present maps.

The new year of the people of Shoa commences on the fourth of September. A very considerable portion of their time is occupied in religious and superstitious fasts. Several of their rites, ceremonies, and customs, are clearly derived from the ancient Hebrew church. They count their leap-year by the names of the four evangelists, adding five days to each of the three first, but six days to the last, (the fourth, or that named after St. John), which addition is called *Pagmie.* They believe in evil spirits, which they call Sarotsh, eighty-eight in number, who are divided into two equal bands, under the command of different leaders. These spirits, they believe, inflict upon men sickness, and other evils; and to deprecate their wrath, they sacrifice at times a red hen, which they afterwards eat, reserving the brain for the person who performed the most material part of the ceremony. · They also smoke, sing, and move their whole body in strange gesticulations, in order to frighten the evil spirit away from them.

The government of Shoa is an absolute despotism. The king claims every thing, holds a monopoly of every thing, and takes the tenth of every thing. The bridge he caused to be constructed over the river Beresa, he claims as exclusively his own, and will not permit any one to pass across it, but himself and his favourites. Justice is administered in an open space, under four judges, but in the presence of the king, who, if he disapproves of the judgment given by the judges, decides the case according to his own judgment. The religion of the population of Shoa is a strange compound of the Christianity, debased, of the Alexandrian church, Judaism, Mahommedanism, and Paganism. A little to the north of Shoa, Mr. Kraaf tells us, there dwells an isolated sect of Jews. The men and the women live in separate houses. He gives us also a list of thirty-six books, in the Amharic and Ethiopic languages, chiefly relating to religious subjects. In the church of St. George, there are seventy books belonging to it. Mr.

Kraaf also gives us many particulars regarding their theology, their customs, and their superstitions, which are very curious and very strange, but which are more the province of the theologian than the geographer. Alluding to geography, Mr. Kraaf states, from the king to the peasant, in Shoa, and amongst travellers who came there from other parts of the country, that every one took a great interest in geographical subjects, and were most anxious to receive instruction on every point relating to this science. The king was particularly inquisitive about the knowledge and works possessed by Europeans, and expressed the greatest astonishment when he was told about our railroads, steamers, ships, &c. &c.

Adverting to steam, the journal of Mr. Kraaf is a remarkable proof of the wonders it is working, and is certain yet further to work in this world. The journal alluded to brings with it a letter, dated Ancobar, on the 5th November last, and which reached London on the 9th March!! Half a century ago it might have taken years to complete the communication.

. The rains commenced at Ancobar on the 21st of June, and continued strong through July and August. They comparatively ceased, it would appear, towards the middle of August, and during the early days of September. From the 20th to the 30th of that month, they became so violent, that Mr. Kraaf remarks, "The rainy season seems to have come again." This, however, is the regular course of the seasons within the Northern Tropic, more especially in the more southern portion thereof, and particularly in continental countries such as Africa.

Mr. Kraaf intended to proceed to Garague in December last, and to remain there for three or four months. We may, therefore, shortly expect to hear some interesting intelligence from him regarding that portion of Africa. He states, that Mr. D'Abadie was last autumn with the chief of Damot.

While engaged in correcting the last pages of the work, an opportunity was afforded me of perusing the journal of the late Mr. Davidson, who was treacherously murdered in the month of November, 1836, a few days' journey to the south of Tatta, when attempting to cross the desert from Wednun to Timbuctoo. From that journal, the following important particulars are gleaned regarding the geography of that part of Africa adjoining Wednun, which has been quite wrongly delineated in all the maps hitherto constructed. Wednun is about twenty-five miles from the sea, and the mouth of a river called the Assaka, formed by the junction of two rivers, first the Boukoukmar, and second, the great Sayad, to the S.W. of Wednun. This river passes to the south of the town mentioned. When full, they roll a fine body of water to the sea; they take their rise in the mountains of Suse; the former to the north, and the latter to the N.E. of Sok Assa. The river Drah, or Draha, which rises in Tafilet, is not lost in the desert, as has hitherto been supposed, but passing to the south-westward, near Tatta and Akka, finds its way to the Atlantic, which it enters about thirty-two miles to the S.W. of Cape Nun. Cultivation is general on its northern bank, and also over a considerable strip on its southern bank. A ridge of hills, called Ab-el-Assel, stretches from the sea on the north side of the Draha. The coast to the north of the Draha is bluff and rocky, but to the south, it has sand hills and shallow water. Another ridge of hills skirts the south bank of the Assaka, near the sea. The country through which the Draha flows is represented to be populous, and tolerably well cultivated, producing immense quantities of oil, wax, hides, and almonds, and is inhabited by the Arab tribes of Errub, Draha, Maraibait, Tajacanth, and Ergebat. The mountains of Lower Suse, a branch of the Atlas chain, approach near Wednun, and are crossed in the road from Tesereet to that place. Being without the limits of the tropical rains, all the rivers mentioned were nearly dry when Mr. Davidson saw them in the month of September, proceeding, as in the case of other African rivers, from evaporation. Sok Assa is one day's journey from Wednun; Akka, four days, and Tatta, five days.

THE END.

LONDON:

RICHARD CLAY, PRINTER, BREAD

Lightning Source UK Ltd.
Milton Keynes UK
UKHW021859191218
334260UK00013B/1232/P